STATES OF EMERGENCY

STATES OF EMERGENCY

States of Emergency

Architecture, Urbanism, and the First World War

Edited by

Erin Eckhold Sassin and Sophie Hochhäusl

LEUVEN UNIVERSITY PRESS

Published with the financial support of the Weitzman School of Design,
University of Pennsylvania and Middlebury College, Vermont.

Figure 1.8: Courtesy Albert Moreau/SPCA/ECPAD/Defense/SPA 322 M 5500.

Figures 1.6, 1.7, 1.9, and 1.10: Courtesy BIU Santé (Paris),
https://www.biusante.parisdescartes.fr/histmed/medica/page?02077.

ISBN 978 94 6270 308 7
e-ISBN 978 94 6166 433 4
D/2022/1869/15
NUR: 448
https://doi.org/10.11116/9789461664334

Cover design: Griet Van Haute
Cover illustration: "Wien, Am Hof," Women waiting in line for food at Hoher
Markt, Vienna, August 17, 1918. Image Archives of the Austrian National Library,
Signature PCH 17879-B.

Lay-out: Friedemann Vervoort

Contents

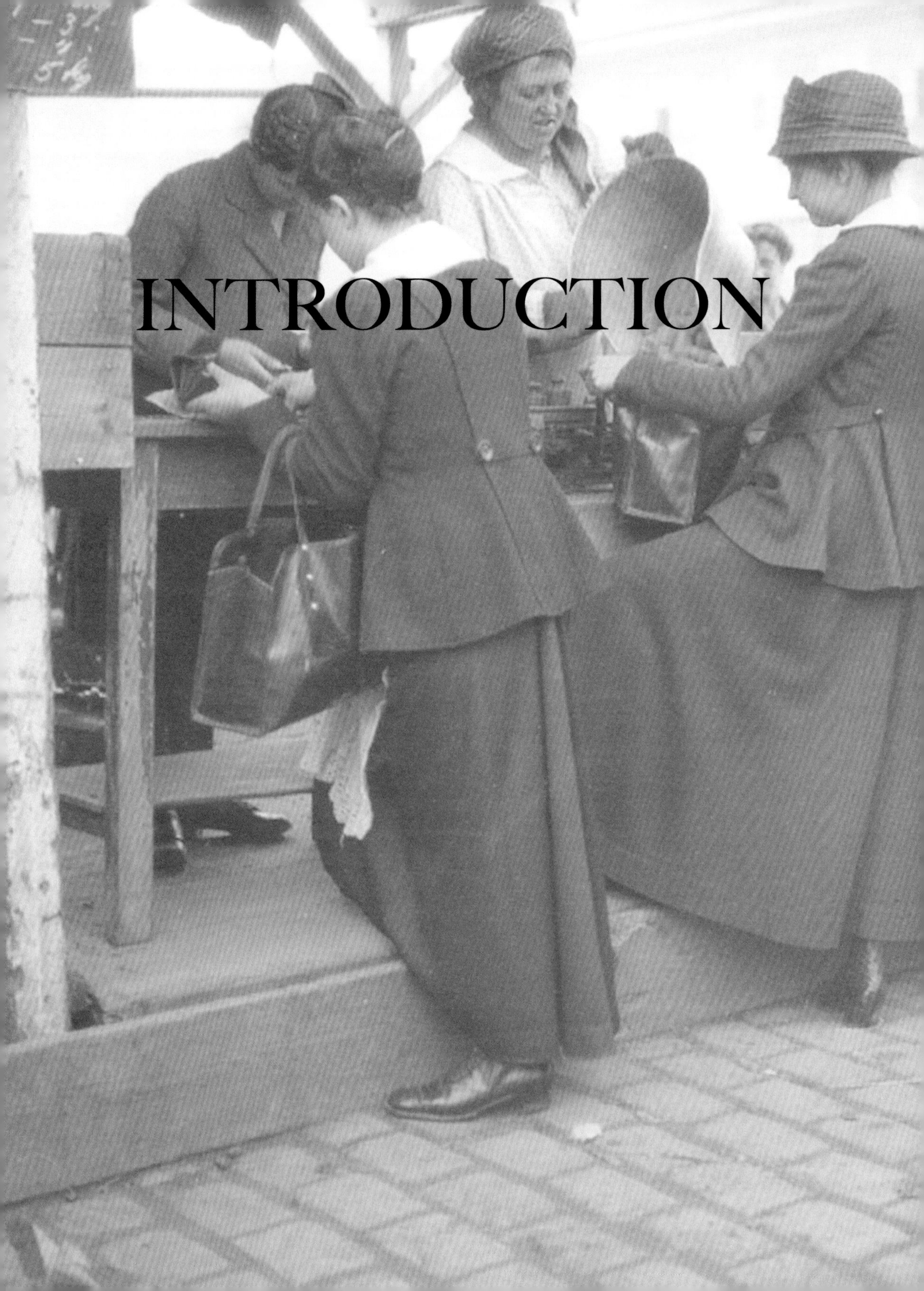

INTRODUCTION

Fig. 1. Potato Sales, *Naschmarkt*, Vienna, September 8, 1917.
Image Archives of the Austrian National Library, PCH 18.128-B.

Introduction

Erin Eckhold Sassin and Sophie Hochhäusl

Ration Cards and the Single File Line

Ration cards reflected one of the most urgent problems throughout World War I, the provisioning of resources including foodstuffs. By 1918, a daily ration of food mandated and policed by the state amounted to 831 calories per person in Vienna. Overall, the average permissible intake of food was bureaucratized as 107 calories of flour, 450 calories of bread, 51 calories of lard, 18 calories of meat, 57 calories of potatoes, 100 calories of sugar, and 48 calories of jam – and those reflected ideal conditions.[1] As the war wore on, many of these basic staples managed through municipal, federal, and philanthropic agencies were no longer available. The single file line in front of food banks and markets mirrored those in front of military barracks and in the trenches and became one of the defining images of World War I. Indeed, merely a few months into the global conflict, World War I had given rise to a managerial circulatory logic that sought to administer bodies and resources equally and under immense pressure. Throughout World War I, these managerial systems remained on the brink of collapse, yet the creation of thousands of public and private agencies and aid programs inscribed and institutionalized the distribution of resources and their reproduction with long-lasting impacts. World War I advanced a new phase in early twentieth century capitalist development, but it also laid the groundwork for discourses about planned and cooperative economies. Both economic debates deeply influenced housing, health, and even urban park systems discourse over the course of the 1920s.

Histories of architecture and design have long emphasized the wartime advances in mechanization and standardization that opened novel fields of inquiry in the aftermath of World War I. They have foregrounded how the global conflict created the technological frameworks for the emergence of interwar modern architecture with its widespread use of material developments in concrete, steel, and communication infrastructures; secondary commentary, too, has highlighted that World War I was not only "a severe dislocation," but also "a unique opportunity for architects, urban planners, and industrialists … an accelerator for new policies and practices."[2] However, rampant militarism, which swept across Europe in the months and years after the summer of 1914, was accompanied by ferocious resource extraction in both cities and the countryside, as well as exploitation of land and labor in the territories Europeans had violently colonized. Between 1914 and 1918, the war economy was characterized by hyper-inflation, underdevelopment, and the logic of governmentality in the state of emergency.[3] Indeed, the first global war of trenches, tanks, and submarines was also one of food banks, bread lines, and ration cards, in which bodies and resources became subjected to scientific and militaristic control. The war literally strained bodies to the point of omnipresent undernourishment, starvation, collapse, and death – overwhelming markets, hospitals, and refugee camps.

States of Emergency: Architecture, Urbanism, and the First World War reassesses what this cataclysmic global conflict meant for architecture and urbanism from a human, social, and economic perspective. Architectural-historical understandings of World War I have long been colored by military histories and the romance or tragedy of specific individuals fighting on the Western Front – from soldier-architects like Erich Mendelsohn, Walter Gropius, and Richard Neutra to literary figures like Siegfried Sassoon, Erich Maria Remarque, and Ernst Jünger.[4] Instead, this volume foregrounds how wartime (under)development manifested spatially, how viewing and mapping techniques were deployed against citizens and subjects, and how military technologies were repurposed by civilians to resist forms of power and control. Joining longstanding and notable efforts by colleagues in closely related fields – historians of disability and trauma, memory and gender studies, as well as those engaged in heritage and preservation studies – our edited volume places an emphasis on the everyday tragedy of war as experienced by combatants *and* civilians across five continents – from cookware to rifles, villages to capital cities, and refugee camps to military barracks.[5] Questions the authors' contributions are concerned with include: how the war recast architectural tropes as they moved from the realm of high art into the everyday, and vice-versa; what the capacities and limitations of this work were and how they were mobilized as forms of propaganda; and how the war economy became entangled with imperial and colonial methods of seeing, marking territory, and reinforcing biopolitical oppression.

Governmentality and Counter-Conduct

Among the political tools employed during World War I was, for example, Austro-Hungarian Emperor Francis Joseph's ordinance of the state of emergency in October 1914. Bypassing other governmental bodies, this state of emergency authorized the sovereign to "give all necessary orders in the area of economy due to the exceptional circumstances caused by the war."[6] On this basis hundreds of organizations were created throughout World War I in the Austro-Hungarian Empire alone, bestowing to them the power to sanction immediate decrees that regulated the distribution and pricing of food as well as all raw materials. In 1917, this state of emergency was bolstered by the Enabling Act for Wartime Economy.[7] More than a decade and a half later, the very same Enabling Act – by then an outdated law on the books – transformed Austria into Engelbert Dollfuß's Austrofascist *Ständestaat*. However, even in 1914 and certainly by 1917, the state of emergency allowed for the consolidation of state power within a massive bureaucratic apparatus that tightly managed everything within its reach – from goods and resources to human life.

In recent years, architectural historians such as Daniel Abramson, Arindam Dutta, Timothy Hyde, Jonathan Massey, and others have emphasized that Michel Foucault's idea of governmentality helps to analyze how architecture, urban systems, and infrastructure become complicit in the management of resources through diffuse forms of biopower. "Foucault developed his conception of governmentality through studies of eighteenth- and nineteenth-century Europe," write Abramson, Dutta, Hyde, and Massey in 2012's *Governing by Design*, "where states and nongovernmental institutions aggregated data to constitute knowledge frameworks and expertise profiles capable of managing populations by regulating their demographics, health, housing, environmental conditions, employment, social lives, and culture," particularly in times of crisis.[8] They continue by noting that governmentality was geared towards providing "security to the processes of life – to tame risk, be it through social insurance schemes, food regulation, or housing norms."[9] World War I marked the culmination of the imperial managerial systems and epistemological frameworks Foucault studied, but also saw their complete dissolution. Due to constant shortages and bottlenecks, governmentality during wartime failed to fulfill its central tenets – the administration of the lives of populations through the enforcement of norms and the willing participation of citizens. Indeed, the collapse of managerial infrastructure gave rise to both more centrally planned and completely pre-capitalist modes of managing economies, including barter systems, which were in essence opposed to the mechanisms of governmentality Foucault theorized.

Moreover, both planned wartime economies on the one hand and barter economies on the other gave currency to theories of cooperation in the interwar period. These theories of cooperation can – to a degree – be understood as forms of resistance to governmentality. Through describing different contexts, architectural historians Anooradha Siddiqi, Ana María León, and Felicity Scott have highlighted that an architecture of counter-conduct (Foucault) or counter-hegemony (Gramsci) is characterized by processes of resistance, cooperation, and "togethering," to use Siddiqi's term.[10] For example, while writing about architecture, war, and migration in the context of post-coloniality, Siddiqi reminds us of Antonio Gramsci's idea of imagining a counter-hegemony, which would indeed enable ideological frameworks contrary to bourgeois and neo-liberal values.[11] Debates on cooperative housing in the 1920s – critiques of their own bourgeois legacies not withstanding – can certainly be understood as belonging within that tradition. Because World War I accelerated both rapid development and widespread underdevelopment, it heightened the logic of governmentality, as well as counter-conduct against it. Even as it thrust the unprecedented management of resources into existence, the war prompted resistance to such managerial logic in the form of alternative economies – both reifying and defying late imperial and colonial thinking.

Architecture and Urbanism in the State of Emergency

While increasingly sophisticated systems and technologies were developed to allocate and distribute much-needed resources during World War I, mobile kitchens, field railways, and do-it-yourself objects were designed by the military industrial complex and civilians alike in the state of emergency. As mechanized trench warfare came to the brink of collapse, hyper-development was accompanied by the re-emergence of systems of underdevelopment in the form of subsistence economies. Aside from the quotidian experiences of citizens and subjects with wartime architecture and urbanism, World War I reshaped the realm within which architects and designers worked, blurring the meaning of what constituted "architecture."

Indeed, the idea of repurposing became one of the defining architectural tenets of World War I. On the home front, for example, women, children, and organizations demanded the creation of food banks, victory gardens, and collective kitchens, thus prompting the re-appropriation of existing buildings, parks, and institutions. Famously, in the midst of World War I, in capitals across Europe all arable urban lands – from construction sites to sports fields and municipal grounds – were used for vegetable production due to an immense food shortage. As the war wore on, art museums became hospitals to care for both wounded soldiers and the victims of epidemics, including the 1918 influenza pandemic. Private individuals and public institutions attempted to feed millions of hungry people, while luxury goods like pianos began to be bartered for potatoes and wheat.[12]

Ephemeral architecture proliferated, too, from tent structures to repurposed infrastructures, and re-appropriated exhibition architectures were reshaped into humanitarian centers.[13] Finally, both the morphology of public and private spaces, as well as urban structures and civic life, started to change as markets overflowed with hungry visitors, intent on scraping their daily rations of food together, from substitute coffee made from acorns to the despised rutabaga. Cookbooks proliferated, instructing housewives on how to make do with limited recourses and how to stock their kitchens with labor- and energy-saving devices. By the end of the war, the outskirts of many cities were deforested, as desperate citizens cut down trees in an effort to harvest firewood, particularly during the harsh winters of 1918 and 1919. In vast territories colonized by Europeans, landscapes were left in a state not dissimilar to that of the front line, as technological systems were deployed under extreme pressure to extract last reserves of natural resources and local populations were subjected to horrific labor conditions. Undergirded by sophisticated systems of management and surveillance utilizing new and old technologies, the physical and psychological coercion of vulnerable people was the logical – albeit intensified – outgrowth of long-established imperial and colonial modes of viewing and control. Borderlands and colonial territories, already highly militarized, became even more subject to the centralizing and bureaucratizing impulses of governments and their allies in industry – essentially functioning as a front between the home and the trenches.

Histories of Architecture, Gender, and Colonialism

While the relationship between the expansion of imperial and military thinking across the globe and the founding of the League of Nations in the aftermath of World War I has been heavily theorized by historians, the colonial frameworks underpinning its material world still deserve historical attention. Recent works in art and performance, such as 2018's "The Head and the Load," a collaboration between composers Thuthuka Sibisi and Philip Miller, performers Ann Masina, Nhlanhla Mahlangu, N'Faly Kouyaté, and artist William Kentridge, are reminders of the horrors people endured in European colonies during World War I. As the title of this collaboration – itself a reference to a Ghanaian aphorism – makes clear, "the troubles of the neck" were inflicted upon the nearly two million porters from Tanzania, Cameroon, Togo, Senegal, Congo, South Africa, Ivory Coast, and Mali coerced and conscripted by German, British, Belgian, and French colonial powers, who bore the brunt of casualties during World War I. Their experiences, as well as the relationship of the war to empire-building, remain widely understudied. Aside from probing how histories of architecture during and after World War I enabled the rise of a new class consciousness, this volume is concerned with histories of difference, including the intersections of gender, race, age, and coloniality.

The volume positions the personal experiences of children, women, and men at its center, and the different modes of oppression citizens and subjects endured under colonial rule. Contributions contained in this volume speak to dimensions of race and gender in conflict on both the front and the home front, and how civilians, in rare instances, resisted being encompassed by military thinking. Importantly, the volume addresses the entanglements between colonialism, imperialism, and militarization and is committed to interrogating the often-violent relationship between front and home front. By following these theoretical considerations about the state of emergency, the histories of architecture presented in this volume imbed the formation of interwar design networks and institutions in broader histories of architectural production as spearheaded by governments, institutions, powerbrokers, and citizens within the framework of imperialism and colonialism.

Finally, at a hundred years' distance *States of Emergency* reassesses what World War I meant for architecture and urbanism from a human, social, economic, and cultural perspective writ large. Casting a wide geographical net to consider World War I in its global context and building on substantial efforts by cultural, social, and political historians, including important work undertaken by urban historians and scholars of memory, disability, and gender studies, the volume probes how civilians were enlisted and forced into the war effort. It charts how institutions were reshaped, military technologies repurposed, and rural and urban landscapes fundamentally remade by extraction.[14] It shows how biopower in the state of emergency came to govern not only flows of capital, building processes, and the circulation of goods, but also bodies through both rapid deployment and the logic of extreme austerity. The war prompted the development of military-architectural knowledge impacting *all* fronts and populations – eastern and western, battle and home fronts, military and civilian populations alike – but not equally, and often at great economic and human cost.

Institutions and Landscapes, Refugees and Civilians in the State of Emergency

An in-depth analysis of the economic underpinnings of both rapidly circulating goods and constant bottlenecks and what these meant for human material and architectural production defines the structure of *States of Emergency*. Overall, the volume is based on four themes: the repurposing of pre-war institutions by civilian and military authorities; the often-forceful reeducation and enlistment of civilian populations; the emergence of wartime cultures of both planning and care, particularly in regards to migrant and refugee populations; and the remaking of wartime and immediate post-war landscapes through forms of cooperation. While these four themes guide a series of essays in each section, they often reverberate across the volume. Topics such as how the state of emergency led to the creation of new institutions and how citizens were forced to contend with everyday scarcity on the ground, moreover, are through lines undergirding the book.

The first section of the volume, *Institutions Repurposed*, traces how the creation of makeshift and ephemeral architecture led to long-lasting, even permanent, institutional change – from the repurposing of exhibition architecture in France to the coordinated reconstruction of East Prussia and its relationship to the creation of mass housing in Weimar Germany. In the first contribution of this section, Aubrey Knox traces how the Grand Palais, designed for the Exposition Universelle in 1900 in Paris, was converted from an exhibition space into a military hospital during World War I. In "The Regulated Body: The Grand Palais as Military Hospital in World War I," Knox takes up the entanglement of circulating wounded bodies, artworks, and spaces, thus positioning the Grand Palais at the center of a history of adaptive reuse in response to overwhelming war casualties. Taking as her subject the wartime and post-war history of East Prussia, Deborah Ascher Barnstone describes how the devastation of large areas of the eastern reaches of the German Empire early in the First World War led the German military – under the auspices of a special *Militärbau Kommando* headed by Berlin architect Paul Kruchen – to mount a coordinated reconstruction effort based on cooperative economies. While "Lessons of War: Architecture of the East Prussian Reconstruction Effort, 1914–1925" lays open the brutal destruction of whole villages, farms, and industrial installations, it also showcases how the War Aid Commission enlisted both military and civilian associations in the development of innovative approaches to architectural design, construction systems, and labor organization – all of which had profound consequences for both wartime and interwar housing production.

Civilians Reeducated, the second section, positions personal experiences of children, women, and men at the fore. Focusing on the enlistment and forceful reeducation of citizens, the essays clarify how World War I was the culmination of imperial managerial thinking, even as individuals were sometimes able to leverage forms of resistance to it. In her article, "Learning to Play the Great Game: American Children and the First "World" War," Emma Thomas describes how American children in the decade leading up to World War I became consumers of visual codes and tropes of imperial politics and arbitration. Through play, children were prompted to understand and become enlisted in abstract concepts such as international alliances, the balance of military power, and the local resonance of geographically distant conflicts. At the same time, they became symbols of the tenuous balance between war and peace through which adults appraised America's role in future global conflicts – reflecting both optimism and anxiety on the eve of World War I. In the same section, Da Hyung Jeong's article, "The First World War and Nationalist Primitivism in Russian Architecture," clarifies the relationship of Russian architects at the outbreak of World War I to rising nativist sentiment, which manifested in an about-face from foreign models and an embrace of the "primitive" Russian provinces in architectural culture – including, but not limited to, competition entries, military structures, printmaking, and treatises. Finally, in the last article of the second section, "International Engagement, International Opportunity: Enlisted Australian Architects and World War I," Julie Willis and Katti Williams highlight the experiences of thousands of young Australian servicemen who saw battle in new and unfamiliar places. Wartime, while traumatic and demanding, also brought opportunity for those who survived relatively unscathed: for enlisted architects, particularly those of limited means and more modest backgrounds, that meant the chance to see buildings and places, and engage with a professional milieu, whilst on leave or at war's end. Such opportunities were further reinforced by the demobilization education programs that were set up late in 1918 for Australian and New Zealand personnel, which enabled many young architects to attend institutions such as the Architectural Association in London, before returning southwards.

The third section, *Refugees and Citizens Resist*, which concentrates on the emergence and expansion of wartime cultures of planning and care, takes individualized responses to trauma and the organizational strategies placed in the service of migrant and refugee populations into consideration. The first article of the section is dedicated to the pushback against military ways of seeing, namely the management of and resistance to one of the most traumatic experiences for civilians in wartime Great Britain. In "Wartime Nightscapes: Zeppelin Night Bombings as Mass Spectacles, 1914–1929," David Caralt describes nocturnal aerial bombings by German Zeppelins (popularly known as "Baby Killers"), which, due in part to their unexpected and silent appearance, induced panic, anxiety, and insomnia, as well as restrictions on nighttime activities. A less somber effect of air raids – given that the civilian population had to rush out of their residences during an attack – was "Zeppelin fashion," or the commercial promotion of women's jacket and pants silk pajamas. Caralt argues that while the threat of raids certainly impacted the morale and effectiveness of the labor force (and nightshift workers in particular), searchlights introduced an entirely new terrifying nocturnal urban landscape, in which the camouflaging of individual civilian bodies functioned as an act of resistance. Taking as his subject the attempted mitigation of civilian suffering through the production of emergency housing, Etien Santiago decodes the historical significance of the 1916 exhibition *La Cité reconstituée*, which took place in the Tuileries Gardens of Paris during World War I. At this exhibition, French architects and builders presented prototypes for lightweight, temporary huts that could rapidly replace the destroyed homes of millions of French refugees. Santiago's "Huts, Houses, and the Industrial Militarization of France, 1914-1917" showcases the development of numerous basic dwelling types based on new building technologies – as well as how the exhibition unfortunately became entwined with wartime France's creeping authoritarianism and militarism. Similarly concerned with the architectural response to the plight of displaced people, Theodossis Issaias's article showcases the "American City" in Pisa – a pilot refugee settlement conceived by the American Red Cross and its permanent Commission in Italy during the First World War. "Humanitarian Relief and Confinement: The American Red Cross Refugee City in Italy during the First World War" shows how American humanitarians merged military technologies with the postulates of modern planning, producing a settlement that carried the socially and racially inflected practices of the colonial camp and operated in the contested space between relief, rehabilitation, and confinement. Issaias's work on the American City in Pisa is thus a paradigmatic case study of the rise of institutional formations, such as modern humanitarian organizations, and their convergence with modern architecture and planning.

Finally, the last section, *Landscapes Remade*, speaks to the making and remaking of wartime and immediate post-war landscapes through both military developmental logic and the ways by which such modes were defied by soldiers and civilians. The section includes Min Kyung Lee's essay "World War I, Aerial Photography and the Emergence of Urbanism in France," which shows that cartography and photography during World War I, while long part and parcel of military and urban planning practices and techniques, saw pioneering uses of these media in aerial reconnaissance. Images from manned observation balloons, blimps, and airplanes provided the means to see and know the terrain in order to identify targets. They functioned to confirm the results of aerial and ground attacks, extending through their reproduction and dissemination the collateral visual effects of warfare. While the Treaty of Versailles may have halted artillery fire, interwar France was no less militarized – it maintained the largest armed forces in Europe and deployed them to consolidate and expand into new territories, including the former Ottoman provinces of Syria and Lebanon, for which photography and cartography continued to function as effective media in French colonial urban projects. Taking the efforts of active military personnel and demobilized soldiers as his point of departure, Massimiliano Savorra's "The "Landscapes" of the Great War: The Role of Italian Engineers and Architects" begins by describing the Italian landscape at the end of the First World War, one that was littered with barbed wire, torched woods, fields turned into graveyards, empty lots invaded by armies of crosses, wasted factories, torn-out churches, and, above all, seemingly endless trench lines and craters. Savorra's contribution then investigates how a generation of young engineers, architects, and artists – all of whom had been or were engaged in various activities at the front – transformed the Italian landscape to mourn and heal both individually and collectively. Linked to both the transformation of the landscape and the emergence of wartime cultures of planning, Antje Senarclens de Grancy's article describes the governmental disposition of refugee "welfare" in the Habsburg monarchy and its relationship to architects. This alliance gave rise to numerous refugee camps and the interning of Austro-Hungarian subjects in barracks. In her essay, "'Camps or Cities': The Urbanism of World War I Refugee Camps in the

Austro-Hungarian Empire," Senarclens de Grancy argues that these camps were city-like spaces reflecting modern urban planning methods and means; on the one hand, they (re)produced modern metropolitan elements of hygiene, order, and control, and on the other, simulated small town and residential colony typologies. Operating in tandem, these two modes allowed inhabitants to identify with and feel "at home" in the camps, while also telegraphing the modernity of the project and functioning as a means of governmental propaganda. Moreover, Senarclens de Grancy shows how these refugee camps reflected and reinscribed imperial logics of both "internal colonization" and colonialism.

Overall, *States of Emergency* thus adds to an evolving, but still limited, discourse on what World War I meant for architecture and urbanism. Building on efforts by colleagues in history, urban, heritage, gender, trauma, and disability studies, the book re-contextualizes architectural oeuvres and institutions – shifting the focus from trenches, officially sanctioned monuments, and imperial building projects to architectures of the everyday. It seeks to broaden and theorize what has traditionally – among architectural historians at least – been a narrow emphasis on individual biography, modular construction, prefabrication, and material technology. As such, this collection addresses what it meant to practice or produce architecture within the state of emergency and which forms of association, production, and urbanism these circumstances created. As a counter position, the book also uncovers what types of architecture and urbanism emerged from or were transformed by the war and which role the makeshift, the ephemeral, and the cooperative played in this effort. This includes, but is not limited to, histories about the role of women, men, and children in the creation of alternative architectures, including the production of objects and foodstuffs, and how architectural agents – from private citizens to governmental actors – mitigated, exacerbated, or actively resisted complicity in this human calamity. Finally, our volume helps to clarify how economic theories both of the war and of underdevelopment gave rise to later political projects of socialization and cooperation. By engaging with these issues, we hope to link the human tragedy that was World War I to the many cultures of education, memory, and care that emerged in the interwar period – even as these systems remained unevenly distributed.

Notes

1   For an in-depth discussion about food provisioning in Vienna during World War I see Maureen Healy, "Food and the Politics of Sacrifice," in *Vienna and the Fall of the Habsburg Empire Total War and Everyday Life in World War I* (Cambridge: Cambridge University Press, 2003), 31–87.

2   Luc Verpoest et al., eds., *Revival after the Great War: Rebuild, Remember, Repair, Reform* (Leuven: Leuven University Press, 2020), 14.

3   See Michel Foucault, *Security, Territory, Population: Lectures at the Collège de France, 1977–78*, ed. Michel Senellart, trans. Graham Burchell (London: Palgrave Macmillan, 2009).

4   For a recent treatment of the impact of the war on Neutra's body of work, as well as that of Patrick Geddes and Adrian Barrington, see Volker M. Welter, "Rebuilding, Recovery, Reconceptualization: Modern architecture and the First World War," in *Revival after the Great War*, 107–122.

5   The disconnection between these fields of study and more canonical architectural-historical work on the First World War is surprising when one considers how closely aligned and interdisciplinary this scholarship can and should be. In particular, the efforts of scholars in heritage/preservation studies have rarely been considered by architectural historians; as Nicolas Bullock and Luc Verpoest put it, "both fields of research – general architectural and urban history and preservation history – seldom really met, if at all" (Nicholas Bullock and Luc Verpoest, eds., *Living with History, 1914–1964: Rebuilding Europe after the First and Second World Wars and the Role of Heritage Preservation* (Leuven: Leuven University Press, 2011), 9). Part of the reason for this is that while "reconstruction architecture" (and planning) has been "the subject of ample academic research" (*Revival after the Great War*, 14), it very rarely employed a modernist architectural or planning language. In fact, most wartime and interwar rebuilding efforts, especially reconstructions of destroyed or "martyred" cities along the Western Front, purposefully leveraged a visual language that rendered them nearly indistinguishable from what had been destroyed. See also Maarten Liefooghe, "'C'est la beauté de l'ensemble qu'il faut viser.': Notes on Changing Heritage Values of Belgian Post-World War I Reconstruction Townscapes," in *Revival after the Great War*, 87–106; Richard Plunz, "Reflections on Leuven as Martyred City and the Realignment of Propinquity," in *Revival after the Great War*, 55–64.

Additionally, architectural historians have paid little scholarly attention to smaller-scale initiatives on the ground during the war; this has been the purview of historians, especially those concerned with the shaping of memory. In fact, those engaged in memory studies have produced a substantial body of work on ephemeral and small-scale initiatives, including, but not limited to, temporary memorials. Please see Paul Fussell, *The Great War and Modern Memory* (Oxford: Oxford University Press, 2000); Jay Winter, *Sites of Memory, Sites of Mourning: The Great War in European Cultural History* (Cambridge: Cambridge University Press, 1995); Leen Engelen and Marjan Sterckx, "Expressing Grief and Gratitude in an Unsettled Time: Temporary First World War Memorials in Belgium," in *Revival after the Great War*, 141–64.

Relatedly, scholars of gender, trauma, and disability – often historians – have been grappling with the "daily physical and mental, individual and communal experiences of people attempting to reclaim and reconfigure their daily lives in dramatically changed circumstances" (*Revival after the Great War*, 15). See also Deborah Cohen,

The War Come Home: Disabled Veterans in Britain and Germany, 1914–1939 (Berkeley: University of California Press, 2001); Tammy M. Proctor, "Reclaiming the Ordinary: Civilians Face the Post-war World," in *Revival after the Great War*, 127–40; Joanna Bourke, *Dismembering the Male: Men's Bodies, Britain, and the Great War* (Chicago: University of Chicago Press, 1996); Sabine Kienitz, *Beschädigte Helden: Kriegsinvalidität und Körperbilder, 1914–1923* (Paderborn: Schöningh, 2008).

6   Reichs Gesetz Blatt (RGBl.), Number 274, October 14, 1914.

7   RGBl., Number 307, July 24, 1917, otherwise known as *Kriegswirtschaftliches Ermächtigunsgesetz.*

8   Daniel M. Abramson, Arindam Dutta, Timothy Hyde, and Jonathan Massey for Aggregate, "Introduction," in *Governing by Design: Architecture, Economy, and Politics in the Twentieth Century* (Pittsburgh: University of Pittsburgh Press, 2012), viii.

9   *Ibid.*

10   Although writing about post-war architecture in war zones and under military dictatorship, Siddiqi's, León's, and Scott's concepts of resistant forms of cooperative architecture are powerful examples of counter-conduct as described here. See, for example, Ana María León's forthcoming work on "counter-architectures," Anooradha Iyer Siddiqi's work on "togethering" and Scott's work on "counterinsurgency." Anooradha Iyer Siddiqi, "Writing With: Togethering, Difference, and Feminist Architectural Histories of Migration," *e-flux architecture*, accessed July 28, 2018, <https://www.e-flux.com/architecture/structural-instability/208707/writing-with/>; Felicity Scott, *Outlaw Territories: Environments of Insecurity – Architectures of Counterinsurgency* (New York: Zone Books, 2016).

11   Siddiqi, "Writing With".

12   Healy, "Food and the Politics of Sacrifice," 31–87.

13   This is not to discount the vast body of scholarship on remembrance and commemoration practices – including both ephemeral and permanent memorials – during and after the cessation of hostilities, even to the present day. However, the shaping of memory related to World War I has only occasionally been the concern of architectural historians. For an overview please see Fussell, *The Great War and Modern Memory*; Winter, *Sites of Memory*; Engelen and Sterckx, "Expressing Grief and Gratitude"; George L. Mosse, *Fallen Soldiers: Reshaping the Memory of the World Wars* (Oxford: Oxford University Press, 1990); David Williams, *Media, Memory, and the First World War* (Montreal: McGill-Queen's University Press, 2009); Martin Löschnigg and Marzena Sokołowska-Paryż, eds., *The Great War in Post-Memory Literature and Film* (Berlin: De Gruyter, 2014); Gordon Hughes and Philipp Blom, eds., *Nothing but the Clouds Unchanged: Artists in World War I* (Los Angeles: The Getty Research Institute, 2014).

14   Urban ruins and subsequent rebuilding/reconstruction efforts in wartime and interwar Europe have long been the focus of urban historians, see Stefan Goebel and Derek Keene, eds., *Cities into Battlefields: Metropolitan Scenarios, Experiences and Commemorations of Total War* (Farnham: Ashgate, 2011); Plunz, "Reflections on Leuven." However, much of this work has focused on the "martyred cities" of Belgium and northern France, which have also been the subject of historical scholarship on the birth of "modern" humanitarianism, including "caritive reconstruction" (Pierre Purseigle, "Catastrophe and Reconstruction in Western Europe: The Urban Aftermath of the First World War," in *Revival after the Great War*, 46). The latter rebuilding efforts were often transnational and undertaken with aid from organizations like the Red Cross, or even privately financed, such as the American organizations and individuals who helped to rebuild the burnt library of Leuven University (John Horne, "Reconstruction, Reform and Peace

in Europe after the First World War," in *Revival after the Great War*, 303). See also Julia Irwin, *Making the World Safe: The American Red Cross and a Nation's Humanitarian Awakening* (Oxford: Oxford University Press, 2013); Bruno Cabanes, *The Great War and the Origins of Humanitarianism, 1918–1924* (Cambridge: Cambridge University Press, 2014); Melanie S. Tanielian, *The Charity of War: Famine, Humanitarian Aid, and World War I in the Middle East* (Stanford: Stanford University Press, 2017). Additionally, rural reconstruction along the Western Front has also been the subject of scholarly investigation, though this is often related to heritage/preservation studies, rather than traditional architectural history for the reasons enumerated earlier (for example, Hugh Clout, *After the Ruins: Restoring the Countryside of Northern France after the Great War* (Exeter: University of Exeter Press, 1996); Dries Claeys and Yves Segers, "Making Good Farmers by Making Better Farms: Farmstead Architecture and Social Engineering in Belgium After the Great War," in *Revival after the Great War*, 65–86).

Bibliography

Aggregate. *Governing by Design: Architecture, Economy, and Politics in the Twentieth Century*. Pittsburgh: University of Pittsburgh Press, 2012.

Bourke, Joanna. *Dismembering the Male: Men's Bodies, Britain, and the Great War*. Chicago: University of Chicago Press, 1996.

Bullock, Nicholas, and Luc Verpoest, eds. *Living with History, 1914–1964: Rebuilding Europe after the First and Second World Wars and the Role of Heritage Preservation*. Leuven: Leuven University Press, 2011.

Cabanes, Bruno. *The Great War and the Origins of Humanitarianism, 1918–1924*. Cambridge: Cambridge University Press, 2014.

Clout, Hugh. *After the Ruins: Restoring the Countryside of Northern France after the Great War*. Exeter: University of Exeter Press, 1996.

Cohen, Deborah. *The War Come Home: Disabled Veterans in Britain and Germany, 1914–1939*. Berkeley: University of California Press, 2001.

Foucault, Michel. *Security, Territory, Population: Lectures at the College de France, 1977–78*. Edited by Michel Senellart. Translated by Graham Burchell. London: Palgrave Macmillan, 2009.

Fussell, Paul. *The Great War and Modern Memory*. Oxford: Oxford University Press, 2000.

Goebel, Stefan, and Derek Keene, eds. *Cities into Battlefields: Metropolitan Scenarios, Experiences and Commemorations of Total War*. Farnham: Ashgate, 2011.

Healy, Maureen. "Food and the Politics of Sacrifice." In *Vienna and the Fall of the Habsburg Empire Total War and Everyday Life in World War I*, 31–87. Cambridge: Cambridge University Press: 2003.

Hughes, Gordon, and Philipp Blom, eds. *Nothing but the Clouds Unchanged: Artists in World War I*. Los Angeles: The Getty Research Institute, 2014.

Irwin, Julia. *Making the World Safe: The American Red Cross and a Nation's Humanitarian Awakening*. Oxford: Oxford University Press, 2013.

Kienitz, Sabine. *Beschädigte Helden: Kriegsinvalidität und Körperbilder, 1914–1923*. Paderborn: Schöningh, 2008.

Kraus, Karl. *The Last Days of Mankind*. Translated by Fred Bridgham and Edward Timms. New Haven: Yale University Press, 2015.

Löschnigg, Martin, and Marzena Sokołowska-Paryż, eds. *The Great War in Post-Memory Literature and Film*. Berlin: De Gruyter, 2014.

Mosse, George L. *Fallen Soldiers: Reshaping the Memory of the World Wars*. Oxford: Oxford University Press, 1990.

Siddiqi, Anooradha Iyer. "Writing With: Togethering, Difference, and Feminist Architectural Histories of Migration." *e-flux architecture*. Accessed July 28, 2018. <https://www.e-flux.com/architecture/structural-instability/208707/writing-with/>

Scott, Felicity. *Outlaw Territories: Environments of Insecurity – Architectures of Counterinsurgency*. New York: Zone Books, 2016.

Tanielian, Melanie S. *The Charity of War: Famine, Humanitarian Aid, and World War I in the Middle East*. Stanford: Stanford University Press, 2017.

Verpoest, Luc, Leen Engelen, Rajesh Heynickx, Jan Schmidt, Pieter Uyttenhove, and Pieter Verstraete, eds. *Revival after the Great War: Rebuild, Remember, Repair, Reform*. Leuven: Leuven University Press, 2020.

Williams, David. *Media, Memory, and the First World War*. Montreal: McGill-Queen's University Press, 2009.

Winter, Jay. *Sites of Memory, Sites of Mourning: The Great War in European Cultural History*. Cambridge: Cambridge University Press, 1995.

PART ONE

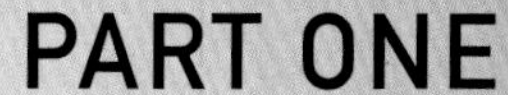

INSTITUTIONS REPURPOSED

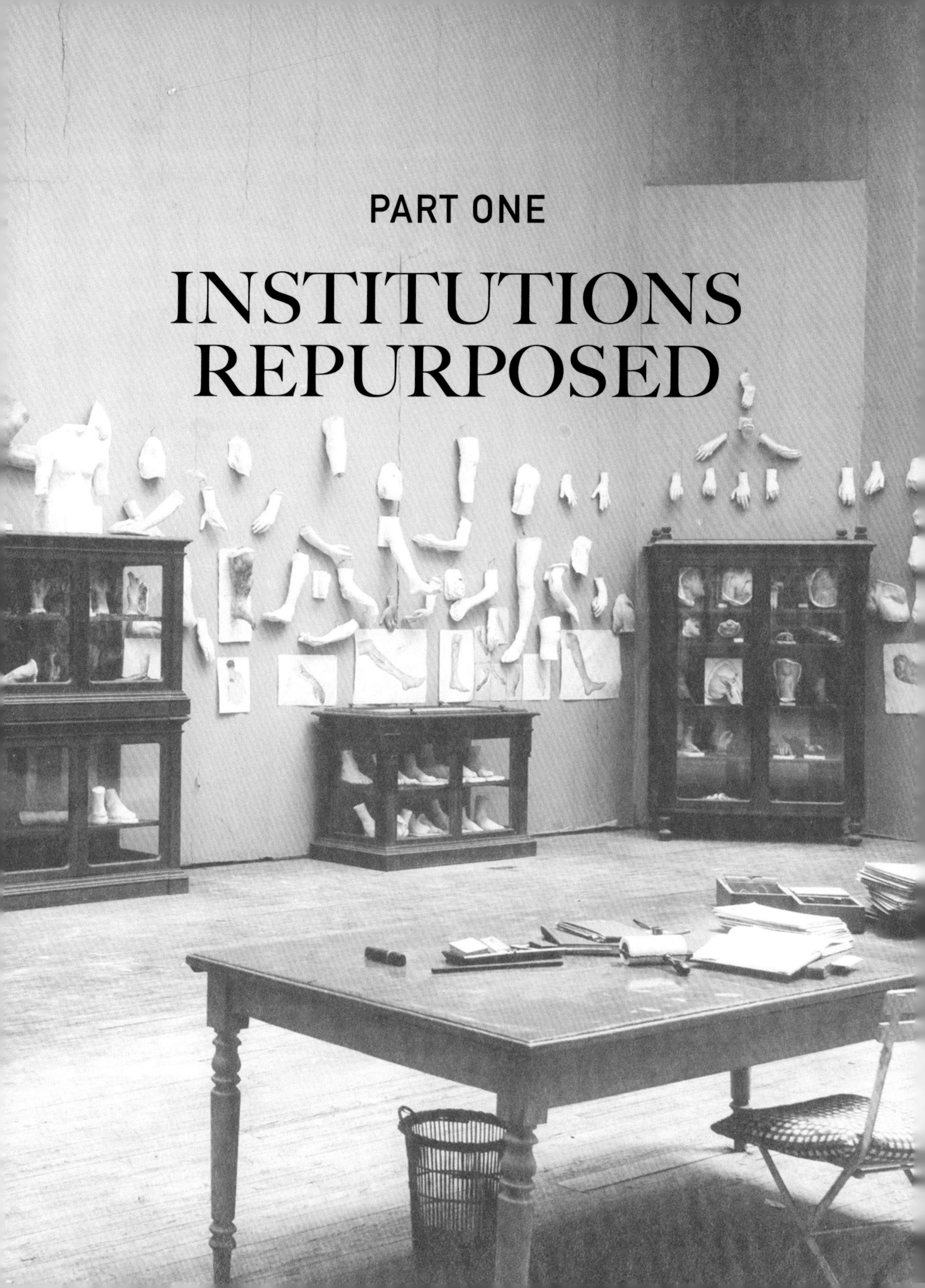

Figure 1.1: *The Great Nave: Wounded Soldiers Performing Arms Drills at the End of Their Medical Treatment* (*La Grande Nef: Le maniement des armes des blessés en fin de traitement*), 1916. Gelatin silver print, 8 5/8 × 11 in. (21.9 × 27.9 cm). The Metropolitan Museum of Art, Gilman Collection, Purchase, Ann Tenenbaum and Thomas H. Lee Gift, 2005 (2005.100.317). Image courtesy The Metropolitan Museum of Art.

The Regulated Body

The Grand Palais as Military Hospital in World War I

Aubrey Knox

Introduction

During the First World War, cultural institutions across Paris were drafted into service. The Grand Palais, designed for the Exposition Universelle in 1900, was converted from an exhibition space into a military hospital.[1] Sculptures and visitors were replaced by the injured and recovering, the regulated space of the exhibition by ordered regiments of soldiers. This study begins with the 1916 photograph *The Great Nave: Wounded Soldiers Performing Arms Drill at the End of Their Medical Treatment* [fig. 1.1]. Taken from a high vantage point, the photograph captured rows of soldiers executing drills in the nave of the Grand Palais. Almost the entire top half of the picture was dedicated to the architecture, soaring ironwork and steel grids giving way to a dome of light that evoked a Gothic cathedral. The structure of the dome echoed the parallel lines of the soldiers as it sloped to an apex that dwarfed the human figure. The sublime beauty of the photograph stood in stark contrast to the building's new function as a receptacle for the human cost of war.

The architecture of the Grand Palais acted as a palimpsest, where the design of the clinical healing space and military operation was overlaid onto the exhibition space. Joining the ranks of temporary hospitals at the front and permanent military hospitals in Paris, the Grand Palais provided an example of adaptive reuse as a strategic response to overwhelming casualties. While smaller churches, schools, and other public buildings were used as hospitals during the war, the Grand Palais was unique among these conversions in its scale and location. Its size made it ideal; it was able to accommodate a hospital and a garage, a nursing school and a rehabilitation center, new technologies and a robust archive. It was also located in the center of Paris in strategic proximity to key buildings in the military-governmental infrastructure. It had been a tribute to the cultural supremacy of France in 1900, and would carry this stature into its new function.

Beyond these practical considerations, this essay seeks to reveal a deeper ideological resonance between the pre-existing structure and its adaptation while resisting familiar narratives that cast the First World War as a moment of total rupture in art and architecture, a break that cleared the way for the next phase of the avant-garde. Rather than the broken bodies of mutilated men leading to radical artistic movements that fractured, alienated, or ridiculed the human form, the case of the Grand Palais revealed the continuity between nineteenth- and twentieth-century narratives of morality and wartime attempts to maintain the integrity of the human body. Nineteenth-century museums and exhibitions were designed to provoke moral goodness, heal the soul, and, alternately, to control movement and behavior. The military hospital of the twentieth century echoed this duality. *The Great Nave* showed a building suspended between two typologies, two eras, and two contemporaneous worlds: the chaos at the front and the ordered response of the home front. The body of the soldier was subject to the ravages of war, as seen in so many narratives of this period, but treatment at the Grand Palais allowed it to be reconstituted. The men in *The Great Nave* of 1916 were shown healed and preparing to return to the front, mid-way through this cycle between disintegration and reintegration. The first line of soldiers was nearly crawling off the picture plane, about to leave the regimented space of the exhibition hall-cum-medical establishment and re-enter the chaos of the unseen war.

The inaugural event for the Grand Palais and its sister building, the Petit Palais, was the great art exhibition of the 1900 Exposition Universelle. The nave of the Grand Palais was given over to the sculptures of the past decade, dominated by French artists. Rather than the horizontal linear quality of *The Great Nave* of 1916, a photograph of the space in 1900 captured the grand central staircase and emphasized the curvilinear form of the exhibition design that led visitors on a circular promenade around sculptures lofted upon thick pedestals [fig. 1.2]. Approaching the scene from a slightly oblique angle, the photographer here reinforced the organization of the exhibition around the central oculus of the dome and the importance of procession to the experience of the show. While not a museum, the configuration of the Grand Palais and the way in which its space was conceived drew much from nineteenth-century museum design. The nineteenth-century exhibition, especially in the case of museums and art display, subverted the overt systems of power previously exerted by princely collectors into an invisible but powerful network of control. The way in which rooms were partitioned and art hung was intended to teach visitors to adjust their behavior as they learned to achieve the higher spiritual ideals of art appreciation and understanding, consume information, engage in intellectual debate, and become more refined citizens.[2]

Figure 1.2: Nave of the Grand Palais during the Exposition Universelle in 1900. "Le Grand Palais – L'exposition de sculpture." Published in Neurdein frères and Maurice Baschet, *Le panorama, Exposition universelle* (Paris: Librairie d'Art Ludovic Baschet, 1900). Collection: *Paris: Capital of the 19th Century*. Brown Digital Repository, John Hay Library, Brown University.

Much has been written on museums and cultural spaces as sites of memory during and after World War I, as places to collect ephemera or erect monuments.[3] While museums were an important codification of this kind of nationalistic sentiment and of memory, this essay instead explores exhibition spaces as sites of bodily regulation and hegemonic control, and considers the interactions of these systems and their built environment with those of the war. Taking the expanded sense of the exhibitionary complex from Tony Bennett, these systems include museums, international exhibitions, and multivalent exhibition spaces such as the Grand Palais.[4] According to Bennett, for whom the work of Michel Foucault and Antonio Gramsci is foundational, the three aspects that link museums with exhibition spaces like the Grand Palais are their mission to display and educate about cultural phenomena, their publicness, and their use of architectural space to create a psychological-physiological connection, and thus promote self-regulation.[5] On this last point, Bennett writes: "Overcoming mind/body dualities in treating their visitors as, essentially, 'minds on legs', each, in its different way, is a place for 'organized walking' in which an intended message is communicated in the form of a (more or less) directed itinerary."[6] From this perspective, the activities within the Grand Palais during the First World War, while appearing to be in opposition to the experience of the 1900 exhibition, were in fact a different point on the same spectrum. Instead of ingrained architectural modalities of control, the war imposed overt systems of discipline, a military ordering of men that externalized regulation. The medical establishment added its own layer of methodology, developed through social systems and hospital design reaching back to the eighteenth century.[7]

Designing the Grand Palais

The Grand Palais was first conceptualized in 1895, when a committee of leading politicians and artists designed the overarching urban structure of the 1900 Exposition Universelle.[8] Believing that Germany might attempt to do the same, France, ever vigilant against its old nemesis, announced in 1892 that it would seize this crucial date, reinforcing its cultural primacy for a new century and foreshadowing the coming conflict with a competitive soft-power preview.[9] The fair had to reflect the progress of the previous century and the optimism of the next, while communicating the position of France as a leader on the world stage. The federal and municipal governments envisioned a reconfiguration of the city for this pivotal moment. Early in the planning process, organizers conceived a new bridge across the Seine, the Pont Alexandre III, and a corresponding thoroughfare, Avenue Nicolas II, which would connect Les Invalides and the seat of the French army to the Palais de l'Élysée, the presidential residence. The existing Palais de l'Industrie, a massive exhibition space built for the 1855 Exposition Universelle, which served as a venue for everything from agricultural exhibitions to horse shows, stood in the way of this new military, social, and political axis. The newly constructed avenue would run directly through it; thus, the planning committee decided to demolish the old building to make way for a new configuration. The Grand Palais and the Petit Palais, facing each other across the Avenue Nicolas II, would take its place. The two buildings formed the final branch of the national trifecta of military, government, and culture [fig. 1.3].

While discussions at planning meetings revealed a split between the artists and industrialists on the matter, it was conceded that the Grand Palais had not only to host the annual Salons of the Société des Artistes Français and the Société Nationale des Beaux-Arts, but the other events evicted from the Palais de l'Industrie as well, such as equestrian shows and exhibitions of machinery.[10] In 1896, an architectural competition put forth an impossibly short timeline to propose and construct the final buildings, which had to be completed in time for the Exposition Universelle just four

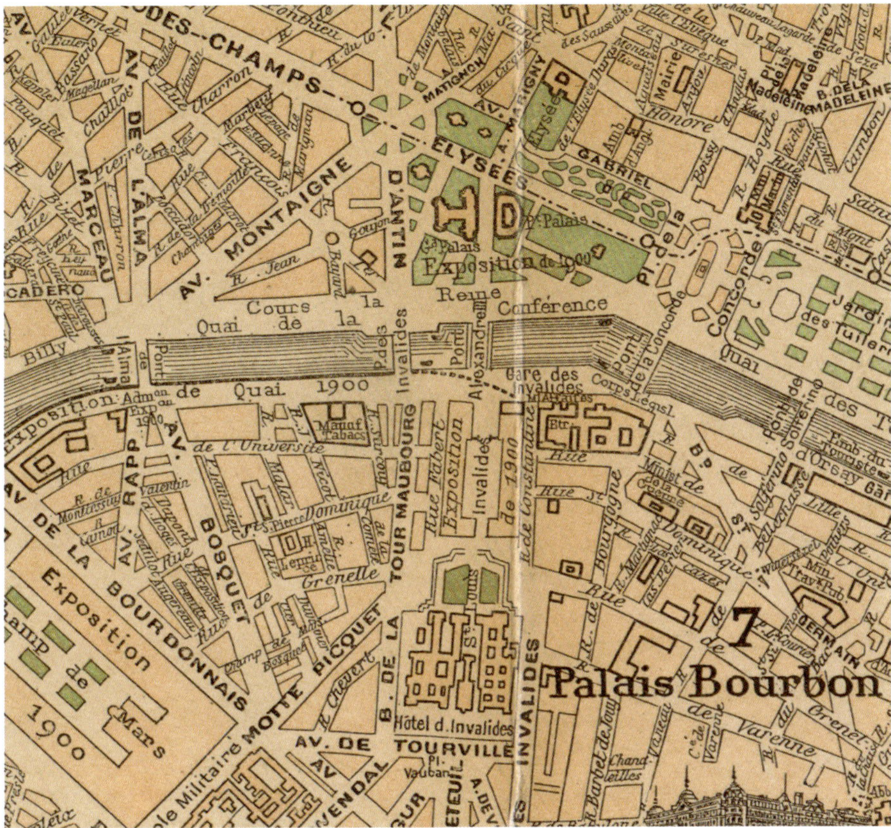

Figure 1.3: Detail of a plan of the 1900 Exposition in Paris released by the Bon Marché department store showing the Pont Alexandre III connecting the Invalides at center bottom to the Palais d'Élysée, with the Grand Palais and Petit Palais just north of the Seine. "Plan de Paris des magasins du Bon Marché." Collection: *Paris: Capital of the 19th Century*. Brown Digital Repository, John Hay Library, Brown University.

years later. The committee in charge set the terms. There were to be two buildings – one large enough to host up to 12,000 visitors at a time for the aforementioned industrial and trade shows (the Grand Palais) and one intended to become a museum of French art (the Petit Palais).[11] The committee received 82 submissions from 59 architects and chose four finalists.[12] Charles Girault was selected as the architect for the Petit Palais and the overall supervising architect for the project. Because of the size of the Grand Palais and the compressed timeline for design and construction, the committee selected three architects to collaborate on the larger building. Henri Deglane was to complete the nave, a soaring dome of steel and glass intended to serve as the primary site of the massive trade shows and the section of the building that would abut the Avenue Nicolas II. Albert-Félix-Théophile Thomas was selected for the smaller Palais d'Antin at the rear of the building, with its own facade and entrance. Louis-Albert Louvet was the junior architect who united the two buildings, navigating between the two more senior architects and creating several grand galleries and a monumental staircase in this liminal space.

The resulting structure was a multipurpose building with two main nodes, two entrances, and two facades, able to accommodate everything from aeronautics to fine arts. While the supporting infrastructure was later often categorized as Art Nouveau, the masonry shell was Neoclassical and Beaux-Arts, dripping with ornament, mosaics, sculptures, and reliefs. The bodies on display were the height of classicism – allegories of the arts and muses, seminude women alongside heroic gods and triumphant men. The building was a true spectacle. The external shell dazzled with its thick colonnades and scalloped corners and the internal space defied gravity with its scale, appearance of lightness, and comparatively sparse ornamentation. The stylistic layering at the Grand Palais demonstrated both industrial progress and cultural primacy; it was France looking to the future with a firm grasp on the past, an apotheosis of Belle Époque ideology that would end with the outbreak of war 14 years later.

An Exhibition Space Repurposed

One day after President Poincaré signed the mobilization order for French troops, on August 2, 1914, the Grand Palais officially entered service as a gathering point for soldiers receiving their arms and assignments. Grand Palais architect and *conservateur* Henri Deglane wrote in 1916 that it was at this point that his building sustained massive damage.[13] In order to accommodate the 2,000 to 3,000 soldiers who constantly rotated through, the exhibition space was hastily adapted into rooms, arms storage, kitchens, and bathrooms [fig. 1.4]. Deglane complained that the army, having no respect for the arts, punched holes through the grand colonnades to vent the apparatus needed for the kitchen, staining the facade mosaics with grease.[14] On August 4, the government requisitioned all heavyweight vehicles for use in the war effort, and the basement of the Grand Palais was transitioned into a garage.[15] This caused more consternation for Deglane, who lamented the oil (*cambouis*) and smoke from the cars.[16] On September 4, 1914, just before the bloody battle of the Marne (September 6–12), Deglane received an order from the military to transform sections of the Palais d'Antin into an *ambulance*, distinct from an *hôpital* in its function as a center for urgent care and triage rather than long-term rehabilitation.[17] The next day, Deglane led an expansion of this requisition to include the galleries to the northwest and southwest of the nave and their attendant bathrooms, slowly pushing out the billeted soldiers until eventually the space was dedicated to the medical facilities. The Grand Palais thus began its conversion into a vast military hospital. Administratively considered an annex of the Val de Grâce military hospital in the fifth arrondissement, the space within the Grand Palais was officially the *Hôpital complémentaire du Val de Grâce*, known by the acronym VG7.[18]

Figure 1.4: Grand Palais auxiliary hospital (Hôpital auxiliaire du Grand Palais) (Champs Elysées), Ludovic Jablonski commandant gestionnaire, October 1914 © *musée du Service de santé des armées, Val-de-Grâce, Paris.*

The choice of this building for the military hospital, made by a committee of army and government officials, was influenced by a number of factors. The committee was struck by the size of the building, the beauty and light in the space, the height of the ceilings and size of the windows, the views onto green gardens and great avenues, the "gaiety and air in abundance."[19] Surely such a striking combination would allow soldiers to heal rapidly and would ensure antiseptic conditions; sunlight was thought to sanitize and be therapeutic.[20] The building's prodigious glass was a major asset for this new life, from its large windows to its towering dome, a benefit to healing and the human spirit. The glass dome, originally constructed to allow light to illuminate the unmoving whiteness of plaster and marble sculpture, would now serve to contain the fallout of the first mechanical war, the progress of nineteenth-century industry turned against itself. Jean Baudrillard writes that "glass's cardinal virtue … is of a moral order: its purity, reliability and objectivity, along with all those connotations of hygiene and prophylaxis which make it truly the material of the future."[21] In purpose-built hospitals, glass was used to allow sunlight to penetrate the walls in the name of disinfection.[22] It was seen as clean and aseptic, and thus moral as Baudrillard notes, but it also allowed medical professionals to continuously observe patients in panopticon designs and medical students to observe procedures in enclosed operating theaters. Originally designed to dazzle, the glass at the Grand Palais became a tool both of healing and of containment.

Despite its clear assets, there were severe structural oversights to the choice of the Grand Palais as well. As Deglane noted, the committee could easily have chosen a school or other building already intended for habitation, containing proper heating and plumbing systems, electricity, a cafeteria, sufficient bathrooms, and other appropriate facilities. The Grand Palais would have to be significantly adapted during a time of great shortage of materials and expertise. Yet other potential sites mentioned by Deglane lacked the ideological strength of the physical position of the Grand Palais. Great parades already marched down the Avenue Nicolas II, and military ceremonies were held in the nave of the Grand Palais from the very early days of the war. Deglane also noted that, between 1900 and 1914, "the Grand Palais served exceptionally, in times of trouble or political ferment, to gather troops to safeguard the [Palais de l'] Élysée."[23] The police had installed a permanent position in the basement in order to maintain contact with the Palais de l'Élysée prior to the war.[24] The building held an ideological and strategic location within the urban space by its proximity to the presidential palace and the seat of the army.

The cultural significance of the Grand Palais was underscored by the burning of the University of Leuven library on August 25, 1914 and the bombing of Reims Cathedral on September 18. These events codified accusations that Germans were barbarians lacking refinement and culture.[25] Alternately, scholars have noted that there were widespread concerns at the turn of the century in France about "decadence" leading to the weakness of the French race.[26] Kenneth Silver cites many contemporaneous sources, such as author and illustrator Lucien Métivet and anti-Dreyfusards such as Maurice Barrès, who believed that a love of beauty and luxury seen as particularly frivolous at the *fin-de-siècle* made France vulnerable.[27] However, when the Grand Palais took the baton from the ruined Reims in 1914, it was with a belief that, rather than a liability, beauty could be France's redemption. The design of the building could restore military might by rehabilitating the souls and bodies of the French fighting force. Similar to the Art Nouveau interiors that the historian Debora Silverman interprets as a salve for the neurasthenic urban dweller, the Grand Palais was art as armor.[28] The masonry shell shielded the soldiers inside, who would be healed by its spectacular interior architecture. If the war was seen as a lapse in so-called "civilizing progress," a concern discussed by Stéphane Audoin-Rouzeau and Annette Becker, then the Grand Palais was an antidote.[29] The primacy of the arts, as the highest form of human cultural achievement, counteracted the basest forms of carnage at the front.

Encapsulating all of this symbolic weight, the Grand Palais was ready to accept patients on October 7, 1914, just one month after the original requisition. Deglane wrote: "There was … a nurturing impression of calm welcoming our sorrowful battle victims; no longer an asylum of pain, but a place of regeneration and hope of returning to life."[30] It was to be a salubrious area where soldiers could heal from the trauma of the front. But it was also to be an extension of the front itself, a chamber of military control within the urban capital. The Grand Palais was a space between – a calm respite for the injured soldier, perhaps, but also a pressing reminder of the war to the Parisian civilian. No longer a spectacular celebration of nationalism in culture and industry open to all, the building was now shuttered and turned inward, its invisibility glaring. Ultimately, while light entered dramatically through the dome in *The Great Nave*, even the glass was a one-way membrane. It allowed the soldiers a view of the sky and sunlight but prohibited access to the urban public, both for the health of the state and the protection of civilians. The glass of the Grand Palais contained this outpost of the war within the city, creating a hermetic seal in an attempt to isolate and neutralize the mayhem of the front. If beauty healed, it also concealed.

While civilians were not permitted entry into the Grand Palais during wartime, soldiers convalescing in the hospital were likewise not allowed to leave.[31] Entrances to the building became checkpoints under strict military control. Only images intentionally shared with the press would have made visible contemporary events inside the Beaux-Arts walls. This isolation thus mirrored that of the soldiers at the front – far removed from daily life, even while close in geographic proximity. In *The Great Nave* of 1916, the front was seen in the center of the city, a reminder of the closeness of the fighting (at once coming within 30 kilometers of Notre-Dame) and the ever-present threat of a German invasion of Paris as in 1870. But if the battlefield could be contained in the Grand Palais, the threat of consumption of the capital city as a whole might be neutralized.

Reinforcing this parallel between the VG7 and the front, mail sent to and from convalescing soldiers in the Grand Palais was subject to the same rules as mail sent to the front; it was both free of charge and censored. Information coming out of the Grand Palais was carefully regulated as the military considered the exposure of poor morale or the realities of sustained injuries threatening to the war effort; they sought to guard against "le mauvais esprit" and criticism.[32] One example of a postcard sent by a soldier in June 1918 appeared as if sent by a tourist, featuring the great facade of the building with no indication of its current function [fig. 1.5]. One would not have been able to determine whether the photograph showed the building in peacetime or in wartime. Printed information only identified the building's name and origin, further obscuring the transformation inflicted by the war.[33] Only the accompanying note provided further clarity, reading "Here is the Grand Palais, transformed into a hospital since the war and where I was treated."[34] The architecture maintained its external grandeur, the context of its adapted state erased.

Figure 1.5: Postcard from a wounded soldier treated at the VG7. Private Collection, Caroline Dubail © Caroline Dubail.

The second of Bennett's three characteristics of the exhibitionary complex, publicness, was here inverted by wartime. The exhibition space was turned away from the public, its regulation all the more robust given its near invisible state. To display to and educate the public, as in Bennett's first characteristic, the newly inhabited Grand Palais utilized propagandistic images and information about medical advances inside of the building, carefully displaying and sharing sections of the accumulated medical records to targeted populations in order to continue the pedagogical function of the venue.[35] Although the public could not enter the building or see the inner workings of the hospital, they were fed carefully released information that assured them this extension of the front was controlled, beneficial, and a great example of the highly functional workings of a powerful state.

The arts were not completely shut out of the medical establishment within the building, though they were often repurposed to meet the needs of the bureaucracy within. The development of new technologies responding to the massive number of wounded men required proportionate documentation to form, define, and communicate this growing body of knowledge. Written records were augmented by photographs, x-rays, drawings, sculptures, plaster casts, and plaster covered with wax and watercolor to appear more lifelike. The records were kept in an archive and some were displayed for fellow medical professionals and military staff in a room called the *musée*, a moniker that harkened back to the building's original function and once more recalled Bennett's characteristics. But now, art was replaced with disjointed fragments of human bodies [fig. 1.6].

Stefanos Geroulanos and Todd Meyers argue that World War I was a turning point in medicine.[36] Just prior to the war, several major medical theories reconceptualized the body as one whole, after many decades of pathology and germ theory had rendered it a kit of parts. But the war brought with it a fundamental challenge – if the body was an integrated whole, it was fragile and susceptible to disintegration by even mild threats. In the face of pathological fragmentation came a reinforcement of a dogged individualism. This shift, as Geroulanos and Meyers explain, relied on the case study. The case study required sensitive illustration, and for this, artists were deployed. Watercolors of wounds were done in great detail by Paul Prévot, who also decorated some of the treatment rooms. The cast studio was run by sculptor Fernand David, who also designed therapeutic apparatus. The classically trained artists employed at the Grand Palais used their previous figurative focus and transformed it into a hyper-focus on anatomy, with the intent of documenting, healing, augmenting, and reintegrating actual bodies that had been broken or threatened with obliteration by the war. While much has been written on artists' reaction to the violence of World War I, from their silence to their changing relationship with abstraction and subject matter, Prévot and David were working on the ground to literally bring threatened forms back from the brink of complete annihilation.[37] Displaced by the conflict, these artists became medical staff, and the arts once housed in the Grand Palais were subsumed within this medical structure.

Figure 1.6: The archives room and the *musée* (*La salle d'archives et le musée*). Published in Henri Deglane, Charles-René Coppin, and Jean Camus, *Le Grand Palais pendant la guerre (1914–1915–1916)* (Paris: Imprimerie L. Fournier, 1916). BIU Santé (Paris).

Crafting Spaces for Healing

Eventually, the *ambulance* inside of the Grand Palais would transform into a "hospital establishment of the highest order, able to compete with the most reputable military hospitals."[38] The hospital was placed under the auspices of Médecin Principal Dr. René Charles Coppin, formerly of the colonial army.[39] In early 1915, Dr. Coppin hired Dr. Jean Camus to direct the department of physiotherapy in the newly formed Corps de Rééducation Physique (CRP). As Dr. Coppin wrote, "the streets of Paris already saw a number of wounded and lame men, healed of their wounds, but in need of outpatient treatment."[40] A visibly worthy cause, the CRP quickly received full funding from private donors.[41] Starting with one expert in Swedish massage in 1914, the physiotherapy apparatus grew to a massive undertaking that attracted international attention and conducted groundbreaking research in a number of rehabilitative fields, including mechanotherapy, radiotherapy, hydrotherapy, electrotherapy, gymnastics, and massage therapy. Though some soldiers moved between the hospital and the rehabilitation spaces of the CRP, many only entered the building for physiotherapeutic

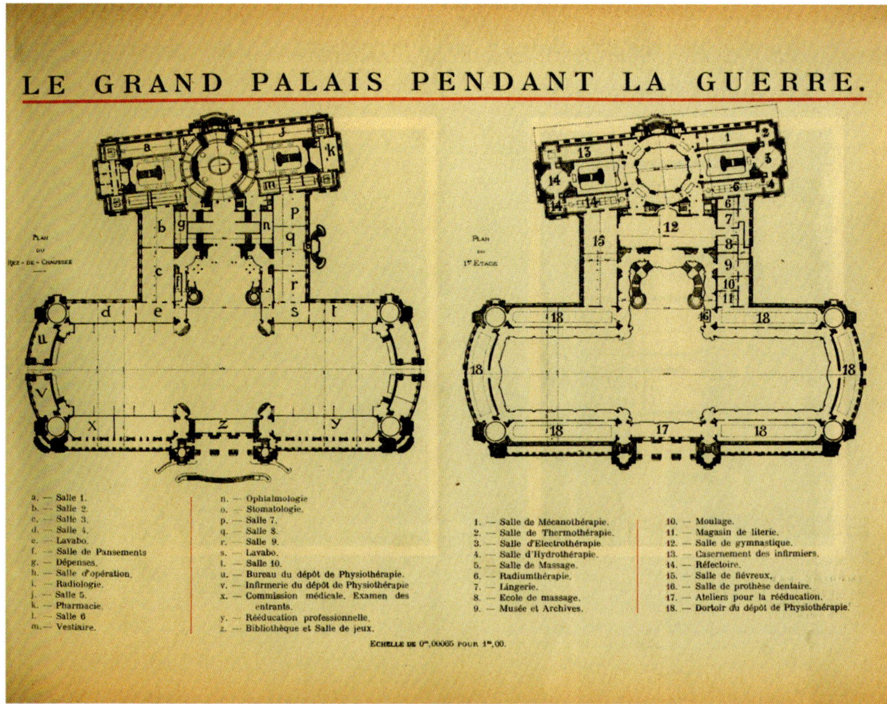

Figure 1.7: Annotated floor plan of the Grand Palais during World War I. Published in Deglane, Coppin, and Camus, *Le Grand Palais*. BIU Santé (Paris).

treatment through the Palais d'Antin at the rear of the building.[42] The therapeutic studios of the CRP were largely housed on the second floor [fig. 1.7]. By 1916, the CRP treated up to 2,200 soldiers at a time from the VG7 and other area hospitals.[43] In total, 80,000 soldiers passed through the CRP, and 80 percent of them were sent back to the front in an average of three to four months.[44] This was an exceptional rate of success in a time when some authors put the ratio of wounded to fighting soldiers at around 40 percent.[45] The soldiers in *The Great Nave* were at the final stage of this process, captured one last time by the camera before being declared fit for duty and returned to battle. Unlike the optimistic rebuilding of the body for economic recovery after the war described by some scholars, this was a death machine.[46] The body was rebuilt in order to return to the site of its most existential threat.

The healing nature of the exhibition space found its literal conclusion in the success of medical technology at the Grand Palais, the spiritual and moral growth intended by the founders of museums translated to physical fitness and national strength. The human body was no longer comprised of a soul reaching to God, awaiting moral instruction from a just state, but was instead a machine, fixable and replaceable, tuned and ready to serve not God, but generals and commanders. Those undergoing treatment at the CRP from the VG7 would remain under the administrative control of the army, overseen here by Captain Bousquet, and their movement throughout the building and across the threshold of the space was carefully regulated. Jean Camus relates:

> Permissions, special authorizations, must, quite frequently, be granted; that is how we quite often give permission to those injured soldiers who have parents, a wife, or children, to sleep in their homes. At first, we were very sparing with these permissions to sleep in the city, but we quickly became convinced that they were not the cause of disorder in Paris: to the contrary, the wounded, the carriers of the sleeping card (*carte de couchage*), showed the best discipline, fearing to be deprived of the favor they enjoyed.[47]

Replacing the moral incentive encoded in the exhibition space, the *carte de couchage* mandated good behavior in exchange for participation in one's own social life. The lucky and well-behaved soldiers granted *cartes de couchage* would be able to obtain a semblance of their former lives as civilian urban dwellers, moving through a membrane that separated the war from home, the front from the home front.[48] In addition, those CRP patients who were not being directly treated at the hospital may have had no cause to traverse the rest of the building, which housed the wards and the surgeries, creating a boundary between the grievously wounded and the walking wounded even within the building. Those allowed to exit and sleep at home were subject to layered visibility regarding the physical devastation of war, both in what they were permitted to see inside of the building and what they carried with them outside; their families, then, were removed even further. The building mediated this space between war and capital city, unseen and seen, unspeakable violence and recovery worth showing. These dichotomies were in tension even within its own walls and among its own soldiers.

As a tool of order, the *carte de couchage* was incredibly effective. In a three-month period in 1916, 29 of a total 390 disciplinary actions at the VG7 were given to holders of the *carte de couchage*; just 29 of the total 600–800 holders stepped out of line.[49] Only 11 of these actions were incurred for misbehavior outside of the building. This was a subverted form of control, wherein incentives were given in order to ensure that soldiers chose to abide by rules, rather than the overt control of the front or the military environment inside of the hospital. These implicit standards ran parallel to the forms of social control that museums hoped to enact at their inception. The *cartes de couchage* also allowed the citizens of Paris to see, in part, what might be going on behind the doors of their former home of the arts.[50] As Coppin pointed out, Parisians already interacted with wounded soldiers on a regular basis; the key was to use these encounters to benefit the war effort, to garner support for the cause rather than to provoke pessimism. The choice to allow those receiving physiotherapeutic treatment to exit the building would permit Parisians to see the wounded in a controlled setting – only the best-behaved and those who were benefitting from the technological progress of the French medical establishment were visible. The soldiers suffering from shock, "neuropaths," those with severe wounds or infections, and those preparing for or recovering from surgery would still be hidden, keeping the most devastating effects of the war out of sight for so many urban dwellers.

The spectacular function of the Grand Palais, now made private, was projected in full force onto its smaller sister building across the street. Throughout the war, the Petit Palais held exhibitions and functions to raise money for the war effort and at times directly for the wounded being treated at such close proximity. The Société des Artistes Français and the Société Nationale des Beaux-Arts replaced their salons at the Grand Palais with regular benefits at the Petit Palais for the cause.[51] Where one building became a contested site navigating the tension between the front and the city, the other took up the cultural baton and reinforced the importance of the French fine arts in national self-definition. Where the public was turned away from the interior of the Grand Palais, they were drawn into the Petit Palais. If suffering was to be hidden, beauty was to entice the eye and spark the heart with national pride. The two buildings, designed as an interdependent complex in 1900, were now opposites, their symbiotic relationship transformed from one of mass exhibitions and fine arts to one of visibility and invisibility, of conspicuous patriotism and carefully hidden violence. They were united in their intent to heal, physically and spiritually, a nation torn asunder by war.

Staging Medical Progress

While a hospital, the Grand Palais did host a number of exhibitions, but instead of the fine arts or industry, they were dedicated to elements of medical progress, from equipment to vehicles. They were also far from public, restricted only to those medical and military staff directly involved in the war effort. These exhibitions, often housed within temporary tented structures in the nave, visually recalled the fairs that were once mounted in this space, regulated systems of ordered movement and display. Now, human bodies were both visitors and subjects of display. One image of such an exhibition in 1918 captured a series of tents arranged in what appears to be the north arm of the nave, a new surgery intended to be deployed to the front [fig. 1.8]. The tents were arranged at right angles with regular entrances, surrounded by ambulances and medical transport vehicles, the temporality of everyday life evoked by the buckets outside of the central tent and the ladder paused mid-construction in the foreground. Here, the tents that might recall pre-war fairs in this space evoked something else – the temporary hospitals at the front, often less than orderly clusters designed for hasty triage and immediate care before sending the wounded on to a hospital away from the fighting or disposing of corpses. No longer a jovial fair or a cluster of spectacular experiences, the ephemerality of the tent denoted instead the constantly shifting status of the body and the built environment in the flux of war. The 1918 exhibition displayed this transient architecture of conflict, the hastily constructed tent, subsumed now within the walls of the capital city and within the vast exhibition space at its heart.

The photograph of the 1918 surgery exhibition described above was taken during a visit from the Undersecretary of State for the Health Service, M. Mourier, who was welcomed in the top right of the image. Similar to *The Great Nave*, taken in this exact space two years prior, the implements of war were fine-tuned, prepared, and ultimately declared fit for duty. The photographer of the 1918 exhibition chose not to include the glass dome in the frame, focusing the lens downward so that the tents became the primary subject and the architecture of the building was obscured. While one understands the space from the visual cues in the background – the sloping staircases, the sinuous iron piers, the intersection at the heart of the nave – the image emphasized the uncanny slippage between the exhibition space and the front. The surgery was here contained within the glass dome and the context of the exhibition but would soon be activated in the chaos of battle. The tents in the foreground, perhaps not completely erected, drooped and sagged, soft cloth windows echoing the downward slope of the fabric. In contrast to the tighter angled forms of the tents in the background, their transience and flimsiness was further heightened. In *The Great Nave* of two years prior, the bodies of the soldiers were featured as an element of the architecture, horizontal lines in parallel with the structure of the dome, appearing rigid, strong, and effective. The individuals in the background, milling about and awaiting their turn to enter the drill space in the foreground, further reinforced the relentlessness of the medical military cycle by reminding the viewer that there were always others to come up behind, to fill the ranks, to be healed and re-deployed. When compared, *The Great Nave* and the image of the 1918 exhibition threaten to expose the paradox within military medicine and its rehabilitative function. The front was not far and was impossible to contain, and ultimately the success of the hospital, the CRP, and the state lay in the percentage of soldiers sent *back* to the front, *back* into harm's way, often to their deaths.

Figure 1.8: Albert Moreau, *Paris, Inauguration of a surgical ambulance, and the tents which compose the service of the surgical ambulance* (*Paris, inauguration d'une auto-chirurgicale, les tentes composant le service de l'auto-chirurgicale*); Undersecretary of State for the Health Service, M. Mourier, visits a surgical outpost installed in the Grand Palais. This outpost is about to be sent to the front to provide the seriously wounded with appropriate care (Sous-secrétaire d'Etat au service de Santé, M. Mourier visite une antenne chirurgicale installée dans le Grand Palais. Cette antenne s'apprête à gagner le front pour offrir aux blessés graves des soins appropriés), August 1918 © Albert Moreau/SPCA/ECPAD/Defense/SPA 322 M 5500.

The temporary form of the tent in 1918 illustrated the ultimate state of the Grand Palais during World War I – adaptive reuse of an existing building, retrofitted to fuel war with human capital. Distinct from purpose-built hospitals, which were designed with great care to respond to the needs of the medical community and to the healing of the patient, the Grand Palais was an exhibition space hastily remade into a receptacle for the detritus of war. A tear in the urban fabric or a reweaving, the structure shifted from its position at the heart of visible Paris, designed to be seen and to display, into an uneasy portal from battle to home, from an injured to a recovered state, from life into death and from the clutches of death back to life.

Conclusion

When the war ended on November 11, 1918, the country turned from a singular focus on the military to recovery, which meant, among other things, rebuilding the economy. The commercial function of the exhibition hall was sorely needed to ensure the country could begin to rebuild and press forward. Likewise, the normalcy of regular salons and exhibitions was required to reset the cultural health of the country after the long war. In January 1919, it was announced that the VG7 would be closed; it was evacuated and returned to an exhibition space later that year.[52] From May 1 to June 30, 1919, the two rival salons (the Société des Artistes Français and the Société Nationale des Beaux-Arts) combined forces and held an exhibition at the newly re-opened Grand Palais to raise money for the recovery effort.[53] The conflagration over, funds were primarily required to repair the damage inflicted on people and the landscape alike.[54] The cultural calendar transitioned from its wartime support of the nation back into its regular salon schedule, this collaborative exhibition evidence of the overlap as the city slid back to normalcy.

In the span of the building's life to this point, from 1900 to 1919 [fig. 1.9-1.11], the containment and order that had originally been imposed on the body in the exhibition hall was taken to its most drastic end. The building that had once been intended to be seen and to display in order to hold up the undercurrent of national strength flowing between the government and the military had been adapted to conceal and contain for the very same reason. When the Grand Palais returned to its expected programming, this period of its life soon became hazy in the national memory. A monument of a *poilu* returning home to a woman and child was erected outside of the Grand Palais in Spring 1919, raised on a tall platform and surrounded by cannons, seemingly intended to be temporary.[55] A sculpture of the Victory of Samothrace atop a tank was displayed between the Grand Palais and the Petit Palais on the occasion of the *salon de l'automobile* in October 1919. Describing its import, *Le Petit Parisian* said of the sculpture: "The small French tank was chosen to glorify the part the automobile had in the victory, and two sculptors of talent, Messrs. Pasche and Pirou, received the mission of realizing a strong and harmonious work to symbolize the triumph of civilization."[56] The building deployed during the war became the passive host of such sites of memory, as so many places of significance in the war did. Once the memories of the war were sanitized with allegory and heroic narratives, codified in sculpture, and acknowledged in ceremony, they were sealed in the past and the city moved on.

Figure 1.9: Arrival of the seriously injured (Return from Germany) (*Arrivée de grands blessés (Retour d'Allemagne)*). Published in Deglane, Coppin, and Camus, *Le Grand Palais*. BIU Santé (Paris).

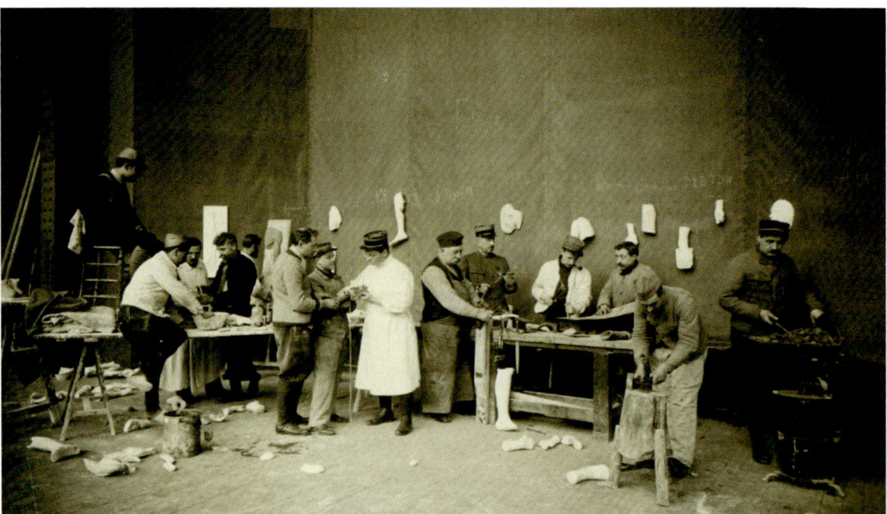

Figure 1.10: The casting room (*La salle de moulage*). Published in Deglane, Coppin, and Camus, *Le Grand Palais*. BIU Santé (Paris).

Figure 1.11: *The Great Nave: Wounded Soldiers Performing Arms Drills at the End of Their Medical Treatment*, 1916. The Metropolitan Museum of Art, Gilman Collection, Purchase, Ann Tenenbaum and Thomas H. Lee Gift, 2005 (2005.100.317).

Notes

1   This research received the generous support of a Doctoral Students Research Grant, a Mellon Travel Fellowship, and an Art Science Connect Research Fellowship from The Graduate Center of The City University of New York. I would like to express my gratitude to Caroline Dubail for sharing her research and for taking me through this remarkable building. I am also indebted to Claire Maingon, Romy Golan, Marta Gutman, Jay Winter, Tobah Aukland-Peck, and Lindsey Knox for the invaluable conversations and feedback. Special thanks to the musée du Service de santé des armées, Val-de-Grâce, Paris, for sharing images and archival material. Unless otherwise noted, all translations are mine.

Caroline Dubail, art historian and historian of the Grand Palais at the Réunion musées nationaux – Grand Palais (Historienne de l'art et du monument Grand Palais à la Rmn-GP), has done critical early research on this period in the building's life; see Caroline Dubail, *1914–1918: L'Hôpital Militaire du Grand Palais: Dossier pédagogique du Grand Palais No. 3* (Paris: Rmn-GP, 2014); Caroline Dubail-Letailleur and Joseph Beauregard, *La Vie de Gabrielle: Infirmière au VG7* (Paris: Rmn-GP, 2015).

2   Charlotte Klonk, *Spaces of Experience: Art Gallery Interiors from 1800 to 2000* (New Haven and London: Yale University Press, 2009); Carol Duncan and Alan Wallach, "The Universal Survey Museum," *Art History* 3, no. 4 (1980): 448–69.

3   See, for example, Gaynor Kavanagh, *Museums and the First World War: A Social History* (London: Leicester University Press, 1994); Claire Maingon, *Le Musée Invisible: Le Louvre et la Grande Guerre (1914–1921)* (Mont-Saint-Aignan and Paris: Presses universitaires de Rouen et du Havre and Musée du Louvre éditions, 2016); Jay Winter, *Remembering War: The Great War between Memory and History in the Twentieth Century* (New Haven and London: Yale University Press, 2006); Jay Winter, *Sites of Memory, Sites of Mourning: The Great War in European Cultural History* (Cambridge: Cambridge University Press, 1995).

4   Tony Bennett, *The Birth of the Museum: History, Theory, Politics* (London: Routledge, 1995).

5   In *The Birth of the Museum*, Bennett draws heavily from Foucault's intellectual framework in *Discipline and Punish: The Birth of the Prison* and *The Order of Things: An Archaeology of the Human Sciences*. To this, he adds Antonio Gramsci's theory of cultural hegemony from *Selections from the Prison Notebooks* and *Selections from Cultural Writings*, extending both to the exhibition space.

6   Bennett, *The Birth of the Museum*, 6.

7   Not cited by Bennett, Michel Foucault's discussion of the formation of the "medical gaze" is critical here. *The Birth of the Clinic: An Archaeology of Medical Perception*, trans. A. M. Sheridan Smith (New York: Vintage Books, 1973). On the history of hospital design, see Jeanne Kisacky, *Rise of the Modern Hospital: An Architectural History of Health and Healing, 1870–1940* (Pittsburgh: University of Pittsburgh Press, 2017); Annmarie Adams, *Medicine by Design: The Architect and the Modern Hospital, 1893–1943* (Minneapolis: University of Minnesota Press, 2008).

8   Alfred Picard, *Exposition Universelle Internationale de 1900, Rapport Général Administratif et Technique*, vol. 2 (Paris: Imprimerie Nationale, 1903), 15-6.

9   Jean Monneret, *Le Grand Palais, regard de Jean Monneret* (Paris: Réunion des musées nationaux, 2006), 23; July 13, 1892 decree detailed in Alfred Picard, *Exposition Universelle Internationale de 1900, Rapport Général Administratif et Technique*, vol. 1 (Paris: Imprimerie Nationale, 1902), 7–10.

10   Picard, *Exposition Universelle*, vol. 2, 17–8.

11   Caroline Dubail, *Le Chantier du Grand Palais: Dossier pédagogique du Grand Palais No. 2* (Paris: Rmn-GP, 2013–14), 5.

12   Picard, *Exposition Universelle*, vol. 2, 18–25.

13   Henri Deglane, "Notice historique par Monsieur Deglane Architecte Conservateur du Grand Palais," in Henri Deglane, René Charles Coppin, and Jean Camus, *Le Grand Palais pendant la guerre (1914–1915–1916)* (Paris: Imprimerie L. Fournier, 1916), 3.

14   Deglane, "Notice historique," 3.

15   Dubail, *1914–1918: L'Hôpital Militaire du Grand Palais*, 6.

16   Deglane, "Notice historique," 3.

17   "Monsieur le Conservateur du Grand Palais est requis de faciliter 'l'exécution d'appropriation et d'aménagement nécessaires pour l'installation d'une ambulance dans l'aile du Palais située en bordure de l'Avenue d'Antin." Deglane, "Notice historique," 3.

18   Dubail, *1914–1918: L'Hôpital Militaire du Grand Palais*.

19   "Mais la place manquait ailleurs, tandis qu'ici, les grandes salles et galeries très spacieuses, très-hautes sous plafond, offrant d'immenses cubes d'air; leurs larges baies avides de soleil, d'échappées sur la verdure des jardins environnants ou des larges avenues, plantées d'arbres, relient les grands espaces bordés des Champs-Élysées et du Cours la Reine; tout cet ensemble de gaieté et d'air à foison, séduisit la Commission de visite et, sans calculer autrement les difficultés de l'adaptation, le Grand Palais fut décrété

apte à sa nouvelle destination." Deglane, "Notice historique," 3.

20   Jeanne Kisacky, *Rise of the Modern Hospital*, 125, 149, 181–2, 196, 373n82; Arthur Downes and T. P. Blunt, "The Influence of Light upon the Development of Bacteria," *Nature* 16 (1877): 218.

21   Jean Baudrillard, *The System of Objects*, trans. James Benedict (New York: Verso, 1996), 43–4.

22   Kisacky, *Rise of the Modern Hospital*, 181–2.

23   "Entre temps, le Grand Palais servait accidentellement, en temps de troubles ou d'effervescence politique, à concentrer des troupes pour la sauvegarde de l'Élysée." Deglane, "Notice historique," 2.

24   Deglane, "Notice historique," 2.

25   Thomas W. Gaehtgens, *Reims on Fire: War and Reconciliation between France and Germany*, trans. David Dollenmayer (Los Angeles: The Getty Research Institute, 2018).

26   Kenneth E. Silver, *Esprit de Corps: The Art of the Parisian Avant-Garde and the First World War, 1914–1925* (Princeton: Princeton University Press, 1989); Sharon Hirsh, "Codes of Consumption: Tuberculosis and Body Image at the Fin-de-Siècle," in *In Sickness and in Health: Disease as Metaphor in Art and Popular Wisdom*, ed. Laurinda S. Dixon (Newark: University of Delaware Press, 2004), 144–65; Barbara Larson, "Curing Degeneration: Health and the Neoclassical Body in Early Twentieth-Century France," in *In Sickness and in Health*, 166–86.

27   Silver, *Esprit de Corps*, 13–27.

28   Debora L. Silverman, *Art Nouveau in Fin-de-Siècle France: Politics, Psychology, and Style* (Berkeley and Los Angeles: University of California Press, 1989).

29   Stéphane Audoin-Rouzeau and Annette Becker, *14–18: Understanding the Great War*, trans. Catherine Temerson (New York: Hill and Wang, 2002), 32–6.

30   "C'était aussi la bienfaisant impression de repos accueillant pour nos malheureuses victimes des batailles; non plus un asile de douleur, mais un lieu de régénérescence et d'espoir de retour à la vie." Deglane, "Notice historique," 5.

31   Dubail, *1914–1918: L'Hôpital Militaire du Grand Palais*, 7, 25.

32   Dubail, *1914–1918: L'Hôpital Militaire du Grand Palais*, 25.

33   "Paris – Grand Palais des Champs-Élysées … Construit par Deglane, Louvet et Thomas pour l'Exposition de 1900."

34   "Voici le Grand Palais transformé en hôpital depuis la guerre et où que je suis soigné."

35   Examples are Deglane, Coppin, and Camus, *Le Grand Palais*; Jean Camus, "Les Services de Physiothérapie du Grand-Palais," *Paris medical: La semaine du clinician*, no. 17 (1915): 53–61; Jean Camus, *Le Corps de Rééducation Physique du Grand Palais* (Paris: Imprimerie L. Fournier, 1916).

36   Stefanos Geroulanos and Todd Meyers, *The Human Body in the Age of Catastrophe: Brittleness, Integration, Science, and the Great War* (Chicago: University of Chicago Press, 2018).

37   Silver, *Esprit de Corps*; Romy Golan, *Modernity and Nostalgia: Art and Politics in France between the Wars* (New Haven and London: Yale University Press, 1995); Philippe Dagen, *Le silence des peintres: Les artistes face à la Grande Guerre* (Paris: Librairie Arthème Fayard, 1996); Claire Maingon, *Mains coupées sur paupières closes: Blessures, mutilations subies et sublimées des artistes en guerres (1914–1930)* (Mont-Saint-Aignan: Presses universitaires de Rouen et du Havre, 2018).

38   "Il est juste de rendre ici hommage à la largeur de ces dons qui permirent de réaliser ces installations de la plus haute utilité, et qui, peu à peu, firent de l'Hôpital du Grand Palais, au début ambulance pour petits blessés ou convalescents, un établissement

hospitalier de premier ordre, capable de rivaliser avec les Hôpitaux militaires les plus justement réputés, et où furent traitées des opérations chirurgicales et thérapeutiques de la plus haute portée." Deglane, "Notice historique," 5.

39   Beyond the scope of this discussion, the status of recalled colonial troops and requisitioned colonial subjects is a significant point of inquiry for future study – these groups seem to have been represented in the personnel and patients at the Grand Palais.

40   "On voyait déjà circuler dans les rues de Paris de nombreux mutilés et éclopés guéris de leurs plaies, mais ayant besoin de traitements externes." René Charles Coppin, "Création et organisation de l'hôpital par le médecin principal Coppin, Médecin Chef," in Deglane, Coppin, and Camus, *Le Grand Palais*, 9.

41   While it is unclear if the CRP received funding from foreign donors, American benefactors were very active in contributing to medical initiatives in France during the war. See a contemporary accounting of one such effort in *Friends of France: The Field Service of the American Ambulance Described by its Members* (Boston and New York: Houghton Mifflin Company, 1916).

42   Camus, "Les Services de Physiothérapie du Grand-Palais."

43   Camus, *Le Corps*, 375.

44   Dubail, *1914–1918: L'Hôpital Militaire du Grand Palais*, 12.

45   Audoin-Rouzeau and Becker, *14–18: Understanding the Great War*, 24.

46   For example, see Luc Verpoest et al., Introduction to *Revival after the Great War: Rebuild, Remember, Repair, Reform* (Leuven: Leuven University Press, 2020).

47   "Des permissions, des autorisations spéciales doivent, assez fréquemment, être accordées; c'est ainsi que nous donnons assez souvent aux blessés qui ont leurs parents, leur femme, leurs enfants, l'autorisation de coucher chez eux. Au début, nous avons été très parcimonieux de ces permissions de coucher en ville, mais nous nous sommes convaincus rapidement qu'elles n'étaient pas la cause de désordre dans Paris: bien au contraire, les blessés, porteurs de carte de couchage se montraient les mieux disciplinés, craignant de se voir retirer la faveur dont ils jouissaient." Camus, *Le Corps*, 369.

48   For a discussion of the dissonance soldiers experienced passing from the violence and chaos of the front to the ordered patriotism of the home front, see Philipp Blom, *Fracture: Life and Culture in the West, 1918–1938* (London: Atlantic Books, 2015).

49   Camus, *Le Corps*, 369.

50   The Louvre was also closed and largely emptied for the protection of the art; see Claire Maingon, *Le Musée Invisible*.

51   For example, the *Exposition organisée sous le patronage de la Ville de Paris au profit des œuvres de guerre de la Société des Artistes Français et de la Société Nationale des Beaux-Arts au Petit Palais des Champs-Élysées*, May–June 1918.

52   It is notable that the influenza pandemic of 1918–19 (the so-called Spanish Flu) was at its peak in France when the war ended; upwards of 7,000 people in Paris died of the flu in 1918, with the greatest number of deaths occurring in October. While over 1,000 Parisians died by the end of February 1919, around the time the VG7 was closing, the epidemic mostly dropped off in Paris after March. Anton Erkoreka, "The Spanish Influenza Pandemic in Occidental Europe (1918–1920) and Victim Age," *Influenza and Other Respiratory Viruses* 4, no. 2 (March 2010): 81–9.

53   *Exposition organisée au profit des œuvres de guerre de la Société des Artistes Français et de la Société Nationale des Beaux-Arts*, May 1–June 30, 1919.

54   Parallels between the restoration of the body and destroyed architecture are numerous. For one example, see Luc Verpoest et al., eds., *Revival after the Great War*.

55   Dubail, *1914-1918: L'Hôpital Militaire du Grand Palais*; "Scene 25. New statue 'The
        Return of the Poilu,' temporarily placed on the Champs Elysees, to stimulate the sale
        of the Fourth French Liberty Bonds," Scenes in Paris: War Trophies [1918-1919],
        Record Group 111, Series: Historical Films, c.1914–c.1936, The US National Archives
        and Records Administration.

56   "Le petit tank français a été choisi pour glorifier la part de l'automobile dans la Victoire,
        et deux sculpteurs de talent, MM. Pasche et Pirou, ont reçu la mission de réaliser une
        œuvre forte et harmonieuse pour symboliser le triomphe de la civilisation." "Le Tank
        Monumental du Salon de l'Automobile," *Le Petit Parisian*, October 1, 1919.

Bibliography

Archives nationales de France.
        Plans de l'Agence d'architecture du Grand palais (CP/102AJ)
Bibliothèque historique de la Ville de Paris.
        Éphémères de la Première Guerre mondial (4-DEP-001)
Établissement de Communication et de Production Audiovisuelle de la Défense (ECPAD).
Le musée Carnavalet – Histoire de Paris.
Musée du Service de santé des armées.
The U.S. National Archives and Records Administration.
        Record Group 111: Records of the Office of the Chief Signal Officer, Series: Historical
        Films, c.1914–c.1936.

1917. Metz: Centre Pompidou-Metz, 2012. Published in conjunction with an exhibition of
        the same title, presented at the Centre Pompidou-Metz, May 26–September 24, 2012.
Adams, Annmarie. *Medicine by Design: The Architect and the Modern Hospital, 1893–1943*.
        Minneapolis: University of Minnesota Press, 2008.
Audoin-Rouzeau, Stéphane, and Annette Becker. *14–18: Understanding the Great War*.
        Translated by Catherine Temerson. New York: Hill and Wang, 2002.
Baschet, Ludovic, ed. *Exposition Universelle de 1900: Catalogue Officiel illustré de
        l'Exposition Centennale de l'art français de 1800 à 1889,* Paris: Imprimeries Lemercier,
        1900.
Baschet, Ludovic, ed. *Exposition Universelle de 1900: Catalogue Officiel illustré de
        l'Exposition Décennale des Beaux-Arts de 1889 à 1900*. Paris: Imprimeries Lemercier,
        1900.
Baudrillard, Jean. *The System of Objects*. Translated by James Benedict. New York: Verso,
        1996.
Bennett, Tony. *The Birth of the Museum: History, Theory, Politics*. London: Routledge, 1995.
Blom, Philipp, *Fracture: Life and Culture in the West, 1918–1938*. London: Atlantic Books,
        2015.
Camus, Jean. *Le Corps de Rééducation Physique du Grand Palais*. Paris: Imprimerie L.
        Fournier, 1916.
———. "Les Services de Physiothérapie du Grand-Palais." *Paris medical: La semaine du
        clinician*, no. 17 (1915): 53–61.
Dagen, Philippe. *Le silence des peintres: Les artistes face à la Grande Guerre*. Paris: Librairie
        Arthème Fayard, 1996.

Deglane, Henri, René Charles Coppin, and Jean Camus. *Le Grand Palais pendant la guerre (1914–1915–1916)*. Paris: Imprimerie L. Fournier, 1916.

Dixon, Laurinda S., ed. *In Sickness and in Health: Disease as Metaphor in Art and Popular Wisdom*. Newark: University of Delaware Press, 2004.

Downes, Arthur, and T. P. Blunt. "The Influence of Light upon the Development of Bacteria." *Nature* 16 (1877): 218.

Dubail, Caroline. *1914–1918: L'Hôpital Militaire du Grand Palais: Dossier pédagogique du Grand Palais No. 3*. Paris: Rmn-GP, 2014.

———.*Le Chantier du Grand Palais: Dossier pédagogique du Grand Palais No. 2*. Paris: Rmn-GP, 2013–14.

Dubail-Letailleur, Caroline, and Joseph Beauregard. *La Vie de Gabrielle: Infirmière au VG7*. Paris: Rmn-GP, 2015.

Duncan, Carol, and Alan Wallach. "The Universal Survey Museum." *Art History* 3, no. 4 (1980): 448–69.

Erkoreka, Anton. "The Spanish Influenza Pandemic in Occidental Europe (1918–1920) and Victim Age." *Influenza and Other Respiratory Viruses* 4, no. 2 (March 2010): 81–9.

Exposition organisée sous le patronage de la Ville de Paris au profit des œuvres de guerre de la Société des Artistes Français et de la Société Nationale des Beaux-Arts au Petit Palais des Champs-Élysées. Published in conjunction with an exhibition of the same title, presented at the Petit Palais, May 1–June 30, 1918.

Exposition organisée au profit des œuvres de guerre de la Société des Artistes Français et de la Société Nationale des Beaux-Arts. Published in conjunction with an exhibition of the same title, presented at the Grand Palais, May 1–June 30, 1919.

Foucault, Michel. *The Birth of the Clinic: An Archaeology of Medical Perception*. Translated by A. M. Sheridan Smith. New York: Vintage Books, 1973.

Friends of France: The Field Service of the American Ambulance Described by Its Members. Boston and New York: Houghton Mifflin Company, 1916.

Gaehtgens, Thomas W. *Reims on Fire: War and Reconciliation between France and Germany*. Translated by David Dollenmayer. Los Angeles: The Getty Research Institute, 2018.

Geroulanos, Stefanos, and Todd Meyers. *The Human Body in the Age of Catastrophe: Brittleness, Integration, Science, and the Great War*. Chicago: University of Chicago Press, 2018.

Golan, Romy. *Modernity and Nostalgia: Art and Politics in France between the Wars*. New Haven and London: Yale University Press, 1995.

Hirsh, Sharon. "Codes of Consumption: Tuberculosis and Body Image at the Fin-de-Siècle." In *In Sickness and in Health: Disease as Metaphor in Art and Popular Wisdom*, edited by Laurinda S. Dixon, 144–65. Newark: University of Delaware Press, 2004.

Kavanagh, Gaynor. *Museums and the First World War: A Social History*. London: Leicester University Press, 1994.

Kisacky, Jeanne. *Rise of the Modern Hospital: An Architectural History of Health and Healing, 1870–1940*. Pittsburgh: University of Pittsburgh Press, 2017.

Klonk, Charlotte. *Spaces of Experience: Art Gallery Interiors from 1800 to 2000*. New Haven and London: Yale University Press, 2009.

Larson, Barbara. "Curing Degeneration: Health and the Neoclassical Body in Early Twentieth-Century France." In *In Sickness and in Health: Disease as Metaphor in Art and Popular Wisdom*, edited by Laurinda S. Dixon, 166–86. Newark: University of Delaware Press, 2004.

Maingon, Claire. *Mains coupées sur paupières closes: Blessures, mutilations subies et sublimées des artistes en guerres (1914–1930)*. Mont-Saint-Aignan: Presses universitaires de Rouen et du Havre, 2018.

———.*Le Musée Invisible: Le Louvre et la Grande Guerre (1914–1921)*. Mont-Saint-Aignan and Paris: Presses universitaires de Rouen et du Havre and Musée du Louvre éditions, 2016.

Marrey, Bernard. *Le Grand Palais: Sa construction, son histoire*. Paris: Picard, 2006.

Massacré. "Isolement et Rééducation des Blessés de Guerre dits 'fonctionnels.'" *Paris medical: La semaine du clinician*, no. 25 (1917): 38–41.

Monneret, Jean. *Le Grand Palais, regard de Jean Monneret*. Paris: Réunion des musées nationaux, 2006.

Paris 1900: La Ville Spectacle. Paris: Paris Musées, 2014. Published in conjunction with an exhibition of the same title, presented at the Petit Palais, Musée des Beaux-Arts de la Ville de Paris, April 2–August 17, 2014.

Picard, Alfred. *Exposition Universelle Internationale de 1900*, Rapport Général Administratif et Technique. 8 vols. Paris: Imprimerie Nationale, 1902–1903.

Plum, Gilles. *Le Grand Palais: L'aventure du Palais des Beaux-Arts*. Paris: Réunion des musées nationaux, 1993.

———.*Le Grand Palais: Un palais national populaire, architectures et décors*. Paris: Éditions du Patrimoine, Centre des monuments nationaux, 2008.

Silver, Kenneth E. *Esprit de Corps: The Art of the Parisian Avant-Garde and the First World War, 1914–1925*. Princeton: Princeton University Press, 1989.

Silverman, Debora L. *Art Nouveau in Fin-de-Siècle France: Politics, Psychology, and Style*. Berkeley and Los Angeles: University of California Press, 1989.

"Le Tank Monumental du Salon de l'Automobile." *Le Petit Parisian*, October 1, 1919.

Verpoest, Luc, Leen Engelen, Rajesh Heynickx, Jan Schmidt, Pieter Uyttenhove, and Pieter Verstraete, eds. *Revival after the Great War: Rebuild, Remember, Repair, Reform*. Leuven: Leuven University Press, 2020.

Winter, Jay. *Remembering War: The Great War between Memory and History in the Twentieth Century*. New Haven and London: Yale University Press, 2006.

———."Shell-Shock and the Cultural History of the Great War." *Journal of Contemporary History* 35, no. 1 (January 2000): 7–11.

———.*Sites of Memory, Sites of Mourning: The Great War in European Cultural History*. Cambridge: Cambridge University Press, 1995.

Wylie, W. Gill. *Hospitals: Their History, Organization, and Construction*. New York: D. Appleton and Company, 1877.

Figure 2.1: Prisoners of war in a street in the destructed municipality of Crossen. © Bundesarchiv, 183-R31894.

Lessons of War

Architecture of the East Prussian Reconstruction Effort, 1914–1925

Deborah Ascher Barnstone

"The visible expressions of culture are the products of art; architecture was, and will be again, the 'mother of the arts.' A strong and purposeful architecture is therefore a major requirement for uplifting and strengthening the culture of the East."[1]

Building Arts Chamber of the East, 1918/1919.[2]

The sudden need to reconstruct large areas of East Prussia early in the First World War led the German military to develop several innovative approaches to architectural design, construction systems, and labor organization that had profound consequences for both wartime and interwar housing production.[3] As the citation from the Building Arts Chamber of the East above makes clear, at the end of the war, architecture was considered the penultimate art form and the salve that could repair physical, spiritual, and cultural wounds suffered during the conflict. Thus, any innovations from wartime architectural efforts were welcomed. Innovations developed in two ways: through federal policy dictated from Berlin and through experience in the military reconstruction effort.

The prosecution of the war took a particularly heavy toll in Germany's easternmost province, East Prussia, where Russian forces mounted an early two-pronged assault in August 1914. East Prussia comprised territory on the easternmost edges of Germany that was bordered by the Baltic Sea to the north and the Russian Empire to the east and south, making it vulnerable to Russian invasion. (Today, it is part of Poland.) The Russians sent the First Army against the well-fortified city of Königsberg in the northeast, and the Second Army around the Masurian Lakes farther south to advance on East Prussia from the south in order to trap Germany's Eighth Army near Allenstein.[4] Although the Russians inflicted considerable casualties on German forces, they were plagued by poor communications, lack of modern equipment – especially aerial reconnaissance capabilities – and an uneducated and unprepared soldiery.[5] Russia appeared to be winning at the beginning of the attack on August 20 and 21, but by the 29th its armies were in disarray. Over 50,000 troops were killed and over 90,000 were captured by the Germans. The unexpected necessity to house so many prisoners-of-war was one catalyst for establishing a special military unit, the Militärbau Kommando (military construction commando), tasked with construction and reconstruction.

As the Russian army retreated from the initial skirmishes, its soldiers brutally destroyed everything in their path – whole villages, farms, and industrial installations.[6] The scale of destruction increased exponentially over the coming years of battle as this was only the first of several incursions made by Russian troops in 1914 and 1915. According to official Prussian tallies, in and around East Prussia over 10,000 structures were either damaged or destroyed during this period. By 1916 official Prussian figures record 41,414 structures completely razed or in severe disrepair and another 60,000 with serious damage.[7] Similar records show that Gumbinnen County suffered the loss of about one-fifth of its entire building stock.[8] Eye-witness accounts describe malicious acts of vandalism as the Russians retreated: "furniture and household appliances smashed, the linen ripped apart, all cupboards emptied, the beds chopped up and the down scattered, letters and other papers thrown about, walls damaged by shots fired in fun, windows and doors smashed, merchandise pointlessly wasted, and the rooms fouled with human excrement."[9] Not only did this wholesale damage render enormous parts of the built environment useless but the Russian soldiers' actions displaced hundreds of thousands of German citizens in the first months of the war alone; contemporary reports place the numbers at about one-sixth of the total provincial population, which would have been over 300,000 people.[10] Although these citizens were forced to flee their homes ahead of advancing Russian troops, and were faced with likely further hostilities to come, the government expected them to remain homeless, without regular employment, and dependent on state aid for the foreseeable future (as long as the war continued).[11] The needs to house displaced citizens and reconstruct the physical infrastructure in order to facilitate the war effort were therefore the other catalysts for creating the Militärbau Kommando. The Kommando was a totally new military entity with no historic precedent and therefore had to imagine whole systems and structures to support its work. Its innovations included the formation of construction teams that integrated skilled, experienced workers with neophytes; inventive use of materials to hand; the pragmatic combination of traditional aesthetics with modern materials and construction systems; and the early adoption of what later, in the interwar period, was called functionalism, the practical design response to design challenges.

The Militärbau Kommando and the Kruchen Labor Organization System

On August 27, 1914, while the Battle of Tannenberg was still underway, Kaiser Wilhelm II ordered the implementation of every possible means with which to "alleviate the emergency" in East Prussia.[12] By mid-September 1914, the federal government had founded the Kriegshilfekommission (War Aid Commission) on the civilian side with an initial budget of 400 million marks and the German military had established the Militärbau Kommando, under the authority of the Berlin architect Paul Kruchen as battalion commander, to mount a coordinated reconstruction effort. The Militärbau Kommando's headquarters were situated in Stallupönen, site of some of the worst fighting and physical destruction in 1914 and 1915.[13] The first cities targeted for reconstruction included Stallupönen and neighboring Pillkallen, Gumbinnen, Eydtkuhnen and Goldap, all located in the northeast corner of East Prussia where the Russian First Army had penetrated. Later, the Kommando worked in Crossen, Gruben and Insterburg. The Kommando's primary aims were two-fold: to replace civilian infrastructure that had been destroyed during the conflict and to build prisoner-of-war camps to house the nearly 100,000 prisoners-of-war in German captivity.[14]

Kruchen shrewdly calculated the benefits of a well-conceived reconstruction effort: reinstatement of necessary German infrastructure including roads, bridges and railways, provision of employment to locals left economically devastated by the conflict, and capitalization on the potential inherent in a prisoner-of-war labor force.[15] Germany suffered a severe labor shortage soon after the start of the war that became more acute with every passing month.[16] Over 13 million Germans mobilized during the prosecution of the war, a figure that represented almost every man of conscript age. Therefore, very quickly, Germany experienced grave labor shortages in industry, agriculture, and mining but also reconstruction. One solution was to forcibly draft prisoners-of-war into these occupations. Kruchen's approach was far more ingenious; he created a jobs training program, with minimal pay and other incentives, for both German citizens and the prisoners-of-war, from which they could gain marketable skills that they could use after the war was over. (Even early on, it was clear that construction skills were going to be in high demand once the war ended.) Kruchen was equally cognizant of the challenges involved in combining local German workers with prisoners-of-war on construction teams; he therefore made his incentive system two-tiered, with lower pay for prisoners and slightly higher, better pay for German citizens (both soldiers and civilians). Kruchen recognized that simply using prisoners-of-war as forced laborers would result in poor-quality work since it is difficult to coerce people into doing good work when they do not want to. He worried that the product of forced labor would be poor quality – any construction projects completed under duress would need to be replaced after the war. If prisoners-of-war were provided proper incentives, however, they would perform well because they would work willingly. He also reasoned that such a benevolent program might turn former enemies into future friends.[17]

Kruchen's system was a coordinated effort between the military and civilian associations active in East Prussia, including the national Deutsche Werkbund, Architektenbund (Architects' Association), and Bund für Heimatschutz (Association for the Preservation of the Homeland), and regional groups like Verband Ostdeutscher Industrieller (Association of East German Industrialists) in Danzig, Königliche Eisenbahndirektion (Royal Railroad Directorate) in Königsberg, and the office of the Oberpräsident Ost Preußen (President of East Prussia). Kruchen strove to integrate local handworkers and craftsmen, wherever available, with soldiers and prisoners in the reconstruction effort, whose watchword was "Civilian Capability with Military Organization."[18] The model that he developed for project delivery was small construction teams that blended experienced craftsmen, preferably local ones, with neophytes in a way that maximized labor potential. By using experienced and novice workmen together, the teams functioned both for training and construction, which made them efficient and effective.

There were challenges to collaborating with the local civilians, partly real and partly the result of prejudices common to Germans from the west of the country. German architect Hans Scharoun, who worked with Kruchen in the Militärbau Kommando, writes, "In the East-Prussian population, an individualistic, crassest form is found, which tends towards the form of egoism, and in its independence, goes so far that, for its own sake, it rejects forms of business that would bring it a financial advantage."[19] In other words, East Germans were seen as being stubborn and difficult to work with, and for cutting off their noses to spite their faces. Scharoun's opinion of the local workforce echoes other contemporary assessments of Germans in East Prussia and Silesia; the eastern provinces were largely rural and backward in comparison with other parts of Germany.[20]

Kruchen created teams that typically had between 16 and 22 people slated for work either outdoors or in workshops.[21] The typical team consisted of two German security guards who were skilled workers supervising 20 unskilled prisoners-of-war. The size of the teams varied depending on the kind of work they were engaged in: masonry and carpentry teams usually had between two and four expert craftsmen together with 12 prisoners-of-war, while teams working outside on infrastructure like roads and bridges tended to be the larger 22- to 24-member ones. The prisoners-of-war were occupied in an impressive range of construction-related tasks, including masonry and carpentry, painting, glazing, plastering, and acting as locksmiths, furniture designers, and furniture makers. Kruchen writes in 1915: "The whole [w]as a basis for the later to be formed cooperatives … [T]he advantage of this device: faster, better, cheaper and more beautiful" construction work.[22]

In another clever organizational decision for his model, Kruchen divided reconstruction expenses between the military and civilian authorities so that the military did not have to shoulder the full burden of the costs but also to encourage local and regional participation in his system. Local and regional support was not only financial, it was also material – some of the operating costs were defrayed by local communities: "for standard accommodation, food, clothing and health requirements, the local county councils (or other interest groups as well as municipalities) have to pay."[23] Localities also contributed second-hand clothing and food.

Within the larger system, Kruchen developed two different models for housing construction teams, depending on where they were employed: a decentralized and a centralized one. Teams working outdoors in the country on large-scale infrastructure projects were scattered and boarded locally in small accommodation. In contrast, those employed in the cities in production workshops or on urban reconstruction projects where large numbers of soldiers and prisoners were occupied were housed together, usually in close proximity to the production workshops.[24]

According to records in the archives, despite initial skepticism on the part of both military and civilian groups, Kruchen's system worked well for the first couple of years. But as the war progressed, there were fewer and fewer civilians available because more citizens had been conscripted into the German army.[25] The dearth of available civilian workers in 1917 and 1918 meant that reconstruction slowed, demand for the limited resources grew, and the composition of the teams had to change.[26] In turn, this forced the Kommando to develop priorities for its work rather than tackle all the different tasks at once. Priority was given first to rebuilding local and regional infrastructure, since these were critical to the war effort. Of secondary importance were buildings that had economic value or that housed functions that supported the war effort in some way, such as factory buildings. Tertiary importance was given to producing ersatz foods to replace lost crops or crops that were impossible to raise during the conflict, as well as ersatz industrial products. "After all, it was first and foremost necessary to support the war that had become an economic war … and above all, to provide for the accommodation of the harvest, the vineyard, and last but not least, the inhabitants in the destroyed area. As a result of the practical and organized establishment, new barns, stables, dairies and schools were built in the shortest possible time and damaged areas were repaired. In addition to ensuring food for the populace, care was also taken to find a substitute for the grain crops … needed for human consumption … In the district of Insterburg, two fat extraction plants were completed, and in the district of Ragnit, a sulfite alcohol factory set up by the Zollstofffabrik."[27] Thus, from the start, the Kommando's strategic value was both military and economic.

Functional Design: Site Strategies, Architectural Form, Innovative Materials, and Construction Methods

The architectural projects that Kruchen's teams worked on ranged in scale and type from relatively small buildings like barracks for prisoners-of-war to large-scale storage depots and industrial installations. The teams of prisoners-of-war built entire prisoner-of-war camps like the ones at Crossen and Gumbinnen, with numerous buildings of many different kinds arranged on a large block of land, as well as single building projects like the 8,000-square-meter provision depot at Frankfurt an der Oder.[28] Each program, coupled with the exigencies of war, demanded a very different approach to building siting, materials, structural systems and spatial organization [fig. 2.1].

The prisoner-of-war camps were arguably the most complex design and construction challenges facing Kruchen's teams because of their sheer scale and variety of building types. They were also the only buildings that the Kommando designed and built from scratch; other buildings were reconstruction projects. The camps usually had to house about 10,000 prisoners-of-war together with 1,000 German soldiers. The camp was a new architectural model, for which there was little, if any, architectural precedent. Instead, Kruchen and his team had programmatic requirements and functional considerations to guide them, along with the rules for prosecution of war outlined in the 1907 Geneva Convention for the Amelioration of the Condition of the Wounded and Sick in Armies in the Field, 11 L.N.T.S. 440, and the 1907 Hague Conventions on Land Warfare.[29] The Geneva Convention outlined humanitarian treatment of prisoners-of-war, whether wounded, sick, or healthy, but did not give any architectural advice as to how to interpret its requirements in built form.[30]

In order to devise an appropriate site layout for the camps, Kruchen's team carefully considered the essentials necessary to a well-functioning camp. Aesthetics had virtually no role to play in these projects because of what the program involved and the limited resources available. The programmatic issues they had to consider were complex. The site layout needed to accommodate both Russian prisoners and German soldiers together yet separately, with adequate provision for surveillance and safety for both groups. The ratio of German soldiers to Russian prisoners was roughly 1:10 early in the war, but worse as the number of prisoners-of-war grew, which meant that building siting had to facilitate surveillance while offering physical protection to the outnumbered German soldiers. Epidemics were rife amongst the prisoners, so the barracks needed to be arranged in a way that would allow for quarantine and care of sick prisoners while keeping them under watch.

Kruchen's team also likely studied the layouts used at other camps around Germany. The one in Meschede typified one common approach to the problem: a surviving contemporary postcard shows rows of cookie-cutter, one-story box structures, two deep, laid out on an orthogonal grid, with a series of unique buildings at one end. While this arrangement is certainly straightforward, and its repetitive strategy would have made construction easy, surveillance is not optimized. The site plan also leaves little space for prisoners to exercise. Kruchen's solutions were more thoroughly considered and therefore even more practical and functional. As at Meschede, his team used repeated building types to maximize efficiency but in place of the Meschede layout they used a modified fan-shaped plan, one far better suited to surveillance.[31]

Merzdorf near Cottbus was a typical camp; it was a series of buildings and courtyards arranged to satisfy requirements for surveillance, security, privacy, exercise, and quarantine of whole companies of captive Russian soldiers.[32] The result was a blueprint for many projects to come.[33] Kruchen used the ancient form of a Greek amphitheater, with its central, half-round stage flanked by seats arranged in outwardly radiating, concentric semi-circles, as inspiration for the site plan, since the form, like Jeremy Bentham's Panopticon, allows for easy observation of every space on the concentric rings from a central point. The core of the fan-shape was a repeated unit made up of public outdoor space, around which were situated six small-sized barracks that served 250 prisoners in total. Five of these barracks could house up to 50 prisoners each, with the sixth reserved for those who were ill; they were served by Russian military medical personnel, usually ones who had been attached to the company. This was one of the provisions of the 1907 Geneva Convention. The central public space was divided into three courtyards – one for quarantined soldiers, one for individuals and another for groups. Five of these six-barrack arrangements, a number that could hold exactly one Russian company, were organized around a larger courtyard. This arrangement, in turn, was repeated again and again in the semi-circular fan until there were enough barracks to house the entire division. The units all had rear gardens that the prisoners could tend. The gardens backed onto a neutral zone that offered security separation. The entire ensemble was ringed with elevated watch towers, often octagonal or round in plan, that afforded clear 360-degree views of the camp and its surroundings[34] [fig. 2.2].

A five-story watch tower, which doubled as a water tower, sat at the heart of the architectural ensemble. Fortified by an earthen rampart, the tower was a multi-story wooden structure whose upper story was an open observation deck fitted out with a machine gun. The middle stories housed the camp water storage, an officers' room below, and an artillerymen's room on the ground floor. The basement contained the kitchen, store rooms, and dining room for the camp [fig. 2.3].

Figure 2.2: One of the prisoner-of-war camps in Crossen constructed using the Kruchen System. © Bundesarchiv R 67 Bild-02-002.

Figure 2.3: The hexagonal watchtower at Crossen. © Bundesarchiv, R 67 Bild-02-003.

The actual buildings were designed to be as easy to erect and as functional as possible. The barracks were simple, long, rectangular boxes with low-slung, pitched roofs. Orthogonal forms are the easiest to build because they do not require complicated joinery. The form is also well suited to holding rows of bunkbeds arranged side-by-side. Windows were placed in the roof so that they did not block placement of the bunks. The pitched roof shed snow reasonably well, a necessity in the East Prussian winter at that time.

Because of material shortages throughout Germany and disruptions to the rail system, which made transport cross-country difficult, Kruchen's designers were forced to use whatever was to hand. The shortages were a result of two interrelated factors: the blockade conducted by the Allied Powers that only intensified as the war continued, and the requisitioning of raw material and manufacturing capacity to the war economy. The result was a dramatic drop in raw material imports to Germany with concomitant scarcities in every industry.[35] Materials used in munitions manufacture, for instance, such as steel, were almost impossible to come by.[36] As Johann Hermann Wilke, who wrote about the reconstruction effort in East Prussia, lamented, "There are neither wall stones nor masons, the war ruined the brickyards, destroyed the building materials, and killed or wounded the craftsmen."[37] More often than not, as at Merzdorf, the material of choice was a combination of mud and wood, materials easily sourced in the area.[38] Teams of prisoners obtained wood in the extensive East Prussian forests, where native species include oak, pine, birch, ash, and Douglas fir, all good for building construction.[39] Kruchen's teams then processed and milled the lumber for use as structural members and cladding. The barracks at Merzdorf were log cabins made of pine roundwood from the surrounding area, felled and stripped of bark but not squared, then sealed with mud slurry.[40] This was an efficient way to build since the wood was not fully milled, making the preparation process less labor intensive and faster.

Roofs and interior walls were finished with boards covered with tar paper. Scharoun writes, "You almost feel like you have travelled back in time when, from buildings towering above, you see the strange little thing close to the earth. Especially with a peek into the hut-like interiors that the dwellers have decorated with many kinds of childlike carvings," made by the prisoners to domesticate the otherwise simple structures.[41] Scharoun also describes the different colors used at the camp to enliven the visual aspect.

In one report on the camp designs, Scharoun acknowledges the difficulty of speaking about aesthetics given the pragmatic nature of the camp architecture. However, he does feel that the urban design solution that Kruchen developed merits recognition as an elegant functional response to the program.[42]

Transition to Peacetime

When the war ended, there was some discussion about using the Militärbau Kommando, already renamed the Bau Kommando (Building Battalion), as a peacetime institution in order to make a seamless transition from wartime to peacetime reconstruction.[43] This idea made sense since it would take advantage of the well-organized and functional Kruchen System with its local labor force and connections to the East Prussian building bureaucracy, functioning workshops, and the immense experience its architects had gained during the war in such areas as functional building design and efficient delivery. The hope was also to transfer the administrative and planning operations developed by the Kommando to civilian institutions. Equally advantageous, new institutions founded by the federal government in 1914 to support the financial and logistical sides of the reconstruction effort were well integrated into Kruchen's system. Along with those organizations named above were the Kriegshilfekasse für Ostpreussen (War Aid Fund for East Prussia), which provided easy credit for building, and the Vermittlungsstelle für Aufträge aller Art (Exchange Office for Orders of all Kinds), which supported local craftsmen.[44]

Although the Bau Kommando never eventuated, architects who had been in the Militärbau Kommando, like Kruchen and Scharoun, did accept civilian appointments in East Prussia after the armistice, which helped smooth the transition from military to civilian order. Scharoun became director of the Bauberatungsamt (Construction Consulting Authority) Insterburg, and a member of the Baukunstkammer des Ostens (Eastern Chamber of Architects). In 1919, he also took over the office in Insterburg that had served as headquarters for the Militärbau Kommando, running it as a private architectural practice and, as an independent architect, he was employed by the Allgemeine Wohnungsbaugenossenschaft Insterburg (Insterburg General Housing Cooperative) between 1920 and 1924.[45]

The suggestion to repurpose the Militärbau Kommando took into account the lack of available local talent, the scope of destruction that far outstripped the experience of most civil construction or engineering companies, and the small number of entrepreneurial firms in East Prussia.[46] In addition, the sheer magnitude of the work required put economic pressures on local government that was beyond their capacity. The federal government hoped that the new Bau Kommando could help bridge the local challenges and that it would succeed since its officers were already well known in East Prussian architectural and construction circles so would not be perceived as total outsiders and interlopers.

The idea was to divide the Bau Kommando into two: an office for reconstruction and another for construction. However, it seems that the plan never materialized and the formal structures of the proposed Bau Kommando were dissolved by April 1919.[47] Most likely, this occurred as other new housing construction programs were legislated by the Weimar government, especially the establishment of housing agencies, and thinking about the best ways to reconstruct evolved. Beyond the transformation of the former Kommando office headquarters into a private practice under Scharoun's direction, it is clear from archival material and the few surviving buildings that accumulated wartime experience was influential in other ways.[48] During the period from 1919–1925, Scharoun executed more than twenty-five building designs in and around Insterburg for the Allgemeine Wohnungsbaugenossenschaft Insterburg, which included large-scale housing developments, villas, estates, settlements and building conversions.[49] One surviving project by Scharoun, Bunte Reihe (Colored Row) in Kamswyk, Insterburg, shows the lessons learnt during the war: economy of scale, functional planning, simple ways to embellish plain design, use of readily available materials and construction systems that even lay people could handle.

Interwar Policy and Projects in East Prussia

The German federal government decided to mount a concerted campaign in 1918–1919 to expand wartime reconstruction programs in East Prussia to include new construction in the cities and countryside, particularly large-scale housing projects for those left homeless by the war. There were a range of reasons for homelessness: returning soldiers whose homes were destroyed during the conflict, displaced citizens who abandoned their homes as they fled the advancing Russian troops, and Germans who were expelled from territory after the armistice.[50] Reconstruction was one part of a larger federal program whose aim was to improve the overall situation in East Prussia. Its goals were the expansion of the province's economic capacity, improvement of utility delivery, and the "implementation of a vigorous settlement policy" to populate border provinces with ethnic Germans in order to strengthen German territorial claims in the present and the future.[51]

A critical aspect of the interwar reconstruction effort was the passage of new laws intended to support design and construction of more housing, delivered as quickly and efficiently as possible. The new laws extended ones that were already in place, which were part of the growing concern for *Sozialpolitik*, the ways in which the state could support its citizens and guarantee a basic quality of life for all Germans. Housing legislation reflected the developing belief that access to affordable, decent housing was a fundamental human right, but also the provision of good housing was seen as a mechanism by which the state could exercise control over the poorer masses. The March 1918 Preussischer Wohnungsgesetz (Prussian Housing Law) at the state level and the 1919 national constitutional guarantee of adequate housing to every German citizen in Article 155 of the Weimar Constitution were the linchpins for interwar housing reform.[52] The Prussian Housing Law created a uniform set of rules to govern financing, design and construction of public housing.[53] It increased public subsidies for new housing projects, restricted support to non-profit housing corporations, provided for public appropriation of land for housing under certain circumstances, established base-line criteria for the quality of design and construction, and prescribed the establishment of local and regional housing authorities to manage finance, design, and construction processes. Article 155 assured every German a "healthful habitation" and "homesteads for living and working that are suitable to their needs." Soldiers were promised special consideration in the forthcoming homestead legislation, what became the Reichsiedlungsgesetz (Reich Settlement Law). In fact, the Reichsiedlungsgesetz of 1919 legislated resettlement in rural parts of Saxony, Silesia, and East Prussia, adding further impetus to reconstruction.[54]

According to Johann Hermann Wilke, who authored a three-page summary describing the politics and practical side of the reconstruction effort during the war and interwar periods, the principal goal for reconstruction from the start in 1914 was providing East Prussians with a house that was "nice and functional."[55] He makes clear that "nice" means acceptable in terms of the amount of space and amenities provided but not in terms of aesthetics. Function is the primary consideration, given the many constraints. In Wilke's view, speed of construction was essential to reconstruction since so many East Prussians were homeless and temporarily housed in the same wood and mud barracks that had been used for prisoners-of-war. Wilke also comments on the exigencies that led to experimentation with materials like concrete block over more traditional ones like brick. For residents of two provinces considered the "border of German culture" and "the bulwark against Eastern and Asian infiltration," however, being denied the comforts of a traditional German brick house would be distressing.

In actuality, guidelines for design were more explicit even than those Wilke reported on: beginning in 1915, federal officials developed a set of artistic principles for reconstruction.[56] In addition to function, new houses should be "comfortable, homey ones whose hearth and garden please the East Prussian people."[57] Design needed to consider economic viability, the agrarian lifestyle, and the character of the province, objectives pushed by the *Heimatschutz* movement. The buildings should be low-rise, to mimic the historic fabric, and use aesthetics that fit this fabric along with modern spatial planning and construction techniques. They should be as small as possible and experimentation with ersatz materials and building techniques was encouraged.[58] The use of ersatz materials had burgeoned during the blockade of Germany in the First World War, so German industry led in this area internationally.[59] Future development was also to be considered. The parameters included forceful advice to avoid styles like Jugendstil that were not typical of local architecture and to carefully consider how to integrate modern design with the historic context. These guidelines prescribe an approach closely followed by Scharoun in East Prussia as well as others like Ernst May in Silesia, who also documented the precepts in numerous issues of the journal *Schlesisches Heim* (*Silesian Home*).[60]

Scharoun's Bunte Reihe in Insterburg is one example of a "nice and functional" project executed soon after the war, whose overall design incorporates many of the wartime innovations. Bunte Reihe was the first solo architecture project Scharoun ran out of the Insterburg office that was not commissioned by the military.[61] Designed and constructed between 1920 and 1924 to house postal and rail workers, the Bunte Reihe development consists of 17 buildings arranged in a loosely formed T along two roads. Parallel facing rows of once-colored housing sit on either side of Bunte-Reihe Street, two smaller single blocks lie further on like punctuation points, and two more long rows of three-story housing extend along Kamswyker Allee to form the top of the T. A second row of small double houses was built parallel to both blocks on Bunte-Reihe Street.[62] All in all, there are 83 units of differing sizes.

The only extant floor plans for Bunte Reihe show tight functional spatial planning.[63] Four units are grouped around a common entry and stair with two units per floor. A typical unit has a small entry foyer, four small rooms, a minimal toilet and bathroom, and a kitchen arranged with the least possible wasted space: the only circulation space is the tiny foyer. The kitchen, toilet and two of the rooms – those for living and dining – are accessed through the foyer, the bedrooms are accessed through the living and dining rooms. The spatial planning conforms to the Existenz Minimum (Existence Minimum), whose goal was to develop the most functional plan using the least space necessary for a comfortable flat, a planning concept that gained popularity in the period.[64] Scharoun's experience in the Bau Kommando taught him economical spatial planning: the bunkers and military service buildings were all planned as efficiently as possible, with as little wasted space in plan or section as could be devised [fig. 2.4].

Although Wilke describes the use of concrete block in many reconstruction projects, Bunte Reihe is made of brick covered over in colored stucco, hence the name. A photograph of another contemporary project in Insterburg, the double house on Pregel Street, shows workers laying brick for a site across the street. There are piles of rubble brick on the ground behind the workers and in a nearby cart, which suggests that some of the reconstruction projects used materials scavenged from ruined buildings.[65] It is likely that Scharoun chose brick because it was locally produced, or readily available as a recycled material from war rubble, which would have made it economical in spite of interwar material shortages. Like the Kommando's choice of wood from local forests for the prisoner-of-war camps, selecting brick was opportunistic. It is also relatively easy to conceal sloppy brick work by covering it with render, another reason that brick might have been deployed.

Figure 2.4: Siedlung Bunte Reihe in Insterburg designed by Hans Scharoun after the war. The view shows the subtle variations in window shapes over the entryways. © Creative Commons.

The housing rows are long orthogonal blocks, essentially rectangular in plan, topped with a gently pitched roof, small dormer windows, and little volumetric articulation. Such straightforward volumes are easier to construct than more complex ones, another likely reason for Scharoun's design. Scharoun did indulge in some modulation of the facade on the rear face where he repeatedly angled two short walls in relationship to the facade in order to create a subtle undulation that originally contained a small balcony. Similarly, the building ends are not flat but two angled planes protruding into space [fig. 2.5]. Visual variation and articulation was almost exclusively limited to the play with colors and the occasional oddly shaped window over an entry. These strategies are similar to the ones that Scharoun had used in his designs for prisoner-of-war camps where embellishment and decoration were rare. At the camps, Scharoun made watch towers and communal buildings in unconventional shapes and sizes, with unusual roof forms so that they served as visual relief and therefore a kind of ornament while rhythmic arrangement of windows was the only element that disrupted the architectural monotony of the barracks.

Figure 2.5: The end of the bar building, Siedlung Bunte Reihe. The angling of the facade to animate the building end and the brick construction are both apparent here. © Creative Commons.

Scharoun also seemed to owe a debt to contemporary publications on reconstruction and preservation. In 1917, 1922, and 1928, Georg Steinmetz published three volumes called *Grundlagen für das Bauen in Stadt und Land* (*Principles for Building in City and Country*) that together sought to catalog the principal historic building types in East Prussia along with modern options in order to facilitate the reconstruction effort.[66] Steinmetz's project was jointly sponsored by the Reichsverbandes Ostpreußenhilfe (Reich Association for East Prussian Aide) and the Deutschen Bund Heimatschutz (German Federation for Homeland Protection). The books feature plans, elevations, site strategies, and photographs with suites of options that include modern adaptations of historic tropes. At the same time, between 1919 and 1925, May published articles in *Schlesisches Heim* on how to design large-scale housing projects with sample types that documented all aspects of design from floor plans to sections to elevations.[67] Steinmetz and May show simple building volumes with traditional pitched roofs, often historic elements like eyebrow windows or ornamented doors, stucco facades, and functional and economic spatial planning. The designs were meant to appeal to uneducated local tastes, to fit in with historic vernacular buildings destroyed during the war, and to be cheap and easy to build, as mandated by government policy.[68]

Scharoun did deploy one strategy that May seems to have ignored but Steinmetz promoted: the use of color. A signatory to Bruno Taut's famous *Ruf zum farbigen Bauen* (*Call to Colored Architecture*) of 1919, Scharoun shared Taut's belief in the power of color to enliven architecture and to stand in for more traditional forms of ornament. Render facades were long-established in Germany, dating at least to the eleventh century, although they were not historically painted the bright and varied palette used at Bunte Reihe but in earthier and more neutral colors. The German word for render, *putz*, has its origins both in "to clean" and "to beautify;" the double entendre might partially explain the material's long-lived popularity. Render is a general term for a range of different compounds with varying consistency and texture. Scharoun originally had the render facades on the two facing parallel blocks painted in bright, primary colors – red, yellow and blue – while the other blocks were apparently painted in more sober colors.[69] Primary colors also featured as accents in the details of doors and windows used to enliven the architectural composition. Color is an extremely economical ornament to use; it was also becoming popular with a segment of the avant-garde at this time.[70] Scharoun did not use color much, if at all, on the sober military architecture he had designed, but he did learn how minimal design embellishments can greatly enhance simple architectural forms. The variations in window shapes, small manipulations of the facades, and restrained use of color were all similar techniques.

It is tragic that most of Scharoun's interwar buildings in East Prussia did not survive the Second World War and that so much of the documentation was lost, since these were the architect's first attempts to develop a unique architectural language. The East Prussian buildings are also the ones most directly influenced by Scharoun's wartime experience, his tutelage under Paul Kruchen, and his work on military architecture. However, the transitional nature of the work for Scharoun is clear from what remains: he used it to test lessons from the war in peacetime and to begin to experiment with new ideas like three-dimensional plastic form and color. His inventive use of materials to hand, early adoption of functional planning yet resistance to oversimplifying solutions or aesthetics, and his ability to enliven a simple design with minimal means were all lessons taken from the war that continued to inform his architecture throughout his life.

Notes

1   Johann Hermann Wilke, *Der Stein des Waisens: Zum Wiederaufbau Ostpreußens* (1915), accessed July 2019, <http://resolver.staatsbibliothek-berlin.de/SBB0000873500000000>; Hans Scharoun, document without name or date, Scharoun Archive, Dokumente vor 1945, Mappe 4.1, Akademie der Künste Berlin (AdK).

2   This essay would not have been possible without the help of the intrepid Jordan Troeller, who generously waded through the files at the Geheimes Staatsarchiv Preußischer Kulturbesitz for me in August 2019.

3   Research into the reconstruction effort is hampered by the destruction of the Reichsarchiv in Potsdam on April 14, 1945. Material has survived in some private archives, such as the Hans Scharoun Archive at the Akademie der Künste Berlin, archives of the Prussian ministries, and regional archives. This essay relies on the material in the Scharoun Archive and material from the Geheimes Staatsarchiv Preußischer Kulturbersitz. An excellent article by Jochen Oltmer, "Unentbehrliche Arbeitskräfte. Kriegsgefangene in Deutschland, 1914–1918," in *Kriegsgefangene im Europa des Ersten Weltkriegs*, ed. Jochen Oltmer (Paderborn: Ferdinand Schöningh, 2006), 67–96, confirmed much of the material from the Scharoun Archive.

4   Since this essay is about the period when East Prussia was German territory, it will use the German names rather than the Polish ones.

5   Anthony Brandt, "Blind Bear at Bay: obligated by treaties to declare war in August 1914, Russia was unprepared to attack, and in East Prussia its vast army soon proved no match for German intelligence, reconnaissance and railways," *MHQ: The Quarterly Journal of Military History* 28, no. 4 (Summer 2016), 44–52.

6   Geheimes Staatsarchiv Preußischer Kulturbesitz (GStPK), XX. HA Rep. 2II, 3576, Bds. 22, 3, and 4 describe the Russian attack on East Prussia; Alexander Watson, "'Unheard of Brutality': Russian Atrocities against Civilians in East Prussia, 1914–1915," *Journal of Modern History* 86, no. 4 (December 2014): 780–825; Holger H. Herwig, *The First World War. Germany and Austria-Hungary, 1914–1918* (London: Arnold, 1997), 127–8.

7   "Der Wiederaufbau Ostpreußens und das ostpreußische Handwerk," Scharoun Archive, Dokumente vor 1945, Mappe 3.2, AdK; Letter of Oberpräsident to Präsident des Staatsministeriums in Berlin, April 9, 1921, and table 2 accompanying it. GStA, Berlin: XX. HA Rep. 2II, 3759, reverse of fols. 56 and 64 – cited in Watson, "'Unheard of Brutality,'" 787.

8   Report by Regierungspräsident Gumbinnen to Unterstaatssekretär Heinrichs, April 21, 1915. GStPK, Berlin: I. HA Rep. 90A, 1064, 7; cited in Watson, "'Unheard of Brutality,'" 788.

9   Report of Regierungspräsident Königsberg, September 16, 1914. GStPK, Berlin: XX. HA Rep. 2II, 3558, fol. 17; cited in Watson, "'Unheard of Brutality,'" 788.

10   Wilke, *Der Stein des Waisens*, 1.

11   "Der Wiederaufbau Ostpreußens und das ostpreußische Handwerk," Scharoun Archive, Mappe 3.2, AdK.

12   "Der Wiederaufbau Ostpreußens als künstlerische Tat," GStPK, XX. HA Rep. 2II, 3584, 4; Wilke, *Der Stein des Waisens*, 1.

13   "Geschichtlich," Scharoun Archive, AdK, 1.

14   The Germans did not expect such rapid success or so many prisoners-of-war so they had nowhere to house all these men.

15   "Der Wiederaufbau Ostpreußens und das ostpreußische Handwerk," Scharoun Archive, Dokumente vor 1945, Mappe 3.2, AdK.

16   Jürgen Kocka, *Klassengesellschaft im Krieg: Deutsche Sozialgeschichte, 1914–1918* (Göttingen: Vandenhock und Ruprecht, 1978), 156; Christian Döring, *Die Bevölkerungsbewegung im Weltkrieg*, vol. 1 (Copenhagen: Luno, 1919), 10; cited in Oltmer, "Unentbehrliche Arbeitskräfte," 68.

17   "Das Arbeitslager im Aufbaugebiet," Scharoun Archive, Mappe 3.5, AdK.

18   Paul Kruchen, "Unseren Kriegsgefangenen und ihre Verwendung beim Wiederaufbau der Provinz Ostpreußen," Scharoun Archive, Dokumente vor 1945, Mappe 3.3, AdK.

19   "Grundstoffe," Scharoun Archive, Mappe 3.1, Nr. 1.

20   The eastern regions of Prussia were a late addition to the province, a fact that may explain the area's long history of marginal identity in relationship to the rest of Germany. See Christopher Clark, *Iron Kingdom: The Rise and Downfall of Prussia, 1600–1947* (Cambridge, Mass.: Belknap Press of Harvard University Press, 2006), 190–210, and Norman Davies and Roger Moorhouse, *Microcosm: Portrait of a Central European City* (London: Pimlico, 2003), 200–18.

21   "Grundstoffe," Scharoun Archive, Mappe 3.1, Nr. 1.

22   Kruchen, "Unseren Kriegsgefangenen und ihre Verwendung beim Wiederaufbau der Provinz Ostpreußen."

23   *Ibid.*

24   "Baubearbeiten mit den deutschen Bauhandwerken in bürgerlicher und militärischer Stellung und mit Kriegsgefangenen Russen," Scharoun Archive, Mappe 3.1, Nr. 2, AdK.

25   "Notwendigkeit, Leistung und Anpassung der Militärbau-Kommando," Scharoun Archive, Mappe 3.3, AdK.

26   *Ibid.*

27   *Ibid.*

28   "Baubearbeiten mit den deutschen Bauhandwerken in bürgerlicher und militärischer Stellung und mit Kriegsgefangenen Russen," Scharoun Archive, Mappe 3.1, Nr. 2, AdK.

29   Convention for the Amelioration of the Condition of the Wounded and Sick in Armies in the Field, 11 L.N.T.S. 440, entered into force August 9, 1907, no longer in force, accessed July 1, 2019, <http://hrlibrary.umn.edu/instree/1906a.htm>.

30   There were an estimated 8 million prisoners-of-war taken by all combatants during the First World War, which led to a small industry not only in Germany but in Russia and Austria-Hungary, and to a much lesser degree in France and Great Britain. All combatants used prisoner-of-war labor in varying conditions; however, the state of the prison architecture is difficult to ascertain. See Heather Jones, "Prisoners of War," *1914–1918 Online., International Encyclopedia of the First World War*, accessed January 24, 2020, <https://encyclopedia.1914-1918-online.net/article/prisoners_of_war>; and Heather Jones, "Prisoners of War," accessed January 24, 2020, <https://www.bl.uk/world-war-one/articles/prisoners-of-war>.

31   Actual drawn site plans of the Kruchen camps have not survived but there is a drawing of the Sachsenhausen Camp site plan from the Second World War, which is very similar to the descriptions of Crossen.

32   "Das Kriegsgefangenenlager," Scharoun Archive, Mappe 3.1, Nr. 4, AdK.

33   *Ibid.*

34   *Ibid.*

35   Marion C. Siney, *The Allied Blockade of Germany, 1914–1916* (Ann Arbor, Mich.: University of Michigan Press, 1957); Marjorie Milbank Farrar, *Conflict and Compromise: The Strategy, Politics and Diplomacy of the French Blockade, 1914–1918* (The Hague: Martinus Nijhoff, 1974); Charles Paul Vincent, *The Politics of Hunger: The Allied Blockade of Germany, 1915–1919* (Athens, Ohio: Ohio University Press, 1985).

36   Roger Chickering, *The Great War and Urban Life in Germany: Freiburg, 1914–1918* (Cambridge: Cambridge University Press, 2007), 130–2. Chickering describes the effects of shortages on local economies.

37   Wilke, *Der Stein des Waisens*, 1.

38 *Ibid.*, 1; not only was this a solution that the Kommando embraced, but the East Prussian parliament recommended exactly the same strategy for general reconstruction.

39 *The Forests in Germany: Selected Results of the Third National Inventory* (Berlin: Federal Ministry for Food and Agriculture, 2015).

40 "Das Kriegsgefangenenlager," Scharoun Archive, Mappe 3.1, Nr. 4, AdK.

41 *Ibid.*

42 *Ibid.*

43 "Der Umwandlung des in Ostpreußen Baukommandos," Scharoun Archive, Mappe 3.3, AdK; "Grundstoffe," Scharoun Archive, Mappe 3.1, Nr. 1; a note from the director of the Ostpreußische Landesgesellschaft dated August 27, 1918 mentions "[t]he War as a teacher of makeshift construction" and suggests that the lessons of the Kommando are worthy of adoption post-war. GStPK, XX. HA, Rep. 2II, 3743, 4.

44 *Nachrichtenblatt*, Nr. 46, May 18, 1918, p. 2.

45 For more on the history of housing cooperatives see, for example, David Kuchenbuch, *Geordnete Gemeinschaft: Architekten als Sozialingenieure – Deutschland und Schweden im 20. Jahrhundert* (Bielefeld: Transcript, 2010); Tanja Poppelreuter, *Das neue Bauen für den neuen Menschen: zur Wandlung und Wirkung des Menschenbildes in der Architektur der 1920er Jahre in Deutschland* (Hildesheim: Olms, 2007); and Axel Schildt and Arnold Sywottek, eds., *Massenwohnung und Eigenheim: Wohnungsbau und Wohnen in der Großstadt seit dem Ersten Weltkrieg* (Frankfurt: Campus, 1988).

46 "Grundstoffe," Scharoun Archive, Mappe 3.1, Nr. 1.

47 Files in the GStPK, XX. HA Rep. 2II, 3704, "An Herrn Reg. Presidenten in Gumbinnen," 57–60 are a series of missives between officials in East Prussia and Berlin about shutting down the Bau Kommando by April 1, 1919.

48 As mentioned at the beginning of the essay, most of the archival material was destroyed on April 14, 1945 during the Second World War when the central archives in Potsdam were bombed.

49 Wilfried Wolff, "Insterburg – Scharoun – Berlin: Ein Puzzle fügt sich," *Baukammer Berlin* (December 2010): 43–8; accessed July 4, 2019, <http://scharoun-gesellschaft.de/projekte/siedlung-kamswyken-insterburg/>.

50 Hermann Christlieb Matthäus von Stein, *Erlebnisse und Betrachtungen aus der Zeit des Weltkrieges* (Leipzig: K. F. Koehler, 1919).

51 Dieter Hertz-Eichenrode, *Politik und Landwirtschaft in Ostpreußen, 1919–1930: Untersuchung eines Strukturproblems in der Weimarer Republik* (Cologne: Westdeutscher, 1969), 170–1.

52 Benedikt Schmittmann, ed., *Preußisches Wohnungsgesetz und Bürgschaftssicherungsgesetz, 1918* (Berlin: Guttentag, 1918). For details about the law, see Frederick F. Blachly and Miriam E. Oatman, *The Government and Administration of Germany* (Baltimore: The Johns Hopkins Press, 1928), 604–5; Richard Bessel, *Germany after the First World War* (Oxford: Oxford University Press, 1993).

53 "Brauchen wir ein Wohunungsamt?," *Bergische Arbeiterstimme*, August 31, 1918, Stadtarchiv Solingen; accessed June 3, 2019, <https://archivewk1.hypotheses.org/tag/preussisches-wohnungsgesetz>.

54 For the background on the resettlement campaign and an account of it in Silesia, see Susan R. Henderson, "Ernst May and the Campaign to Resettle the Countryside: Rural Housing in Silesia, 1919–1925," *Journal of the Society of Architectural Historians* 61, no. 2 (June 2002): 188–211.

55 Wilke, *Der Stein des Waisens*, 2.

56 "Der Wiederaufbau Ostpreußens als künstlerische Tat," GStPK, XX. HA Rep. 2II, 3584, 4.

57   *Ibid.*

58   "Niederschrift," 1918, GStPK, XX. HA Rep. 2II, 3743, 3–4; "Bericht," August, 26 1918, GStPK, XX. HA Rep. 2II, 3743, 5–8.

59   For more on the history of Ersatz in Germany see "Die Welt des Ersatzes," *Neue Freie Presse*, November 29, 1917; "Die Ersatzmittelausstellung," *Neue Freie Presse*, June 8, 1918; and Lena Hallwirth, "Die Versorgung der Zivilbevölkerung mit Lebensmitteln und Ersatzlebensmitteln während des Ersten Weltkriegs," Masterarbeit, Institute of Social Ecology, Vienna, Alpen-Adria-Universitaet Klagenfurt Vienna, Graz, 2016. (Thanks to Erin Maynes for these references.)

60   Henderson, "Ernst May and the Campaign to Resettle the Countryside." Claudia Quiring, Wolfgang Voigt, Peter Cachola Schmal, and Eckhard Herrel, eds., *Ernst May: 1886–1970* (Munich: Prestel, 2011).

61   Unfortunately, the original drawings were all lost during the Second World War. For information on the Bunte Reihe, see Carsten Krohn, *Hans Scharoun: Bauten und Projekte* (Basel: Birkhäuser, 2018); Dimitri Suchin, "Baugeschichte der Bunten Reihe," accessed July 21, 2019, <http://de.instergod.ru/biografiya-domov/istoricheskaya-sprav-ka-pyostryiy-ryad.html>; Wolff, "Insterburg – Scharoun – Berlin"; Benedikt Hotze, "Bunte-Reihe Scharoun in Ostpreußen," *Baunetzwoche*, no. 180 (2010): 3–17. The German architect, Dimitri Suchin, has been the most active advocate for historic preservation and restoration of the surviving Scharoun projects in Insterburg including Bunte Reihe.

62   Photographs from the Scharoun Archive; reproduced in Krohn, *Hans Scharoun*, 34–5.

63   Reproduced in Krohn, *Hans Scharoun*, 35; and reproduced in Wolff, "Insterburg – Scharoun – Berlin," 44 from a photograph taken by Dimitri Suchin.

64   One well-known example is Hans Scharoun's design for the Ledigenheim in Breslau, completed in 1929. The units were about 27 square meters!

65   Photograph of Siedlung Pregelstrasse, Scharoun Archive, AdK, Mappe MV 20; reproduced in Krohn, *Hans Scharoun*, 33.

66   Georg Steinmetz, *Grundlagen für das Bauen in Stadt und Land*, vol. 1, *Körper und Raum* (Berlin and Munich: Georg D. Callwey, 1917); *Grundlagen für das Bauen in Stadt und Land*, vol. 2, *Besondere Beispiele* (Berlin and Munich: Georg D. Callwey, 1917); *Grundlagen für das Bauen in Stadt und Land*, vol. 3, *Praktische Anwendungen* (Berlin and Munich: Georg D. Callwey, 1922).

67   Typical articles by Ernst May include "Siedlungspläne," *Schlesisches Heim* (1919): 7–10; "Kleinwohnungtypen," *Schlesisches Heim* (1919): 14–7; and "Notheime," *Schlesisches Heim* (1920): 1–11.

68   Henderson, "Ernst May"; Deborah Ascher Barnstone, *Beyond the Bauhaus: Cultural Modernity in Breslau, 1918–1933* (Ann Arbor, Mich.: University of Michigan Press, 2016).

69   A simulation of the paint scheme can be found at <http://scharoun-gesellschaft.de/projekte/siedlung-kamswyken-insterburg/>.

70   Scharoun was a signatory to Bruno Taut's "Ruf zum farbigen Bauen" (Call to Colored Architecture) in 1919, so Scharoun's use of primary colors in Insterburg is not surprising.

Bibliography

Hans Scharoun Archive, Papers:
 "Baubearbeiten mit den deutschen Bauhandwerken in bürgerlicher und militärischer Stellung und mit Kriegsgefangenen Russen," 3.1, Nr. 2, AdK.
 "Das Arbeitslager im Aufbaugebiet," Mappe 3.5, AdK.
 "Das Kriegsgefangenenlager," Mappe 3.1, Nr. 4, AdK.
 "Der Umwandlung des in Ostpreußen Baukommandos," Mappe 3.3, AdK.
 "Der Wiederaufbau Ostpreußens und das ostpreußische Handwerk," Mappe 3.2, AdK.
 "Der Wiederaufbau Ostpreußens als künstlerische Tat," GStPK, XX. HA Rep. 2II, 3584, 4.
 "Geschichtlich," AdK, 1.
 "Grundstoffe," Mappe 3.1, Nr. 1.
 "Notwendigkeit, Leistung und Anpassung der Militärbau-Kommando," Mappe 3.3, AdK.
 "Oberpräsident to Präsident des Staatsministeriums in Berlin, April 9, 1921."

"An Herrn Reg. Presidenten in Gumbinnen," 57–60, Files in the GStPK, XX. HA Rep. 2II, 3704.

Barnstone, Deborah Ascher. *Beyond the Bauhaus: Cultural Modernity in Breslau, 1918–1933*. Ann Arbor, Mich.: University of Michigan Press, 2016.

"Bericht," August26, 1918, GStPK, XX. HA Rep. 2II, 3743, 5–8.

Bessel, Richard. *Germany after the First World War*. Oxford: Clarendon Press, 1993.

Blachly, Frederick F., and Miriam E. Oatman. *The Government and Administration of Germany*, 604–5. Baltimore: Johns Hopkins, 1928.

Brandt, Anthony. "Blind Bear at Bay: obligated by treaties to declare war in August 1914, Russia was unprepared to attack, and in East Prussia its vast army soon proved no match for German intelligence, reconnaissance and railways." *Quarterly Journal of Military History* 28, no. 4 (Summer 2016): 44–52.

"Brauchen wir ein Wohunungsamt?" *Bergische Arbeiterstimme*, August 31, 1918. Stadtarchiv Solingen. Accessed June 3, 2019. <https://archivewk1.hypotheses.org/tag/preussisches-wohnungsgesetz>

Chickering, Roger. *The Great War and Urban Life in Germany, Freiburg, 1914–1918*. Cambridge: Cambridge University Press, 2007.

Clark, Christopher. *Iron Kingdom: The Rise and Downfall of Prussia 1600–1947*. Cambridge, Mass.: The Belknap Press of Harvard University Press, 2006.

Convention for the Amelioration of the Condition of the Wounded and Sick in Armies in the Field, 11 L.N.T.S. 440, entered into force August 9, 1907, no longer in force. Accessed July 1, 2019. <http://hrlibrary.umn.edu/instree/1906a.htm>

Davies, Norman, and Roger Moorhouse. *Microcosm: Portrait of a Central European City*. London: Pimlico, 2003.

"Der Wiederaufbau Ostpreußens als künstlerische Tat, GStPK, XX. HA Rep. 2II, 3584, 4.

"Die Ersatzmittelausstellung," *Neue Freie Presse*, June 8, 1918.

"Die Welt des Ersatzes," *Neue Freie Presse*, November 29, 1917.

Döring, Christiane. *Die Bevölkerungsbewegung im Weltkrieg*. Vol. 1. Copenhagen, 1919.

Farrar, Marjorie Milbank. *Conflict and Compromise: The Strategy, Politics and Diplomacy of the French Blockade, 1914–1918*. The Hague: Martinus Nijhoff, 1974.

The Forests in Germany: Selected Results of the Third National Inventory. Berlin: Federal Ministry for Food and Agriculture, 2015.

Hallwirth, Lena. "Die Versorgung der Zivilbevölkerung mit Lebensmitteln und Ersatzlebensmitteln während des Ersten Weltkriegs." Master's thesis, Institute of Social Ecology, Vienna, Alpen-Adria-Universitaet Klagenfurt Vienna, Graz, 2016.

Henderson, Susan R. "Ernst May and the Campaign to Resettle the Countryside: Rural Housing in Silesia, 1919–1925." *Journal of the Society of Architectural Historians* 61, no. 2 (June 2002): 188–211.

Hertz-Eichenrode, Dieter. *Politik und Landwirtschaft in Ostpreußen, 1919–1930: Untersuchung eines Strukturproblems in der Weimarer Republik*. Wiesbaden: Springer, 1969.

Herwig, Holger H. *The First World War. Germany and Austria-Hungary, 1914–1918*. New York: St. Martin's Press, 1997.

Hotze, Benedikt. "Bunte-Reihe Scharoun in Ost Preußen." *Baunetzwoche* 180 (2010).

Jones, Heather. "Prisoners of War." In *1914–1918 Online. International Encyclopedia of the First World War*. <https://encyclopedia.1914-1918-online.net/article/prisoners_of_war>

———."Prisoners of War." <https://www.bl.uk/world-war-one/articles/prisoners-of-war>

Kocka, Jürgen. *Klassengesellschaft im Krieg: Deutsche Sozialgeschichte, 1914–1918*. Göttingen: Vandenhock und Ruprecht, 1978.

Krohn, Carsten. *Hans Scharoun: Bauten und Projekte*. Basel: Birkhäuser, 2018.

Kruchen, Paul. "Unseren Kriegs gefangenen und ihre Verwendung beim Wiederaufbau der Provinz Ostpreußen." Scharoun Archive, Dokumente vor 1945, Mappe 3.3, AdK.

Kuchenbuch, David. *Geordnete Gemeinschaft: Architekten als Sozialingenieure – Deutschland und Schweden im 20. Jahrhundert*. Bielefeld: Transcript, 2010.

May, Ernst. "Siedlungspläne," *Schlesisches Heim* (1919): 7–10.

———."Kleinwohnungtypen," *Schlesisches Heim* (1919): 14–7.

———."Notheime," *Schlesisches Heim* (1920): 1–11.

"Niederschrift," 1918, GStPK, XX. HA Rep. 2II, 3743, 3–4.

Oltmer, Jochen. "Unentbehrliche Arbeitskräfte: Kriegsgefangene in Deutschland, 1914–1918." In *Kreigsgefangene im Europa im Ersten Weltkriegs*, edited by Jochen Oltmer, 67–96. Paderborn: Ferdinand Schöningh, 2006.

Poppelreuter, Tanja. *Das neue Bauen für den neuen Menschen: zur Wandlung und Wirkung des Menschenbildes in der Architektur der 1920er Jahre in Deutschland*. Hildesheim: Olms, 2007.

Quiring, Claudia, Wolfgang Voigt, Peter Cachola Schmal, and Eckhard Herrel, eds. *Ernst May, 1886–1970*. Munich: Prestel, 2011.

Report by Regierungspräsident Gumbinnen to Unterstaatssekretär Heinrichs, April 21, 1915. GStPK, Berlin: I. HA Rep. 90A, 1064, 7.

Report of Regierungspräsident Königsberg, September 16, 1914. GStPK, Berlin: XX. HA Rep. 2II, 3558, fol. 17.

Scharoun Gesellschaft. Accessed July 4, 2019. <http://scharoun-gesellschaft.de/projekte/siedlung-kamswyken-insterburg/>

Schildt, Axel, and Arnold Sywottek, eds. *Massenwohnung und Eigenheim: Wohnungsbau und Wohnen in der Großstadt seit dem Ersten Weltkrieg*. Frankfurt: Campus, 1988.

Schmittmann, Benedikt, ed. *Preußisches Wohnungsgesetz und Bürgschaftssicherungsgesetz 1918*. Berlin: Guttentag, 1918.

Siney, Marion C. *The Allied Blockade of Germany, 1914–1916*. Ann Arbor, Mich.: University of Michigan Press, 1957.

Stein, Hermann. *Erlebnisse und Betrachtungen aus der Zeit des Weltkrieges*. Leipzig: K. F. Koehler, 1919.

Steinmetz, Georg. *Grundlagen für das Bauen in Stadt und Land*. Vol. 1, *Körper und Raum*. Berlin and Munich: Georg D. Callwey, 1917.

———.*Grundlagen für das Bauen in Stadt und Land*. Vol. 2, *Besondere Beispiele*. Berlin and Munich: Georg D. Callwey, 1917.

———.*Grundlagen für das Bauen in Stadt und Land*. Vol. 3, *Praktische Anwendungen*. Berlin and Munich: Georg D. Callwey, 1922.

Suchin, Dimitri. *Baugeschichte der Bunten Reihe*. Accessed July 21, 2019. <http://de.instergod.ru/biografiya-domov/suchin.html>

Vincent, Charles Paul. *The Politics of Hunger: The Allied Blockade of Germany, 1915–1919*. Athens, Ohio: Ohio University Press, 1985.

Watson, Alexander. "Unheard of Brutality: Russian Atrocities against civilians in East Prussia, 1914–1915." *Journal of Modern History* 86, no. 4 (December 2014): 780–825.

Wilke, Johann Hermann. *Der Stein des Waisens: Zum Wiederaufbau Ostpreußens* (1915). Accessed July 2019. <http://resolver.staatsbibliothek-berlin.de/SBB0000873500000000>

Wolff, Wilfried. "Insterburg – Scharoun – Berlin: Ein Puzzle fügt sich." *Baukammer Berlin* (December 2010): 43–8. Accessed July 4, 2019. <http://scharoun-gesellschaft.de/projekte/siedlung-kamswyken-insterburg/>

PART TWO

CIVILIANS
REEDUCATED

Figure 3.1: Cavendish Morton, *L'Entente Cordiale: Japanese and British boys and Flags*, inscribed 1911. Color lithograph, ink on card stock. Photograph © 2021 Museum of Fine Arts, Boston.

Learning to Play the Great Game

American Children and the First "World" War

Emma Paige Thomas

Introduction: "A Wonderful Game"

In October 1917, 25-year-old Lieutenant Basil Beebe Elmer of Ithaca, New York wrote a letter to his parents before departing for France with the 165th Infantry Regiment of the American Expeditionary Forces. "Please be glad and happy for me in this great adventure," he urged them.[1] "The whole thing is so teeming with excitement and interest and romance that I occasionally thrill at the thought of it and long to get at it. It is a wonderful game."[2] In another note home, Elmer again used the metaphor of a game to describe the experience of mobilizing for war, assuring his parents that "[f]or me the whole game is the best of sport every minute. The life is ideal from every viewpoint, and agrees with me perfectly."[3] Even after experiencing the horrors of battle, when Elmer reflected upon his transfer to a desk job in intelligence in 1918, he looked back at his experience as a combat officer with nostalgic longing, lamenting that "[t]hat great game is over."[4]

It is, of course, impossible to fully discern the complexity of Lieutenant Elmer's psychology from only these brief remarks.[5] Perhaps his apparent eagerness was merely youthful bravado fueled by the pursuit of romanticized violent masculinity; or perhaps it was a ploy to soothe the anxieties of worried family members who were receiving his letters. Yet Elmer's jovial tone is hardly unique among letters and memoirs penned by American soldiers and nurses during the First World War. As historians such as David Kennedy and Mark Meigs have observed, the documents left behind by American soldiers are particularly striking for their "baffling optimistic qualities."[6] In his classic cultural history of World War I, Paul Fussell similarly notes how the language used by the early waves of British forces deployed in 1914 recalled that of enthusiastic sportsmen; however, the tenor of British dispatches from the front shifted considerably as troops became increasingly demoralized by the harrowing reality of total war.[7] In comparison, Kennedy remarks upon the surprisingly "unflaggingly positive, even enthusiastic tone" that many American soldiers who experienced combat continued to adopt in their accounts of the war.[8] Such observations of patterns of emotional expression can indeed be sweeping and prone to oversimplification, promoting an inaccurate perception of the diverse individuals who composed the American Expeditionary Forces as a homogenous mass. Nonetheless, this prevalence of optimistic language among American troops remains striking, particularly to the cultural historian of the First World War. One explanation is that such language reflects youthful perceptions of immortality and exceptionalism that transcend any particular historical moment. So too did the late arrival of the American Expeditionary Forces to the war mean that while their experiences of battle were still traumatic, Americans were not subjected to the same relentless physical and psychological battery of years-long trench warfare experienced by their European counterparts.[9]

American soldiers also derived the language that they used to describe their wartime experience from the currents of mass culture. Kennedy has demonstrated how recruits were excellent students of propagandistic slogans and jargon, whether provided by the YMCA, the pages of *Stars and Stripes*, or tales from their childhood storybooks and novels. He remarks that the language of many American soldiers of the First World War is distinctly reminiscent of a type of antiquated, knights-on-crusade variety of romance that was yanked from the pages of well-loved copies of Sir Walter Scott and deposited on the battlefields of France.[10] This impulse to look back at the adolescence of these participants in the war is an astute one. In order to attempt the impossible task of reconstructing the lived experience of the men and women of the First World War, it makes sense to consider their consumption of mass culture not only at the moment of mobilization but also in the many psychologically formative years that preceded it.[11]

Doing so reveals that it was not just a romantically nostalgic vision of war that pervaded American childhood at the turn of the century – young Americans had also been introduced to a distinct perspective on how military conflicts of the modern global landscape should unfold. In particular, this study analyzes the youth culture related to a conflict that some historians argue ought to be considered the actual First "World" War: the Russo-Japanese War of 1904–1905.[12] At this moment, a variety of different media, from toys and comics to books and pictures, attempted to familiarize American children with the many intricate layers of their geopolitical landscape and shaped their expectations of and assumptions about diplomacy and war. This culture suggested that even though America might be a distant observer of conflict for the time being, a silent, invisible puppeteer, it might one day have a crucial role to play if the fragile web of alliances that were at once uniting and dividing the globe were to collapse. It provided young Americans with a model of the type of attitude adopted by Lieutenant Elmer in 1917: the notion that the business of preserving democracy abroad was an adventure that Americans were destined to take up. Their initial task would be to participate in the game of detached diplomacy as invested non-combatants; should this task fail, they should feel themselves prepared to deal the decisive blow on the battlefield.

The Russo-Japanese War in America

Young men like Lieutenant Elmer had never witnessed a war on American soil, but that does not mean that they came of age oblivious to international conflict. The young men aged 21–30 who were required to register for the first round of the draft by the Selective Service Act of June 5, 1917 would have been between eight and 17 years of age in 1904, the year that marked the beginning of the Russo-Japanese War. Although not nearly as large in geographical scope or devastation as World War I, this series of bloody battles waged between Russia and Japan in a bid for control over the Liaodong Peninsula of Northeast China could be understood as the first global conflict of the era of industrialized warfare.[13] As David Wells and Sandra Wilson have noted, while the significance of the Russo-Japanese War was deeply and uneasily perceived by those who followed it even from a distance in 1904–1905, its memory has typically been engulfed by the scale of the First World War, which has in turn rendered the earlier conflict a largely niche subject of interest to mainly military historians. Yet they observe that just as a cultural history of the Great War emerged in the 1990s, so too can scholarship retrieve a rich "social, intellectual and imaginative history" of the Russo-Japanese War that will further illuminate its grand strategy and diplomatic narratives.[14] Such history will also serve to frame the Russo-Japanese War not only as a military precursor to the First World War, but also as a culturally intertwined antecedent.

While works such as Wells's and Wilson's have significantly contributed to the necessarily interdisciplinary task of reconstructing the Russo-Japanese War in the Russian and Japanese imagination, this study further expands the geographical boundaries of this cultural history. As Russia and Japan faced each other on the battlefields of China, Britain, France, Germany and the United States offered support to the warring nations with varying degrees of boldness. Japan and Britain were established allies, having drawn up the First Anglo-Japanese Alliance in 1902. The Alliance did not obligate Britain to enter the war on Japan's behalf. Rather, it was understood that if Russia were to enlist another powerful Western ally, Britain would order its large and powerful military to China. As such, while sympathetic to Russia, Germany remained a largely removed spectator of the conflict. France navigated similar concerns when Russia requested financial assistance to prepare its Baltic fleet. The majority of French politicians unequivocally expressed support for Russia, but France's long history of strained relations with Britain had only just come to an end with the *Entente Cordiale* of 1904, making many hesitant to officially intervene on Russia's behalf. Nonetheless, numerous French trade unions, political groups, and private individuals sent financial and humanitarian aid to Russia, and the French press frequently referred to the nations' friendship in wartime journalism.

Technically, the United States remained neutral throughout the war, reflecting an ambivalence rooted in weighing the potential effects of Russian encroachment into China with America's own nascent imperial ambitions. On the one hand, President Theodore Roosevelt hoped that Japan could serve as a buffer against the rapid expansion of Russia into the Far East. On the other hand, with the recent annexations of Hawai'i and the Philippines and looking forward to its own potential extension into the Pacific, the US was also wary of encouraging the further growth of the Japanese Empire. American public sentiment at large, however, roundly favored Japan. Japan also financed nearly half of its war effort with the assistance of a well-publicized loan from private American banker Jacob Henry Schiff, a Jewish investor who both deplored Russia's anti-Semitic pogroms and felt particular affinity towards the plight of Japan.[15] Ultimately, Roosevelt assured America of its own seat at the imperial table by facilitating the resolution of the war with the Treaty of Portsmouth, signed in Portsmouth, New Hampshire on September 5, 1905.[16]

While multiple nations entangled themselves both officially and unofficially in the war in China, an international audience eagerly consumed news of the war's progress. A small but significant body of material aimed at a youthful American audience suggests that it was not only adults who consumed wartime news and propaganda.[17] As studies of the material culture of childhood such as that of Juliet Kinchin have shown, the twentieth century was a moment in which many adults emphasized the unique innocence of children and cast them as emotionally fragile beings that needed to be shielded from the adult complexities of politics and war. At the same time, the child became a frequently politicized symbol as well as a consumer of materials that were specifically aimed at inculcating young people with specific sociopolitical or ideological values.[18] During the Russo-Japanese War, young people in nominally neutral America consumed a range of products that encouraged them to understand themselves as informal allies of Japan, and to develop conviction in the success of American diplomacy and allyship on a global stage.

Little Ambassadors

Historians of the First World War have observed how Roosevelt's negotiation of the Treaty of Portsmouth in 1905 led many American observers of the early years of the Great War to assume that their nation could maintain is role as a powerful but peaceful facilitator of arbitration.[19] During the Russo-Japanese conflict, Americans consumed a visual culture that emphasized peacekeeping and diplomacy as a sort of American birthright, and children in particular appeared as prominent symbols of international cooperation. As it provided persuasive emblems that served as an optimistic barometer of healthy diplomatic relations, such imagery suggested that international negotiation was a key responsibility of the youthful generation.

Such imagery had already emerged and was continually consumed in the context of the Anglo-Japanese Alliance, signed in 1902 and renewed in 1905 and 1911. Throughout this period, British and Japanese manufacturers alike produced collectible images that celebrated the friendship between Japanese and British children. For instance, in a postcard that was captioned "L'Entente Cordiale," two young boys, one Japanese and one British, stand beside each other. To the left, a somewhat smaller, shorter Japanese boy wears a kimono, and to the right, a British boy wears a vaguely military-looking nautical outfit. They clasp their right hands in a firm handshake, while holding the flags of their respective nations in their left hands. Staring directly at the camera, their expressions are serious [fig. 3.1]. A handshake conducted in the presence of the Japanese and British flags was a common pose used to illustrate the Anglo-Japanese Alliance. The composition of this postcard, for instance, mirrors that of a political poster for Britain's pro-Alliance Conservative Party which depicted a handshake between two adults, a figure who is presumably to be read as a British politician and a Japanese soldier [fig. 3.2]. Viewed alongside this poster, as the boys shake hands, the postcard provides a glimpse of the passage of time and a preview of the politicians of the future. We are reminded that one day, these boys will be men, and it will be their job to continue to maintain the health of the alliance. As such, it is in the best interest of both nations to train their children to look favorably upon each other. The youthful subjects of the postcard also gesture at the notion that the relationship between Japan and Britain was part of a new era of diplomacy; as the countries did not have longstanding ties of friendship, the alliance was still quite young and immature, and would require time to become stronger and more confident.

The imagery of the Anglo-Japanese Alliance was not exclusively male, and women and girls also appeared as evidence of goodwill in both Japanese and British images. The tone and rhetoric of these images, however, differed considerably from depictions of boys. A 1903 oil painting by British painter William Logsdail embodies this contrast [fig. 3.3]. The work was titled *An Anglo-Japanese Alliance,* but the content of the scene is more subtly political than *L'Entente Cordiale*. Here, friendship with Japan is expressed through the young girl's Orientalized toys: her tea set, her kimono-clad doll, and her parasol. The girl rehearses the way in which she will be expected to contribute to Britain's imperial project as a female – in this case, through her domestic work in the home and by means of aesthetic appreciation.[20] Logsdail's painting attempts to temper some of the threat of militarized Japan by reinforcing a familiar, longstanding stereotype of a feminized Asia and Asia as an exotic commodity to be consumed by the West.[21]

Figure 3.2: E. Huskinson, printed by Hill, Slifken and Co., "Vote for the Conservatives who Gave You the Alliance," 1905–1906. Courtesy LSE Digital Library.

Figure 3.3: William Logsdail, *An Anglo-Japanese Alliance*, 1903. Oil on board, 41 × 31 cm. ©
Calderdale Borough Council / Bridgeman Images.

Just as Britain and Japan renewed the Anglo-Japanese Alliance in 1905, a picture
postcard employed children as symbols of America's more informal alliance with
Japan. In this image, Japanese children tussle with each other in a playful melee, half
brandishing Japanese flags, the other half Russian [fig. 3.4]. Seated off to the side
is a child who does not participate in the game but instead waves a Japanese and
an American flag as he watches the fight. Counting the number of flags in this play
battle reveals at an interesting balance of power –there are five Japanese flags vs. six
Russian. However, if the American flag becomes part of Japan's overall count, it is
an equal fight, with six flags on either side. This detail may be coincidental, but the
general reference towards America as an unofficial ally is clear. As an undated image,
it is unclear whether this postcard was produced before or after Roosevelt negotiated
the Treaty of Portsmouth. Thus, the presence of the American flag could speak to

America's assistance in securing Japan's victory by means of negotiating the treaty, but it might also serve as an acknowledgement of broader American goodwill and the support of American citizens. Overall, the imagery of *L'Entente Cordiale* remains a much more overt assertion of friendship. But then again, Britain was much bolder in declaring the official nature of its alliance with Japan.

Figure 3.4: Artist unknown, *Children Holding Japanese and Russian Flags,* 1904–1906. Lithograph with hand coloring, ink on card stock. Photograph © 2021 Museum of Fine Arts, Boston.

The subject matter of the postcard – Japanese children playing war games – was one that also appeared in the international illustrated press during the Russo-Japanese War. Throughout the war, the Western press provided readers with detailed descriptions of the military fervor of Japanese society and of its youth in particular.[22] Japanese cultural historian Sabine Frühstück has noted that prior to the late nineteenth century, Japanese adults were actually largely ambivalent about children's war games. Opinions on the topic shifted by the time of the Russo-Japanese War, during which Japanese schools actively promoted mock battles and implemented military drills as part of their curriculum.[23] In 1904, French illustrator Georges Ferdinand Bigot depicted one such battle in the illustrated supplement to the magazine *Le Petit Parisien*[24] [fig. 3.5]. This battle is not the random chaos of playfully raucous youth – in addition to the visible surveillance of the adult supervisor, who stands in a pose of concentrated scrutiny with his brow furrowed and arms crossed, we see other marks of organization and discipline, from the caps that delineate the members of each side (naval caps for the "Japanese" and fur hats for the "Russians"), to the use of a single, standardized "weapon" consisting of a long wooden club with a heavy knob at the end. It is not so much a spontaneous game as it is an organized exercise. Although surviving descriptions of these games suggest that girls were sometimes included, this image also presents the game as a strictly masculine affair, as the female students huddle together in the back of the scene, watching the battle unfold well out of harm's way.[25] In a fashion similar to Logsdail's *Anglo-Japanese Alliance*, the children rehearse the gendered roles expected during a military conflict.

Figure 3.5: Georges Ferdinand Bigot, "La petite guerre dans les écoles japonaises." Printed in the *Supplément Littéraire Illustré* of *Le Petit Parisien*, September 4, 1904. © Look and Learn / Bridgeman Images.

Inherent in Bigot's description of Japanese children's war-themed play was the uneasy question regarding the militarized Japanese child as a proxy for the nation at large. Some Western observers of Japanese school drills preferred to frame the practice as a relatively innocuous means of physical education. The caption to Bigot's print, for instance, emphasized the "harmless" nature of the children's wooden clubs. But Westerners also consumed images that provided a more intimidating glimpse of the supposed war-fever of Japanese children, as in the case of a stereoscopic print from 1905 that was captioned "Japanese School Boys with Dummy Guns, the Nation's Future Defense" [fig. 3.6]. Here, a sense of military preparation supersedes the suggestion of play. It is a jarring image, somewhat surreal in its vacillation between childhood and adulthood, innocence and seriousness, aggression and restraint, make-believe and reality.[26] A mass of boys – young men, really – crowds together, brandishing wooden rifles. Staring straight ahead, they make direct, unflinching eye contact with the camera. With the boys cocking their weapons and poised to "shoot," the viewer looks directly down the barrel of their guns, a confrontation that would have been further intensified by the illusion of viewing the image through the eyepieces of a stereoscope, a device that produced a three-dimensional effect. With as many "armed" boys packed into the frame as possible, the group instantly evokes the idea of a battalion of soldiers, awaiting the order to charge.

Figure 3.6: Artist unknown, "Japanese school boys with dummy guns, the nation's future defense," c.1905. Stereograph photo. Courtesy of the Library of Congress, LC-DIG-stereo-1s31617.

Even minus the military paraphernalia, the densely crowded composition reflects the anxiety of a subset of Americans who kept a wary eye on the waves of Japanese immigrants arriving in the US around the time of the Russo-Japanese War. Many fearfully imagined the growth of a de-facto colony of Japanese on America's west coast which would drain jobs and resources from native-born Americans. They argued that these immigrants would refuse to accept American law and order, remaining loyal only to the Empire of Japan, and thus America would soon discover that it had been silently invaded by the Japanese.[27] This assumption of the inherently inassimilable nature of Asians into American society had already been used to validate policies of Chinese exclusion since the 1880s. By 1907, these racialized tensions would come to a head as US Executive Order 589 attempted to stem the flow of Japanese immigration into the United States.[28] In the same year, race riots broke out along the Pacific coast in which white activists violently targeted East and South Asian communities and businesses. As Erika Lee has noted, the years following the Russo-Japanese War marked the global coalescence of anti-Asian sentiment across the United States, Canada and Britain. The supposed "Yellow Peril" therefore came to be understood as a potential global catastrophe, rather than a more localized threat.[29]

As such, the picture postcard in which the Japanese child waves the stars and stripes in a sea of Russian and Japanese flags served to dissipate some of the anxiety about the United States' potential to check the rise of imperial Japan. The American flag alters the tone of the image such that it presents a different message than Bigot's vision of war games. These children are not just foreign belligerents – they are grateful allies in need of American support and guidance. And in turn, American children were also offered as reciprocal diplomatic evidence of the nation's good-will toward Japan. In 1905, Baron Kaneko Kentaro, a Harvard-educated diplomat, was dispatched to the United States to manage Western public opinion concerning the recent war. There, he attended the Independence Day celebrations in Portland, Maine, not too far from the eventual site of the signing of the Treaty of Portsmouth. At these celebrations, he watched as several hundred children staged mock battles between Russia and Japan. According to the local newspaper, "[t]he Japanese army was very well disciplined, while the Russian one was a rabble. When they clashed the latter soon began to lose, threw away their colors and drums, and fled." The paper suggested that these American children were doing more than simply play fighting – they were actively processing the current events around them. It noted that "[t]hough this was only done in play it was evidence that even innocent children seem to know of the Russian army's weakness and the bravery of the Japanese army."[30] From this description, it is clear that this battle was more than spontaneous child's play – it was an instance of diplomatic pageantry staged on Kaneko's behalf.[31] Evidently, the performance was successful, as, observing the children's enthusiasm, Baron Kaneko happily concluded that "[t]he sympathy of the American people for Japan will not be easily reduced. Now in all classrooms the upper to the lower, even the children earnestly hope for Japan's victory."[32]

The child's voice – with its connotation of innocence, honesty and simplicity – therefore became a useful counter to otherwise tense diplomatic relations. By viewing the modern geopolitical landscape through the lens of children and their play, adults could indulge in a reassuringly simplified version of current events. Such a psychological strategy suggested that if the snarl of politics could be distilled down to the level of a child's comprehension, surely it was not actually so very complex or so ominous. In this light, children were metaphorically ideal for diffusing delicate diplomatic situations. Indeed, from 1906 to 1909, as tensions between Japan and the US soared, children became a key part of the pageantry arranged by the Japanese government as an expression of friendliness between the nations. When, in 1907, Roosevelt ordered the battleships of America's "Great White Fleet" to tour the Pacific

Figure 3.7: Artist unknown, *Postcard Commemorating the Great White Fleet*, c.1908. Collection of the author.

as a blatant expression of the extent of America's military reach into the region, Japan lined the sailors' 18-mile train ride to Tokyo with cheering children and waving flags. Arriving at the station platform, the American officers walked through a chorus of 10,000 school children singing the *Star Spangled Banner*."[33] And once again, children appeared on commemorative postcards. On one such postcard, a Japanese baby plays with a doll with curly blonde hair, flanked by the Japanese and America flags [fig. 3.7]. In response to Roosevelt's threat, the image leveraged the stereotype of Japan as America's innocent child, incapable of causing harm. Seated by his little doll, largely understood as a girls' plaything, this baby is hardly the warmongering Japanese youth that American viewers feared. As he interacts with the doll, he also acts out friendship with an imaginary Western friend. This figure hovered as the embodiment of the delicate and tenuous balance between innocence and corruption and between war and peace.

In the year following the Great White Fleet's visit to Japan, Japanese-American lawyer Masuji Miyakawa would likewise evoke the metaphor of Japan as an obedient child, and would also reiterate Japanese youths' commitment to peace over war. During a series of lectures delivered to American public school children, Miyakawa delivered a "special message" of goodwill on behalf of the public school children of Japan to those of the United States. The audiences were told that author of the message was a sixth-grade Tokyo schoolboy, who wrote:

> We have in the meantime, been told that there is a certain sentiment which looks upon war between the two countries as inevitable, just as our older brothers who passed before us in our schools thought war with China and the late war with Russia inevitable. In view of our teaching at school and at home that "the American people are the foster mothers of Japan's present progress and prosperity," we, the public school children in convention assembled, with the permission of our fathers, brothers, and teachers, passed the following resolution: Resolved, That we, the pupils of the Imperial public schools, shall never raise our swords against, but shall emulate the pupils of the Public Schools of the United States as perfect examples of brotherhood and sisterhood.[34]

Miyakawa was keen to emphasize that the message "was considered by American and European officials and diplomats, as the greatest, the most unprecedented and the shrewdest piece of diplomacy in all history."[35] Certainly, this assessment bordered on the hyperbolic, but it is true that the American press did frame the children's message as a new and interesting form of diplomacy that had not yet been deployed in world affairs.[36]

Child's Play

In this visual and performative culture of diplomacy that emerged in the years surrounding the Russo-Japanese War, we therefore observe that the child became a political symbol for adult consumption; the examples discussed thus far were largely directed at an adult audience, although children likely would have had access to them. But even more explicitly, as they became part of diplomatic pageantry, children themselves were also imbued with conviction in America's powerful role as a detached ally in the Russo-Japanese conflict through a range of media directed specifically towards young consumers.

Figure 3.8: *Advertisement for Parker Games,* c.1895–1897. Collection of the author.

A key form that introduced American children to the visual codes and tropes of imperial politics was the war-themed board game. This was not a new form of entertainment in 1904. American families had enjoyed board games during the Civil War as well as during the more recent conflicts of the Spanish American War (1898) and Philippine-American War (1899–1902), as demonstrated by games like Parker Games' "The War in Cuba" and "The Battle of Manila."[37] A turn-of-the-century advertisement for "The Battle of Manila" demonstrates how these games were more than just amusing children's playthings [fig. 3.8]. In this image, a mother, father, son, and daughter are comfortably seated around a table as they enjoy the game laid out before them. They lean excitedly towards the game board as the daughter smiles and claps her hands while her father moves a piece. The family's attire as well as the furnishings of the home is to the latest refined taste, contributing to the image's overall air of idealized Victorian domesticity and thereby conveying an intrinsic social message of supposed middle-class decency. Over the course of the mid- to late nineteenth century, the parlor had become a site in which the American middle class attempted to differentiate itself from what it perceived as the disorderly, unschooled masses. By performing certain kinds of social choreography – for instance, by taking tea at five o'clock or choosing fashionable home décor from a catalog – middle-class Americans indicated that they had internalized the habits of what they considered good taste and self-control. Entertainment and leisure were part of this performance, and games were one means by which parents instructed children in the intellectual, social and moral values of "respectable" society.[38]

The Parker Games advertisement therefore illustrated multiple aspects of successful middle-class parenting: the children are at home under their parents' watchful supervision rather than roaming the streets; they are animated, but not unruly, as the family takes turns and cooperates in game-play; the family values an education in geography and current events. Curiously, although the advertisement specified that "The War in Cuba" was a game for boys, the company did not apply this particular designation to all of its war-themed games, including "The Battle of Manila." It does appear that such toys *did* primarily target a largely male audience, as suggested by the writings of a small but vocal peace movement that protested the production of war toys for children, almost exclusively framing its arguments around young boys' use of such toys.[39] However, as demonstrated by the family portrayed by Parker Games, such games were not universally played by boys or men. Both adult men and women followed news of the Russo-Japanese War in illustrated magazines, picture postcards, and newspapers. During the World's Fair of 1904, the *Saint Louis Republic* suggested that mapping the war could be both entertainment and an exercise in citizenship applicable to the entire family. It published a map that readers could assemble and mount on a piece of cotton cloth, to which they could then pin cardboard ships and armies to track the progress of the war.[40]

Compared to some of the photographic imagery published during this era, much of which was unflinchingly graphic in its portrayal of violence, gruesome injuries, and death, family games still provided a sanitized, idealized vision of war.[41] But just because the imagery of these games was not graphic does not mean that it was ideologically unsophisticated. Looking more closely at several games produced during the time of the Russo-Japanese War reveals a visual culture that assumed that children were actually quite capable of consuming much of the same visual propaganda as their elders. Consider, for instance, Milton Bradley's strategy game "Across the Yalu." Released in 1904, this game was a variation on *xiangqi*, or "Chinese Chess." Whether or not an East Asian game was chosen to complement the theme of an East Asian conflict is unclear. The metaphor of chess, was, however, occasionally used within contemporary textual descriptions of the contested region.[42] As in traditional *xiangqi*, the game represents two opposing armies which attempt to capture the enemy's general on the other side of the board. On this particular board, the armies are divided by the Yalu River, the site of the first major land battle of the Russo-Japanese War. The selection of this particular battle is significant in understanding the political slant of this game. It was Japan's triumph in the Battle of the Yalu that led many Westerners to question Russia's overwhelming assurance that it would easily crush a much weaker Japanese military.[43] Along with the selection of a decisive Japanese victory as the game's background, the illustrated game box also subtly shaped players' perception of Japanese soldiers [fig. 3.9]. Depicting two armies leveling their weapons at one another across the river, the box is visually similar to other war-themed board games produced around this time, such as Parker Brothers' "The Philippine War" [fig. 3.10].

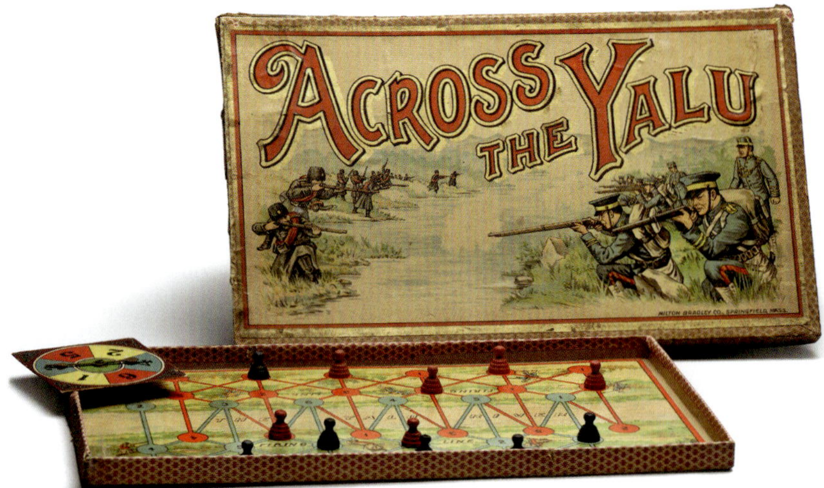

Figure 3.9: Milton Bradley Company, *Board Game: Across the Yalu*, 1904. Cardboard. Photograph © 2021 Museum of Fine Arts, Boston.

Figure 3.10: George S. Parker, *Board Game: The Philippine War: Crushing the Rebellion in Luzon*, 1900. Courtesy of The Strong, Rochester, New York.

Compared to much of the popularly consumed imagery of Japanese soldiers produced during the era of the Russo-Japanese War, the imagery of this game relies less on exaggerated, racially-based caricature. In fact, there is little to distinguish Milton Bradley's Japanese soldiers from the American ones that appear on the Parker Brothers box. The armies seem to be equally powerful, matched in physicality, skill, and preparation. This message was quite different than that delivered by toys produced in pro-Russia France, which, according to one contemporaneous writer, tended to "represent the Japanese getting the worst of it." To support his point, the writer described in detail a toy that depicted "a brave Russian who with a single shot lays flat a file of ten Japanese, on whose painted faces is an expression of abject fear."[44]

In its departure from racialized caricature, the imagery of "Across the Yalu" operated similarly to a type of postcard that was disseminated throughout Europe and the United States that depicted leaders of the Japanese military in Western-style portrait busts [fig. 3.11]. The postcards portrayed these men as leaders of a distinguished nation, no different than Western military leaders or dignitaries.[45] A child playing "Across the Yalu" who considered the game box would have received through images a message that President Roosevelt had already delivered in words: "While I am President the Japanese will be treated just exactly like the English, Germans, French, or other civilized peoples … I think it will be the permanent policy of our Government."[46] Images such as these postcards presented a very different vision of a non-Western nation than that which many American consumers would have been accustomed to. Even images that took a pro-Japan stance often relied on caricatures that were still mocking, infantilizing, or blatantly racist in their portrayal of the Japanese, as in the case of the board game "The Great Japanese Puzzle"[47] [fig. 3.12]. The lid of "The Great Japanese Puzzle" depicts a Japanese soldier locked in combat with a white "Russian" bear amidst a shower of exploding shells. The game itself portrays a critical moment in which battleships have blown a hole in the side of the bear's fort; having lost his crown, he finds himself surrounded by a battalion of Japanese

Figure 3.11: Artist unknown, published by Misch & Stock's, *Admiral Togo, In Command of the Japanese Fleet, from the series In Far East no. 216*, 1904–1905. Color lithograph, ink on card stock. Photograph © 2021 Museum of Fine Arts, Boston.

soldiers wielding bayonets. The text on the lid asks young players: "Can you get the Japs in the Fort and drive the bear out?" To play the game, players placed a white marble representing the bear into the center of a circle of upright nails representing the "fort"; then, colored marbles representing Japanese soldiers were placed outside the fort. Players were to tilt the box, manipulating the colored marbles into the fort. Finally, once all of the marbles were inside, in order to win the entire game, the player had to guide the white marble out of the ring, expelling the bear from the fort.

Figure 3.12: J. Ottmann Lithography Co, *Board Game: The Great Japanese Puzzle*, 1904–1905. Courtesy of The Strong, Rochester, New York.

Like "Across the Yalu," the imagery of "The Great Japanese Puzzle" recalls the war's broader propaganda, as small Japanese soldiers fending off a ferocious Russian bear was a common motif that appeared in cartoons and picture postcards [fig. 3.13]. Even more so than "Across the Yalu," "The Great Japanese Puzzle" introduced players to the conventions of the mocking, more abstract variety of propaganda originally conceived for a more mature audience. That the imagery of adult propaganda trickled down into children's culture is also evidenced by a set of paper dolls that appeared in the French children's magazine *La joie des enfants* [fig. 3.14]. The magazine provided cartoons of a Japanese soldier and a rotund, red-nosed "John Bull" fleeing a menacing Russian bear. The child was to cut out the pieces of each figure – which were divided up into a torso, arms and legs – and paste them onto cardboard to create a puppet with articulated, moveable limbs that could then be used in his own puppet show. The magazine did not give any explanation of the figures beyond how to assemble them; presumably, young French readers were already familiar with these tropes. Like "The Great Japanese Puzzle," these paper dolls placed the child in a position of control and power, as the master of his own little empire. As the French child played, he could make his Russian, Japanese and British puppets do as he pleased. As the American child tipped the box of "The Great Japanese Puzzle" back and forth, he shifted the positions of the Japanese "soldiers." It was only with the child's help that his Japanese soldiers could defeat the bear – quite literally, without his momentum, they remained stagnant, unable to act. It was a subtle reminder of the notion that America's unofficial support was tipping the balance of Japan's victory.

Figure 3.13: Dudley Hardy, published by Davidson Brothers, *Waking Him Up, from the series 3015,* 1904–1905. Color lithograph, ink on card stock. Photograph © 2021 Museum of Fine Arts, Boston.

Figure 3.14: Paper dolls from the French children's magazine *La joie des enfants*, c.1904–1905. Collection of the author.

Viewed together, "Across the Yalu" and "The Great Japanese Puzzle" are indicative of a larger struggle in which Americans young and old began to grapple with their existing conception of a hierarchy of "civilized" and influential nations. Throughout the nineteenth century, Americans and Europeans had enjoyed a variety of around-the-world-themed board games that introduced them to non-white, non-Western cultures. Couched in the language of "adventure" or appreciation of "exoticism," the imagery of these board games prompted largely white, middle- to upper-class Americans to identify themselves as innately different from and superior to non-white foreigners.[48] However, Japan's victory and declarations such as Roosevelt's regarding the similarities of the Japanese and Westerners destroyed many of these comforting distinctions between "us" and "them." Implicit in Japan's victory over Russia and Roosevelt's insistence on sameness was the ominous question: if Japan could defeat Russia, what would prevent it from pursuing similar victories over other Western nations? Thus, unlike "Across the Yalu," the cartoons of "The Great Japanese Puzzle" quelled some of this anxiety by still casting Japan as a caricature for Western consumption and amusement. American players could still find reassurance in the otherness of Japan, even as they helped its soldiers to victory.

War and Peace

While games like "Across the Yalu" or "The Great Japanese Puzzle" belonged to a middle-class culture of educational entertainment that was mediated by adults, the events of the Russo-Japanese War also infiltrated more informal, unruly youth culture. On February 15, 1904 – only one week after the Battle of Port Arthur – *The New York Times* described the mayhem caused by a pack of boys who selected the Sunday services of a New York City church as the site of a prank battle. The paper explained that the boys "represented themselves to be the Japanese contingent, while the congregation of the faithful were designated as the Russian foe, and for fully twenty minutes, during two separate clashes, the boys dropped playful but noisy torpedoes on the mosaic aisles of the church, much to the amazement and discomfort of the worshippers."[49] Overall, writing with a tone of rueful chagrin, the *Times* cast this incident as simply boyish mischievousness. Yet, at this moment, adult observers also examined children's war games as a serious matter that could provoke long-reaching consequences. Aligning with a growing international peace movement, American educator Lucia Ames Mead, for one, had much to say on the subject in her anti-imperialist, pacifist primer *Patriotism and the New Internationalism*, published in 1906. In addition to arguing that school teachers must "tolerate no phrases like 'our dominance of the Pacific,' or 'the dominance of the Anglo-Saxon race,'" Mead was repulsed by the nonchalance with which American parents allowed their children to play war. "Why should one encourage boys to fight sham battles with toy guns any more than he would let them play at execution and burial with toy gallows and coffins?" she argued.[50] R. F. Outcault, author of the popular children's cartoon *Buster Brown*, espoused a similar opinion through the medium of his own work. In a comic vignette titled "Buster Brown Plays David and Goliath," published in 1905, young Buster Brown imagines himself as the biblical shepherd boy, slinging a rock at a dummy he has created to play the role of Goliath. Instead of hitting the dummy, his stone strikes a passer-by, who angrily chases after him, forcing Buster Brown to run for his life [fig. 3.15]. Eventually forgiven, the young hero concludes:

> Resolved: That David was right in his time – but fighting is going out of fashion now. Some day people will read of war like we read of the tower of Babel. The same men who advocate war would wallop their sons for fighting out their disputes. If every body were honest, there wouldn't be any war. I am awfully sorry I hit that man, and I apologized to him. He forgave me. Now it takes the real stuff in a man to forgive a fellow who has just socked him in the head with a rock. It takes a man to forgive. ANY chump can get mad and fight. [fig. 3.16]

Figure 3.15: R.F. Outcualt, Illustrations from "Buster Brown Plays David and Goliath," in *Buster Brown Goes Shooting* (New York: New York Herald), 1905. Collection of the author.

Figure 3.16: R.F. Outcualt, Illustrations from "Buster Brown Plays David and Goliath," in *Buster Brown Goes Shooting* (New York: New York Herald), 1905. Collection of the author.

This cartoon does not *directly* address the Russo-Japanese War, but the David and Goliath motif clearly associates it with the conflict. As it became increasingly apparent that Japan would achieve victory over Russia, the imagery of the boy David defeating the giant Goliath became a common means of framing the young empire's triumph for Western readers and viewers.

In addition to its generalized anti-war stance, this particular edition of *Buster Brown* pointedly took a few ruthless jabs at President Theodore Roosevelt's carefully cultivated image of violent masculinity and scoffed at his vision of the "strenuous life." Even though he was awarded the Nobel Peace Prize for brokering the Treaty of Portsmouth, Roosevelt was highly concerned about the declining state of military enthusiasm and physical aggressiveness among young American men and boys, especially as it pertained to the nation's ability to maintain an army and navy that were sufficiently threating to be used as persuasive tools in arbitration. As Gail Bederman has explained, Roosevelt was attracted to a "more violent masculinity," the type of masculinity that drove him to promote himself as an emblem of the rough-riding, hunting, athletic, physically superior American male.[51] According to Roosevelt's line of thinking, war toys, along with sports, hunting trips, and participation in proto-military boys' clubs like the Boy Scouts of America, founded in 1910, would help cultivate a martial spirit that was declining among American males. Outcault specifically rejected this version of preparedness. Another cartoon in the same volume, "Buster Brown Goes Shooting," mocked "the idea of a president going out armed with a gun and a camera and a press agent to shoot helpless and unarmed animals." Addressing young readers, Buster asked: "Can a great man destroy the works of his creator, and take a life which he can't replace? Just to get his picture in the papers for small boys to look at?" As far as Outcault was concerned – and a small but vocal subset of champions of disarmament agreed – masculinity had little to do with the arts of war. The new world order called for a new kind of man. They argued that lack of military enthusiasm in a society was not to be understood as decline, but as reaching a higher state of evolution.[52]

Amidst such calls for pacifism, and even as conviction in the efficacy of diplomatic negotiation and the exertion of unofficial political influence grew, concern regarding the military preparedness of American children nonetheless deepened in the years following the Russo-Japanese War. At the onset of the conflict, the symbolic language of visual culture largely attempted to quell latent anxiety that Japan might actually become a serious threat to nations that were already more established on the imperial stage. But with Japan's victory, many Westerners began to question the fittingness of applying imagery characterized by connotations of innocence, guilelessness or helplessness to the Japanese. Even prior to the Russo-Japanese conflict, an author writing in the American political and literary magazine *The Dial* observed Japan's emergence as a world power during the First Sino-Japanese War of 1894–1895, and argued that "[t]he Chino-Japanese war has made it painfully evident that the fanciful notions long-current regarding the 'child of the world's old age,' stand badly in need of revision. To go on patronizingly viewing Japan as a clever child mimicking the ways of its elders and amusing itself for a space with its toy army, toy fleet, toy railroads, telegraph, etc. is out of the question since Yalu and Port Arthur."[53] For this writer, the metaphor of the innocent, precocious child no longer seemed apt when applied to Japan.

As Americans considered the spectrum of depictions of Japanese children and absorbed the intrigues of the Russo-Japanese War, they implicitly and explicitly pondered the now less unthinkable possibility of the failure of diplomacy and the possibility of war in an imperial world. How would American youths measure up? American educators, for instance, debated the usefulness of military drills in the nation's schools. Some supported the idea that, as in Japan, military instruction should be a mandatory part of public education from the elementary to the university level as a means of bolstering the reserves of Uncle Sam's army.[54] But in general, proponents of military drills in schools skirted around the question of whether they were intended to prepare American children to face a real, active threat from abroad. Instead, they tended to emphasize the drills' benefit in fostering a generalized sort of discipline that could be applied to any part of a young person's life. Others argued that it was simply another way of keeping children interested in physical activity by harnessing the child's natural enthusiasm for playing soldier – as one Massachusetts teacher attending an educational conference on the matter put it simply, "[t]hey love to drill, and I think it better than football."[55] In the case of girls, military drill groups did exist, but descriptions were careful to emphasize that the experience was an aesthetic one in which the girls painted a pretty picture of patriotism. Writers who described such drills were careful to note that violence or anticipation of war was not the impetus behind girls' drills. Carefully chosen costumes, graceful movement and good posture combined in a performance akin to a ballet. Some descriptions were also tinged with a degree of titillating amusement at the topsy-turvy notion of young women playing at men's work.[56] An implied takeaway was that to train up a military battalion was not, in fact, that difficult; if 12-year-old girls could master drills as a means of recreation – in some cases, shouldering feather dusters, dainty parasols or long-stemmed flowers instead of wooden rifles – then surely if need arose, the training of fully grown men would require little time or effort.[57]

By 1909, Frank G. Carpenter, a journalist and author of children's geographical readers, suggested outright in *The Boston Daily Globe* that American children should exercise a healthy amount of respect and wariness where their Japanese counterparts were concerned. In an article intended for young readers, Carpenter explained that despite their differences in appearance, Japanese boys and girls were "just like Americans." However, he added, Japanese children were especially quick to pick a fight, and their smaller statue should not be cause to underestimate their strength. He also was fascinated by the sheer number and variety of war toys enjoyed by Japanese children. He argued that these, in combination with the extensive military drilling that took place within the public schools and with the recent victory against Russia, Japanese boys had developed a sort of swaggering pugnaciousness. He explained: "Just now the boys think the Japanese people could whip any other nation, and that the United States would have a poor show in a fight with their country. We are friendly to them, but we must keep our eyes open, for no one can tell but that we may have to fight them by and by."[58]

Carpenter's words vacillated between anxiety and dismissiveness. Since the nineteenth century, pseudoscientific theories had argued that Japanese bodies were stunted and weak compared to the ideal Western body. In turn, these theories lent support to eugenic arguments that justified Western imperialism as the natural and unavoidable course of societal evolution.[59] Such arguments also troubled Japanese intellectuals and government officials who themselves accepted such reasoning as scientifically accurate. Even after Japan's success in the Russo-Japanese War, they carefully considered how the Japanese body could be improved and strengthened so as to accurately reflect the political robustness of Japan. As the nation's future resources, the bodies of children were particular sites of interest, hence the implementation of programs such as compulsory military drill.[60] On the one hand, Carpenter rejected this type of thinking by suggesting that the smaller physicality of Japanese children was *not* indicative of inferior military or national strength. On the other hand, he attempted to temper this somewhat ominous admission by injecting it with humor. He offered his young American readers to share in a joke – to be amused by the Japanese boys' conviction that they could "whip" an American if they were teased enough, like a toddler or small puppy who overestimates its strength. Much like the exaggerated caricature of the game "The Great Japanese Puzzle," Carpenter's joke attempted to alleviate some of the unease surrounding the difficulty of understanding this new, modern, Japanese Other. Words like his suggested to young Americans, via a racially-based undercurrent, that they would perform at *least* as well as their Japanese counterparts if called to take up arms.

Conclusion: Uncle Sam Picks the Right Side

Thus, the voice of the child emerged out of the tensions of the first decade of the twentieth century as a key part of American diplomatic propaganda. By the time the US entered World War I, the frequency with which children appeared as coercive political symbols had increased exponentially. Countless images of children beseeching adults to participate in any number of activities – to enlist in the army, buy war bonds, or plant a garden – are part of the well-known imagery of the First World War, as the child's supposed innocence, vulnerability and moral simplicity made him the darling of wartime propaganda offices.[61] But at the same time, the men and women who were old enough to serve by 1917 had been consumers of a culture that had introduced the complex task of observing and assessing the shifting balance of geopolitical power and global alliances since they themselves had been "innocent" children in 1904–1905.

Having been used as symbols of international cooperation during the era of the Russo-Japanese War, young Americans had for some time absorbed the message that peacekeeping and diplomacy were a key responsibility of youth and of their generation. As they observed the conflict in China, both mass culture at large as well as a specific youth-directed culture attempted to bolster conviction of America's value as an ally and the nation's ability to tip the scales of an armed conflict towards peace. By co-opting Japan's victory as America's own, the American propaganda of the Russo-Japanese War inculcated the confidence-building suggestion that the United States *had* been on the winning side before in the era of modern warfare, even though American boots had not been on the ground.

Perhaps it is no wonder, then, that Lieutenant Basil Beebe Elmer expressed enthusiasm as he prepared for his opportunity to play the game of war. The same message that "The Great Japanese Puzzle" had conveyed to 10-year-olds as they beat back the

Russian bear in 1904–1905 was now repeated to them as 22-year-olds in the pages of the *Stars and Stripes*: "Our Uncle Samuel, be it remembered, is a cautious old gent, and looks well on both sides before getting into a scrap; but once he gets in – and the canny old customer always picks the right side – he's in to stay until the whole job is cleaned up, and he's in right up to his shoulderblades."[62] As they had grown up observing America's geopolitical ascendancy on the fringes of international conflict, many of the young men who headed to the front – or indeed, the young women who found themselves taking up nursing, operating switchboards, or otherwise mobilizing the home front – had been inculcated with a language of confidence surrounding America's ability to provide decisive victory as an ally. It assured them that when the time came, the game of world affairs would be theirs to play and to win.

Notes

1   Basil Beebe Elmer, Letter to his parents, October 14, 1917, 3-4. Basil Beebe Elmer Correspondence 1917–1919, SC23224, New York State Library.

2   Basil Beebe Elmer, Letter to his parents, October 14, 1917, 4. Basil Beebe Elmer Correspondence 1917–1919, SC23224, New York State Library.

3   Basil Beebe Elmer, Letter to his parents, October 27, 1917, 2. Basil Beebe Elmer Correspondence 1917–1919, SC23224, New York State Library.

4   Basil Beebe Elmer, Letter to his parents, August 5, 1918. Basil Beebe Elmer Correspondence 1917–1919, SC23224, New York State Library. In his letter of August 5, 1918, Elmer described the front as "all a dream – a nightmare."

5   On the complexities of soldiers' letters as a category of analysis see Jay Winter, *Remembering War: The Great War between Memory and History in the Twentieth Century* (New Haven: Yale University Press, 2006), particularly Chapter 4, "War Letters: Cultural Memory and the 'Soldiers' Tale' of the Great War."

6   Mark Meigs, *Optimism at Armageddon: Voices of American Participants in the First World War* (London: Macmillan, 1997), 5. See also David Kennedy, *Over Here: The First World War and American Society* (Oxford: Oxford University Press, 1980), 212–4.

7   Paul Fussell, *The Great War and Modern Memory* (Oxford: Oxford University Press, 2000), 9. Fussell notes of this "sporting spirit:" "The ensuing maneuvers during late October and early November are variously named 'The First Battle of Ypres,' and 'The Race to the Sea' – that is, to the Belgian seaports. The journalistic formula 'The Race to the ______' was ready to hand, familiar through its use in 1909 to describe Peary's 'Race to the (North) Pole' against Cook. Rehabilitated and applied to these new events, the phrase had the advantage of a familiar sportsmanlike, Explorer Club overtone, suggesting that what was happening was not too far distant from playing games, running races, and competing in a thoroughly decent way."

8   As Kennedy notes, "Almost never in contemporary accounts do the themes of wonder and romance give way to those of weariness and resignation, as they do in the British."

9   Kennedy, *Over Here*, 205.

10   *Ibid.*, 212–3.

11   This study therefore embraces continuing attempts to expand the scope of scholarship of the First World War beyond the chronological boundaries of 1914–1918 and to

engage in further topical diversification, as articulated, for instance, by Steven Sabol in the inaugural issue of the journal *First World War Studies*. See Steven Sabol, "A Brief Note from the Editor," *First World War Studies* 1, no. 1 (2010). So too do I model my methodology in light of works such *Revival after the Great War* with its attention to "focusing on daily life in all its facets against the background of major political, economic, and societal transformations." See Luc Verpoest et al., eds., *Revival after the Great War: Rebuild, Remember, Repair, Reform* (Leuven: Leuven University Press, 2020), 12.

12   On the multitude of reasons why the Russo-Japanese War could be considered the first truly global conflict of the modern era, see the introduction to John W. Steinberg et al., *The Russo-Japanese War in Global Perspective: World War Zero*, vol. 1 (Leiden: Brill, 2005), xix–xxiii.

13   David Wells and Sandra Wilson, eds., *The Russo-Japanese War in Cultural Perspective, 1904–1905* (London: Macmillan, 1999), ix–x: "The ramifications of Japanese victory over Russia in 1905 thus ranged from a fundamental change in the balance of power in Asia to a clear challenge to prevailing notions of white, European superiority throughout the world."

14   *Ibid.*, x.

15   On the transnational scope of the Russo-Japanese War, see Iriye Akira, "The Russo-Japanese War in Transnational History," in *The Russo-Japanese War in Global Perspective*, vol. 2, ed. David Wolff et al. (Leiden: Brill, 2007), 1–9. On Jacob Schiff, see Adam Gower, *Jacob Schiff and the Art of Risk: American Financing of Japan's War with Russia 1904–1905* (Cham: Springer International Publishing, 2018).

16   Norman E. Saul's chapter "The Kittery Peace," provides an overview of the Treaty of Portsmouth in *The Russo-Japanese War in Global Perspective*.

17   The material culture of childhood is notoriously difficult from a historiographic standpoint; as Juliet Kinchin notes of scholarly hesitation regarding these kinds of objects in *Century of the Child: Growing by Design 1900–2000* (New York: Museum of Modern Art, 2012), 16: "One answer lies in the overlay of adult nostalgia, sentiment, and angst onto anything to do with children, which inhibits dispassionate and rigorous analysis." See also Megan Brandow-Faller, "Introduction: Materializing the History of Childhood and Children," in *Childhood by Design: Toys and the Material Culture of Childhood, 1700–Present*, ed. Megan Brandow-Faller (New York: Bloomsbury, 2018), 1–27.

18   Kinchin, *Century of the Child,* 121.

19   Michael S. Neiberg, *The Path to War: How the First World War Created Modern America* (Oxford: Oxford University Press, 2016), 9.

20   On the confluence of America's imperial agenda and the work of domesticity, see Amy Kaplan, *The Anarchy of Empire in the Making of US Culture* (Cambridge: Harvard University Press, 2002), especially Chapter One, "Manifest Domesticity."

21   On the clash between stereotypes of Orientalized femininity and ascendant Japanese military power, see Miya Elise Mizuta, "'Fair Japan': On Art and War at the Saint Louis World's Fair, 1904," *Discourse* 28, no. 1 (2006): 28–52.

22   International writer Lafcadio Hearn, for instance, described in detail the military enthusiasm and play of Japanese children in "A Letter from Japan," *Atlantic Monthly* (November 1904): 627–8.

23   Sabine Frühstück, *Playing War: Children and the Paradoxes of Modern Militarism in Japan* (Oakland: University of California Press, 2017), 31–2. As Frühstück explains, the Russo-Japanese War marked a moment in which war became perhaps more concrete

than ever before in Japanese childhood, especially when it came to viewing the child as a future soldier.

24 A similar version of Bigot's illustration titled "War Fever Among Japanese Boys" also appeared in the *Chicago Tribune* on March 2, 1904, but minus the figure of the school teacher and the Russian hats and flags, producing a more chaotic, frenetic scene.

25 Frühstück, *Playing War,* 32–3.

26 As argued by the introduction to *Children's Literature and Culture of the First World War*, the child dressed as a soldier in the early twentieth century is an example of a sort of surreal spectacle, "simultaneously jarring and arresting in the inherent contradictions of innocence and experience, adult and child, work and play." See Lissa Paul, Rosemary Ross Johnston, and Emma Short, eds., *Children's Literature and Culture of the First World War* (New York: Routledge, 2016), 1.

27 For one of many examples of this type of thinking, see "The Yellow Peril," *Nevada State Journal*, February 28, 1905, p. 3.

28 Executive Order 589 drastically limited Japanese and Korean immigration from Hawai'i, Mexico, and Canada, key entry points to the US besides the west coast.

29 Erika Lee, "The 'Yellow Peril' and Asian Exclusion in the Americas," *Pacific Historical Review* 76, no. 4 (November 2007): 554–5.

30 Kaneko Kentaro, Extract from Foreign Office Records, quoted in Masayoshi Matsumura, *Baron Kaneko and the Russo Japanese War (1904–1905)*, trans. Ian Ruxton (Morrisville, N.C.: Lulu Press, 2009), 152.

31 Anne Nishimura Morse, "Exploiting a New Visuality: The Origins of Russo Japanese War Imagery," in *A Much Recorded War: The Russo-Japanese War in History and Imagery*, by Frederic A. Sharf, Anne Nishimura Morse, and Sebastian Dobson (Boston: MFA Publications, 2005), 46.

32 Matsumura, *Baron Kaneko,* 206.

33 *The New York Times* described how 1,000,000 Japanese children were supposed to take part in the week's celebration in an article from October 20, 1908, noting that "[t]he children's choruses were evidently a part of a carefully thought out plan."

34 Masuji Miyakawa, *Life of Japan* (New York: Neale Publishing, 1910), 242–3.

35 *Ibid.*, 44.

36 Several newspaper articles framed Miyakawa's lectures as an interesting diplomatic gesture; representative examples include "A Brand New Diplomacy: School Children of Tokio are Instructed to be Friendly," *Santa Cruz Evening News*, December 27, 1909, p. 4 and "To Educated Americans Japanese Resort to Novel Methods," *Boston Globe*, December 18, 1909, p. 4.

37 Susan Asbury, "A Plethora of Games for a Splendid Little War: Parker Brothers Invades the Parlor," *Play Stuff Blog*, March 29, 2018, the Strong National Museum of Play, <https://www.museumofplay.org/blog/play-stuff/2018/03/a-plethora-of-games-for-a-splendid-little-war-parker-brothers-invades-the>.

38 Melanie V. Dawson, "From Carnival to Nostalgia: The Play of Cultural Literacy in the Nineteenth Century Parlor" (PhD diss., University of Pittsburgh, 1997), 329–30.

39 See, for instance, "Toys Teach Art of Cruelty Declares a Chicago Woman," *Chicago Daily Tribune*, November 5, 1904 and "Ban to Universal Peace: the boy of the world still wants to play with warlike toys," *Washington Post*, November 26, 1904.

40 "War Chart with Movable Warships and Soldiers," *St. Louis Republic*, March 6, 1904. As the paper declared, "Every man, woman and child reader of the *Republic* will ob-

tain instructive amusements by following the Russo-Japanese War by the aid of this innovation in war maps."

41   John Dower, "Yellow Promise/Yellow Peril: Foreign Postcards of the Russo-Japanese War," MIT Visualizing Cultures, <https://visualizingcultures.mit.edu/yellow_promise_yellow_peril/yp_essay01.html>.

42   See Homer B. Hulbert, "Korea, the Bone of Contention," *Century Illustrated Monthly Magazine* 68, no. 1 (1904): 151. "Nothing encourages the study of geography like war. It was in 1871 that Americans began to look up Korea on the map, for at that time we were at war with her, but there was only one battle, ad only one man was killed – on our side. And now again, in this year of grace, she is to be made, though much against her will, the chess-board for another game."

43   The American press cast the defeat of Russia at the hands of Japan as particularly historic. As the author of an eye-witness account explained to readers of *Leslie's Monthly Magazine*, "[n]ever before in the history of the world's military operations have we heard that the Russian laid down his arms on the field of battle, his belt full of cartridges and his comrades fighting about him." "The Battle of the Yalu River as I Saw It," *Leslie's Monthly Magazine* 58, no. 6 (October 1904): 634.

44   "Paris Dealers Turn to Russo-Japanese Conflict for New Ideas," *Pittsburgh Daily Post*, December 4, 1905, p. 6.

45   Dower, "Yellow Promise/Yellow Peril."

46   Theodore Roosevelt, letter to Lloyd Griscom, July 15, 1905, quoted in Ki Jung Kim, "The War and US-Korean Relations," in *The Russo-Japanese War in Global Perspective*, 477.

47   Dower, "Yellow Promise/Yellow Peril."

48   Dawson, "From Carnival to Nostalgia," 379–80.

49   "Played War in Church," *New York Times,* February 15, 1904, p. 9.

50   Lucia Ames Mead, *Patriotism and the New Internationalism* (Boston: Ginn and Company, 1906), 58–9.

51   Gail Bederman, *Manliness and Civilization: A Cultural History of Gender and Race in the United States, 1880–1917* (Chicago: University of Chicago Press, 2008), 170.

52   John Fiske, "The Strong and the Weak," in *Patriotism and the New Internationalism*, 50.

53   "The Japan of To-Day," *Dial* 19, no. 225 (1895): 257. The First Sino-Japanese War resulted in a shift in East Asian power from China to Japan, with China's recognition of Korean independence as a Japanese protectorate and cession of Taiwan and Liaodong Peninsula to Japan.

54   "Boys Trained for War 11,000 Graduated Annually," *Chicago Daily Tribune*, June 26, 1904, p. D1.

55   "School Military Drill," *Boston Daily Globe*, November 26, 1904, p. 7.

56   "Military Girls Drill like Uncle Sam's Regulars," *Boston Daily Globe*, March 6, 1904, p. 5.

57   See "Pretty Girl Zouaves Win Military Honors," *Chicago Daily Tribune*, March 6, 1905, p. C10, and Henry Symes, "How to be Healthy and Beautiful: A Feather Duster Drill for Little Girls," *Los Angeles Times,* November 1, 1903, p. E8.

58   Frank G. Carpenter, "Boy and Girls of Japan: Frank G. Carpenter Writes a Letter for the Children of New England About the Children of the Mikado's kingdom," *Boston Daily Globe*, March 28, 1909.

59   Izumi Nakayama, "Gender, Health and the Problem of 'Precocious Puberty' in Meiji Japan," in *Gender, Health and History in Modern East Asia*, ed. Leung Angela Ki Che

and Nakayama Izumi (Hong Kong: Hong Kong University Press, 2014), 47. Early Social Darwinists argued that certain non-white races such as the Japanese ceased to grow physically taller after reaching puberty earlier in childhood than Westerners, which they correlated with associated intellectual stunting.

60   Nakayama, "Gender, Health and the Problem of 'Precocious Puberty,'" 37–40. Nakayama looks at the work of Mishima Michiyoshi, explaining how his comparison of Japanese and Western children's bodies aligned with the assumption of "the physical growth of children as corresponding to the development of the nation."

61   Justin Nordstrom, "'A Salesman for Uncle Sam': Images of Childhood in US Food Conservation, 1914–1919," in *Children's Literature and Culture of the First World War*, 179. As Nordstrom notes, in times of national crisis, childhood becomes a crucial trope for influencing adult behavior, as "mirrors" of the values that adults should strive for.

62   "No Delay about Moving In," *Stars and Stripes*, February 8, 1918, p. 1.

Bibliography

Asbury, Susan. "A Plethora of Games for a Splendid Little War: Parker Brothers Invades the Parlor." *Play Stuff Blog*, March 29, 2018. The Strong National Museum of Play. <https://www.museumofplay.org/blog/play-stuff/2018/03/a-plethora-of-games-for-a-splendid-little-war-parker-brothers-invades-the>

"Ban to Universal Peace: the boy of the world still wants to play with warlike toys." *Washington Post*, November 26, 1904.

"The Battle of the Yalu River as I Saw It." *Leslie's Monthly Magazine* 58, no. 6 (October 1904): 632–4.

Bederman, Gail. *Manliness and Civilization: A Cultural History of Gender and Race in the United States, 1880–1917*. Chicago: University of Chicago Press, 2008.

"Boys Trained for War 11,000 Graduated Annually." *Chicago Daily Tribune*, June 26, 1904.

"A Brand New Diplomacy: School Children of Tokio are Instructed to be Friendly." *Santa Cruz Evening News*, December 27, 1909.

Brandow-Faller, Megan, ed. *Childhood by Design: Toys and the Material Culture of Childhood, 1700–Present*. New York: Bloomsbury, 2018.

Carpenter, Frank G. "Boy and Girls of Japan: Frank G. Carpenter Writes a Letter for the Children of New England about the Children of the Mikado's kingdom." *Boston Daily Globe*, March 28, 1909.

Dawson, Melanie V. "From Carnival to Nostalgia: the play of cultural literacy in the nineteenth century parlor." PhD diss., University of Pittsburgh, 1997.

Dower, John. "Yellow Promise/Yellow Peril: Foreign Postcards of the Russo-Japanese War." MIT Visualizing Cultures. <https://visualizingcultures.mit.edu/yellow_promise_yellow_peril/yp_essay01.html>

Frühstück, Sabine. *Playing War: Children and the Paradoxes of Modern Militarism in Japan*. Oakland: University of California Press, 2017.

Fussell, Paul. *The Great War and Modern Memory*. Oxford: Oxford University Press, 2000.

Gower, Adam. *Jacob Schiff and the Art of Risk: American Financing of Japan's War with Russia 1904–1905*. Cham: Springer, 2018.

Hearn, Lafcadio. "A Letter from Japan." *Atlantic Monthly* (November 1904): 627–8.

Hulbert, Homer B. "Korea, the Bone of Contention," *Century Illustrated Monthly Magazine* 68, no. 1 (1904): 151–4.

"The Japan of To-Day." *Dial* 19, no. 225 (1895): 257–8.

Kaplan, Amy. *The Anarchy of Empire in the Making of US Culture.* Cambridge: Harvard University Press, 2002.

Kennedy, David. *Over Here: The First World War and American Society.* Oxford: Oxford University Press, 1980.

Kinchin, Juliet, and Aidan O'Connor, eds. *Century of the Child: Growing by Design 1900–2000.* New York: Museum of Modern Art, 2012.

Lee, Erika. "The 'Yellow Peril' and Asian Exclusion in the Americas." *Pacific Historical Review* 76, no. 4 (November 2007): 537–62.

Matsumura, Masayoshi. *Baron Kaneko and the Russo Japanese War (1904–1905).* Translated by Ian Ruxton. Morrisville, N.C.: Lulu Press, 2009.

Mead, Lucia Ames. *Patriotism and the New Internationalism.* Boston: Ginn and Company, 1906.

Meigs, Mark. *Optimism at Armageddon: Voices of American Participants in the First World War.* London: Macmillan, 1997.

"Military Girls Drill like Uncle Sam's Regulars." *Boston Daily Globe,* March 6, 1904.

Miyakawa, Masuji. *Life of Japan.* New York: Neale Publishing, 1910.

Mizuta, Miya Elise. "'Fair Japan': On Art and War at the Saint Louis World's Fair, 1904." *Discourse* 28, no. 1 (2006): 28–52.

Mosse, George L. *Fallen Soldiers: Reshaping the Memory of the World Wars.* Oxford: Oxford University Press, 1990.

Nakayama, Izumi. "Gender, Health and the Problem of 'Precocious Puberty' in Meiji Japan." In *Gender, Health and History in Modern East Asia,* edited by Leung Angela Ki Che and Nakayama Izumi, 37–60. Hong Kong: Hong Kong University Press, 2014.

Neiberg, Michael S. *The Path to War: How the First World War Created Modern America.* Oxford: Oxford University Press, 2016.

"No Delay about Moving In." *Stars and Stripes,* February 8, 1918.

"Paris Dealers Turn to Russo-Japanese Conflict for New Ideas." *Pittsburgh Daily Post,* December 4, 1905.

Paul, Lissa, Rosemary Ross Johnston, and Emma Short, eds. *Children's Literature and Culture of the First World War.* New York: Routledge, 2016.

"Played War in Church." *New York Times,* February 15, 1904.

"Pretty Girl Zouaves Win Military Honors." *Chicago Daily Tribune,* March 6, 1905.

Sabol, Steven. "A Brief Note from the Editor." *First World War Studies* 1, no. 1 (2010): 1–2.

Schmidt, Jan, and Katja Schmidtpott, eds. *The East Asian Dimensions of the First World War: Global Entanglements and Japan, China, and Korea, 1914–1919.* Chicago: University of Chicago Press, 2020.

"School Military Drill." *Boston Daily Globe,* November 26, 1904.

"War Chart with Movable Warships and Soldiers." *St. Louis Republic,* March 6, 1904.

Sharf, Frederic A., Anne Nishimura Morse, and Sebastian Dobson. *A Much Recorded War: The Russo-Japanese War in History and Imagery.* Boston: MFA Publications, 2005.

Steinberg, John W., Bruce Menning, David Schimmelpenninck van der Oye, David Wolff, and Shinji Yokote, eds. *The Russo-Japanese War in Global Perspective: World War Zero.* Vol. 1. Leiden: Brill, 2005.

Symes, Henry. "How to be Healthy and Beautiful: A Feather Duster Drill for Little Girls." *Los Angeles Times,* November 1, 1903.

"To Educated Americans Japanese Resort to Novel Methods." *Boston Globe*, December 18, 1909.

"Toys Teach Art of Cruelty Declares a Chicago Woman." *Chicago Daily Tribune*, November 5, 1904.

Verpoest, Luc, Leen Engelen, Rajesh Heynickx, Jan Schmidt, Pieter Uyttenhove, and Pieter Verstraete, eds. *Revival after the Great War: Rebuild, Remember, Repair, Reform.* Leuven: Leuven University Press, 2020.

Wells, David, and Sandra Wilson, eds. *The Russo-Japanese War in Cultural Perspective, 1904–1905.* London: Macmillan, 1999.

Winter, Jay. *Remembering War: The Great War between Memory and History in the Twentieth Century.* New Haven: Yale University Press, 2006.

Figure 4.1: Leningrad House of Commerce (formerly House of the Imperial Guard Economic Society), 1907. Saint Petersburg, Russia. Photograph reproduced in G. K. Lukomskii, *Sovremennyi Petrograd : Ocherk istorii vozniknoveniia klassicheskogo stroitel'stva. 1900-1915 gg.* (Petrograd: Izdatel'stvo "Svobodnoe Iskusstvo," 1916).

The First World War and Nationalist Primitivism in Russian Architecture

Da Hyung Jeong

During the First World War, Russia focused its propaganda efforts on the cultivation of anti-Germanic sentiment and the romanticization of the countryside. Wartime fervor gave the provinces bordering enemy territory a new significance as a site of patriotic heroism, and their architecture, modest but honest, came to be viewed as an antidote to eclecticism, or uncritical reliance on foreign models. Resistance to the German *Werkbund*[1] and the Vienna Secession was particularly strong and produced a stylistic nationalism, while the interest in provincial architecture delineated a special kind of "primitivism." If the West relegated the "primitive" strictly outside its geographical confines, Russians located it among themselves and cherished it. This self-fetishization motivated historians to examine the architecture of contested border regions like Galicia, Podolia, Bukovina and Lithuania in search of marks of Slavic identity. At the same time, British models came to the fore after the invalidation of German and Austrian ones, revealing an intention not to reject foreign influence entirely but simply to accept it with greater discernment.[2] Additionally, timber's amenability to the fulfillment of wartime construction needs was explored alongside the symbolic potential that it possessed as Russia's traditional building material.

In a wartime issue of the *Arkhitekturno-khudozhestvennyi ezhenedel'nik* (*Architecture and Art Weekly*), architect and theorist Georgii Gints emphatically asserted that "only war could put an end" to the "falsification" of architecture that Germanophilia, an incorrect "artistic idea," had caused, bringing about the proliferation of "misshapen" constructions.[3] Only war, that is, could ensure a radical severance of ties to Germany and Austria-Hungary and eliminate the "*meisterzingerstvo*" characteristic of Russian architecture, replacing it with a search for authentic expressions of national identity.[4] The peculiar term referred to the German Meistersinger tradition, which for Russian literary critics had become synonymous with insincerity and facetiousness, qualities increasingly ascribed to German and Austro-Hungarian architecture with war looming on the horizon. To be sure, neo-Byzantinists had long been mounting "waves of protest" against Jugendstil, but German and Austro-Hungarian construction firms, very strongly present in Russia, had been insistently favoring the style.[5] Gints was right – only after the war broke out and an embargo was imposed would they leave Russia and bring an end to the "tyranny of Jugendstil."

In 1907, the German company Wayss & Freytag invited Otto Wagner to Saint Petersburg to serve on the jury for an international competition for the design of a department store, and an Art Nouveau scheme by Ernest F. Virrikh, an ethnic German from Odessa, was chosen as the winning entry [fig. 4.1].[6] The middle-aged male officers of the Russian Imperial Guard were the target clientele of the store, which was to "supply them with the essentials, from uniforms and equipment to shoes and linen," and none other than the Russian war minister Vladimir A. Sukhomlinov led the inauguration of the building.[7] The camaraderie suggested by this joint venture involving a German firm, an Austrian architect, a Russian architect of German heritage and a Russian military organization was, however, a precarious one that would soon give way. The war commenced in 1914, and at its height in March 1916, Sukhomlinov was arrested for treason. His close association with Sergei A. Myasoedov, a notorious German spy, had laid him open to this charge – "pro-German Russians who wished to enlist in the German spy organization in Russia and betray their country were always referred to Myasoedov."[8]

As for the new German Embassy designed by Peter Behrens with the assistance of the young Mies van der Rohe, the Russian reception switched dramatically from enthusiastic approval to deep skepticism. Upon its completion in 1913, *Moskovskii arkhitekturnyi mir* (*The Moscow Architecture World*) and *Peterburgskaia gazeta* (*The Petersburg Gazette*) lavished highly favorable assessments on the building, paying attention to how "the simplicity and the severity of the architectural lines" seemed to guarantee "the integrity and unity of the architectural impression," qualities sought as an antidote to eclecticism.[9] The semantics of the building was wholly unambiguous – the stern neoclassical facade hearkened back to Karl Friedrich Schinkel, to the Prussian classicism that Arthur Moeller van den Bruck would, with nationalist motives, celebrate in his 1916 book *Der preußische Stil*. If, all the same, a commentator could speak of a "marvelous ensemble" that St. Isaac's Cathedral formed with the new German Embassy and Fyodor Lidval's Hotel Astoria in the January 27, 1913 issue of *Zodchii* (*Architect*), a drastic shift in tone soon occurred.[10] Russians increasingly projected their fear of German militarism onto the Embassy building, problematizing its "Teutonic" character and thus echoing "the suspicions of certain foreign observers at the 1914 *Werkbund* congress who had contended that the movement was too closely tied to the German cause."[11] The uneasiness intensified and culminated upon the outbreak of the war when a group of "patriotic demonstrators" stormed the building and, climbing onto its roof, dismantled the bronze Dioscuri, which are rumored to have been dumped in the Moika River.[12] Melissa Kirschke Stockdale, in *Mobilizing the Russian Nation: Patriotism and Citizenship in the First World War*, has observed that, from the "very start of hostilities," the demonization of the enemy was used as a means of winning popular support for the war effort, with "stories of German and Austrian atrocities and violations of the rules of warfare" constantly filling the pages of the Russian press and creating an object of hatred "around which everyone could unite" and come to the realization that "internal differences paled in comparison before the terrible, external foe."[13]

The patriotic culture emergent in war-stricken Russia conditioned the total invalidation and rejection of German and Austrian models, in lieu of which British practice became the primary source of inspiration for Russian architects. In a letter addressed to the Saint Petersburg branch of the Russo-British Chamber of Commerce and reproduced in the February 25, 1915 issue of the *Ezhenedel'nik*, a representative of the British Architectural Association underscored the "desire" expressed among "architects and art circles in Russia ... to remove Germanic influence on the architectural and decorative arts in this country and to replace it with British influence."[14] Hoping to "free the Russian market from dependence on models of Germanic origin," the Chamber of Commerce contemplated organizing exhibitions of British "artistic journals, catalogs, prospectuses and individual architectural examples."[15] Here, it becomes evident that the Triple Entente was not simply a military alliance among Russia, Britain, and France, as it also constituted a shared cultural sphere that facilitated the circulation of ideas and the mutual reinforcement of different propaganda campaigns. For instance, Russian poet Aleksandr Roslavlev, in his "Reims Cathedral" of 1915, shared Gustave Le Bon's outrage at the German bombardment of the church expressed in *Enseignements psychologiques de la guerre européenne*, which ascribes the vandalism to Wilhelm II's intense hatred for Catholicism. As for the popularity enjoyed by the music of the Russian composers Sergei Rachmaninoff, Igor Stravinsky and Sergei Prokofiev in Britain, it led to the formation of the Russian Music Committee in that country, where "Holy Russia" was a dominant propaganda theme. British propaganda was wont to portray the tsar as a modern crusader struggling against Wilhelm the "German Antichrist," and this mirrored the production, undertaken among others by the Riga publishing house Gempel', of "high-quality photomontages" in which "the tsar, the tsarina and the tsarevich are embraced by the wings of the double-headed eagle," the Russian state emblem, with the imperial crown placed in the center "beneath the first line of the anthem 'God Save the Tsar.'"[16]

If the ubiquity of anti-German and anti-Austrian sentiment throughout the Entente ensured the emergence of an international culture, nationalism, no less powerful a driving force, engendered a sense of caution within Russian artistic circles. In his commentary on the letter from the British Architectural Association, Gints warned against the uncritical adoption of the new, British models. "We are ready to, following Peter the Great's example, learn from our neighbor [Britain] …, but the suppression of our millennial art that is unique in this world … would be ludicrous," he said, holding that a strong sense of self was necessary for the cultivation of a "serious" devotion to architecture.[17] Gints's nationalist primitivist position – that is, his insistence on the uniqueness of Russian art and its rootedness in a tradition stretching back a millennium – corresponded to the view held by avant-garde artists like Natalia Goncharova, who had stated in 1912 that Cubism, while a "positive phenomenon," was not altogether a new one.[18] "The Scythians' stone images, the painted wooden dolls sold at fairs are cubist works," she memorably declared, while Voldemārs Matvejs, in a 1912 article titled "Principles of the New Art" and published over two issues of the journal of the avant-garde group *Soiuz Molodezhi*, asserted that "the symbols that we find … in the *lubok* … are flashes of beauty and divinity."[19] The *lubok*, plural *lubki*, is an illustrated popular print specific to Russia. A traditional medium originating in the seventeenth century, it had always served to enlighten the illiterate peasantry, conveying both religious and secular messages, but the start of the twentieth century saw its transformation into a propaganda tool. The first boom of so-called war *lubki*, circulated with the aim of reporting the heroism of Russia's own military while ridiculing the enemy, occurred during the Russo-Japanese War of 1904–1905. Countless battle scenes "containing hundreds of soldiers, explosions, smoke and light beams" were printed "with almost photographic accuracy and in a host of colors."[20] Meanwhile, the Russian artistic avant-garde took a great interest in the distinct formal characteristics of the traditional *lubok*, which was a fetish for Goncharova, Matvejs, and others in much the same way as the Japanese woodcut and the African mask were fetishes for their Western counterparts. The self-othering performed by Russian artists paradoxically helped them arrive at a stronger sense of self, motivating a search for uniquely Russian modes of expression, but they at the same time took a firm stance against cultural isolation. If they admitted that foreign influences were inevitable and sometimes even desirable, they left open the questions of where these influences should be coming from and to what degree they should be adopted.

The garden city, a British invention, had a significant appeal in Russia, where it functioned as an ideal, as a desideratum that seemed within reach but always remained elusive. Garden cities required a highly sophisticated rail system, which Russia did not yet possess. The basis of Alfred von Schlieffen's firm belief in German military superiority was the perceived "inadequacy" of Russian railways, which he correctly predicted would make swift and efficient mobilization difficult in the event of war.[21] Indeed, the Russian Empire entered the war with the "least capable rail network in Europe by every measure," barely managing the transportation of one army corps when Germany could manage three or four.[22] Precisely this lack of transportation infrastructure was what seemed to utopian urban planners to be hindering Saint

Petersburg's transformation into the "organizational center" of a constellation of garden cities.[23] An editorial in the September 28, 1916 issue of the *Ezhenedel'nik*, revealingly titled "Ot goroda-kreposti k gorodu-sadu" ("From a Walled City to a Garden City"), claimed that the inherent "regularity" of the imperial capital, which reflected its origins as a planned city, justified the pursuit of the Howardian ideal, but its dramatic expansion "from 20 square *versts* under Peter the Great's rule to 258 square *versts* in 1901" called for a thorough reconceptualization of movement from one district to another.[24] Civil engineer Fedor E. Enakiev, in his 1912 *Zadachi preobrazovaniia Peterburga* (*Goals of Transforming Saint Petersburg*), put forth a "rationally" planned underground rapid transit that would link up with the Primorskaya railway to the north and extend southward in the direction of Oranienbaum.[25] While optimistic that the electrification of the lines was "altogether possible," he acknowledged the exorbitant expenses that the enterprise as a whole would entail – indeed, it proved too ambitious for its time, and the construction of the Saint Petersburg metro would not begin until 1941, only to be interrupted again by the Second World War. In fact, Ebenezer Howard had voiced the same concerns in *Garden Cities of To-Morrow*, warning that the £4,000 cost projected for every mile of road in the Garden City would be "doubtless inadequate if subways are constructed."[26]

Garden Cities of To-Morrow was translated into Russian only in 1911, seven years after Georges Benoit-Lévy's French edition and four years after Maria Wallroth-Unterlip's German edition. The foundation of the Russian Society of Garden Cities (Russkoe obshchestvo gorodov-sadov) in 1913 was also a belated event – its German and French counterparts, Deutsche Gartenstadtgesellschaft and l'Association des cités-jardins, had formed respectively in 1902 and 1904. The Russian Society, at the height of war in 1916, announced a competition for the design of a garden city to be named Mirolino and planned around the Miaglovo train station on the Saint Petersburg–Rybinskii line. The brief called for a "trinity," or "the organization of three districts, each with a clearly defined center, into a whole that shares a common arterial road extending into the capital."[27] A theater, a cinema, a library, a reading room, a stadium, a hydrotherapy center, and a gymnasium would ensure the well-being of the residents, who would also have access to an abundance of greenery. There was also to be an "open-air museum" where "national architectural monuments, that is to say detailed reproductions of the *izbas* and wooden churches that have remained," would be exhibited – here, the overlap between the Russian garden city movement and a nationalist devotion to folk architecture becomes clear.[28]

If the war and, eventually, the Revolution brought this and numerous other garden city projects to a premature end, one did materialize to an extent. Prozorovka, located 40 kilometers southeast of Moscow on the Moscow–Kazan line, was designed by architect Vladimir N. Semenov. After a politically motivated stay in England, Semenov returned to Russia in late 1912 and published the decidedly Howardian

Blagoustroistvo gorodov (*Improvement of Cities*) and began work on what is a rare example of a realized garden city. In Prozorovka, an attempt was made to give the garden city ideal a concrete, Russian form. The three axes radiating from the train station, which was both the geographical center and economic heart of the town, are a clear homage to the "trident" of Saint Petersburg. As for the division of the residential area into a part occupied by wooden houses and a part occupied by stone houses, it was consistent with the traditional bifurcation of Russian towns into "a center dominated by masonry construction and a periphery dominated by timber construction."[29]

For the Russian architect, timber and stone were not just different materials but also carriers of different meanings. In February 1916, the All-Russian Society for the Remembrance of the Fallen organized a design competition for memorials for soldiers killed in action, inviting proposals for either a "wooden chapel" or a "stone chapel" and requiring that the proposed chapel must be in either the "Russian vernacular" style or the "Russian classicist" style.[30] Curiously, the submitted designs for the wooden chapel show a preference for the vernacular, while those for the stone chapel are classicizing. Russian architects evidently believed that different styles call for the use of different materials, though, under war conditions, a general material shortage usually forced them to make do with whatever was readily available and lent itself to quick and easy construction. Georgii A. Golubev's stone chapel, for instance, would have been a monumental stone dome superimposed on an Ionic order, whereas Mikhail P. V'iushkov's wooden chapel, much more modest in scale, would have featured folk elements like *kokoshniki*, though both would have been centrally planned and alluded to Byzantine architecture.

The impact of wartime pragmatism on the Russian garden city discourse merits discussion. Pre-war engagements with Howard's ideas generally did not go beyond simple recapitulation and focused predictably on familiar issues like the establishment of "the necessary hygienic system," the provision of "easy and affordable connections" between communities, the relocation of industry "outside urban centers" and the creation of "squares, gardens and parks," but the war brought with it additional challenges.[31] At the first All-Russian Congress for the Beautification of Cities, organized by the Russian Technical Society in 1916, special emphasis fell on "public health" and "the education and training of the public," war conditions having sharpened the demand for "hospitals, emergency treatment points …, sanatoria and bacteriological laboratories" and "auditoriums and reading rooms" intended for dissemination of information, though there was tight control over the kinds of news that could circulate about the war.[32] For instance, "full military censorship" was established in "zones of military activity," which included active fronts as well as regions contiguous to them, and distribution in these zones of a periodical publication "not given prior approval by the censors" could draw fines "ranging from 100 to 2,000 rubles." The contents of letters and telegrams from the front, especially those describing "Russian losses in materiel or personnel," were placed under special scrutiny.[33]

Meanwhile, very different circumstances prevailed in the Russian Far East. The preponderance of maritime battles in the Asia-Pacific region – the siege of the German-occupied Chinese port of Tsingtau (Qingdao) was the only major land battle – meant that inland cities continued to prosper under relative peace and that ambitious urban plans unimaginable in gravely war-stricken European Russia could be put forth. Harbin is a case in point [fig. 4.2]. Established in 1898 as the administrative center of the Russian-owned Chinese Eastern Railway, it soon grew into a cosmopolis, in particular after absorbing the exodus from Lüshun and Dalian, warm-water ports that Russia was forced to cede to Japan at the conclusion of the 1904–1905 Russo-Japanese War. In its heyday, Harbin was dubbed "a Manchurian Petersburg." Home to Russians, Chinese, Japanese, Germans, Armenians, Georgians,

Figure 4.2: Chinese Eastern Railway, *Map of Harbin and its Surroundings, Within the Limits of the Right of Way of the Chinese Eastern Railway* (*Plan Kharbina i okrestnostei: v predelakh polosy otchuzhdeniia Kitaiskoi vostochnoi zheleznoi dorogi*), 1903. The Library of Congress.

Jews, Estonians, Latvians, Lithuanians, and others, it possessed a sophisticated urban culture and seemed to many to be a microcosm of the empire with its ethnically diverse subjects. Revealingly, a journalist wrote in 1910 that "if a colony implies a land … which represents a particle of fatherland transplanted to a foreign country, then Harbin with the Chinese Eastern Railway is now the first and so far the only Russian colony."[34] As is characteristic of colonial cities, Harbin's layout is a purportedly rational one determined by metropolitan planners. An annotated map reproduced in S. M. Fomenko's 1911 *Sputnik po dal'nemu vostoku* (*Guide to the Far East*), for instance, shows two discrete neighborhoods, one adjacent to the Sungari River (Songhua River) and the other further along the railway line. The former contains a club for railway mechanics, a synagogue, a park, and a city hall, while the latter, radially arranged, includes a hospital, a market, a post office, and a military base. In 1916, a scheme for a greater Harbin was proposed that would have, if realized, unified the neighborhoods by integrating them into an extensive network of new garden city-type settlements planned for the surrounding countryside. Seen as a kind of *tabula rasa*, the Russian Far East held an attraction for ambitious planners who dreamed of implementing garden city ideals on a large scale, the ongoing war having helped promote these ideals by revealing the shortcomings and limitations of pre-existing urban forms and traditional approaches to planning.[35]

In European Russia, dire circumstances required that architecture temporarily suspend its symbolic function for a fuller confrontation with concrete needs. Journals devoted special attention to fireproofing amid growing anxiety about enemy bombardment and urban conflagrations that it might cause – in December 1916, a Zeppelin raid on Saint Petersburg was thwarted only by bad weather and an engine failure. Commenting on a particularly disastrous fire in Saint Petersburg in the June 22, 1916 issue of the *Ezhenedel'nik*, Architect Aleksandr A. Staborovskii attributed the complete incineration of many new, supposedly modern buildings to construction inadequacies resulting from frequent mobilizations of laborers and a pervasive lack of familiarity with fireproofing, calling for immediate attention to these issues. Staborovskii used photography, a medium thought to guarantee objectivity, to respond to the demand for reliable information sharpened by war conditions, believing that the use of the medium and the "archaeological" approach taken to the analysis of remnants from the fire gave his report a "scientific" character.[36] Other subjects of interest to pragmatists included, strikingly, the architecture of trenches. The same Georgii Gints who had problematized the "falsification" of Russian architecture examined the plan of a typical German trench in the December 14, 1916 issue of the *Ezhenedel'nik*, and Anglophilia made itself felt even in this context, for Gints concluded that the "more *primitive*, shallow English trenches" were superior to their German counterparts, which were more extensive and better protected but yielded a poorly ventilated environment where soldiers were far more susceptible to infectious diseases.[37] However, he acknowledged that if the Germans planned entire subterranean "villages," this was because they bore in mind the possibility of having to wait in the trenches for a long time, as well as because these "villages" had the status of "officially sanctioned" architectural projects.[38]

Military architecture was not limited to battlefields, and "urban barracks" intended as temporary lodging for soldiers formed an entirely new addition to existing city-scapes.[39] Initially, the mobilization department of the Saint Petersburg City Council earmarked various private and public buildings in the city center for this purpose, but it soon became apparent that, should these be put to use, invasive interventions and additions would become necessary if servicemen's needs were to be properly met. After this option proved impracticable, the attention shifted to Vasilyevsky Island. Brand-new buildings modern in character – in other words, well ventilated, hygienic, and fireproof – were to go up in this then largely undeveloped area, in addition to buildings of the "tent type" (*shatrovyi tip*). The emperor himself had proposed this new type, which was to be built entirely of timber and, as if this were not enough of a reference to tradition, to have a roof identical to the "tented roofs" (*shatër*) of pre-Petrine wooden churches, now celebrated as the purest architectural expression of Russian identity. Of course, a staunch modernist would have problematized the material's combustible character and advised against its use despite its powerful symbolism, but the same modernist would not have failed to notice the wartime advantages offered by construction using standardized timber parts.

The ubiquity of military architecture was just another sign that the distinction between the battlefront and the home front was becoming meaningless. Most of the actual fighting took place in the countryside, and as government propaganda increasingly romanticized it as a site of heroism, the traditional hierarchy privileging the city began to crumble. Nationalist primitivist critics dismissed city dwellers as cowardly and the eclectic architecture that they inhabit as "degenerate" and even anti-Russian. They homed in on the fact that architects of Germanic heritage have traditionally enjoyed a high profile in Russian cities and especially in Saint Petersburg, where Andreas Schlüter, Georg Friedrich Veldten, and Leo von Klenze served as court architect respectively to Peter the Great, Catherine the Great, and Nicholas I. As for Fedor (Franz) Shekhtel, a key representative of Russian Art Nouveau, he grew up in a close-knit community of German immigrants in the Volga town of Saratov. This was enough to conclude that his work was of dubious quality.

In 1915, architectural historian Georgii K. Lukomskii published *Galitsiia v ee starine. Ocherki po istorii arkhitektury XII–XVIII vv.* (*Galicia and its Antiquities: Essays on Architectural History from the Twelfth Century to the Eighteenth Century*). Richly illustrated with drawings by the author himself, the book was at once histor-ical, ethnographic, ideological, and propagandistic. Endorsing pan-Slavism, or the expansionist belief that it was Russia's mission to protect – and therefore annex – all

Іорданов. *Дома на площади.*

лыни. Хаты бѣлёныя, крыты четырехскатными соломенными крышами *). Архитектура гуцульскихъ жилищъ, въ частности, не имѣетъ ничего подобнаго на всей территоріи Украины. Это довольно большія сооруженія, состоящія изъ просторной хаты и другихъ помѣщеній—и все это покрыто общимъ скатомъ, между которымъ— небольшой дворикъ. Такая гуцульская „гражда“ является—защитой хозяйства отъ воровъ, при изолированности своего положенія.

Несмотря, однако, на всю свою архитектурную оригинальность—„гражда“ близка по внутреннему расположенію къ украинскому общему типу. Эта замкнутость помѣщеній встрѣчается, вѣдь, также въ равнинѣ Галицкой и на Волыни.

Жилища бойковъ много интереснѣе. „Они отличаются своею величиною, тремя окнами съ фасада, крытой галлереей вдоль передней стѣны, причемъ эта галлерея въ наиболѣе старинныхъ хатахъ прихотливо украшена рѣзьбой (точеные столбики, нарѣзка на фризахъ). Прекрасны огромныя, съ большимъ свѣсомъ, крыши, въ видѣ ступенекъ изъ подстриженной соломы, подымающіяся до гребня“. На конькахъ часто стали появляться за послѣднее время вышки, главки—совсѣмъ маленькія копіи главокъ церковныхъ. Но это ничто иное какъ фальшивыя трубы. Закономъ запрещается выводить дымъ „подъ стрыхи“, т. е. черезъ потолокъ въ особое отверстіе. И вотъ, жители устраиваютъ „для полиціи“ подобныя трубы, на самомъ дѣлѣ продолжая выводить дымъ изъ

---

*) Но срубъ изъ горизонтальныхъ бревенъ постепенно уступаетъ мѣсто упрощенной конструкціи изъ стоекъ и обрѣзковъ дерева, пространство между которыми набивается глиною.

110

Figure 4.3: Page from Lukomskii's *Galicia and Its Antiquities* (1915) showing houses on the town square in Jordanów, Galicia. New York Public Library.

lands inhabited by Slavic peoples, *Galitsiia v ee starine* uses architecture as material evidence supporting the legitimacy of this belief, of Russia's claim to Galicia, then part of the Austro-Hungarian Empire [fig. 4.3]. Lukomskii goes to great lengths to demonstrate that Galician architecture is distinctly Slavic in character, that it is readily comparable to traditional Russian architecture, before proceeding to justify the military actions undertaken by the Russian Empire in the region. After the Battle of Galicia ended in a decisive Russian victory in September 1914, it remained under Russian control until the summer of 1915, when a combined German and Austro-Hungarian offensive forced the Russians into retreat. Writing shortly thereafter, Lukomskii held that "the latest shifts in boundaries are completely meaningless" from the perspective of someone privy to the region's "architectural history" and with the understanding that Austria-Hungary was unnaturally planting itself in an alien soil.[40] Centuries of Austro-Hungarian rule had resulted in a gross "neglect" and "oppression" of the region's fine specimens of "Ruthenian" architecture, which were "deeply national and picturesque," and Lukomskii hoped that a more "favorable political situation" would soon put an end to this abuse.[41] Only after Russia established permanent dominance in the region could Galician architecture be saved, for sincere preservationist efforts necessitated an empathetic response to the architecture. Remarkably, Lukomskii's drawings soon began to circulate in non-architectural contexts as well, appearing for instance in general news periodicals like *Letopis' voiny* (*The War Chronicles*) and *Otechestvo* (*Fatherland*).

Meanwhile, the Segodniashnii Lubok (Today's Lubok) group – avant-gardists like Kazimir Malevich, Vladimir Mayakovsky, Aristarkh Lentulov, and David Burliuk were among its members – produced primitivist lithographs that were conscious imitations of traditional *lubki* and meant to be circulated as "patriotic propaganda."[42] One of these glorifies the valor of the residents of the Galician town of Galich, or Halych in Ukrainian, where local peasants took the Russian side and fought against their Austro-Hungarian overlords. The lighthearted image depicts a triumphant peasant soldier. The accompanying text reads, "jauntily we go about safeguarding our beloved Galič, so that we may finally crush the enemy one day." In another one, a larger-than-life peasant woman has run her hayfork through a minuscule Austro-Hungarian soldier. "An Austrian soldier made his way into the Radziwiłł realm and ended up on the lady's pitchfork," the text reads – the Radziwiłł family originated in Kernavé, the medieval capital of Lithuania, another one of the disputed regions [fig. 4.4]. As for *Austrians in the Carpathians…*, it tells of an episode from the Battle of Galicia. Helpless in the face of a sudden attack by the Russians, an Austro-Hungarian regiment is seen hurriedly preparing for flight, having abandoned the bodies of fallen comrades as well as an unmistakably phallic canon, which begs to be read as a token of masculinity.

Figure 4.4: Kazimir Malevich, *An Austrian Went to Radziwiłł…* (*Shel avstriets v Radzivily…*), 1915. Color lithograph, 41 × 57.2 cm. New York Public Library.

Andrew M. Nedd has characterized Segodniashnii Lubok's lithographs as "mythic" images that existed at one remove from the harsh and often disheartening reality faced by Russian troops throughout the war.[43] Indeed, the group's recourse to folklore seems escapist, but the desire for the "mythic" was only part of what defined wartime visual culture in Russia. Media like drawing and printmaking, while familiar and firmly grounded in tradition, ultimately failed to satisfy an equally strong desire for the factual, in pursuit of which many turned to photography. Due to its indexical relationship to reality, photography, at least in theory, left no room for doubt as to the accuracy and objectivity of the information that it conveyed and increasingly attracted propagandists. If Staborovskii used photography for the sake of "science," explicitly propagandistic uses of the medium were also made, for instance by the author of the photographic essay "Around Galicia" published in the September 14, 1916 issue of the *Ezhenedel'nik*. The anonymous author deliberately juxtaposed photographs of buildings before and after they suffered vandalism at the hands of the enemy with the aim of "painting a dolorous picture" that could "excite the strongest nerves," and if many of his claims, like the one that Galicia suffered "destruction on a scale completely unprecedented in human history," seem hyperbolic, the photographs, serving as tokens of factuality, would have at least partly dispelled the skepticism of the incredulous.[44]

Specialist journals like the *Ezhenedel'nik* presumed a sophisticated readership, and that even these should have come to embrace photography, despite the medium's association with popular journalism, is telling. It seemed that, under war conditions, all publications had to function as propaganda, that journals should use all available resources to try to reach as wide an audience as possible. Indeed, one did not need to belong to an exclusive professional circle or even be literate to understand the message of "Around Galicia," for the sight of buildings in ruin would have elicited an empathetic response from anyone, especially when the buildings were supposed to be embodiments of one's identity. The Russian peasantry struggled to grasp the abstract notion of the Russian nation and, for the most part, "cared nothing for the politics of France, or Germany, or Austria or Serbia …, having no interest in the German Kaiser or the assassinated Archduke Franz Ferdinand," but it would have readily cathected the image of, for instance, a vandalized Orthodox church.[45] The potency of such images would not have gone unnoticed by those responsible for implementing so-called "rural enlightenment projects," ambitiously undertaken by Imperial Russia in the hope of "nurturing patriotic identity," of resolving the problem, among others, of illiteracy – despite all efforts, illiteracy would remain prevalent in Russia until the Soviets aggressively pursued *likbez* (*likvidatsiya bezgramotnosti*, or liquidation of illiteracy). Scott J. Seregny has noted the existence of adult education programs specifically targeting illiterate villagers, such as biweekly "public readings" where large numbers of men and women would gather to hear "local teachers read aloud from the latest newspapers."[46] As their fingers travelled on *lubok* maps "from L'viv to Kraków, from Warsaw to Berlin and back again" and blackened the battlefields, peasants grew more and more eager to learn about "the geography and history of nations," and illustrated books and newspapers became a primary source of information for these nascent literate subjects.[47] The transformation of peasants into modern subjects organized around an ideology was underway.

Concomitant to this newfound subjecthood was a novel creative agency, the most notable manifestation of which was perhaps the activity of those amateur photographers who, "armed with easy-to-use hand-held cameras," went to remote areas that could not be easily reached and took pictures, which they then sold to mainstream media.[48] However, there were also exceedingly personal images not intended for wide circulation, like those belonging to the Italian architect Giovanni Tiella. Born an Austro-Hungarian subject in Trentino, he trained under Otto Wagner in Vienna, where he let the "vivacious polemics surrounding … the dominant styles of architecture" leave a profound mark on him, the drawings from his student years demonstrating a thorough familiarity with the vocabulary of the Vienna Secession.[49] During the war, Tiella fought on the wrong side of the Battle of Galicia and found himself in captivity under the Russians. Eventually, he ended up at a military post in Antonowka, where an officer took note of his exceptional draftsmanship and

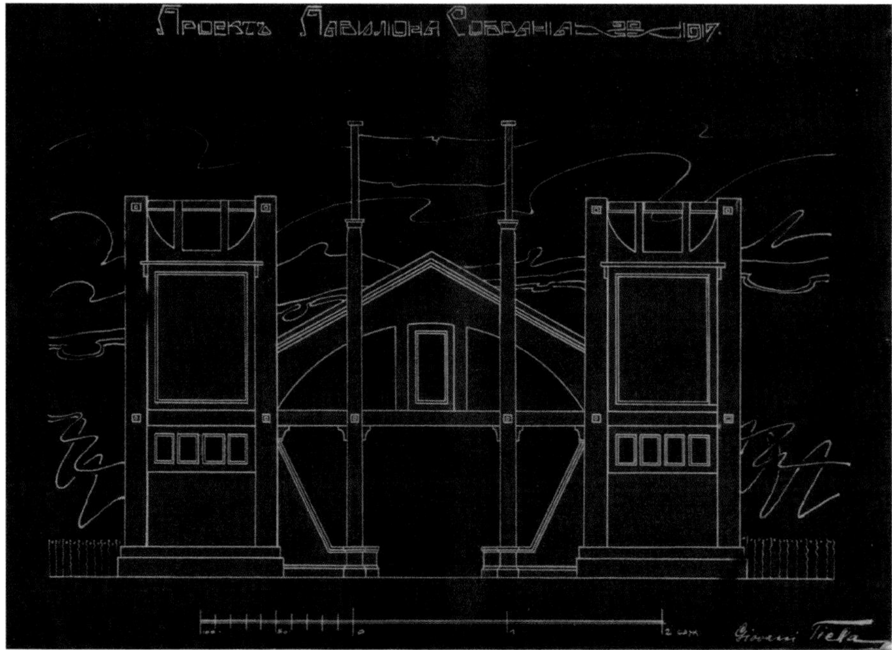

Figure 4.5: Front elevation of Giovanni Tiella's assembly pavilion (*pavil'on sobraniia*), Galicia, Ukraine, 1917. Collezione Tiella Rovereto.

Figure 4.6: Photograph of Giovanni Tiella's assembly pavilion (*pavil'on sobraniia*), Galicia, Ukraine, 1917. Collezione Tiella Rovereto.

allowed him to join the Second Railway Construction Battalion as a designer and a constructor. Architectural plans made in this context have survived and reveal that Tiella experimented with the design not only of train stations but also of a variety of other building types, most notably the assembly pavilion, an example of which is shown surrounded by a crowd in a 1917 photograph [fig. 4.5-4.6]. The imperative "Unite!" written across the banner clearly announces the building's function, and as for the use of timber, it must have been prompted by war conditions, though it could also have been a conscious reference to local material culture. The numerous sketches that Tiella made of the Galician landscape reveal a contextualism, and, in the diary that he kept in Antonowka, a sketch of a vernacular structure forms an intriguing contrast with the reproduction of Aristarkh Lentulov's painting *Minaret* on the following page.

Nearly a decade after the conclusion of the war, the exiled Russian general Yuri Danilov remembered it as a propaganda war. By his account, the Great War hinged on propaganda from start to finish. The anti-Austrian propaganda mounted by Serbian nationalists started it, and it culminated in a devastating defeat for Russia in 1917 because widespread illiteracy made the germination of a "healthy nationalism" impossible there, making the country defenseless against enemy propaganda.[50] A pervasive lack of psychological preparation for the war added to the problem. If rural communities responded to calls to arms, this was simply because they were "accustomed to doing everything that the authorities told them to do," not because they felt any real sense of urgency.[51] Danilov lamented that, in the face of enemy propaganda, Russians were like "capricious children" while the French could maintain an "iron tenacity."[52] In France, organizations like the Union des grandes associations françaises contre la propagande ennemie rigorously checked all forms of communication originating in enemy territories, but no real mechanism was in place to check them in Russia. As a result, German and Austro-Hungarian propaganda flyers could easily penetrate it "by way of neutral countries, often alongside photographs or chocolate bars."[53] By the time Russia took steps to address the issue, it was already too late. The balance had already tipped irreversibly, and the Revolution soon dealt a death blow to a regime barely sustaining its war efforts.

Notes

1   For an account of the influence of German, Austro-Hungarian, French, and Italian models on the emergence of Art Nouveau in Russia, see John E. Bowlt, *Moscow and St. Petersburg in Russia's Silver Age: 1900–1920* (London: Thames and Hudson, 2008), 129. The Russian reception of the German *Werkbund* is discussed in Joan Campbell, *The German Werkbund: The Politics of Reform in the Applied Arts* (Princeton: Princeton University Press, 1978), 82–103.

2   Not to be confused with the autonomous community of the same name in north-western Spain, Galicia (Halychyna in Ukrainian) is today a region in modern Ukraine bordering Poland, having been the site of one of the most important battles fought on the Eastern Front during the First World War. Motivated by a racial ideology, Imperial Russia took it upon itself to "liberate" the local Slavic population from what it perceived to be oppressive rule by Austria-Hungary, managing to win a decisive victory there in 1914. In the midst of war, the region acquired an exceptional symbolic status on which propagandists could capitalize.

3   G. E. Gints, "Fal'sifikatsiia arkhitektury v Moskve," *Arkhitekturno-khudozhestvennyi ezhenedel'nik*, December 7, 1916, p. 469.

4   G. Gevirts, "Spory ob arkhitekture," *Arkhitekturno-khudozhestvennyi ezhenedel'nik*, December 23, 1915, p. 460.

5   Selim O. Khan-Magomedov, *Alexandr Vesnin and Russian Constructivism* (New York: Rizzoli, 1986), 15.

6   B. M. Kirikov, *Ulitsa Zheliabova* (Leningrad: "Svecha," 1990), 53. Today, the department store is located at the intersection of Volynskii Pereulok and Bolshaia Koniushennaia Street and called Dom leningradskoi torgovli (Leningrad House of Commerce). Its original name, Dom Gvardeiskogo ekonomicheskogo obshchestva (House of the Imperial Guard Economic Society), makes evident its former association with the Russian Imperial Guard.

7   Boris I. Antonov, *Imperatorskaia gvardiia v Sankt-Peterburge* (St. Petersburg: Glagol, 2001), 209.

8   Roger Lewis, "Russia's Enemy Within: The Amazing Story of German Propaganda and Intrigue," *Collier's Weekly*, December 22, 1917, p. 9.

9   William C. Brumfield, "*Mitteleuropa* to Moscow: Germanic Links with Russian Architecture," in *Cold Fusion: Aspects of the German Cultural Presence in Russia*, ed. Gennady Barabtarlo (New York: Berghahn Books, 2000), 181.

10   "Khronika–Peterburg," *Zodchii: Zhurnal arkhitekturnyi i khudozhestvenno-tekhnicheskii*, January 27, 1913, p. 45.

11   Joan Campbell, *The German Werkbund: The Politics of Reform in the Applied Arts* (Princeton: Princeton University Press, 1978), 98.

12   Viktor G. Tiukavkin, *Istoriia SSSR, 1861–1917* (Moscow: Prosveshchenie, 1990), 353.

13   Melissa Kirschke Stockdale, *Mobilizing the Russian Nation: Patriotism and Citizenship in the First World War* (Cambridge: Cambridge University Press, 2016), 49.

14   G. E. Gints, "Nedorazumenie," *Arkhitekturno-khudozhestvennyi ezhenedel'nik*, February 25, 1915, p. 466.

15   "Vystavki," *Zodchii: Zhurnal arkhitekturnyi i khudozhestvenno-tekhnicheskii*, February 15, 1915, p. 71.

16   Hubertus F. Jahn, *Patriotic Culture in Russia during World War I* (Ithaca: Cornell University Press, 1995), 41.

17   Gints, "Nedorazumenie," 466, 468.

18   John E. Bowlt, ed., *Russian Art of the Avant-Garde: Theory and Criticism, 1902–1934* (New York: Viking Press, 1976), 78.

19   *Ibid.*, 37.

20   Jahn, *Patriotic Culture in Russia during World War I*, 13.

21   Holger H. Herwig, *The First World War: Germany and Austria-Hungary, 1914–1918*, 2nd ed. (London: Bloomsbury Publishing, 2014), 48.

22   Dale C. Rielage, *Russian Supply Efforts in America during the First World War* (London: McFarland and Company, 2002), 76.

23   Martell, "Ot goroda-kreposti k gorodu-sadu," *Arkhitekturno-khudozhestvennyi ezhenedel'nik*, September 28, 1916, p. 384.

24   *Ibid.* A *verst* is a pre-revolutionary unit of measurement equal to 1.07 kilometers.

25   Fedor E. Enakiev, *Zadachi preobrazovaniia Peterburga* (St. Petersburg: n.p., 1912), 43.

26   Ebenezer Howard, *Garden Cities of To-Morrow* (London: Routledge, 2007), 83.

27   "Usloviia konkursa na planirovku 'goroda-sada,' ob"iavliaemogo obshchestvom Gorodov-Sadov v Petrograde," *Arkhitekturno-khudozhestvennyi ezhenedel'nik*, July 20, 1916, n.p.

28   *Ibid.* An *izba* is a traditional Russian log house.

29   E. I. Kirichenko, *Gradostroitel'stvo Rossii serediny XIX–nachala XX veka*, vol. 2, *Goroda i novye tipy poselenii* (Moscow: Progress, 2001), 537.

30   "Imperatorskoe Obshchestvo Arkhitektorov Khudozhnikov … ob"iavliaet shest' konkursov," *Arkhitekturno-khudozhestvennyi ezhenedel'nik*, February 24, 1916, p. 112.

31   Enakiev, *Zadachi preobrazovaniia Peterburga*, 20–1.

32   E. I. Kirichenko, *Gradostroitel'stvo Rossii serediny XIX–nachala XX veka*, vol. 1, *Obshchaia kharakteristika i teoreticheskie problemy* (Moscow: Progress, 2001), 123.

33   Stockdale, *Mobilizing the Russian Nation*, 39.

34   A. Rykachev, "Russkoe delo v Man'chzhurii," *Russkaia mysl'* XXXI, no. 8 (1910): 122, cited in Olga Bakich, "A Russian City in China: Harbin before 1917," *Canadian Slavonic Papers* 28, no. 2 (June 1986): 131.

35   For more information on the establishment of garden city-type settlements in the Russian Far East undertaken throughout the 1910s, see Svetlana S. Levoshko, *Russkaia arkhitektura v Man'chzhurii: konets XIX–pervaia polovina XX veka* (Khabarovsk: Izdatel'skii dom "Chastnaia kollektsiia," 2003).

36   A. A. Staborovskii, "Kartiny razrusheniia pozharami kamennykh domov v Petrograde," *Arkhitekturno-khudozhesvennyi ezhenedel'nik*, June 22, 1916, p. 267.

37   G. E. Gints, "Arkhitektura germanskogo okopa," *Arkhitekturno-khudozhestvennyi ezhenedel'nik*, December 14, 1916, p. 481. My italics.

38   *Ibid.*, 479.

39   V. N. Kuritsyn, "Gorodskie baraka dlia vremennogo postoia voisk v Petrograde," *Arkhitekturno-khudozhestvennyi ezhenedel'nik*, August 24, 1916, p. 339.

40   G. K. Lukomskii, *Galitsiia v ee starine. Ocherki po istorii arkhitektury XII–XVIII vv.* (Petrograd: Izdanie tva R. Golike i A. Vil'borg, 1915), 10.

41   *Ibid.*, 114.

42   E. A. Dinershtein, *Maiakovskii i kniga: iz istorii izdaniia proizvedenii poeta* (Moscow: "Kniga," 1987), 42.

43   Andrew M. Nedd, "*Segodniashnii Lubok*: Art, War and National Identity," in *Picture This: World War I Posters and Visual Culture*, ed. Pearl James (Lincoln, Nebr.: University of Nebraska Press, 2009), 243.

44   V. S., "Po Galitsii, ot sobstv. korrespondenta," *Arkhitekturno-khudozhestvennyi ezhenedel'nik*, September 14, 1916, p. 364.

45   W. Bruce Lincoln, *Passage Through Armageddon: The Russians in War and Revolution, 1914–1918* (New York: Oxford University Press, 1994), 45–6.

46   Scott. J. Seregny, "Zemstvos, Peasants and Citizenship: The Russian Adult Education Movement and World War I," *Slavic Review* 59, no. 2 (Summer 2000): 291, 302.

47   *Ibid.*, 294.

48   Christopher Stolarski, "Press Photography in Russia's Great War and Revolution," in *Russian Culture in War and Revolution, 1914–22, Book 1: Popular Culture, the Arts, and Institutions*, eds. Murray Frame et al. (Bloomington: Slavica, 2014), 141.

49   Marco Tiella et al., *Giovanni Tiella: Architettura in tempo di Guerra, 1915–1919* (Rovereto: Museo storico italiano della guerra, 2005), 11.

50   Youri Danilov, *La Russie dans la guerre mondiale, 1914–1917* (Paris: Payot, 1927), 49.

51   *Ibid.*, 156.

52   *Ibid.*, 157.

53   *Ibid.*, 381.

Bibliography

Antonov, Boris I. *Imperatorskaia gvardiia v Sankt-Peterburge*. St. Petersburg: Glagol, 2001.

Bakich, Olga. "A Russian City in China: Harbin before 1917." *Canadian Slavonic Papers* 28, no. 2 (June 1986): 129–48.

Bowlt, John E. *Moscow and St. Petersburg in Russia's Silver Age: 1900–1920*. London: Thames and Hudson, 2008.

———.*Russian Art of the Avant-Garde: Theory and Criticism, 1902–1934*. New York: The Viking Press, 1976.

Brumfield, William C. "*Mitteleuropa* to Moscow: Germanic Links with Russian Architecture." In *Cold Fusion: Aspects of the German Cultural Presence in Russia*, edited by Gennady Barabtarlo, 169–84. New York: Berghahn Books, 2000.

Enakiev, Fedor E. *Zadachi preobrazovaniia Peterburga*. St. Petersburg: n.p., 1912.

Campbell, Joan. *The German Werkbund: The Politics of Reform in the Applied Arts*. Princeton: Princeton University Press, 1978.

Danilov, Youri. *La Russie dans la guerre mondiale, 1914–1917*. Paris: Payot, 1927.

Dinershtein, E. A. *Maiakovskii i kniga: iz istorii izdaniia proizvedenii poeta*. Moscow: "Kniga," 1987.

Gevirts, G. "Spory ob arkhitekture." *Arkhitekturno-khudozhestvennyi ezhenedel'nik*, December 23, 1915.

Gints, G. E. "Arkhitektura germanskogo okopa." *Arkhitekturno-khudozhestvennyi ezhenedel'nik*, December 14, 1916.

———."Fal'sifikatsiia arkhitektury v Moskve." *Arkhitekturno-khudozhestvennyi ezhenedel'nik*, December 7, 1916.

———."Nedorazumenie." *Arkhitekturno-khudozhestvennyi ezhenedel'nik*, February 25, 1915.

Herwig, Holger H. *The First World War: Germany and Austria-Hungary, 1914–1918*. 2nd ed. London: Bloomsbury Publishing, 2014.

Howard, Ebenezer. *Garden Cities of To-Morrow*. London: Routledge, [1898] 2007.

"Imperatorskoe Obshchestvo Arkhitektorov Khudozhnikov…ob"iavliaet shest' konkursov."

Arkhitekturno-khudozhestvennyi ezhenedel'nik, February 24, 1916.

Jahn, Hubertus F. *Patriotic Culture in Russia during World War I.* Ithaca: Cornell University Press, 1995.

Khan-Magomedov, Selim O. *Alexandr Vesnin and Russian Constructivism.* New York: Rizzoli, 1986.

"Khronika—Peterburg." *Zodchii: Zhurnal arkhitekturnyi i khudozhestvenno-tekhnicheskii,* January 27, 1913.

Kirichenko, E. I. *Gradostroitel'stvo Rossii serediny XIX–nachala XX veka.* Vol. 1, *Obshchaia kharakteristika i teoreticheskie problemy.* Moscow: Progress, 2001.

———.*Gradostroitel'stvo Rossii serediny XIX–nachala XX veka.* Vol. 2, *Goroda i novye tipy poselenii.* Moscow: Progress, 2001.

Kirikov, B. M. *Ulitsa Zheliabova.* Leningrad: "Svecha," 1990.

Kuritsyn, V. N. "Gorodskie baraka dlia vremennogo postoia voisk v Petrograde." *Arkhitekturno-khudozhestvennyi ezhenedel'nik*, August 24, 1916.

Levoshko, Svetlana S. *Russkaia arkhitektura v Man'chzhurii: konets XIX–pervaia polovina XX veka.* Khabarovsk: Izdatel'skii dom "Chastnaia kollektsiia," 2003.

Lewis, Roger. "Russia's Enemy Within: The Amazing Story of German Propaganda and Intrigue." *Collier's Weekly*, December 22, 1917.

Lincoln, W. Bruce. *Passage Through Armageddon: The Russians in War and Revolution, 1914–1918.* New York: Oxford University Press, 1994.

Lukomskii, G. K. *Galitsiia v ee starine. Ocherki po istorii arkhitektury XII–XVIII vv.* Petrograd: Izdanie tva R. Golike i A. Vil'borg, 1915.

Martell. "Ot goroda-kreposti k gorodu-sadu." *Arkhitekturno-khudozhestvennyi ezhenedel'nik*, September 28, 1916.

Nedd, Andrew M. "*Segodniashnii Lubok*: Art, War and National Identity." In *Picture This: World War I Posters and Visual Culture*, edited by Pearl James, 240–71. Lincoln, Nebr.: University of Nebraska Press, 2009.

Rielage, Dale C. *Russian Supply Efforts in America during the First World War.* London: McFarland & Company, 2002.

Seregny, Scott. J. "Zemstvos, Peasants and Citizenship: The Russian Adult Education Movement and World War I." *Slavic Review* 59, no. 2 (Summer 2000): 290–315.

Staborovskii, A. A. "Kartiny razrusheniia pozharami kamennykh domov v Petrograde." *Arkhitekturno-khudozhesvennyi ezhenedel'nik*, June 22, 1916.

Stockdale, Melissa Kirschke. *Mobilizing the Russian Nation: Patriotism and Citizenship in the First World War.* Cambridge: Cambridge University Press, 2016.

Stolarski, Christopher. "Press Photography in Russia's Great War and Revolution." In *Russian Culture in War and Revolution, 1914–22, Book 1: Popular Culture, the Arts, and Institutions*, edited by Murray Frame et al., 139–64. Bloomington: Slavica, 2014.

Tiella, Marco, et al. *Giovanni Tiella: architettura in tempo di Guerra: 1915–1919.* Rovereto: Museo storico italiano della guerra, 2005.

Tiukavkin. Viktor G. *Istoriia SSSR, 1861–1917.* Moscow: Prosveshchenie, 1990.

"Usloviia konkursa na planirovku 'goroda-sada,' ob"iavliaemogo obshchestvom Gorodov-Sadov v Petrograde." *Arkhitekturno-khudozhestvennyi ezhenedel'nik*, July 20, 1916.

"Vystavki." *Zodchii: Zhurnal arkhitekturnyi i khudozhestvenno-tekhnicheskii,* February 15, 1915.

V. S. "Po Galitsii, ot sobstv. korrespondenta." *Arkhitekturno-khudozhestvennyi ezhenedel'nik*, September 14, 1916.

Figure 5.1: Unknown Australian official photographer, two unidentified soldiers admiring the statuary of the exterior of a church [Notre-Dame de la Neuvelle], France, May 15, 1918. Australian War Memorial: E02458. Australian War Memorial, Canberra.

International Engagement, International Opportunity
Enlisted Australian Architects and World War I

Julie Willis and Katti Williams

Introduction

World War I drew thousands of young men into military service and action in new and unfamiliar places. Although Australia had become a nation in its own right in 1901, it remained a dominion of the British Empire. Therefore, when Britain declared war on Germany in 1914, Australia was at war as well: in response, the Australian Imperial Force (AIF) was formed within two weeks of declaration and young men flocked to enlist as soon as they could.[1] For many, it was their first travel experience outside their home country, albeit under horrifying and tragic circumstances, and under conditions that were very remote from their daily existence.[2] For practicing architects and students alike, the conflict meant a reduction in the capacity to practice, with hundreds seeing active service in the many theaters of war across Europe and the Middle East. Despite some incidents closer to home as Australia helped secure German colonial outposts in the Pacific, including sites in New Guinea and Micronesia, the focus of Australia's war effort was sending troops *en masse* to the Middle Eastern and European battlegrounds.

For reasons that might be expected, the impact of the wartime on Australian architecture and architects was significant, yet in contrast to other belligerent nations such as Germany, France, and Great Britain, this was not due to the physical destruction of its towns and cities, nor the complete disruption of building. In contrast to the Australian experience of World War II, there were no significant building or material restrictions or a significant direct threat of invasion or attack on the Australian mainland. Instead, the youngest members of the profession were sent away to a war being waged on the other side of the globe. Change was wrought on and by the profession in two key ways: by major changes to the education and qualification of architects (which provided opportunity for women to qualify in significant numbers for the first time and has been documented elsewhere);[3] and through the experiences of enlisted architects, returning with further education and new knowledge. Drawing on a range of military records and personal accounts, this work conceptualizes the experience of World War I on the Australian architectural profession through travel, collegiality, military employment, and post-war opportunity. For many Australian architectural professionals, participation in the war enabled a level of international engagement that underpinned and greatly enhanced their subsequent professional success.

The Impact of War

The impact of war on the Australian architectural profession can be measured in terms of physical or psychological trauma: deaths incurred, missing limbs, or inter-rupted careers.[4] From a population of less than five million, over 400,000 Australians enlisted (3,000 of whom were women);[5] the AIF itself sustained casualties of more than 200,000, of which some 65,000 were killed. Several hundred Australian archi-tects, architectural draftsmen, and architectural students – all males – enlisted for service in World War I with Australian and other Imperial forces. Of a sample of 340 practitioners, compiled from a survey of the AIF's embarkation rolls and individ-uals' service records, over 10 percent were killed in action or died due to accidents, wounds suffered, or disease.[6]

Initial enlistment criteria targeted relatively young, able-bodied men, so it is little surprise that the most casualties were suffered by those who were at the beginning of their careers.[7] The losses were felt across the Australian continent. Queensland architect William Belson (1892–1915) died at 22 years of age during the Gallipoli landings on April 25, 1915.[8] Promising Victorian student Herbert Affleck (1891–1917), articled to respected practitioner Arthur Peck and a member of the Victorian Architectural Students' Society (VASS), survived the same event, only to be "blown asunder" – in the words of an eye-witness – near Ypres in August 1917.[9] His fellow VASS member Zavel Freadman (1895–1917) died in an accident while training with the Australian Flying Corps in Britain.[10] Herbert Brough (1892–1917), who had trained with the Sydney firm of Kent, Budden & Greenwell, died of wounds in France; his compatri-ots erected a wooden cross over his grave near Bapaume.[11] The body of 23-year-old Perth architectural draftsman David Jackson (1892–1915), on the other hand, was not recovered; he is commemorated on the Memorial to the Missing at Lone Pine on the Gallipoli Peninsula. After overcoming disease and significant injuries, Adelaide architect Elwyn Gould (1893–1917) was eventually killed in action near Broodseinde, Belgium.[12] Of course, there were also more senior casualties; just six days before the armistice, Sydney architect George Owen (c.1885–1919) succumbed to influenza in a casualty clearing station in France.[13]

Further numbers suffered significant physical injuries as a result of their war service; the loss of a hand, reduction to partial vision, or even a lack of ability to sit comfortably at a drawing-board were significant disabilities for those engaged in a predominantly visual profession such as architecture. While Douglas McMurtrie's *The Disabled Soldier*, published in 1919, suggested that architects, as conceptual or "head workers," were less affected by disability than those in manual occupations,[14] the reality is somewhat harder to assess. For one, McMurtrie's optimistic view did not take psychological injury into account; "shell shock" and "neurasthenia" appear on the service records of several practitioners, but the long-reaching and personally devastating effects of such are difficult to quantify. Certainly, there are some examples of personal triumph over physical adversity: Cobden Parkes (1892–1978), an architectural draftsman from Leichhardt, New South Wales, for example, lost three fingers from his right hand on the Gallipoli Peninsula in 1915, yet returned to practice, eventually becoming Government Architect for the State of New South Wales.[15] Similarly, William Blackett Forster (1885–1947) of Melbourne continued an already successful career despite the amputation of his left arm, using a modified drawing board.[16] Henry D. Berry (1894–1976), also from Melbourne, lost his right eye as a result of a shell burst; a subsequent professional photograph in *Who's Who in Australia* selectively depicts the unblemished left side of the architect's face in profile.[17] However, for John Southern Harrison (1887–?), a British-born architectural draftsman employed in Melbourne before the war, his injuries proved catastrophic. In the early months of 1919 he was resident at St. Dunstan's Hostel for Blinded Soldiers and Sailors in England: suffering total loss of vision and a degree of deafness, he was unable to return to his profession, and was instead being retrained as a poultry farmer.[18]

While not exhaustive by any means, these examples of death and disability provide a snapshot of broad-ranging deleterious effects on individual designers and the Australian architectural profession as a whole. Yet the opposite, positive, effects of participation in the war are well worth considering – particularly as regards the Australian architectural fraternity. World War I, while traumatic and demanding, also brought unparalleled opportunity to some enlisted architects. Service overseas meant the chance to see buildings and places, and to engage with a professional milieu whilst on leave during the hostilities, or at war's end. Some also had the opportunity to continue practicing during hostilities, often in engineering units, where their skills in drawing and planning were highly valuable. Ultimately, the positive effects of wartime service can be conceptualized in four ways: through travel, collegiality, military employment, and post-war opportunity.

Travel

Technically, Australians were British nationals at the time of World War I. Joining the AIF did not mean that personnel were Australian by birth, though it did indicate that the candidate was resident in Australia at the time of enlisting. While some AIF personnel had been born in the British Isles, or in other imperial dominions, such as New Zealand, the vast majority of AIF enlistees had never travelled any major distance from Australia. The sense of wonder at taking in new scenery is encapsulated in an imaged captured by an official Australian war photographer in France, which depicts two Anzacs pausing to contemplate the exterior of a French church [fig. 5.1]. Official photographers were commissioned to capture the Australian experience of war for posterity, including the day-to-day experiences of the troops as well as more prominent events such as the aftermath of battle: the soldiers are unidentified, but their identity is of less importance than their absorption and interest in their surroundings. The church is the late fifteenth- to early sixteenth-century Notre-Dame de la Neuville, near the Somme town of Corbie, which is remarkable for the large carved tympanum above the doors on its facade, and which has arrested the soldiers' attention.[19] To the locals, these churches were part of the everyday scenery, but for Antipodean visitors, who were used to considering their own country as "young" in implicitly colonialist terms, such old and ornate structures were a novel source of fascination.

Travel, if it could be achieved, was considered an important part of an architect's education. Prior to World War I, training in Australia was gained through indenture, or serving articles, with an established practitioner. Articled students learnt through instruction from their master, but often added supplementary formal classes in drawing and building construction available through working men's colleges to their education. A lucky few would have the opportunity to travel to expand their knowledge and understanding of architecture, an honor usually reserved for the best and brightest. For instance, in 1893 the Sydney Architectural Association provided one scholarship for overseas travel for a promising young architect in which sketching key buildings was a required component, but most students of the time could only dream of such an opportunity, unless they had ample funds at their disposal.[20] Nevertheless, the inherent belief in the importance of travel is demonstrated by the nomination forms for Associateship of the Melbourne-based Royal Victorian Institute of Architects (RVIA) of the time, which included a section for applicants to detail any travel they had undertaken alongside details of their training. The Institute's May 1914 examination for Associateship also required candidates to possess the ability to conceptualize and articulate the formal qualities of canonical international architectural examples, through instructions to elucidate the difference between Ancient Greek and Roman architecture, as well as sketch three examples from a list including the Great Temple at Karnak, the Madeleine in Paris, one of Christopher Wren's parish churches in

England, St. Apollinare in Ravenna, and a New York skyscraper.[21] Students would have gained familiarity with these structures through photographic reproductions and measured drawings, but as an art specifically designed for human occupation, architecture is meant to be experienced as well as viewed. First-hand experience of iconic examples of architecture was a tremendous and keenly cultivated advantage.

Yet, for Australian practitioners, travel before, and certainly post-, qualification was largely out of reach because of geographic distance and the attendant cost. Enlisting for active service thus meant a great opportunity to see a large portion of the architecturally significant sites of the world. Where they served was ultimately determined by which army unit they belonged to, but it was possible during the earlier years of the war, for example, for a man to arrive at one of several training camps in Egypt, proceed to the Dardanelles, and then – providing he survived – be sent on to France and Belgium. Training camps were also established in the United Kingdom, and troops travelled back and forth across the English Channel for both active service and recreational leave.

Suddenly, a much larger slice of the profession was mobile. Arthur Peck, erstwhile master of Herbert Affleck, described the long-term benefits for the profession in an article in the RVIA's *Journal of Proceedings*. "Of those returning," he enthused, "I trust that many will rise to eminence in the professions. They must have benefited considerably in having been able to see many of the wonderful works of the old Masters … It was a wonderful chance for a student in Architecture to see the old world, have all his expenses paid, be clothed and fed, paid a weekly wage and at the same time to fight for his country."[22] By September 1916, VASS reported that 49 of its 69 student members were at war, a figure which continued to grow as the war progressed.[23]

Individual service records sketch an itinerary for each soldier – charting movements to and from training camps and detailing time spent on leave and under medical attention – while unit diaries give more specific locations during periods of active service. The most revealing accounts, though, are personal, in the form of diaries, letters, photographs, and sketches. Herbert Affleck's characteristically spartan diary for December 13, 1914 describes a delightful day shortly after the 2nd Field Artillery Brigade's arrival in Egypt: "Slept in till 9am, did not attend church parade, went up Pyramid (Cheops)."[24] Hugh L. Peck (1888–1965), son of Arthur Peck, sent a postcard to the RVIA, writing humorously that "[t]his is how they interest us in the 'History of Architecture,' on Sunday mornings, by giving us a route march past architectural remains."[25] An image in the photographic collection of George Earp (1891–1950) – a fellow Victorian architect with the 5th Battalion – shows the striking Egyptian landscape around Mena Camp: two pyramids dominate an otherwise empty horizon, their silhouette echoed by the conical tents in the foreground [fig. 5.2].[26]

Figure 5.2: George H. Earp, photographic view of the 1st Battalion tents at Mena Camp, Egypt, 1915–1916. State Library of Victoria Pictures Collection: H40883. State Library of Victoria.

Travel also allowed for comparison with home: after spending time in France with the 10th Field Company Engineers, Lynn Rule (1891–1941) found that Australian cities and buildings were more "wholesome, clean and progressive" than their overseas counterparts.[27] Others noted methods of construction peculiar to different locations. Hospitalized for some weeks in Malta in 1915, Arthur S. Williams (1887–1916) managed to observe the recently constructed buildings on the island nation, which were predominantly made of sandstone. Writing home, he described ceilings "of 4-inch stone slabs, supported by timber or steel beams. Over the slabs are laid a few inches of stone chips, and then a composition of lime and finely-ground terracotta. This makes an excellent fire-resisting and waterproof roof. The cost is about one-third of building in Australia."[28] The differences in climate – and clientele – also made an impression on Australian Flying Corps pilot Stanley Garrett (1894–1958), who wrote frequently to his family in Melbourne from England. Quartered on Lord Monson's Lincolnshire estate while training at a nearby aerodrome, he noticed the absence of wooden houses. Instead, he noted that "all [were constructed in] either stone or brick, with either tiles or a slate roof. Every little shanty has a tile roof, in fact the dog kennel here is about 6ft × 4ft & about 4 ft high built of stone, & it has a slate roof."[29] After a visit to Oxford he wrote to his father, a successful Melbourne builder, that he had seen "some very quaint ideas, which would look very good if developed & worked into modern Aust[ralian] houses," words which clearly indicate an eye to future building projects that they could undertake on his return.[30] Garrett also visited major English landmarks: of a visit to Lincoln Cathedral, he wrote to his sisters that "the service was worse than dry, but the building most interesting."[31] Immediately after the armistice, Garrett pursued travel further, journeying to Italy, visiting Pompeii, Naples, Rome, Florence, Venice, and Milan, as well as a portion of southern France. A further tour, partially taken by air, took him northeast through Brussels, Antwerp, Cologne, and Bonn. He described this post-war travel as "beneficial," explaining to his family that "living as we were in ruined villages & devastated country, it effects [sic] the nerves."[32] The pursuit of architecture and beauty, his words suggest, could provide a panacea for war's horror.[33]

When Garrett finally applied for Associateship of the RVIA in the late 1930s, his travel log – like that of many returned servicemen – was extensive. In his own nomination papers, Leighton Irwin (1892–1962), later a celebrated member of the Australian architectural fraternity, emphasized that he had "travelled through England Scotland & the Continent purely for Architectural studies" after the armistice.[34] Similarly, George Beech (1893–1939) gave a detailed list of 27 different cities seen in Egypt, France, Italy, England and Scotland, implying that he had gained a wealth of visual experience throughout his service.[35]

Collegiality

War also brought opportunity for national and international professional collegiality gained through one's own personal networks and within individual units. While some practitioners were scattered within AIF units, seemingly at random, others appeared in clusters. These patterns are revealed when examining the embarkation rolls, which list all Australian servicemen who left to serve overseas as well as which ships they travelled on. The collegiality on board these vessels, after weeks of training, with a lengthy voyage ahead, and with the tantalizing prospect of travel on arrival, can well be imagined. Some clusters may be due to social influence via professional association: for example, George F. Addison (1889–1954), Robert W. L. Chambers (1893–1916), and William Belson, all from Brisbane, enlisted within days of each other and embarked on HMAT *Omrah* with the 9th Battalion on September 24, 1914.[36] Addison and Chambers were both students, and the sons of well-established Queensland architects. Belson, as previously mentioned, went missing at Lone Pine; Chambers was killed in action in France in 1916. Other clusters are more predictable, such as those in the Australian army's engineering units, which (as will be seen) made use of specialized professional knowledge. Among these units, the 5th and 6th Field Company Engineers included a particularly high concentration of at least 17 architectural professionals, including prominent Melburnians William A. Henderson (1882–1949) and Philip B. Hudson

(1887–1951) – all of whom embarked on the same troop transport, HMAT *Ceramic*, in November 1915.[37] The camaraderie among architects continued throughout the war, as is demonstrated by personal accounts, which indicate practitioners seeking each other out. For example, Herbert Affleck's diary for 1916 records meetings with Hugh L. Peck while both were stationed in Egypt; as well as being an architect, Peck was also the son of Affleck's architectural master.[38] Stationed on aerodromes behind the front lines in France and Belgium, Garrett received a succession of visitors keen to inspect the airplanes, including Henderson, who knew his builder father.[39] Hudson, too, reported meeting several practitioners.[40]

While informal professional networks were continuing overseas, links with home were also being strengthened, through ongoing contact with professional institutions and the dissemination of publications. The November 1916 issue of the Sydney-based professional journal *Building* boasted that the publication was "posted free to students located on active service."[41] It also published a letter of thanks from Lynn Rule, then serving on the Western Front, who stated that he would pass his own copy of the journal on to the other interested architects and engineers in his unit.[42]

Travel also enabled deeper and more tangible connections with international professional networks, an opportunity which was anticipated before embarkation, with several taking letters of introduction overseas. Writing to the secretary of the RVIA while on leave in London, Arthur S. Williams – a partner in the firm Ashworth & Williams, and who pre-war was studying for a diploma in architecture at the University of Melbourne – reported that "at last [I] have been able to present your letter … to the RIBA [Royal Institute of British Architects]. I have had a most enjoyable week visiting various schools and buildings. I went through the Architectural School at University College this morning, and visited the Architectural Association School yesterday."[43] Addison made contact with his father's old classmate from the Royal Academy, Professor William Lethaby, and enjoyed a meeting with him, asking him "what modern buildings I ought to see."[44] Lethaby recommended just one exemplar, John Francis Bentley's Catholic cathedral at Westminster, much to Addison's gratification, as he had already had admired it. "[Lethaby] hopes they will not get the money to finish it, as he thinks it perfect as it is. Certainly, one can't imagine a better effect than the interior as it is – just the plain brickwork," he wrote.

Employment

The trope of World War I as a relentless machine permeates the modern perception of the conflict; it is a commentary on the expendability of life and the dehumanizing nature of mechanized warfare. Yet such tropes also nuance the enormity and complexity of the task of providing for a massive multi-nation army. Troops had to be trained, housed, fed, bathed, relocated, protected, and tended to medically. To facilitate the workings of this machine, military engineering units – such as Britain's Royal Engineers, the United States' Corps of Engineers, and the Australian Pioneers and Field Company Engineers, among others – were responsible for the design and construction of intricate infrastructural systems. Trenches, dugouts, hangars, observation posts, kitchens, hospitals, laundries and bath-houses, train lines, bridge construction and destruction, and even barbed-wire arrangements were all crucial components in which professional knowledge in designing and construction, as well as skills in drawing, were highly valuable.

In late 1918, Arthur Peck, then President of the RVIA, waxed lyrical in anticipation of the coming end of the war, musing that students would "again take up the pencils they laid down when they picked up the rifle."[45] However, many had kept their pencils firmly in hand throughout the war; the army had provided numerous opportunities to practice and hone professional skills, with a large proportion of architects and draftsmen serving alongside civil, mechanical, and hydraulic engineers in the engineering units of the AIF – including the 17 who had departed on HMAT *Ceramic.* In a letter to the Secretary of the RVIA, dated January 1917, Melbourne architect John Toone (1887–1918) described the work undertaken by the 3rd Pioneers – then based in France – as "repairing trenches, drainage, reinforced concrete work, etc., etc., under shell and rifle fire continually."[46] Arthur S. Williams described how, in Turkey in late 1916, "a rough shed served as a drawing office. Occasionally … a few rounds of shrapnel would drop in amongst the plans and instruments. Excepting these interludes, and the whispering of bullets overhead, one might be back at work in Collins-street."[47] Sadly, this observation foreshadowed his own death at Pozières, France, in July 1916; "he had been drawing a plan of new trenches, and as he flashed his torch on his work for a moment a sniper shot him," the University of Melbourne's *Varsity Engineer* reported.[48]

The types of plans, diagrams, and sketches executed by Williams and his colleagues can be found in the AIF's engineering unit diaries, and these are typically anonymously produced technical delineations, although a few do indicate a deeper architectural knowledge. Of these, a further few are signed, enabling identification. One such example is a drawing made in January 1918 for a drying room at Palmer Baths near Neuve Eglise, Belgium [fig. 5.3], produced by George Fenwick (1887– 1960), a Victorian draftsman who had trained with the Geelong firm Messrs Tombs & Durran, for the 10th Field Company Engineers, and which appears in the unit's diary for that month.[49] Bathing and laundry facilities were an important component of the machine of war, helping to smooth its operation by assisting the control of the spread of disease, and improving morale. While soldiers bathed, clothing would be cleaned and deloused, and in the extreme cold of a European winter, rapid drying facilities were essential. Fenwick's handwritten notes which accompany the drawing describe the stages in construction of a "Nissen hut minus the ends and floor," the ends instead appearing to be made of brick, and housing an arrangement of wires from which the uniforms would be hung.[50]

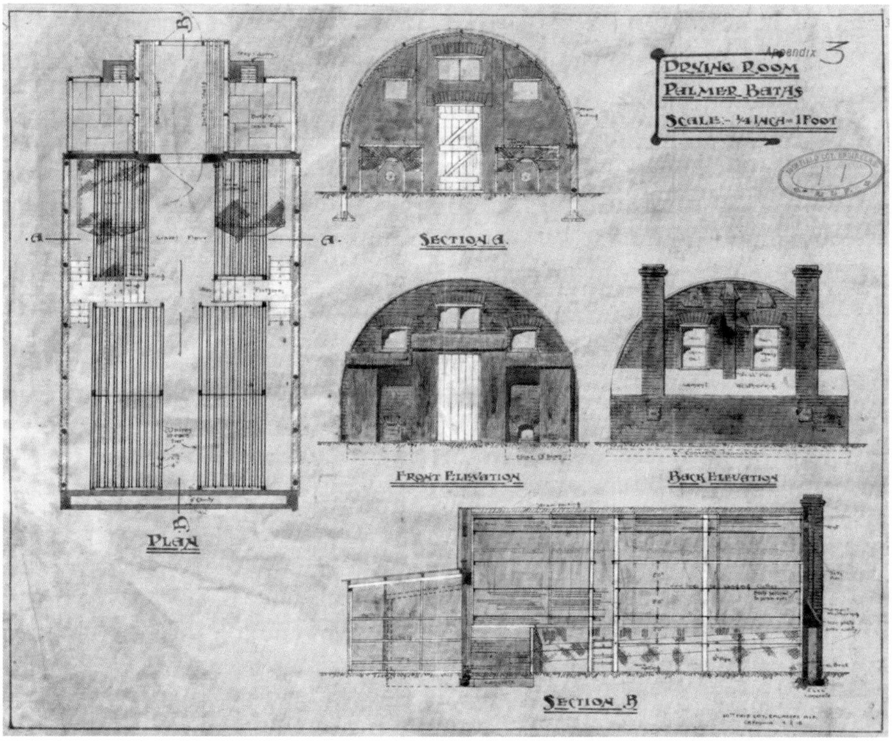

Figure 5.3: George Fenwick, plans for a drying room at Palmer Baths, January 1918. Australian War Memorial: AWM4, 14/29/13. Australian War Memorial, Canberra.

The art of architecture – the depiction of a tangible and interpretable space – could embellish even these pragmatic tasks; engaging upon these allowed a degree of continuation of practice even during the war, at a time of expediency and innovation. What distinguishes Fenwick's drawings from the majority of designs found in the unit diaries is the quality of his renderings: the characteristically ornate lettering of architectural plans at the time, the careful indication in color of the various materials employed for construction, and the delicate touches of shadow. These techniques transform the indicated structure from an ordinary technical plan into a conceivable work of architecture. Similarly, a sketch of a ruined bridge made on site in August 1918 by New Zealand-trained and Melbourne-based Harold Coates (1888–1954) of the 3rd Pioneers is more a lively description than a delineation, clearly indicating its different materials and components, and demonstrating the extent of the destruction through a use of perspective [fig. 5.4].[51]

Figure 5.4: Harold Coates, sketch of ruined bridge, August 10, 1918. Reversed image from blueprint. Australian War Memorial: AWM4, 14/15/22. Australian War Memorial, Canberra.

Architectural practice and the acquisition of knowledge could also transcend enemy lines, with professional architectural knowledge proving of real value. After the battle of Messines, Philip B. Hudson, an accomplished architect and teacher, was directed to investigate and report on German reinforced concrete pillbox design, so that the Australians could learn from a professional examination of the enemy's superior defenses in order to improve their own. "Direct hits from shells had very little damaging effect" on the Germans' most recent version, Hudson concluded; "[t]he ground around is a mass of interlocking shell holes, and yet no concrete is destroyed beyond the layer of steel bar reinforcement. From the proportion of void to solid in the section it can be seen that for the purposes of destruction, the shelter must be considered a solid block of reinforced concrete."[52] Experiences and observations like those of Fenwick, Coates, and Hudson, gained under conditions of expediency, and disseminated among their peers, would inevitably give these architects greater technical skill and knowledge of materials that would prove invaluable not only on the battlefield, but also for their post-war careers.[53]

Post-war Opportunity

Four years of war brought opportunities for travel, collegiality, and innovation to architects, albeit with the constant risks brought by active service. As the hostilities ended, architects' thirst for education continued, but with greater formality, supported by the demobilization education programs that were set up late in 1918 for Australian and New Zealand enlisted personnel. After the armistice, the AIF granted leave for servicemen to participate in a scheme of Non-Military Employment (NME), and even paid for the associated fees, as well as the participants' subsistence.[54] Australian architects relished such opportunities, with many taking up employment in key London practices and the greatest number – nearly 50 in total – securing a place at the Architectural Association (AA) in London. Attending classes at the School's premises in Bedford Square, as well as lectures and site visits, the attendees were catapulted into what would in the vast majority of cases be their first taste of formal institution-based training. Several of these Australian AA attendees would take the opportunity to prepare for and sit the examination for Associateship of the RIBA while they were based in England before returning southwards – a qualification which, if taken from home, would require extensive preparation and lengthy time delays, as well as limited chances for educational support. Some took a longer route home, travelling via America. Others extended their stay from months to years, taking full advantage of the AA's courses of education.

In several instances, this opportunity would be transformative, allowing those in traditionally lower-status trades to upgrade their professional positions to those of architects. William Lawrie (1887–1972) and Charles V. Howard (1894–c.1980) gave their professions on their attestation papers as "carpenter" and "joiner" respectively, but both managed to secure NME at the AA, and then continued to build successful architectural careers with the Australian public service. Howard took full advantage of his good fortune: after completing eight months of study at the Architectural Association and gaining Associate RIBA membership in 1919, he travelled around Italy before being appointed as an architect with the British Government in Egypt in 1921–1925. Howard's return to Australia in 1925 saw him appointed to the Commonwealth Department of Works, where he rose to chief designing architect by 1939.[55] The experience was also profound for Stanley Garrett, who had stated his occupation on enlistment as "architect," but was in reality a junior builder who had gained some knowledge of architectural methods through attending the night courses in "architectural drawing and building construction" taught by Philip B. Hudson at the Swinburne Technical School in Melbourne.[56] Garrett's use of the term "architect" was probably strategic, made in order to gain a commission with the Australian Flying Corps, which privileged higher standards of education.[57] For Garrett, who already knew a range of practitioners through his father, an established builder, the opportunity to take up NME was decisive; he explicitly stated in a letter to his father in March 1919 that, rather than return to "the old game," namely building, he "intended to go in for architecture," and had secured a place at the AA. He was delighted that his pre-war acquaintances "[William] Hughie Craig & young [W. Alan] Devereaux [sic] are doing the same course as I am."[58] Both Craig and Devereux were architectural students; Craig had lived near Garrett in Melbourne, and had been articled to prominent Melbourne architect W. A. M. Blackett.[59] Garrett's persistence paid off. On March 5, 1920 he wrote to tell his father that "[i]t is just a year since I started at the school, & one might say architecture, I am now competing with students who have had many more years of office or school training, & I find that my work is equal to theirs, & in some cases better. It has certainly been a year of hard work, & yet I have found it much more pleasant than boring, & only wish that I could put in another year & progress as satisfactorily."[60]

Others followed their time at the AA with further travel. Sydney architect Cyril Ruwald (1895–1959) was granted special leave by military authorities to travel to Italy "to enable him to continue his studies in architecture in Rome & Venice for a period of three weeks," shortly before his return to Australia.[61] A further number were demobilized in London, with several travelling on to America before returning home. Established practitioner Carlyle Greenwell (1884–1961) – of the firm which had trained the deceased Herbert Brough – asserted the need to travel to America as "essential" to his immediate career. Pre-war, Greenwell had studied at the University of Pennsylvania, explaining on his application for discharge in the UK that this education had enabled him to "specialis[e] in [American methods] … they gave me the standing I held in Sydney. It is important for my future to refresh on these and therefore ask you to help me in getting this knowledge by allowing me to take about 6 weeks in America before my return."[62] Stanley Rickard (1883–1976) also made a case for transatlantic travel, explaining that "the American methods for steel and concrete structures in large cities, and Bungalow styles in California for domestic work are especially adapted to our Australian climate and will be of great benefit in modernising the Architectural profession in Australia."[63] Letters of support from both Greenwell's and Rickard's employers back home further emphasized the value of such experiences, while Frederick Deane's (1891–1960) own application was endorsed by the Principal of the Architectural Association, Robert Atkinson; he took with him a letter from Atkinson to C. H. Whitaker at the American Institute of Architects' *Journal*.[64]

Further travel also meant conveying these architects back home. Echoing the voyage of HMAT *Ceramic* in 1915, in 1920, HMAT *Megantic* carried seven AA attendees home. Of them, four – Charles V. Howard, Leighton Irwin, William Lawrie, and Arthur Stephenson – would become extremely successful practitioners; Stephenson, Howard, and Lawrie had used their wartime opportunities to transition from building- and contracting-based roles pre-war to fully fledged architects. Wartime had thus wrought significant personal change for these men, but it also had a profound impact on Australian architectural culture.

Returning to Home Shores

On their return, these practitioners' accumulated knowledge was disseminated to the Australian architectural fraternity in a variety of ways. The newly established Architectural Atelier at the University of Melbourne, for example, took the Architectural Association as its model, while informally published sketches and public lectures shared these architects' experience with a wider audience. On his return from London and study at the AA, Lieutenant Leighton Irwin was appointed Assistant Director of the Architectural Atelier late in 1919. As the only member of the Atelier's board who had experienced formal institution-based architectural education, it is perhaps unsurprising that he set about creating the Atelier in the AA's image, importing the curriculum, structure, and marking schema into the Atelier course.[65] The Atelier offered advanced study of architectural design to students, with entry only for those who had already completed a diploma of architecture or completed their articles, and was the most advanced architectural education available in Australia in the inter-war period. Irwin was not the only one using his wartime experiences to influence architectural education in Australia: in Sydney, John D. Moore (1888–1958), who had joined the Royal Engineers in London in 1915 after having spent several years working in the USA, also used drew upon his AA experience as the Architectural Design and Draughtsmanship Instructor for the Bachelor of Architecture course at the University of Sydney.[66] As Irwin put it:

> With numbers of our young men returning from the old world, this [the need for education in architectural design] was even more strongly emphasised. Some of them had actually attended courses in England, while all had had the opportunity of studying first hand the building productions of France, England and other parts of Europe.[67]

Philip B. Hudson, of the 5th Company Engineers, also shared his war experience through a lecture to fellow RVIA members at the Institute's General Meeting in May 1919.[68] He not only described conditions on the Front, but also shared the findings of his report into the construction of German pillboxes. A precis of his presentation was published in that month's journal, accompanied by some illustrations, which not only included structural diagrams of the fortifications, but also some more informal sketches of civilian architecture that he had made in moments of leisure. One of these was a pencil sketch of an open-air pulpit at Magdalen College, Oxford [fig. 5.5]. Its publication was significant: in November 1919, Hudson would address the VASS with a paper on sketching, emphasizing "the important part that sketching should play in the development of their studies … 'To be able to sketch is to be able to learn,'" he explained, sharing further images that had been created during the war years.[69] Like the Australian soldiers captured by the official photographer in front of Notre-Dame de la Neuville, near Corbie, on the Somme, at Magdalen College Hudson had been absorbed by an ornate architectural detail, once only accessible through photographic reproduction or illustration, and now viewed first-hand. Being an architect, though, Hudson took out a pencil to record what he saw, capturing the detail before him and cementing the structure within his own visual and intellectual memory – and thereby learning and extending his professional knowledge in the process.

Figure 5.5: Philip B. Hudson, sketch of open-air pulpit at Magdalen College, Oxford, September 1917. *Journal of Proceedings: Royal Victorian Institute of Architects* (May 1919). National Library of Australia.

Conclusion

The networks and experience gained through the enforced travel of wartime enabled these Australian architects to attain a level of international engagement that subsequently underpinned and greatly enhanced their professional success. For a number of these men, war provided not only an opportunity to travel, but the chance to reset their professional horizons. These experiences would have a profound influence on the Australian architectural profession, ranging from personal development to the establishment of a fresh trajectory for Australian architectural education, particularly at the key institutions of the universities of Melbourne and Sydney. Above all, the wartime experiences of these young men demonstrate mostly clearly that their engagement with the profession did not cease during wartime. Rather, the experience enhanced their opportunities, bringing new and unexpected benefits to their professional careers and, as a consequence, to Australian architecture.

Notes

1   The Australian war effort has attracted significant, copious, and diversely focused scholarly attention over the century since the armistice. The 12-volume *Official History of Australia in the War of 1914–1918* (Sydney: Angus and Robertson), edited by Charles Edwin Woodrow (C. E. W.) Bean and published in instalments between 1920 and 1942, remains an important source for historians, while Joan Beaumont's wide-ranging *Broken Nation: Australians in the Great War* (Sydney: Allen and Unwin, 2013) provides a modern and nuanced reading of the war and its aftermath.

2   First-hand accounts have been valuable in documenting both the Australian war effort and its impact. See, in particular, Bill Gammage's *The Broken Years: Australian Soldiers in the Great War* (Canberra: Australian National University Press, 1974), and Alistair Thompson's *Anzac Memories: Living with the Legend*, 2nd ed. (Melbourne: Monash University Publishing, 2013).

3   See Julie Willis, "Architecture and Wartime," in *The First World War, the Universities and the Professions*, ed. Kate Darian-Smith and James Waghorne (Parkville: Melbourne University Press, 2019), 291–308. See also Julie Willis and Bronwyn Hanna, *Women Architects in Australia, 1900–1950* (Canberra: Royal Australian Institute of Architects, 2001).

4   For a broader Australia-specific study of the effects of war-inflicted physical and psychological injuries on both servicemen and their families, see Marina Larsson's *Shattered Anzacs: Living with the Scars of War* (Sydney: University of New South Wales Press, 2009).

5   There were no Australian women architects engaging in a formal war effort during this particular conflict.

6   Australian War Memorial (AWM): AWM8, Unit Embarkation Rolls, 1914–1918 War. National Archives of Australia (NAA): B2455, First Australian Imperial Force Personnel Dossiers, 1914–1920. This sample is drawn from a larger ongoing project by the authors of this paper.

7   At the outbreak of war, the requirements for enlistment included an age range of 19–38 years, which was increased to 45 years in June 1915. Minimum weight and health standards were also relaxed as the war progressed and demand for troops increased. "Enlistment Standards," Australian War Memorial, Canberra, Australia, accessed April 29, 2020, <https://www.awm.gov.au/articles/encyclopedia/enlistment>.

8   NAA: B2455, Belson, William Charles.

9   AWM: 1DRL/0428, Australian Red Cross Society Wounded and Missing Enquiry Bureau Files, 1914–1918 War, 871 Lance Sergeant Affleck, Herbert.

10   NAA: B2455, Freadman, Zavel Ephraim.

11   NAA: B2455, Brough, Herbert William. A photograph of this grave marker is held by the Australian War Memorial in Canberra; AWM: H16018.

12   NAA: B2455, Gould, Elwyn Samuel.

13   NAA: B2455, Owen, George Burgoyne.

14   Douglas McMurtrie, *The Disabled Soldier* (New York: MacMillan, 1919), 61, accessed September 10, 2019, <https://openlibrary.org/books/OL7205266M/The_disabled_soldier>. This work comprised a post-armistice survey of rehabilitation and occupation in the Allied nations.

15   NAA: B2455, Parkes, Cobden.

16   NAA: B2455, Forster, William Blackett.

17   NAA: B2455, Berry, Henry David. International Press Service Association, ed. "Berry, Henry David," *Who's Who in Australia* (Sydney: International Press Service Association, 1929), 614.

18   NAA: B2455: Harrison, John Southern. Harrison was later discharged in the United Kingdom, but further details of his fate are unclear.

19   The tympanum, which depicts Christ's entry into Jerusalem, is located just beyond the statuary shown in the photograph.

20   See, for instance, the article on Harry (H. C.) Budden and his success in gaining the scholarship: "A Clever Student," *National Advocate* [Bathurst, NSW], January 27, 1899, 2.

21   "Royal Victorian Institute of Architects Examination to Qualify for Candidature as Associate, May, 1914," *Journal of Proceedings: Royal Victorian Institute of Architects* [Melbourne, Australia] 12, no. 2 (May 1914): 85.

22   Arthur Peck, "War and Architects," *Journal of Proceedings: RVIA* 16, no. 5 (November 1918): 144.

23   "Federal Parliament House Competition," *Journal of Proceedings: RVIA* 14, no. 4 (September 1916): 410.

24   AWM: 1DRL/0026, Diary of Herbert Alexander Affleck, December 13, 1914.

25   "Along the Bye-Paths," *Journal of Proceedings: RVIA* 13, no. 1 (March 1915): 28.

26   Earp later became a farmer in country Victoria, Australia. NAA: B73, Personal case files, World War 1, Earp, George Howard.

27   "'Building' in the Trenches," *Building: The Magazine for the Architect, Builder, Property Owner and Merchant* [Sydney, Australia] 20, no. 116 (April 1917): 94, extract of a letter from Rule to the editor. Rule was invalided home later in 1917, having been gassed, and suffering shell shock. NAA: B2455, Rule, Lynn Breakspear.

28   "Along the Bye-Paths," *Journal of Proceedings: RVIA* 13, no. 6 (January 1916), 241–2, partially paraphrased letters from Williams.

29   State Library of Victoria (SLV): MS10762, Stanley George Garrett, letters, October 30, 1916–June 18, 1920, fol. 1a, Garrett to his sisters Mabel and Edie, December 31, 1916. For further discussion of Garrett's observations, see Katti Williams, "Learning

to Fly: Distance and the Wartime Experience of Australian Architect Stanley George Garrett," in *Proceedings of the Society of Architectural Historians, Australia and New Zealand 36, Distance Looks Back*, ed. Victoria Jackson Wyatt, Andrew Leach, and Lee Stickells (Sydney: SAHANZ, 2020), 415–29.

30   SLV: MS10762, fol. 1b, Garrett to his parents Thomas and Elizabeth, March 5, 1917.

31   SLV: MS10762, fol. 1a, Garrett to Mabel and Edie, January 8, 1917.

32   SLV: MS10762, fol. 4a, Garrett to Thomas and Elizabeth, December 30, 1918.

33   For further discussion of the healing role of architecture after war, and its potential denial of trauma, see Ana Carden-Coyne, *Reconstructing the Body: Classicism, Modernism and the First World War* (Oxford: Oxford University Press, 2009).

34   SLV: MS9454, Records of the Victorian Chapter of the Royal Australian Institute of Architects, past member files, Box 88, Irwin, Leighton Francis, nomination forms for associateship.

35   SLV: MS9454, Box 85: Beech, George Alexander, nomination forms for associateship.

36   AWM: AWM8, 23/26/1, 9th Infantry Battalion, September 1914. See also "Roll of Honor (Queensland)," *The Salon: The Official Journal of the Institute of Architects of New South Wales* 4, no. 5 (June 1915): 181, and no. 6 (July 1915): 201.

37   AWM: AWM8, 14/24/1, 5th Field Company Engineers, November 1915.

38   AWM: 1DRL/0026, Diary of Herbert Alexander Affleck, March 11 and 18, 1916.

39   SLV: MS10762, fol. 3a, Garrett to Thomas and Elizabeth, March 13, 1918.

40   Philip B. Hudson, "Life in France," *Journal of Proceedings: RVIA* 17, no. 2 (May 1919): 37.

41   "The Architects of To-Morrow," *Building* 20, no. 111 (November 1916): 118.

42   "'Building' in the Trenches," *Building* 20, no. 116 (April 1917): 94.

43   "Along the Bye-paths," *Journal of Proceedings: RVIA* 14, no. 3 (July 1916): 373.

44   "Roll of Honour," *The Salon* 5, no. 5 (December 1915): 112. Addison's father's letter of introduction had been "lost … with everything else, at the Dardanelles."

45   Peck, "War and Architects," 144.

46   "Letters from France," *Journal of Proceedings: RVIA* 15, no. 1 (March 1917): 38.

47   "Along the Bye-Paths," *Journal of Proceedings: RVIA* 13, no. 6 (January 1916): 241–2, partially paraphrased letters from Williams.

48   Melbourne University Engineering Society, *The Varsity Engineer: War Memorial Number, 1914–1919* (Melbourne: Anderson Gowan, c.1919), 96.

49   AWM4: Australian Imperial Force Unit Diaries, 1914–18 War. 14/29/13, 10th Field Company, Australian Engineers, January 1918.

50   AWM4: 14/29/13, January 1918. The Nissen Hut was designed by Major Peter Norman Nissen, of the British Army's Royal Engineers. The hut was made of corrugated steel with a slightly splayed semi-circular sectional profile. The advantage of these over other structures that they could be prefabricated and were very efficient in the use of materials.

51   AWM4: 15/15/22, 3rd Australian Pioneers, August 1918.

52   Philip B. Hudson, "Life in France," *Journal of Proceedings: RVIA* 17, no. 2 (May 1919): 36–7.

53   For an understanding of the impact of war on architectural production in Australia post-WWII, see Philip Goad and Julie Willis, "Invention from War: A Circumstantial Modernism for Australian Architecture," *Journal of Architecture* 8, no. 1 (Spring 2003): 41–62.

54   For the AIF's education schemes, including NME, see Bean, *Official History*, vol. 6, 1062–72. Bean, 1070, gives the figure of "460 [men] studying architecture, town-planning,

building and engineering" within the part of the scheme overseen by the Technical Section of the AIF's Education Scheme, but no further breakdown in numbers is given.

55 Joseph A. Alexander, ed., "Howard, Charles Vincent," *Who's Who in Australia* (Melbourne: Colorgravure Publications, 1950), 344.

56 NAA: B2455, Garrett, Stanley George. The course title is taken from an advertisement for Swinburne Technical College's night classes, *The Age* [Melbourne, Australia], February 15, 1913, p. 5. SLV: MS9454, Box 87, past member files, Garrett, S. G.

57 See Michael Molkentin, "Culture, Class and Experience in the Australian Flying Corps" (Hons thesis, University of Wollongong, 2004), 7; also Michael Molkentin, "Quite the Right Type: Recruiting and Reinforcing Australia's Effort in the Air, 1914–1918," paper presented at *By the Seat of their Pants,* RAAF Museum, Point Cook, November 12, 2012.

58 SLV: MS10762, fol. 4b, Garrett to Mabel and Edie, April 13, 1919. Garrett and Craig would end up in partnership in the 1930s with a third Anzac, Bennet D. Reynolds.

59 SLV: MS10762, fol. 4b, Garrett to Mabel and Edie, April 13, 1919. Garrett and Craig would end up in partnership in the 1930s with a third Anzac, Bennet D. Reynolds. Both Garrett and Craig were Presbyterians and may have also known each other through local church communities. NAA: B2455, Garrett, Stanley George, and Craig, William Hughston.

60 SLV: MS10762, fol. 5b, Garrett to Thomas, March 15, 1920.

61 NAA: B2455, Ruwald, Cyril Christian.

62 NAA: B2455, Greenwell, Carlyle.

63 NAA: B2455, Rickard, Stanley Noble.

64 NAA: B2455, Deane, Frederick George.

65 Julie Willis, "The Architectural Association and the Architectural Atelier," in *Papers from the Thirtieth Annual Conference of the Society of Architectural Historians, Australia & New Zealand* (Gold Coast, QLD: SAHANZ, 2013), 961–72.

66 Willis, "Architecture and Wartime," 291–308.

67 L. F. Irwin, "The University of Melbourne: Architectural Atelier," *Journal of Proceedings: RVIA* 19, no. 1 (March 1921): 20.

68 "Minutes," *Journal of Proceedings: RVIA* 17, no. 2 (May 1919): 43. Only Hudson's paper – a partial precis which included sections from his report on pillboxes – was reproduced in print. Hudson, "Life in France."

69 "Architectural Sketching," *Journal of Proceedings: RVIA* 17, no. 6 (January 1920): 146.

Bibliography

Australian War Memorial, Canberra, Australia
    AWM4, Australian Imperial Force Unit War Diaries, 1914–18 War.
    AWM8, Unit Embarkation Rolls, 1914–18 War.
    1DRL/0026, Diary of Herbert Alexander Affleck.
    1DRL/0428, Australian Red Cross Society Wounded and Missing Enquiry Bureau Files, 1914–1918 War.
National Archives of Australia, Canberra, Australia.
    B2455, First Australian Imperial Force Personnel Dossiers, 1914–1920.

State Library of Victoria, Melbourne, Australia.
  MS9454, Records of the Victorian Chapter of the Royal Australian Institute of Architects.
  MS10762, Stanley George Garrett, letters, October 30, 1916–June 18, 1920.
The Age [Melbourne, Australia]
Building: The Magazine for the Architect, Builder, Property Owner and Merchant [Sydney, Australia]
Journal of Proceedings: Royal Victorian Institute of Architects [Melbourne, Australia]
National Advocate [Bathurst, NSW]
The Salon: The Official Journal of the Institute of Architects of New South Wales [Sydney, Australia]

Alexander, Joseph A., ed. "Howard, Charles Vincent." *Who's Who in Australia*. Melbourne: Colorgravure Publications, 1950.
Australian War Memorial. "Enlistment Standards," *Australian War Memorial*, Canberra, Australia. Accessed April 29, 2020. <https://www.awm.gov.au/articles/encyclopedia/enlistment>
Bean, C. E. W., ed. *Official History of Australia in the War of 1914–1918.* 11th ed. Sydney: Angus and Robertson, 1941.
Beaumont, Joan. *Broken Nation: Australians in the Great War*. Sydney: Allen and Unwin, 2013.
Carden-Coyne, Ana. *Reconstructing the Body: Classicism, Modernism and the First World War*. Oxford: Oxford University Press, 2009.
Gammage, Bill. *The Broken Years: Australian Soldiers in the Great War*, Canberra: Australian National University Press, 1974.
Goad, Philip, and Julie Willis. "Invention from War: A Circumstantial Modernism for Australian Architecture." *Journal of Architecture* 8 (Spring 2003): 41–62.
Hudson, Philip B. "Life in France." *Journal of Proceedings: Royal Victorian Institute of Architects* 17, no. 2 (May 1919): 33–7.
International Press Service Association, ed. "Berry, Henry David." In *Who's Who in Australia*. Sydney: International Press Service Association, 1929.
Irwin, L. F. "The University of Melbourne: Architectural Atelier." *Journal of Proceedings: RVIA* 19, no. 1 (March 1921): 20–1.
Larsson, Marina. *Shattered Anzacs: Living with the Scars of War*. Sydney: University of New South Wales Press, 2009.
McMurtrie, Douglas. *The Disabled Soldier*. New York: MacMillan, 1919. Accessed April 29, 2020. <https://openlibrary.org/books/OL7205266M/The_disabled_soldier>
Melbourne University Engineering Society. *The Varsity Engineer: War Memorial Number, 1914–1919*. Melbourne: Anderson Gowan, 1919.
Molkentin, Michael. "Quite the Right Type: Recruiting and Reinforcing Australia's Effort in the Air, 1914–1918." Paper presented at *By the Seat of their Pants,* RAAF Museum, Point Cook, November 12, 2012.
———."Culture, Class and Experience in the Australian Flying Corps." Hons. thesis, University of Wollongong, 2004.
Peck, Arthur. "War and Architects." *Journal of Proceedings: RVIA* 16, no. 5 (November 1918): 144–5.

Thompson, Alistair. *Anzac Memories: Living with the Legend*. 2nd ed. Melbourne: Monash University Publishing, 2013.

Williams, Katti. "Learning to Fly: Distance and the Wartime Experience of Australian Architect Stanley George Garrett." In *Proceedings of the Society of Architectural Historians, Australia and New Zealand 36, Distance Looks Back*, edited by Victoria Jackson Wyatt, Andrew Leach, and Lee Stickells, 415–29. Sydney: SAHANZ, 2020.

Willis, Julie. "Architecture and Wartime." In *The First World War, the Universities and the Professions*, edited by Kate Darian-Smith and James Waghorne, 291–308. Parkville: Melbourne University Press, 2019.

———. "The Architectural Association and the Architectural Atelier." In *Papers from the Thirtieth Annual Conference of the Society of Architectural Historians, Australia and New Zealand*, 961–72. Gold Coast, QLD: SAHANZ, 2013.

Willis, Julie, and Bronwyn Hanna. *Women Architects in Australia, 1900–1950*. Canberra: Royal Australian Institute of Architects, 2001.

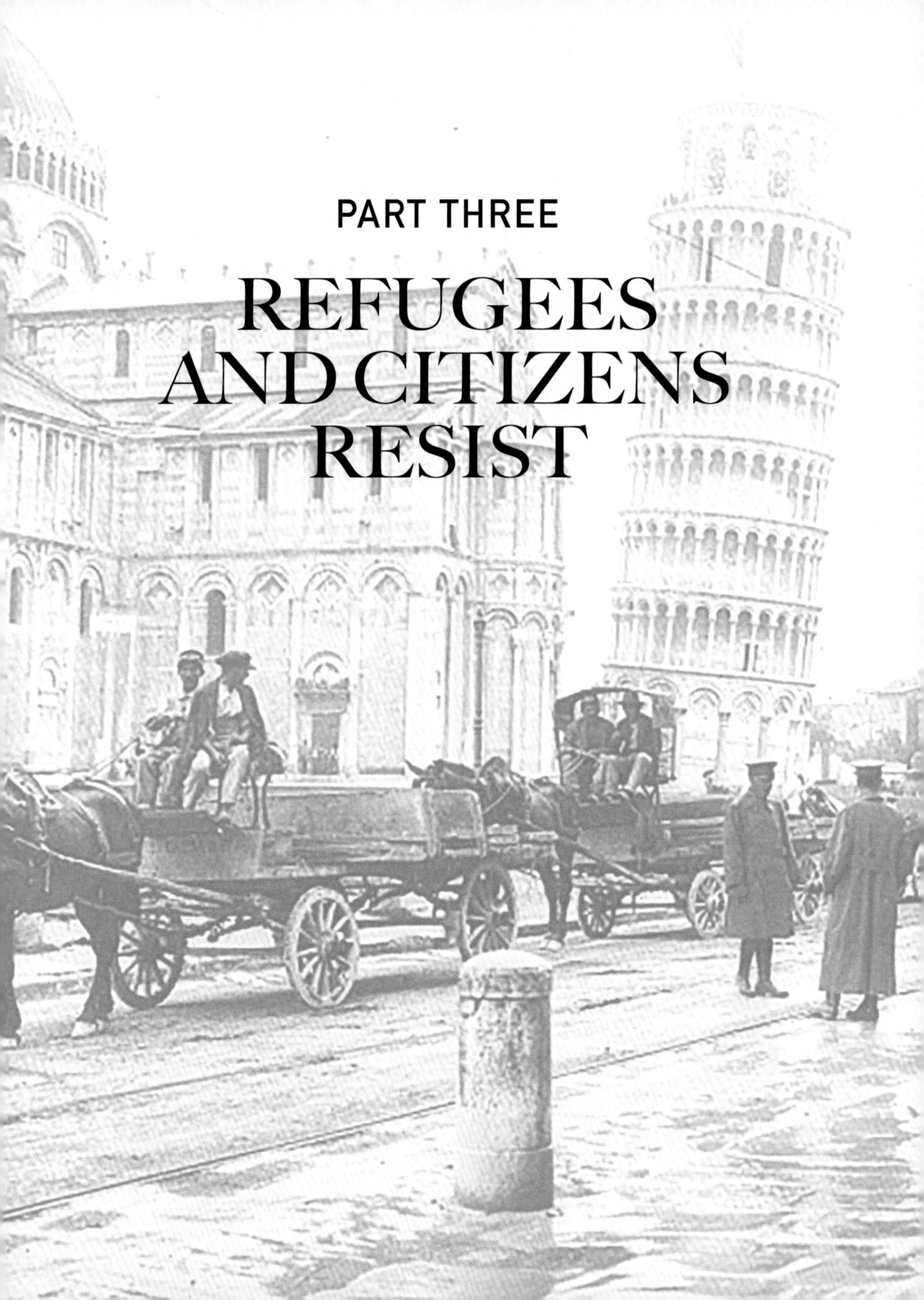

PART THREE

REFUGEES
AND CITIZENS
RESIST

Figure 6.1: "The Raider, publication sanctioned by Official Press Bureau."
(A German Zeppelin over London). Real Photo Postcard, 1915. Author's collection.

Wartime Nightscapes

Zeppelin Night Bombings as Mass Spectacles, 1914–1929

David Caralt

In February 1909, the science magazine *Popular Mechanics* published the image of an airship on its cover. The airship was flying over a city and the caption for the image read: "First (Tactical) Destruction of a Great City." The accompanying article explained: "To demonstrate how easily a fortified city could be destroyed by bombs dropped from airships at night, Roy Knabenshue sailed over Los Angeles on the night of December 18 [1908], and dropped confetti bombs onto the heads of the thousands of people" for an hour and a half.[1] This illustration accurately foreshadowed one of the most surprising and spectacular actions of the First World War [fig. 6.1]: Zeppelins flying over the historic centers of London and Paris amidst the light beams of searchlights. Night would become the preferred space-time to bomb cities by air.

Night bombing as a divertimento first occurred in 1908, the same year in which crowds in New York and Paris saw an airplane flying.[2] It was also the year of publication for *The War in the Air*, a novel by H.G. Wells with illustrations by A.C. Michael, which imagined New York bombed from the air.[3] Speculation about the possibilities of urban aerial bombardment had existed since the first motor-driven airplane lifted off to fly 40 meters in 12 seconds on December 17, 1903 at 10:35 a.m.[4]

Despite the prohibition of air warfare agreed to in the Second Peace Conference in The Hague (1907), real aerial bombardment as a military tactic began at the end of 1911, when the Italians bombed the surroundings of Tripoli. During the First World War the Germans, the French, the English, the Italians, and the Russians flew airplanes over several European cities. This essay is dedicated to the history of air warfare and its relationship with architectural, urban, and popular culture.[5] It argues that night bombings often resulted in an ambivalence – shared by thousands of citizens – between horror and spectacle. Taking a close look at both technology and everyday urban life, moreover, the essay clarifies the intimate relationship between electric lighting technologies and air warfare. Finally, it considers transformations in visual culture, as well as the sounds of night-time urban landscapes in wartime.

Pre-War: The Searchlight Display

Today, the theater is considered to have been the first laboratory to test the effects of electric light, both in illuminating bodies on stage and in the creation of illusions and artificial landscapes.[6] In fact, the evolution of this lighting technique can be followed – in its multiple forms and functions – through the history of such displays and resulting integrated control systems. The transfer of different lightening scenarios to the battlefield – in other words, from culture to war – was an obvious step.[7] "In the Searchlight," a cartoon published in the newspaper *Punch* in 1915, illustrates this process by depicting an opera singer highlighted on the stage and a young man whose brother belongs to the "Anti-Craft Corps," who says: "Mother, they think she's a zeppelin."[8] This cartoon is a reminder of communication between the theater and the theater of war.

Searchlights are devices that project a powerful beam of light of almost parallel rays with a long-distance range, configured by electric arc lights equipped with parabolic reflectors. This application of electrical technology, which was used since the mid-nineteenth century for night work and theater shows, soon began to be utilized in a military context for land reconnaissance and maritime surveillance. With the beginning of the First World War, the lighting of the skies with searchlights became one of the hallmarks of the twentieth century.

From the beginning, the searchlight was a moving image linked to the development of increasingly fast means of transportation – ships, railways, and cars – until the arrival of the airplane. Representations of aircraft equipped with searchlights were widely popular from the end of the nineteenth century, as in Jules Verne's science fiction novels, Albert Robida's *Le Vingtième Siècle* (1883), or George Griffith's *The Angel of the Revolution* (1893), among many others, and usually related to the "city of the future," a city of lights.

In parallel with military research and development, universal exhibitions popularized and released technological and scientific advances to the public. They were an authentic urban laboratory, whose ephemeral tests could potentially be transferred permanently to cities. The first use of searchlights for aesthetic purposes took place in the 1893 World's Columbian Exposition, using General Electric equipment.[9] Especially significant, San Francisco's 1915 Panama–Pacific International Exhibition took place when Europe was already at war and searchlights had begun to work to identify enemy airplanes. The most spectacular lighting effect of the San Francisco fair was the "Scintillator," a multiple searchlight display, one of the hallmark installations of Walter D'Arcy Ryan (1870–1934). Ryan was the founder and first director of General Electric's Illuminating Engineering Laboratory, and his "Scintillator" was a battery of 48 searchlights with interchangeable color filters located in a corner of the port of San Francisco, manipulated – not by chance – but by marine personnel. The powerful beams of light, crisscrossing and creating an aurora, projected skyward against the usual fog of the San Francisco Bay; if the nights were clear, a locomotive provided smoke and steam in lieu of fog. This replicated some characteristic elements of First World War battlefields: searchlights manipulated by the military and the creation of artificial gas clouds occurred simultaneously in the trenches of Europe and in a universal exhibition on the other side of the world.

The collapse of spatial distance and the simultaneity of events – the mobile panoramic gaze, radio and television communications, even the possibilities of using electric light to erase the distinction between day and night – were among the fundamental characteristics of the experience of modernity.[10] Thus, as the nineteenth century gave way to the twentieth, modernity was not only purely spectacular technological progress, but also a sign of fundamental changes in the perception of time and space experienced by people throughout the world.

Wartime

During the First World War, there was an effort to pedagogically explain the conflict to the civilian population through "illustrated alphabet" books, in which each letter corresponded to an image of war – for example, K for Kaiser, or S for Spy. The Z – a difficult letter to match with anything – was usually represented by the Zeppelin. In *An Alphabet of the War*, published in *Punch's Almanack* in 1915, "Z is a Zeppelin, right overhead." The drawing by George Morrow is accompanied by the caption "Isn't it luck to have something for Z?" In this illustration citizens are looking towards the sky and the dark profile of a city in the background – presumably London.[11]

In a belligerent country, looking at the sky with fear would become part of the daily routine of war for civilians.[12] When the war began, the German army had 15 Zeppelins destined for observation or bombing missions. After all, the first flight with a Zeppelin – an airship with a rigid structure conceived by the German count Ferdinand von Zeppelin (1838–1917) – had already taken place over a decade before, on July 2, 1900. Compared to airplanes, by 1914 Zeppelins were nearly as fast, better armed, could carry a much larger bomb load, and had a higher range of action. The Zeppelins' main bombardment zone was the United Kingdom, where its presence in the skies had severe psychological effects: 51 raids killed 577 people and injured

1,358 over the course of the war. Zeppelins also carried out two raids in Paris: the first one, the night of March 20–21, 1915, when four zeppelins dropped seven bombs; the second, on the night of January 29–30, 1916, when a Zeppelin dropped 18 bombs.[13]

Overall, the number of night bombings during the war was almost double that of daytime bombings. This indicates that the night was a preferred time to attack, as it gave the pilots greater security. Thus, one of the first anti-aircraft defense strategies were blackouts.[14] In England, the first blackout orders were to darken ports (August 1914), which were followed by the blackouts of strategic areas of London (September 1914) until they extended to the entire English territory (February 1916). Paris began its blackouts at the beginning of the Zeppelin campaign (the fall of 1915) and reintroduced them in the fall of 1918. The French capital even planned a replica of the city in 1917, which was to be intensely illuminated at night in order to deceive the German bombers.[15] These blackouts were combined with alarms and warnings, as well as the use of metro stations in London and Paris by frightened civilians. Despite such precautions, an abundance of rumors and false alarms created great anxiety and insomnia. This affected workers' morale and effectiveness, especially nightworkers; in addition, the underground stations used as bomb shelters often provided unhealthy conditions.[16] As is well known, these incipient defense strategies were perfected during World War II.

On the nights of bombing runs, artificial lighting in public spaces was dimmed and the windows of houses were covered with cardboard and special opaque curtains, while the sky was brightly illuminated with reflectors. The juxtaposition of dark streets and a bright sky was an unprecedented and characteristic image of the First World War, one that would be further emphasized during the next World War. A dark urban silhouette and a sky furrowed by beams of light was how air warfare transformed the night cityscape. As Asan Mond states, this physical manifestation was also accompanied by a new soundscape. Public clocks – such as Big Ben, the most famous symbol of London – were silenced, giving the city a new temporal dimension during the night. But when the raids arrived, the stillness and silence became rumbling and tumult in the street, the sounds of broken glass, screams and cries, shots: the sound of panic – a transformation of the soundscape.[17]

As Virginia Woolf recalls in her diaries, the contrast between empty streets and crowded train stations were part of London's nightlife.[18] Victoria and Waterloo stations became centers of prostitution where impoverished women entertained men going to or returning from the front. The blackout regime considered severe restrictions on pub closing hours to limit alcohol consumption – which had increased – and improve labour productivity, while cinemas tripled their audience. A feeling of carpe diem floated over the city.[19]

The reactions to Zeppelin raids in Britain[20] (as in France) were "typified by a doubleness: the intertwined aspects of threat and spectacle, fascination and dread."[21] During and after the war, the cultural responses reflect this ambivalence, as in Violet Hunt and Ford Madox Hueffer's *Zeppelin Nights* (1917) – an updated version of Boccaccio's *Decameron* based in a London cellar. Similarly, in John Buchan's *Mr Standfast* (1919), the crowd were "torn between fear of their lives and interest in the spectacle."[22]

In the private sphere, the night bombings also had an effect on daily routines. Bedtime was pushed back and even the most private of places, the bedroom and the bed, underwent changes. Many people had a medical kit ready in their bedroom, to be used if it became necessary. As Lucy Adlington explains, a more unexpected and unintended effect was "Zeppelin fashion," the commercial promotion of women's silk jacket and pants pajamas. These upscale pajamas were sought after items since during an attack a house had to be evacuated quickly.[23] The society magazine *The Tatler* reflected on these practices when it featured an illustration of a woman running in smart pajamas, while an illuminated Zeppelin can be seen through the window.[24] Such widespread commercial use of the image of the Zeppelin also reveals a prevanlent impetus to trivialize death in the midst of great suffering.

Representation

As historian Guillaume de Syon has argued, World War I was fought not only with new industrial weapons, such as Zeppelins, but also with a plethora of popular images and ephemera, such as cartoons, posters and postcards. In such illustrations, aircraft as a theme abounded, alongside messages of mixed anger and humour.[25] After the first bombings, propaganda began from both sides. Among the Allies, the Zeppelin was a symbol of German brutality. The representation of the night raid (a Zeppelin illuminated by searchlights) served to involve the public in the war's cause, from posters for recruitment to the promotion of the use of underground shelters, even sales of special insurance against material damage.

In Germany, by contrast, the Zeppelin was presented as a means to break the stagnation of the trenches and as a symbol of aerial supremacy.[26] The artist Arthur Thiele produced a series of postcards with the pre-war leitmotiv *Zeppelin Kommt!* ("The Zeppelin is coming!") that show the German population cheerfully greeting the passage of such aircraft through their town during the day. After the first bombings of London and Paris, the same artist used this leitmotiv to illustrate scenes of panic and night chaos among Londoners, who were shown hurriedly trying to go down into the sewers or metro stations. Parisians were depicted climbing inside a fountain or, in awe of the spectacle, colliding with a car.[27] There were also an abundance of German postcards with the themes *Über London* (often accompanied by the faces of Count von Zeppelin), and *Gott Strafe England!* ("God punish England") – that divinized the aircraft as half God, half animal. On other side of the English Channel, the Zeppelin was ridiculed by British cartoonists as an animal in the form of a pig, whale or wiener dog (*dachshund*).[28]

Figure 6.2: London in War Time: Piccadilly Circus and St. Pauls. Postcards c.1915. Author's collection.

In addition, a series of special postcards, such as *London in War Time,* showed different areas of the city obscured or with low-intensity light, but with active searchlights. Such images of lights travelling the sky in search of aircraft illustrates how the city turned into a battlefield. [fig. 6.2]. However, just as commonplace are representations of civilians contemplating, from their house's window or balcony, the night visits of the Zeppelin as a fascinating distant spectacle, rather than a source of terror. The bombings were even used as a commercial incentive for tourism during holiday periods, as in the publicity of the English railroad company: "Be in the movement and go to Northend-on Sea: Frequent Zeppelin Displays" (July 1915).[29] "During leisure time (holidays) we continue to attend the theater of war but now as the passive audience of the great spectacle of destruction."

The Mobilization of Children

In the context of total war and the involvement of civilians as targets, the mobilization of children took place through publications (the *War Books for the Youth*), toys, and school lessons. In the pre-war years, popular fascination with the flying machine played a role in nationalist agendas. Representations of children and Zeppelins during the war were closely associated with a child's supposed relationship to aviation writ large. As de Syon noted, flight was infantilized to help adults accept the new technology's unprecedented destructive power.[30] But, at the same time, it reinforced what historian George Mosse has called the trivialization of war.[31]

Furthermore, the war modified teaching content on both sides of the conflict, and children were instructed in the pedagogy of war by studying war maps, the position of troops, and the evolution of the latest battles. Patriotic songs were sung and children read poems. Children even had to write essays and diaries about their war experience, and classroom walls were filled with maps, photographs of aircrafts, Zeppelins, submarines, and battle drawings.[32] New technologies were a topic of interest among children, and Zeppelins held particular allure for boys. Indeed, the fascination with the airship was so great that during the war people thought that any aircraft in the sky was a Zeppelin.[33]

The influence of official propaganda became noticeable in the works of children, who hated the enemy and anticipated victories. The essay "How I made a nightly attack on London with my Zeppelin" (1915), written and drawn by I. Biberl, a student at a secondary school in Graz, Austria, explains a bombardment with three Zeppelins and six planes, and the triumphant return to the base in Antwerp, Belgium.[34] The reality of the destruction of the city became a playful and exciting matter, empty of meaning. While some games for children were inspired by real events, even if they were not, the memory and thinking of young people were nonetheless indoctrinated through these invented victories. Even so, while the initial euphoria among the young for the war was widespread, it devolved into tiredness and exhaustion. Classes were cancelled and the heroism depicted in drawings and essays gave way to representations of horror and death.[35]

Moreover, while the drawings of German children at the beginning of the war were often dedicated to airships destroying cities at night, in French schools the motif had always been the opposite: the destruction of the Zeppelin, trapped in the net of the light beams of searchlights. While German children played at bombing London with toy Zeppelins, by 1916 in England games such as *Bombarding the Zepps* and *The Anti-Zepp* were created.[36]

The Raids in Paris

The bombings of Paris were carried out mainly with airplanes and artillery, but two raids did involve Zeppelins. The first raid, conducted by four Zeppelins on the night of March 20, 1915, produced extensive material damage. In the second, on the night of January 29, 1916, a Zeppelin dropped 17 bombs on Paris, killing 26 and wounding 41.[37] A few days after the raid, *Le Journal* published practical advice on protecting oneself if the Zeppelin returned. These included being alert for warning signs, not meeting in groups and on first floors, ways to put out a fire, and the use of metro stations as a refuge.[38]

Far from creating collective panic, the first bombings in Paris generated great curiosity, and Parisians went out to public spaces with chairs and binoculars to observe the sky.[39] An illustration depicting viewers watching the sky from Montmartre, published in *The Graphic* in 1916, stated:

> As soon as the 'garde à vous' of the firemen resounds through Paris there is a general stampede to the Butte Montmartre to see the Zeppelins … [This] is a splendid coign of vantage for observers. Everybody climbs as high as possible – on roofs, ladders or tables.[40]

It seemed that for Parisians the Zeppelin was not yet a deadly weapon but a spectacle. The pre-war attraction towards aircraft partly continued during the conflict, and reactions were often a mixture between fascination and repulsion.[41] For Marcel Proust, the Zeppelin raids in Paris looked like a Wagnerian *Valkyrie* produced by sirens, squadrons, and the relentless movement of lights in search of the enemy. One could have a good view of this "piece of great aesthetic beauty" as if going to the theater to see a celestial technological ballet. Proust stated, "in some ways the simile was not misleading. The town from being a black shapeless mass seemed suddenly to rise out of the abyss and the night into the luminous sky."[42] The relationship suggested by Proust – between the music of Wagner and Paris in terms of the nocturnal visit of the Zeppelins – conceived of total war as a total work of art. Famously this idea was glorified by Ernst Jünger in his war novel *The Storm of Steel* (1920) and his piece *Total Mobilization* (1930).[43]

The Russian poet Maximilian Voloshin was perhaps the only one who gave a simultaneous written and painted expression of the Zeppelins over the sky of Paris. Voloshin published a poem and a drawing entitled *Les Zeppelins sur Paris* in *L'Élan*, the Cubist war magazine founded by Amédée Ozenfant in 1915.[44] The drawing follows the same scheme as most representations: in the lower half, the dark silhouette of the city, and at the top, the sky with the Zeppelin illuminated by two searchlights. This double expression of the writer (the illustrated poem) shows that the Zeppelin theme is fundamentally visual.

Although the Zeppelin raids in Paris were insignificant compared to those in London, they produced other popular representations. A 1915 souvenir, *Les Zeppelins sur Paris*, consists of a "[t]ableu en profondeur avec plans intermediaires pouvant se poser sur un meuble." It is a diorama composed of three pieces of cardboard that fit together to create a three-dimensional canvas. The main drawing shows the city skyline with the Eiffel Tower lighting up three Zeppelins. It is combined with two drawings that show Parisians in the windows and on roofs of the buildings, saluting, oblivious to danger, making mocking gestures, and observing the sky with telescopes or binoculars.[45] The visit of the Zeppelins even provoked musical compositions, such as Claude Rohand's piano piece, *Bochade nocturne* (1915). The piece features an illustration by Edouard Halouze that captures the scene of an illuminated Zeppelin and a family in pajamas (mom, dad, two children, a domestic servant and a cat) enjoying the show from their house's balcony [fig. 6.3].[46] Thus the sky became the

Figure 6.3: "Bochade nocturne pour piano par Claude Rohand" (music sheet). Illustration by Édouard Halouze, 1915. <imagesmusicales.be>

location of a daily night show, like a big screen, and a balcony or window, the comfortable place from which to enjoy it: "And to think that after the war we will have to pay to see the aircraft!" remarked one woman to another, while lying in an armchair on her Parisian balcony. Interestingly, this fascination with the illuminated sky of Paris also led to suspicions of espionage. Parisians denounced dubious lights, signals, and headlights coming from the roofs of neighboring houses, any of which could be leading German planes.[47]

The 1920s: Illuminated Heavens as Mass Spectacles

In the interwar period there was an awareness of being held in suspense between the horrors of the past and a possible future war. The psychological effects on citizens did not end with the conclusion of the war: in the war's aftermath, imagining that a sudden noise could be an explosion, or that a dark object in the sky was a Zeppelin, signaled the reorganization of perceptual reflections caused by the bombings.[48] A predisposition to see and hear things in the light of recent past violence was common and a transformation of the daily urban landscape had clearly taken place; its sounds and images were rewritten under the sign of the raid.

According to German scholar Janet Ward, electric light advertising played a crucial role in national self-promotion in the Weimar Republic, and as early as 1918 one saw the beginnings of a new battle – of materials derived from recycled war technology.[49] The electric lighting of the metropolis as a spectacular advertisement with an inherited psychological identity from the Great War (the aesthetics of shock, urban expressionism with its agonies and ecstasies, and graphic visual propaganda) played a key role in the advertising discourse of public space due to the German need for international acceptance. The residual transference of aerial battle scenes to the illuminated metropolis are found – for example – in the night tours of commercial airplanes during light festivals (a practice that allowed the air ministry to keep pilots trained) or even in the reappearance of the Zeppelin – after its conversion into a commercial aircraft covering international routes[50] – in the skies over world's fairs.

For the cultural critic Siegfried Kracauer, the forms of entertainment favoured by Weimar Germany's new Taylorized middle and working classes coincided with a psychological need for metropolitan distractions on the same scale.[51] In Berlin's Lunapark, he noted that entertainment was organized according to the rules of the production line and that searchlights continued to play a role alongside military music, even though the war was over.[52] After the war, the use of searchlights also found intensive aesthetic use in several engineering meetings and military demonstrations, activities that were often intermingled.[53] For example, at the sixteenth annual convention of the Illuminating Engineering Society held in Swampscott, Massachusetts in 1922, the US Army operated a battery of big searchlights against the dark sky, so placed that they formed the initials of the society "I.E.S." in a fiery red color.[54] On both sides of the Atlantic during the 1920s, the US Army, the Royal Air Force, and their respective naval fleets carried out multiple demonstrations using increasingly powerful searchlights, while newspapers and illustrated magazines amplified the worldwide circulation of these light shows.[55]

During the 1925 British Imperial Exhibition in the grounds of Wembley, a simulation of the bombings on London was organized. Entitled *London Defended* and performed between May 9 and June 1, commentators deemed it "a stirring torchlight and searchlight spectacle."[56] Large-scale war games became even more commonplace during the 1930s, and were wildly popular. *London Defended* recalls the confetti bombing of Los Angeles with an airship in 1908, and preceded, among other military spectacles, the incredible reenactment of the dropping of the atomic bomb performed at the Los Angeles Coliseum on October 27, 1945, just two and a half months after the bombing of Hiroshima.[57] Such total destruction performances recall the final comment of Walter Benjamin in his essay on the work of art: "mankind, turned into a spectacle of itself, experienced its own destruction as a supreme aesthetic pleasure."[58]

In the field of exhibitions, D'Arcy Ryan's "scintillator" operated at the Centennial Exposition of Brazil in Rio de Janeiro between 1922 and 1923 and at the 1929 Edison Golden Jubilee. A similar system was presented at Philadelphia's 1926 Sesqui-Centennial Exposition, with fourteen high-intensity searchlights supplied by the US Army.[59] From the second half of the 1920s, various festivals of light (termed light holidays or light weeks) were held across Europe, transfiguring nocturnal cities. One of the most important was 1928's *Berlin im Licht*[60] which featured different installations, such as luminous sculptures, a light baldachin, and a tower. Though the project remained unbuilt, the Russian artist Naum Gabo proposed a group of wooden constructions equipped with strictly vertically oriented searchlights, whose light beams could themselves create different formal and spatial configurations.[61]

In any case, this chapter of history is less one of individual geniuses than of multiple and anonymous collaborations[62] (engineering teams, the military and politicians, architects and cultural agents). It is also one of unstoppable technological development and increasingly monumental spectacles. "First in the US, next in Europe, searchlights enter the culture of architecture, advertising and communications … invade the realm of spectacle from stadium performances to mass pageants to new distinctively industrial era forms of religious practice and political showmanship," writes cultural historian Jeffrey Schnapp.[63] Schnapp further explains "public spaces expand vastly during the 1930s as they become networked and electrified." They expand not only in the physical sense, but also in the sensorial and networked sense.[64] In addition, illuminated monuments were erected on colossal scales, from *Cristo Redentor* (1931) in Rio de Janeiro to the Morelos statue built on Janitzio Island in Michoacán, Mexico (1934). Nearly forgotten today, the Columbus Memorial Lighthouse project in Santo Domingo (1928–1930) was one of the most important international competitions during the interwar period. In partnership with the *Chicago Tribune*, the winner, Joseph Lea Gleave, designed a giant cross projected in light onto the night sky to guide airplanes and airships.[65]

The Zeppelin Returns

During the war, spectacular representations of the battles on the home front as entertainment proliferated. A paradigmatic example is the famous Sarrasani Circus in Dresden, which successfully combined traditional circus attractions (animals and acrobats, among other elements) with the use of new technologies (such as film projections and war machines). From 1915, the circus produced *Europa in Flammen*, a war game with real war equipment. Between June and September 1918, the Sarrasani Circus organized its most monumental show in Berlin; *Torpedo-los!* staged the explosion of a shipyard, an underwater war, and the bombing of London with Zeppelins.[66] The war in the trenches was recreated as a circus on the home front.

It took just over ten years after the armistice until Hollywood producers began recreating the spectacular scenes of night bombings over London. The first movie to reflect on the bombing war was *Sky Hawk* (John G. Blystone, 1929) and later *Hell's Angels* (Howard Hughes, 1930).[67] *Sky Hawk* was one of the first aviation films with sound.[68] It tells the story of a British aviator who manages to bring down a Zeppelin. The climax of the film is the Zeppelin bombardment sequence. To capture this scene, the special effects coordinator Ralph Hammeras, a pioneer in techniques and effects for the film industry, designed a giant 30 × 60 meter model of London[69] in the hangar of the Fox Studios airfield, and used mechanical and lighting effects, a model Zeppelin, and miniature airplanes amid clouds, as well as fog created in the studio.[70] The night bombing scene in *Sky Hawk* is the closest recreation of the real attacks over London made in that period.

The posters that publicized the film illustrate the night battle between the fighters and the Zeppelin with headlines such as "Sirens screaming! Stupendous searchlights slashing London's black night! A titan dirigible, bomb laden … the mighty metropolis … six million people terrified." The drama suffered by civilians in war was used as raw material for the entertainment of the masses. The poster designed by Eric Rohman to advertise the premiere of the film in Sweden as *Luftens Ornar* is also of relevance and was inspired by the original Hollywood poster. It shows the dark profile of a city in two planes, and a Zeppelin and airplanes amid the beams of the searchlights [fig. 6.4].

Figure 6.4: *The Sky Hawk*. Swedish movie poster by Eric Rohman, 1929. <ha.com>

While the cinema reproduced scenes of the illuminated Zeppelin over the city, the real action took place simultaneously in the city of Barcelona, on the occasion of the International Exhibition. The so-called German Week was celebrated between October 19–25, 1929, and the climax of this celebration was the arrival of the Graf Zeppelin. The airship arrived at noon on October 23. At night it reappeared unexpectedly over the gardens of the exhibition while the searchlights of the National Palace focused on it, producing an unprecedented light show. The play of lights was completed with the reflector of the Königsberg cruise ship docked at port, which had arrived in Barcelona especially for the occasion: "Above the light fires of the Exhibition, the Zeppelin, silvered by the searchlights, looked like a huge fish swimming over the blue sea of the sky," a journalist wrote.[71] This was a war landscape in peacetime.

Epilogue

World War I confirmed the triumph of aviation as a technology for the destruction of cities and the night as a preferred space-time for the bombing, which had consequences in different everyday environments (schedules, habits, psychology, among others). It entailed the visual and sonic transformation of the night-time urban landscape into that of a darkened city and an intensely illuminated sky set in silent suspense, waiting for the appearance of enemy aircraft. The peculiar shape of Zeppelins floating in a darkly illuminated sky had been an image of fiction exploited in the years before the war (mainly since the end of the nineteenth century). During World War I they became a testimonial representation of the first systematic bombardments of civilians. Such scenes began to be used commercially even during the conflict. In the interwar period they were transformed into pure spectacle and advertising, even fashion and toys. As Walter Benjamin famously put it, these were documents of culture at the same time as they were documents of barbarism.[72]

Figure 6.5: "Wonderful supra-oceanic landscape, seemingly chimerical but brimming with upcoming realities." Illustration by Bocquet, in *La Ilustración Iberoamericana*, 1930. Author's collection.

Using the logic of the record, the same night-time spectacle could also be indefinitely repeated. A postcard of a transoceanic nightscape populated by illuminated monuments and floating islands in the middle of the Atlantic represents the aestheticization of night bombings at the beginning of the 1930s. Search lights guide airplanes and Zeppelins once again [fig. 6.5]: "Mankind is preparing to outlive culture … and the main thing is that it does so with a laugh," Benjamin noted.[73]

Notes

1   "Los Angeles Attacked from Airship," Popular Mechanics, February 1909, pp. 151–2.

2   Robert Wohl, The Spectacle of Flight: Aviation and the Western Imagination, 1920–1940 (New Haven: Yale University Press, 2005).

3   H. G. Wells, The War in the Air, and Particularly How Mr. Bert Smallways Fared While it Lasted (London: George Bell and Sons, 1908).

4   Sven Lindqvist, A History of Bombing (New York: The New Press, 2000), 39.

5   Roger Chickering and Stig Förster, eds., Great War, Total War: Combat and Mobilization on the Western Front, 1914–1918 (Cambridge: Cambridge University Press, 2000), 35.

6   Wolfgang Schivelbusch, Disenchanted Night: The Industrialization of Light in the Nineteenth Century (Los Angeles: University of California Press, 1998), 50.

7   Friedrich Kittler, "A Short History of the Searchlight," Cultural Politics 11, no. 3 (2015): 384–90; see 387.

8   See "In the Searchlight," Punch, or the London Charivari, January 20, 1915, p. 47.

9   K. G. Beauchamp, Exhibiting Electricity (London: Institution of Electrical Engineers, 1997), 137.

10   Stephen Kern, The Culture of Time and Space, 1880–1918, 2nd ed. (Cambridge, Mass.: Harvard University Press, 2003), 6–7.

11   See An Alphabet of War (London: Jarrold and Sons, 1915). Other War Alphabets also used the letter Z for the Zeppelin, see Olivier d'Allard, Alphabet de la Guerre pour les grands et les petits (Brussels: Maurice Lamertin, 1920); Henri Lanos, Alphabet de la Guerre (Paris: Hachette, 1916).

12   On fear and bombings, see Brett Holman, The Next War in the Air – Britain's Fear of the Bomber, 1908–1941 (London: Ashgate, 2014); Michele, Haapamäki, The Coming of the Aerial War: Culture and the Fear of Airborne Attack in Inter-War Britain (London: Tauris, 2014).

13   For a good synthesis of the Zeppelin raids, see Martin Gilbert, "The War in the Air," in The Routledge Atlas of the First World War, 3rd ed. (London and New York: Routledge, 2009), 64–73.

14   Marc Wiggam, The Blackout in Britain and Germany, 1939–1945 (Cham: Springer, 2018), 12–5.

15   The project was conceived by the engineer Fernand Jacopozzi. See Xavier Boissel, Paris est un leure: La véritable histoire du faux Paris (Paris: Inculte, 2012).

16   Thomas Fegans, The Baby Killers: German Air Raids on Britain in the First World War (Barnsley: Pen and Sword, 2002), 45.

17   Assaf Mond, "'It is at night-time that we notice most of the changes in our life caused by the war': War-time, Zeppelins, and Children's Experience of the Great War in London," in War Time: First World War Perspectives on Temporality, ed. Louis Halewwod, Adam Luptak, and Hanna Smyth (London: Routledge, 2018), 91–110; see 95–6, 98.

18   Ariela Freedman, "Zeppelin Fictions and the British Home Front," Journal of Modern Literature 27, no. 3 (2004): 47–62; see 52.

19   See Jerry White, Zeppelin Nights: London in the First World War (London: Bodley Head, 2014).

20   On Britain's responses to the initial air raids, see Susan R. Grayzel, At Home and under Fire: Air Raids and Culture in Britain from the Great War to the Blitz (Cambridge: Cambridge University Press, 2012), 20–63.

21   Leo Mellor, Reading the Ruins: Modernism, Bombsites and British Culture (Cambridge: Cambridge University Press, 2011), 14.

22   Quoted by Mellor, Reading the Ruins, 15.

23   Lucy Adlington, Great War Fashion: Tales from the History Wardrobe (Stroud, Gloucestershire: The History Press, 2013).

24   The illustration "Pyjamas suitable for Zeppelin raids" by Olive Hewerdine was published in The Tatler, October 27, 1915.

25   Guillaume de Syon, Zeppelin!: Germany and the Airship, 1900–1939 (Baltimore: The Johns Hopkins University Press, 2002), 88.

26   Peter Fritzsche, A Nation of Fliers: German Aviation and the Popular Imagination (Cambridge, Mass.: Harvard University Press, 1992).

27   This postcards included a patriotic song on the back to terrify Londoners. See David Marks, Let the Zeppelins Come (Stroud, Gloucestershire: Amberley Publishing, 2017), 33, 37.

28   Mark Bryant, "Flying Pigs and Cabbage Crates: Zeppelins and Other Aircraft of World War I in Cartoons," Revue Roumaine d'Histoire de l'Art. Serie Beaux-Arts 53 (2006): 101–9.

29   See Punch, July 7, 1915, p. 23.

30   Guillaume de Syon, "The Child in the Flying Machine: Childhood and Aviation in the First World War," in Children and War, ed. James Marten (New York: New York University Press, 2002), 116–34; see 116.

31   George L. Mosse, Fallen Soldiers: Reshaping the Memory of the World Wars (Oxford: Oxford University Press, 1990), 126–56.

32   Carolyn Kay, "War Pedagogy in the German Primary School Classroom During the First World War," War & Society 33, no. 1 (February 2014): 3–11.

33   De Syon, Zeppelin!, 103.

34   Judith Fritz, "The Politicization and Mobilization of School Children," online exhibition "The First World War and the End of the Habsburg Monarchy," accessed August 15, 2021, <https://ww1.habsburger.net/en/chapters/school-front>; Stacy Gillis and Emma Short, "Children's experiences of World War One," The British Library, accessed January 29, 2014, <https://www.bl.uk/world-war-one/articles/childrens-experiences-of-world-war-one#>.

35   Helmut E. Lück and Miriam Rothe, "Kinder erleben den Weltkrieg: Empirische Untersuchungen zu Beginn des Krieges," Journal für Psychologie 25 (2017): 111–42.

36   Sonja Müller, "Toys, Games and Juvenile Literature in Germany and Britain during the First World War. A Comparison," in Untold War: New Perspectives in First World War Studies, ed. Heather Jones, Jennifer O'Brien, and Christoph Schmidt-Supprian (Leiden and Boston: Brill, 2008), 249.

37   During the conflict, a total of 702 projectiles were launched on Paris, causing 869 civilian victims, of whom 265 died.

38   Lucien Chassaigne, "Si le Zeppelin revenait … Les leçons du raid: Quelques conseils pratiques pour se protéger, " Le Journal, February 4, 1916, p. 1.

39   The British journalist Helen Pearl Adam wrote: "Our first Zeppelin raid was on March 21, and caused great excitement but no panic." See Helen Pearl Adam, Paris Sees it Through: A Diary, 1914–1919 (London: Hodder and Stoughton, 1919), 52.

40   "Paris in War-Time: A Zeppelin Night on the Butte Montmartre," Graphic, February 12, 1916, p. 221.

41   For some reactions in a humorous way in Paris, see "A Night with the Zeppelins as personally experienced by the Bystander in Paris," Bystander, March 31, 1915, pp. 444–5.

42   Marcel Proust, In Search of Lost Time, vol. 6, Time Regained, trans. Andreas Mayor and Terence Kilmartin (New York: Modern Library, 2000), 99.

43   The war as total work of art was an idea conceived by the Italian futurist Filippo Tomasso Marinetti before the Great War. On Jünger's idea of the war as a "captivating spectacle," see Jeffrey Herf, Reactionary Modernism: Technology, Culture, and Politics in Weimar and the Third Reich (Cambridge: Cambridge University Press, 1986), 70–108.

44   Maximilien Volochin, "Les Zeppelins sur Paris, " L'Élan 5, June 15, 1915, pp. 3–4.

45   Colored lithography on cardboard, attributed to Georges Morinet; Pellerin & Cie, Epinal, 1915. 14/18 L'enfant découpait des images, ed. Martine Sadion (Epinal: Musée de l'image, 2014), 228–9.

46   Bochade nocturne pour piano par Claude Rohand, Paris: Marcel Lion Editeur, 1915. "M. Claude Rohand viente d'éditer, en souvenir de la première nuit du printemps 1915, où les zeppelins nous rendirente visite, une Bouchade nocturne, fantaisie musicale, dont les bénéfices de la vente serviront à secourir nos soldats blessés." Excelsior: Journal Illustré Quotidien, September 10, 1915, p. 10.

47   See André Loez, "'Lumières suspectes' sur ciel obscur: La recherche des espions et le spectacle de la guerre dans Paris bombardé en 1914–1918," in Vrai et faux dans la Grande Guerre, ed. Christophe Rochasson and Anne Rasmussen (Paris: La Découverte, 2004), 166–88.

48   Paul K. Saint-Amour, "Air War Prophecy and Interwar Modernism," Comparative Literature Studies 42, no. 2 (2005): 130–61; see 140–1.

49   Janet Ward, Weimar Surfaces: Urban Visual Culture in 1920s Germany (Berkeley: University of California Press, 2001), 93.

50   De Syon, Zeppelin!, Chapter 4.

51   Siegfrid Kracauer, "Cult of Distraction," in The Mass Ornament: Weimar Essays, ed. Thomas Y. Levin (Cambridge, Mass.: Harvard University Press), 323–30.

52   Ward, Weimar Surfaces, 181.

53   Jeffrey Schnapp, "Luminotectonics (An Archaeology of the Searchlight)," Perspecta 51 (2018): 7–19.

54   Bernard G. Priestley, "Largest Incandescent Lamp in the World," Popular Mechanics 38, no. 6 (December 1922): 841–2.

55   See, for instance, "Monster Searchlights Are Eyes of Fleet," Popular Mechanics 41, no. 2 (February 1924): 198–200; "Fleets' Lights Transform Harbor into Fairyland," Popular Science 107, no. 6 (December 1925): 50.

56   London Defended Torchlight and Searchlight Spectacle, The Stadium Wembley May 9 to June 1, 1925 official programme (London: Fleetway Press, 1925).

57 Gene Sherman, "Coliseum Throng Views Tableau of War Scenes," Los Angeles Times, October 28, 1945, p. 2; see also Paul Boyer, By the Bomb's Early Light: American Thought and Culture at the Dawn of the Atomic Age (Chapel Hill, N.C.: University of North Carolina Press, 2005), 181.

58 Walter Benjamin, The Work of Art in the Age of its Technological Reproducibility, and Other Writings on Media, ed. M. W. Jennings, B. Doherty, and T. Y. Levin (Cambridge, Mass.: Harvard University Press, 2008), 42.

59 Dietrich Neumann, Architecture of the Night: The Illuminated Building (Munich: Prestel, 2002), 122; Schnapp, "Luminotectonics," 17.

60 Berlin im Licht: 13. Bis 16 Oktober 1928. Festprogramm mit Lichtfürher durch Berlin (Berlin: R. Mosse, 1928).

61 The design was published in Bauhaus magazine. See Naum Gabo, "Gestaltung?" Bauhaus 2, no. 4 (1928): 2–6. Gabo's design is on p. 6.

62 Neumann, Architecture of the Night, 45.

63 Jeffrey T. Schnapp, "Projections: Some Notes on Public Space in the 1930s," in Encounters with the 30s, ed. Jordana Mendelson (Madrid: La Fábrica, Museo Nacional Centro de arte Reina Sofía, 2012), 32.

64 Ibid., 31.

65 Albert Kelsey, Program and Rules of the Second Competition for the Selection of an Architect for the Monumental Lighthouse… (Pan American Union, 1930). See also Robert Alexander González, Designing Pan-America: U.S. Architectural Visions for the Western Hemisphere (Austin: University of Texas Press, 2011), Chapter 3.

66 Eva Krivanec, "Staging War: Theatre, 1914–1918," in 1914–1918 Online. International Encyclopedia of the First World War, ed. Ute Daniel et al. (Berlin: Freie Universität Berlin, 2014), <https://encyclopedia.1914-1918-online.net/article/staging_war_theatre_1914-1918>.

67 The Hell's Angels production cost $4 million, the most important investment until 1940. Although it shows a battle scene between airplanes and the Zeppelin, the panorama of the city with the Zeppelin in focus does not appear. On the montage for this scene, recorded in the same hangar as the Sky Hawk, see Dick Cole, "Crashing a Zeppelin for fun," Modern Mechanix, May 1931, pp. 76–9.

68 The film was produced by Fox Film Corporation and premiered on December 11, 1929 in New York. When 20th Century Fox was created in 1935, artist Emil Kosa Jr. painted a monumental monolith amidst searchlights as a logo.

69 The model cost about $20,000.

70 Stephen Pendo, Aviation in the Cinema (Metuchen, N.J.: Scarecrow Press, 1985), 83–4.

71 "El 'Conde Zeppelin' en Barcelona," La Vanguardia, October 24, 1929, p. 6.

72 Walter Benjamin, "On the concept of History," in Selected Writings, vol. 4, 1938–1940, ed. Howard Eiland and Michael W. Jennings (Cambridge, Mass.: Belknap Press of Harvard University Press, 2003), 389–400.

73 Walter Benjamin, "Experience and Poverty," in Selected Writings, vol. 2, pt. 2, 1931–1934, ed. Michael W. Jennings, Howard Eiland, and Gary Smith, trans. Rodney Livingstone et al. (Cambridge, Mass.: Belknap Press of Harvard University Press, 1999), 735.

Bibliography

Adlington, Lucy. *Great War Fashion, Tales from the History Wardrobe*. Stroud, Gloucestershire: The History Press, 2013.

An Alphabet of War. London: Jarrold and Sons, 1915.

d'Allard, Olivier. *Alphabet de la Guerre pour les grands et les petits*. Brussels: Maurice Lamertin, 1920.

Beauchamp, K. G. *Exhibiting Electricity*. London: Institution of Electrical Engineers, 1997.

Benjamin, Walter. *Selected Writings*. Vol. 2, Pt. 2, *1931–1934*. Edited by Michael W. Jennings, Howard Eiland, and Gary Smith. Translated by Rodney Livingstone et al. Cambridge, Mass.: The Belknap Press of Harvard University Press, 1999.

———.*Selected Writings*. Vol. 4, *1938–1940*. Edited by Howard Eiland and Michael W. Jennings. Cambridge, Mass.: The Belknap Press of Harvard University Press, 2003.

———.*The Work of Art in the Age of Its Technological Reproductibility, and Other Writings on Media*. Edited by Michael W. Jennings, Brigid Doherty, and Thomas Y. Levin. Cambridge, Mass.: The Belknap Press of Harvard University Press, 2008.

Berlin im Licht: 13. Bis 16 Oktober 1928. Festprogramm mit Lichtfürher durch Berlin. Berlin: R. Mosse, 1928.

Boissel, Xavier. *Paris est un leure: La véritable histoire du faux Paris*. Paris: Éditions Inculte, 2012.

Boyer, Paul. *By the Bomb's Early Light: American Thought and Culture at the Dawn of the Atomic Age*. Chapel Hill, N.C.: University of North Carolina Press, 2005.

Bryant, Mark. "Flying Pigs and Cabbage Crates. Zeppelins and Other Aircraft of World War I in Cartoons." *Revue Roumaine d'Histoire de l'Art. Serie Beaux-Arts* 53 (2006): 101–9.

Chassaigne, Lucien. "Si le Zeppelin revenait … Les leçons du raid: Quelques conseils pratiques pour se protéger." *Le Journal,* February 4, 1916.

Chickering, Roger, and Stig Förster, eds. *Great War, Total War: Combat and Mobilization on the Western Front, 1914–1918*. Cambridge: Cambridge University Press, 2000.

Cole, Dick. "Crashing a Zeppelin for fun." *Modern Mechanix*, May 1931.

"El 'Conde Zeppelin' en Barcelona." *La Vanguardia*, October 24, 1929.

Excelsior: Journal Illustré Quotidien, September 10, 1915.

Fegans, Thomas. *The Baby Killers: German Air Raids on Britain in the First World War*. Barnsley: Pen and Sword, 2002.

"Fleets' Lights Transform Harbor into Fairyland." *Popular Science* 107, no. 6 (December 1925).

Fritz, Judith. "The politicization and mobilization of school children." Online exhibition "The First World War and the End of the Habsburg Monarchy." Accessed August 15, 2021. <https://ww1.habsburger.net/en/chapters/school-front>

Fritzsche, Peter. *A Nation of Fliers: German Aviation and the Popular Imagination*. Cambridge, Mass.: Harvard University Press, 1992.

Freedman, Ariela. "Zeppelin Fictions and the British Home Front." *Journal of Modern Literature* 27, no. 3 (2004): 47–62.

Gabo, Naum. "Gestaltung?" *Bauhaus* 2, no. 4 (1928): 2–6.

Gilbert, Martin. *The Routledge Atlas of the First World War*. London and New York: Routledge, 2009.

Gillis, Stacy, and Emma Short. "Children's experiences of World War One." The British Library. Accessed January 29, 2014. <https://www.bl.uk/world-war-one/articles/childrens-experiences-of-world-war-one#>

Grayzel, Susan R. *At Home and under Fire: Air Raids and Culture in Britain from the Great War to the Blitz.* Cambridge: Cambridge University Press, 2012.

Haapamäki, Michele. *The Coming of the Aerial War: Culture and the Fear of Airborne Attack in Inter-War Britain.* London: Tauris, 2014.

Herf, Jeffrey. *Reactionary Modernism: Technology, Culture, and Politics in Weimar and the Third Reich.* Cambridge: Cambridge University Press, 1986.

Holman, Brett. *The Next War in the Air – Britain's Fear of the Bomber, 1908–1941.* London: Ashgate, 2014.

"In the Searchlight." *Punch, or the London Charivari,* January 20, 1915.

Kay, Carolyn. "War Pedagogy in the German Primary School Classroom during the First World War." *War & Society* 33, no. 1 (February 2014): 3–11.

Kelsey Albert. *Program and rules of the second competition for the selection of an architect for the Monumental Lighthouse, which the nations of the world will erect in the Dominican Republic to the memory of Christopher Columbus. Together with the report of the international jury, the premiated and many other designs submitted in the first contest.* Pan American Union, 1930.

Kern, Stephen. *The Culture of Time and Space, 1880–1918.* 2nd ed. Cambridge, Mass.: Harvard University Press, 2003.

Kittler, Friedrich. "A Short History of the Searchlight." *Cultural Politics* 11, no. 3 (2015): 384–90.

Krivanec, Eva. "Staging War: Theatre 1914–1918." In *1914–1918 Online. International Encyclopedia of the First World War.* <https://encyclopedia.1914-1918-online.net/article/staging_war_theatre_1914-1918>

Lanos, Henry. *Alphabet de la Guerre.* Paris: Hachette, 1916.

Lindqvist, Sven. *A History of Bombing.* New York: The New Press, 2000.

Loez, André. "'Lumières suspectes' sur ciel obscur: La recherche des espions et le spectacle de la guerre dans Paris bombardé en 1914–1919." In *Vrai et faux dans la Grande Guerre*, edited by Christophe Rochasson and Anne Rasmussen, 166–188. Paris: La Découverte, 2004.

London Defended Torchlight and Searchlight Spectacle, The Stadium Wembley May 9 to June 1, 1925 official programme. London: Fleetway Press, 1925.

"Los Angeles Attacked from Airship." *Popular Mechanics,* February 1909.

Lück, Helmut E., and Miriam Rothe. "Kinder erleben den Weltkrieg: Empirische Untersuchungen zu Beginn des Krieges." *Journal für Psychologie* 25 (2017): 111–42.

Marks, David. *Let the Zeppelins Come.* Stroud, Gloucestershire: Amberley Publishing, 2017.

Mellor, Leo. *Reading the Ruins: Modernism, Bombsites and British Culture.* Cambridge: Cambridge University Press, 2011.

Mond, Assaf. "'It is at night-time that we notice most of the changes in our life caused by the war': War-time, Zeppelins, and children's experience of the Great War in London." In *War Time: First World War Perspectives on Temporality*, edited by Louis Halewwod, Adam Luptak, and Hanna Smyth, 91–110. London: Routledge, 2018.

"Monster Searchlights Are Eyes of Fleet." *Popular Mechanics* 41, no. 2 (February 1924).

Mosse, George L. *Fallen Soldiers: Reshaping the Memory of the World Wars*. Oxford: Oxford University Press, 1990.

Müller, Sonja. "Toys, Games and Juvenile Literature in Germany and Britain during the First World War. A Comparison." In *Untold War: New Perspectives in First World War Studies*, edited by Heather Jones, Jennifer O'Brien, and Christoph Schmidt-Supprian, 233–57. Leiden and Boston: Brill, 2008.

Neumann, Dietrich. *Architecture of the Night: The Illuminated Building*. Munich: Prestel, 2002.

"A Night with the Zeppelins as personally experienced by the Bystander in Paris." *Bystander*, March 31, 1915.

"Paris in War-Time: A Zeppelin Night on the Butte Montmartre." *Graphic*, February 12, 1916.

Pendo, Stephen. *Aviation in the Cinema*. Metuchen, N.J.: Scarecrow Press, 1985.

Priestley, Bernard G. "Largest Incandescent Lamp in the World." *Popular Mechanics* 38, no. 6 (December 1922).

Proust, Marcel. *In Search of Lost Time*. Vol. 6, *Time Regained*. Translated by Andreas Mayor and Terence Kilmartin. New York: The Modern Library, 2000.

Punch, or the London Charivari, July 7, 1915.

Sadion, Martine, ed. *14/18 L'enfant découpait des images*. Epinal: Musée de l'image, 2014.

Saint-Amour, Paul K. "Air War Prophecy and Interwar Modernism." *Comparative Literature Studies* 42, no. 2 (2005): 130–61.

Schivelbusch, Wolfgang. *Disenchanted Night: The industrialization of light in the nineteenth century*. Los Angeles: University of California Press, 1998.

Schlör, Joachim. *Nights in the Big City: Paris, Berlin, London, 1840–1930*. London: Reaktion Books, 1998.

Schnapp, Jeffrey. "Luminotectonics (An Archeology of the Searchlight)." *Perspecta* 51 (2018): 7–19.

———. "Projections: Some Notes on Public Space in the 1930s." In *Encounters with the 30s*, edited by Jordana Mendelson, 30–9. Madrid: Museo Nacional Centro de Arte Reina Sofía, La Fábrica, 2012.

Sherman, Gene. "Coliseum Throng Views Tableau of War Scenes." *Los Angeles Times,* October 28, 1945.

Syon, Guillaume de. "The Child in the Flying Machine: Childhood and Aviation in the First World War." In *Children and War*, edited by James Marten, 116–34. New York: New York University Press, 2002.

———. *Zeppelin!: Germany and the Airship, 1900–1939*. Baltimore: The Johns Hopkins University Press, 2002.

Volochin, Maximilien. "Les Zeppelins sur Paris." *L'Élan* 5, June 15, 1915.

Ward, Janet. *Weimar Surfaces: Urban Visual Culture in 1920s Germany*. Berkeley: University of California Press, 2001.

Wells, H. G. *The War in the Air, and Particularly How Mr. Bert Smallways Fared While it Lasted*. London: George Bell and Sons, 1908.

White, Jerry. *Zeppelin Nights: London in the First World War*. London: Bodley Head, 2014.

Wiggam, Marc. *The Blackout in Britain and Germany, 1939–1945*. Cham: Springer, 2018.

Wohl, Robert. *The Spectacle of Flight: Aviation and the Western Imagination, 1920–1950*. New Haven: Yale University Press, 2005.

CITÉ RECONSTITUÉE

m pavil-
t disposi-
tecte qui

aux ar-

Chambre
nes agri-
ume, puis
la toiture

e Paume,
tre salles
essante.
extension
urbanis-
: Reims,
: Paris,
)écoration

n d'Har-
térêt, des
s détruits
e est ap-
ies.
droite, à
les confé-

ition du
ministère
te et qui
s détruits
0 ; à côté
plus haut
a Gouver-

ire, etc...
sitée éga-
droite en
tour, de
Concorde

où de nombreux pavillons retiennent l'attention. Une école (n° 15), une petite chapelle de
village (n° 12), une maison en nouveaux pro-
duits de ciment et dont l'intérieur est aménagé
par un de nos maîtres modernistes (n° 13), puis
une habitation en bois très simple (n° 11). Des
petites maisons en nouveaux matériaux (numé-
ros 9, 7, 5 attirent l'attention. Une maison dé-
montable (n° 8 abrite le « Bon Gîte », œuvre
excellente, puis un pavillon type colonial (nu-
méro 6) fort bien aménagé, il faut remarquer
sur un des côtés des échantillons de bois de
nos colonies qui montrent les ressources de notre domaine colonial.

Il faut aller jusqu'au bout : les Pavillons 3,
2, 1, retiennent vivement l'attention. Une exposition des machines de la ferme, actionnées
par l'électricité, mérite qu'on s'y arrête.

Sur la rampe d'accès, un bâtiment est édifié
par la « Société des Amis », Société Anglaise
bien connue de nos réfugiés, par le bien qu'elle
a déjà fait.

Le « Village France » retiendra notre attention, les pavillons sont très intéressants à visi-
ter.

Un bureau de poste où les philatélistes peuvent envoyer des correspondances dont les
timbres sont oblitérés avec la mention « Cité
Reconstituée », une cabine téléphonique publi-

que fonctionne également de 11 heures à 6 h.

Le kiosque à musique où un excellent or-
chestre dirigé par Joubert (de l'Opéra), donne
tous les jours des auditions symphoniques de
2 h. 1/2 à 5 h. 1/2. Les visiteurs peuvent se re-
poser un instant à l'Auberge Bon Accueil —
qui ne débite que des boissons hygiéniques, i:
faut pénétrer nos réfugiés de l'obligation de ne
se servir d'alcool qu'en médecine.

L'église Saint-Jean qui dresse son clocheton,
mérite une visite spéciale.

Nous entrons dans la Galerie « D » que nous
traversons en entier pour nous retrouver à no-

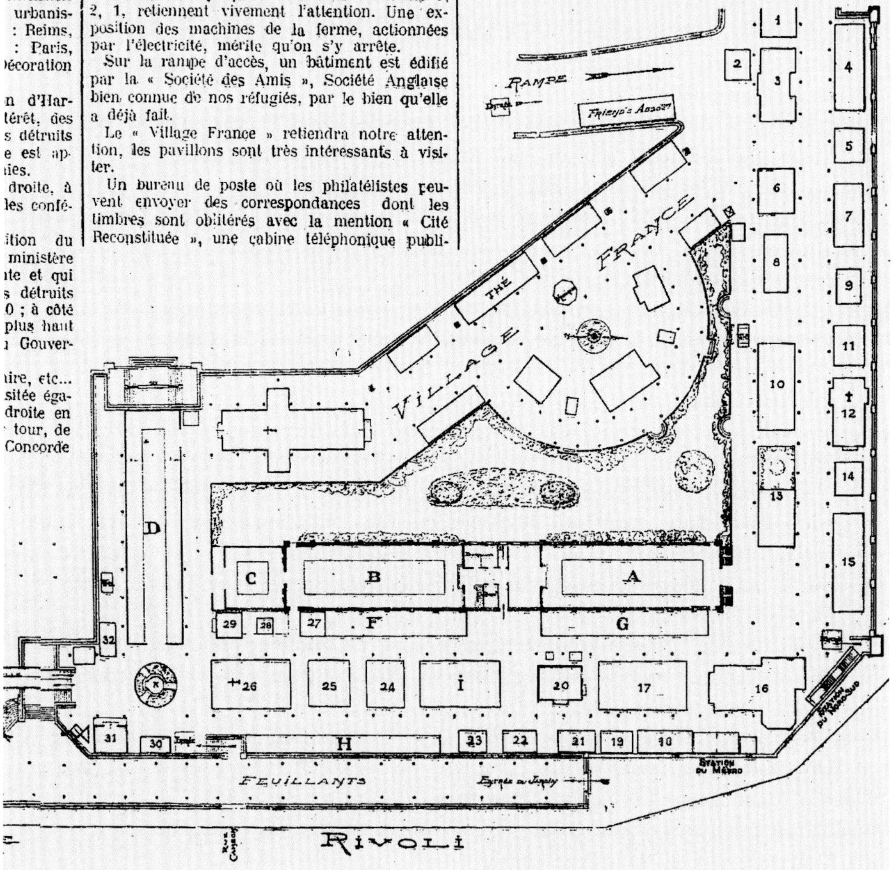

Figure 7.1: Plan of the exhibition La Cité reconstituée, 1916.
"Une Visite à la Cité reconstituée," *La Cité reconstituée* 1, no. 1 (July 2, 1916): 7.
Bibliothèque nationale de France.

Huts, Houses, and the Industrial Militarization of France, 1914–1917

Etien Santiago

On May 24, 1916, the French President Raymond Poincaré inaugurated a large exhibition in the Tuileries Gardens in Paris, directly adjoining Place de la Concorde.[1] Known as La Cité reconstituée, this exhibition focused on how to rebuild the northeastern French provinces destroyed in a brutal war that, for almost two years, had pitted the armies of France and Great Britain against those of Germany. A professional syndicate of civil engineers, the Association générale des hygiénistes et techniciens municipaux de France et des pays de la langue française, had organized La Cité reconstituée. It benefited from the "high patronage" of President Poincaré as well as no fewer than four national ministries: the Ministry of the Interior, the Ministry of Agriculture, the Ministry of Public Instruction and the Beaux-Arts, and the Ministry of Commerce, Industry, Posts and Telegraphs. A slew of high-ranking military officials and government dignitaries accordingly accompanied President Poincaré on his inaugural visit to the exhibition. That ceremonial visit put a seal on the close affiliation of La Cité reconstituée with the wartime rulers of France.

The core of La Cité reconstituée occupied the rooms of the existing Jeu de Paume exhibition building, inside which visitors could admire large drawings of urban masterplans.[2] On the walls of these rooms, leading French architects – graduates of the Parisian École de Beaux-Arts – displayed their proposals for new and improved city layouts.[3] Yet it was the jumble of different huts that encircled the Jeu de Paume, and which were put up specifically for La Cité reconstituée, that chiefly captured the attention of visitors [fig. 7.1]. Accounts of the time report that the public flocked to see the temporary huts, while generally overlooking the dusty exhibition rooms of the Jeu de Paume.[4]

These multifarious huts were not containers for additional displays, but rather objects on show as part of the exhibition. Each hut constituted a life-size sample of a house or utilitarian building that might eventually be erected in the war zone. Their inventors had scrambled to participate in La Cité reconstituée with the hope that the publicity might trigger sales of these huts during the first "emergency" phase of post-war reconstruction. A few months earlier, the French government had decreed that reconstruction would take place in two phases: a lightning-fast temporary resettlement of the devastated areas would precede a slower permanent reconstruction of their built environment with longer-lasting materials.[5] The reasoning behind the two-phase approach was that residents of the numerous towns and large territories damaged during the war should be able to repopulate these places as quickly as possible. Because the national economy relied heavily on the exploitation of these resource-rich, more thoroughly industrialized areas of France, it would suffer dearly if they were not rapidly restored to productivity following the end of hostilities. Moreover, the crushing number of refugee families that had fled the war zone was putting a strain on the French cities to which they had escaped. Mayors and prefects of unoccupied France were eager for their provisional guests to return home long before any permanent houses might be ready for them.[6] Thus, the national government deemed it necessary to prescribe and plan for a first, temporary wave of reconstruction so that the entire country could more rapidly get back on its feet after the war had ended.[7]

Most of the huts displayed at La Cité reconstituée were accordingly demountable. This followed the precedent of nineteenth-century hut-building systems, which Europeans had extensively tested in their colonies and foreign military encampments.[8] In those remote and sometimes unfamiliar locations, Europeans could not necessarily count on sufficient, dependable access to familiar materials as well as trained carpenters or masons. Colonizers and soldiers increasingly turned, throughout the nineteenth century, to demountable huts sourced from Europe as a solution to quickly erect new buildings in places they wanted to control. These huts tended to be made of modular parts prefabricated in workshops or factories in the imperial mainland, shipped across the ocean in compact packages, and then assembled in situ using unskilled labor.

Shortly after the war of 1914 began, some Frenchmen began to argue that similarly radical approaches toward construction might be necessary for the first, short-term resettlement of areas destroyed by fighting. For example, Max Ringelmann, an agricultural expert who had authored books on techniques to help French farmers settle colonial territories, redeployed his knowledge as early as 1915 toward the problem of how to repair northeastern France.[9] He found that its razed towns, fields, and forests mirrored the harsh, "undeveloped" lands of far-away colonies. The war zone, like some colonies, would also surely lack enough skilled builders as well as traditional building materials to meet internal demands once the war had ended. With its array of demountable huts, La Cité reconstituée promoted the idea that innovative technical solutions used to "better" colonize remote lands could also jumpstart the reconstruction of historically French areas ruined during the war.

This momentary equivalence between French colonies and war-torn parts of France hints at political questions that lurked behind the issue of which building systems worked best for post-war reconstruction. Because kit-of-parts huts had developed hand-in-hand with nineteenth-century colonialism and military campaigns, ideas about how to subjugate foreign territories, minds, and bodies permeated this kind of building.[10] Proposing the large-scale deployment of similar huts in areas of the imperial mainland therefore presented several conceptual problems. Would war-ravaged areas of northeastern France lose legal rights as the national government strove to expedite the first phase of reconstruction there? Would rebuilding efforts prolong the ongoing militarization and war-related industrialization of France, even after the war had ended? And finally, if the recovery zone made up of historically French lands could be equated with a colony, how might this equivalence disrupt dominant definitions of French identity and citizenship?

Although La Cité reconstituée did not explicitly address these questions, its exhibits were rife with implicit views about them. Reactions to the exhibition betray doubts about these views and apprehension that, after the war, the distribution of power in France might forever change for the worse. This essay examines how La Cité reconstituée and the responses to it grappled with political ideas latent in architectural or engineering proposals to deploy advanced building technologies to replace the thousands of edifices destroyed during the Great War.

In the past quarter-century, historians have increasingly studied events, like La Cité reconstituée, that took place on the home fronts of World War I.[11] Scholars such as Jay Winter, John Horne, and Kenneth Silver pioneered this trend with cultural histories of the war.[12] The resulting publications revealed how the conflict was fought not only on the front lines, but also in the ethereal realm of beliefs and ideas. Cultural historians have also spotlighted the wartime experiences of disenfranchised populations, whom prior scholars of the Great War often overlooked as they focused on elite military and political decision-makers.[13] Studying French reactions to La Cité reconstituée builds on contributions by cultural historians of World War I while bringing these contributions to bear on the adjoining disciplines of architectural history and construction history.

Retracing the polemic around La Cité reconstituée also reveals an important intersection between the history of modern, lightweight construction and the history of modern architecture. Historians such as Jean-Louis Cohen (in his *Architecture in Uniform: Designing and Building for the Second World War*) have already described the varied roles that architects played during World War II, a conflict that prompted many designers to explore lightweight, rapidly deployable construction systems used by armies.[14] Yet La Cité reconstituée demonstrates that architects had begun to engage with military technologies several decades earlier, during World War I.[15] Those encounters laid the groundwork for the well-documented proliferation, during the 1920s and 1930s, of architectural designs tied to the latest highly mechanized forms of construction.[16] At La Cité reconstituée, a heated French debate about the pros and cons of wartime governmental power became tacitly enmeshed with French attempts to co-opt cutting-edge military and colonial construction systems for architectural purposes.

Basic and Improved Huts

One prefabricated building system on view at La Cité reconstituée, the so-called "Village France" by Charles Roux of the Société des ateliers Borel, proved particularly popular with the public.[17] This exhibit occupied a semicircular clearing in the trees of the Tuileries [fig. 7.2]. A simulated town hall, post office, market, gazebo, small church, and various residences formed a picturesque tableau of what a temporarily reconstructed village in the war zone might look like. All of its buildings featured the same modular system of one-meter-wide windows, doors, and solid plywood panels slotted into a visible wooden frame made up of relatively small studs. According to an enthusiastic journalist, a visitor experiencing this "cheerful" mock village "receives the impression of an original fantasy, a pleasing paradox. The setting is so pretty [*coquet*], the presentation is so fairytale-like, and the village is so droll with all of its miniature services, that one believes oneself to be in the presence of toys for adults."[18] Several critics, however, were not at all amused by the sample huts and faux village

Figure 7.2: Photograph of the "Village France" at La Cité reconstituée, 1916. "L'Exposition de la cité reconstituée," *L'Image de la guerre* no. 94 (August 1916): n.p. Bibliothèque nationale de France.

displayed at La Cité reconstituée. "This exhibition … only shows wooden houses to its visitors," complained Ernest Picard in *L'Architecture*, the official publication of the Société centrale des architectes. "Is this therefore the reconstituted city?"[19] He expounded with another rhetorical question:

> Poor refugees, or soldiers on leave who have come to spend a moment at the Tuileries, eager to see the new, healthy, and comfortable dwellings destined to replace your ruined homes, were you not disappointed to be offered so many demountable houses, so many wooden houses, which do not shelter their residents well from bad weather, which cost a lot today, which come from abroad, and which are not safe since they are flammable …?[20]

As it happens, the war had already elevated huts to a new level of prominence in France. Military dictates had led to a large-scale campaign to build rudimentary huts, which were desperately needed as were new barracks and hospitals as well as prisons for captured enemy soldiers. Because France suffered from a housing shortage that predated the war, huts also constituted the de-facto wartime solution for lodging refugees, orphans, and colonial subjects brought to the mainland to replenish the labor force [fig. 7.3].[21] In 1915, a year before La Cité reconstituée, the French army had sponsored a competition for the design of a multipurpose, demountable wooden hut that could be mass-produced in large quantities.[22] A second lieutenant named Louis Adrian won the competition, after which the architect-builder Gustave Perret helped him to perfect his design.[23] Over the following years, about 100,000 so-called "Adrian huts" were erected all over France – and abroad in other theaters of war – from standardized kits of rectangular panels and frames manufactured in series at Vincennes, near Paris [fig. 7.4].

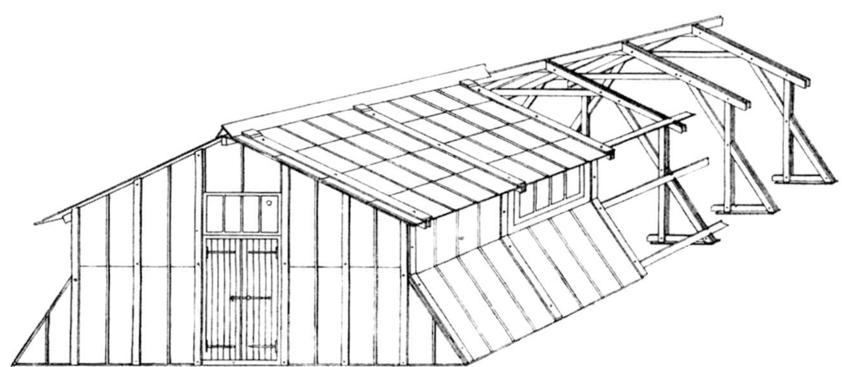

Figure 7.3: Drawing of an Adrian hut, c.1915. *Ministère de la Guerre, Baraquement système Adrian* (Paris: Draeger, n.d.), 20. Bibliothèque nationale de France.

Figure 7.4: Illustration of Adrian huts in a prisoner camp at Île Longue, Brittany, c.1916. Postcard. Author's collection.

The resulting prevalence of industrially fabricated wooden huts meant that greater numbers of French citizens became cognizant of their intrinsic deficiencies. "Thin walls of wood let in the cold, humidity, and not much breathable air," reported a French captive trapped in a German prisoner camp comprised of wooden huts.[24] Elsewhere, a nurse complained in a letter that "it rained everywhere in our hut … It rained along the walls and, thanks to the violent southerly wind, I received a true shower on my head and shoulders."[25] To make matters worse, the unpleasantness of such typically permeable hut construction rivaled the lack of privacy and cleanliness within: "Men, women, and children are piled pell-mell in the most repugnant promiscuity. … Needless to say, it [the hut] is crawling with vermin," wrote a visitor scandalized by a temporary hut settlement for war refugees.[26] The French thus tended to agree that basic wooden huts such as the Adrian hut were execrable places to live.

Despite these widespread negative opinions, certain designers wished to take advantage of the thousands of huts that had already been produced for wartime uses. They dreamed of reconverting these huts into temporary houses by first disassembling them once the war had ended, reassembling them in the former war zone, and upgrading them with new parts. At La Cité reconstituée, for example, the architect Gustave Jacqz and an interior decorator named Gustave Louis Jaulmes exhibited a retrofitted Adrian hut. They had lined its structure with a second wall of wooden planks separated from the first by an air gap that served as thermal insulation. This kind of double wall was a common feature of more luxurious military and colonial huts at the time. Jacqz and Jaulmes also outfitted their Adrian hut with custom built-in furniture [fig. 7.5]. Their conversion of an Adrian hut at La Cité reconstituée fueled a discussion, which had already begun in 1915, about whether or not France should recycle military huts to accelerate the resettlement of devastated regions once the fighting had stopped.[27] Yet some observers were evidently not swayed by Jacqz and Jaulmes's demonstration, countering that even improved versions of Adrian huts were not fit for living in and would only get in the way of the more important task of permanent reconstruction.[28]

Figure 7.5: Photograph of the interior of an Adrian hut, with Gustave Jacqz and Gustave Louis Jaulmes's modifications, displayed at La Cité reconstituée, 1916. Charles Du Bus, "Deux Aspects de l'art urbain; II. Vers la cité prochaine," *Gazette des beaux-arts*, no. 688 (August 1916): 381. Bibliothèque nationale de France.

Critics of La Cité reconstituée aimed their displeasure not only at its apparent celebration of huts, but also at the fact that the exhibition repeatedly blurred the line between the usually distinct realms of hut-building and permanent construction. Two architects named Crevel and Maigrot wrote that:

> Penetrating inside of the exhibition, our eyes do not experience the satisfaction of finding, separate from one another, the two categories of the provisional, on one hand, and the definitive, on the other. This mixture has given to the ensemble the aspect of a poorly laid-out village that has been realized only with difficulty.[29]

The authors lamented that "the juxtaposition of wooden buildings next to pavilions made of resistant materials – bricks or reinforced cement – compounds this markedly unfavorable impression." Indeed, not all of the huts displayed in La Cité reconstituée were made out of wood. Some used reinforced concrete panels or hollow masonry blocks, materials typically associated with permanent construction, as their primary structure. These heavier edifices were primarily designed to provide greater protection from the cold and rain than wooden huts, even though their simple volumes, minimal ornamentation, and ease of assembly followed the example of wooden huts. Crevel and Maigrot, however, disliked the visual commingling of traditional wooden huts with masonry versions of those huts sporting thicker walls.

Crevel and Maigrot similarly criticized another hybrid breed of huts that debuted at La Cité reconstituée. Like standard wooden huts, these innovative huts were lightweight and demountable, but they substituted lumber for more resistant modern materials such as asbestos, metal, or enamel-coated particleboard. This new kind of hut constituted a longer-lasting version of the basic wooden hut. With its decades-long lifespan, it qualified neither as a short-term edifice meant to last only a few years nor as a long-term one meant to last for centuries.[30] The main advantage of this kind of dwelling over a wooden hut is that it would hold up better over time while providing more comfort to its inhabitants. Yet it also cost much more to build than a typical wooden hut. As Crevel and Maigrot explained, the high cost of these improved demountable huts made them almost as expensive as traditionally built houses, nullifying the premise that huts should be nothing more than a cheap and fleeting intermediary solution. Not only did such "semi-definitive" designs upend longstanding custom, but their high price would also, as Crevel and Maigrot saw it, leave fewer funds available for building regular permanent edifices in the devastated areas of France.[31] The art critic Léon Rosenthal agreed with this diagnosis, expressing in *L'Humanité* his displeasure about the fact that "temporary constructions will swallow up considerable sums that are so necessary for the final works."[32]

By contrast, designers and advocates of the semi-definitive house projects displayed at La Cité reconstituée saw great promise in their fusion of temporary and permanent construction methods. In articles penned during the Great War, the military engineer Georges Espitallier urged his compatriots to expand the use of light construction systems from the realm of the temporary to that of the permanent, outlining the economic benefits of doing so in a context marked by severe shortages of materials and manpower.[33] He especially focused on the technique of building thin double walls separated by an air gap. Deploying the same technique with more robust materials would hypothetically achieve maximum durability and thermal performance without relying on stone, brick, or skilled masons. Espitallier thus regretted that, "in current construction practices, it is only too rarely that we take advantage of this [double-wall] system that, in many cases, could favorably replace thick walls."[34] "Temporary buildings," he reasoned, "can last."[35]

Espitallier justified this line of thinking by acknowledging that, due to the formidable challenges standing in the way of permanent reconstruction, provisional shelter for the devastated regions would likely remain in use far longer than anyone had anticipated. Rather than endorsing the officially sanctioned approach of first lodging homeless families in poor-quality temporary huts until these huts, after an indefinite delay, could be replaced with more costly and substantial permanent structures, Espitallier proposed an alternative. He argued that the government should immediately set about building houses that, like huts, are made of light materials, contain elementary standardized parts, and do not take long to erect but, unlike huts, better protect their occupants from the weather while also withstanding the test of time. In other words, he advocated for a superior kind of lightweight dwelling. "What the interested parties are looking for is not a barrack made of badly assembled boards," wrote Espitallier. "[L]et us wish them to have a house – a lightweight house, to be sure, and one that is as economical as possible, but a comfortable one enhanced with an agreeable appearance."[36] At La Cité reconstituée, his company exhibited precisely such a lightweight house. Its walls were made of waterproofed particleboard panels that wrapped around a structural metal frame.[37]

This amalgamation of temporary and definitive construction methods harbored not just practical implications, but also political, theoretical ones. To accept that civilian houses would increasingly borrow from the building systems of demountable huts was tantamount to accepting the premise that militaristic thinking would long continue to shape French society and culture in its image.

Military Takeover of Civilian France

It is important to recall that the First World War triggered a sharp restriction of personal liberties in France. This loss of liberties resulted from an extensive government takeover of civil society. Arguing that it needed every tool at its disposal to fend off the enemy, the French government had passed laws in the fall of 1914 that allowed it to take command of private industry and property.[38] In theory, these martial laws were meant to remain in effect only for the duration of the war. Yet the mostly unspoken concern lingering amongst some French men and women was that these laws might not be fully rolled back once peace returned. The French public might conceivably never regain certain hard-won constitutional freedoms, just as it might never rid itself entirely of heavy-handed state and military involvement in all sectors of society.

After consolidating power over their nation, French wartime leaders had embraced the latest theories of streamlined management – including the scientific organization of labor propounded by the American researcher Frederick Taylor – and French engineers' technical knowledge of how to maximize efficiency.[39] Henceforth, militaristic thinking and objectives began to dictate all aspects of civilian life. Hut-building programs like that of the Adrian hut emerged from this new hierarchical system of control, which allowed the government to marshal all its people, raw materials, money, and machines toward centralized objectives set by the army.[40] Thousands of regular wooden huts proliferating across France since 1914 constituted the built embodiment of this technocratic political structure, which only further consolidated power as the war dragged on.

The wartime political integration of the military, government, and business sectors closely resembled a similar integration that had already long been underway in Germany prior to the war, and which the French tended to eye with suspicion.[41] By 1914, the Germans enjoyed a decisive lead over the French in industrial manufacturing, top-down socioeconomic prescriptions, and the concentration of powers at the national level.[42] Many French citizens thus linked these phenomena with everything that they disliked about their ostensibly bellicose neighbor.[43] Ironically, the wartime French government was mimicking its enemy to better vanquish it on the battlefield.

Caught in a tide of nationalistic fervor, most of the French did not publicly criticize their leaders' plans to win the war by drastically reorganizing the nation around precepts of top-down governance and rabid industrialization – even if this meant imitating the roundly disliked Germans.[44] The much-celebrated *union sacrée* had, after all, persuaded traditionally opposed factions of French society to rally behind their government and military during these extreme circumstances in which the very existence of the nation was deemed to be at risk.[45] Yet the dearth of open debate about how the home front was being governed, as well as about the dangers of the militarization and industrialization engulfing the nation at the time, did not mean that French people harbored no simmering concerns about these topics. Superficially harmless discussion of the designs proposed in La Cité reconstituée allowed these concerns to seep to the surface, wittingly or not, without incurring the wrath of a French state that wielded considerable censorship over its citizens at that time.[46]

One can accordingly detect political undertones in the comments that observers published about the building systems exhibited at La Cité reconstituée. Through their language and argumentation, critics of the innovative, lightweight, and modular houses repeatedly associated them with the downsides of totalitarian government control. By contrast, supporters of these designs often implied that a strong, centralized national government had proven to be a boon for France. They hoped that this transformation and its accompanying top-down political structure would persist after the war. Thus, the historical context surrounding La Cité reconstituée prompted the French to address a commercial array of built prototypes – assemblages of wood, metal, concrete, and other materials – within the frame of lofty theoretical questions regarding the role of the state in civil society. This conflation is evident in the words of Charles Roux, the inventor of the "Village France." He defended, for example, the fragile appearance of his wooden huts by pointing to lightweight military buildings and infrastructures erected as part of the war effort:

> Take a look at industrial buildings that are cropping up all over France to harbor new war factories; they are only made up of metallic and trussed frames of surprising lightness, and which rest, for the most part, on frail pillars of reinforced concrete. These frames have nothing in common with the ancient timber frameworks whose beams would require several cubic meters of oak or pine and which would rest on piles of masonry whose volume was more considerable than the totality of the walls in a modern construction of the same surface area.[47]

Wartime shortages had indeed compelled the French army corps of engineers (the *génie*) to design new factories, hangars, and storage depots such that they consumed the smallest possible quantity of building materials. The sober aesthetics of these constructions only underscored their exceptionally efficient use of materials. As Roux saw it, proposing lightweight, flimsy-looking houses as part of reconstruction was analogous to admiring the wartime dependence on engineering and its relentless pursuit of efficiency. Like him, backers of this position insinuated that the modernization occurring in wartime France should continue into peacetime.

By the same token, critics of La Cité reconstituée such as Crevel and Maigrot harbored an implicit bias against the militarized and engineering mindset that was sweeping over France. "We can only regret," the two architects stated in a slightly condescending tone, that the French construction industry failed to provide a satisfactory answer to the exhibition prompt in part because this industry was presently "monopolized by wartime needs."[48] Crevel and Maigrot clearly thought that the business of war could only divert attention away from the task of designing proper housing because wartime work does not contribute to that task in any way. As they saw it, military work and civilian housing should have nothing in common.

On more than one occasion, Crevel and Maigrot furthermore deplored the "lightness and fragile appearance" of most houses on view at La Cité reconstituée. They correspondingly lavished praise on a demonstration hut – built by the British Quaker Society of Friends – characterized by a "solid" and "serious, robust appearance."[49] Crevel and Maigrot believed that residential architecture should display reassuringly hefty tectonics evocative of immobility and prolonged durability. Their words suggest that, just as a house should promote a stable family life, ensuring the continued survival of a nation by protecting its offspring raised within that building, so should it express those ideals of stability through solid-looking aesthetic forms. Such tectonics were appropriately characteristic of peacetime construction activity, whereas delicate and flimsy tectonics were, at that moment, intrinsically linked to wartime constructions and the military-political autocracy that was churning them out in large numbers.

Regionalist Critique of Light Construction

Hitching their wagons to wartime ideals of maximum efficiency, designers of the huts and semi-provisional houses displayed at La Cité reconstituée had trampled over basic regionalist principles. The term *régionalisme* first gained steam to designate a turn-of-the-century French political movement that opposed the concentration of power in Paris and its national institutions.[50] It championed the view that every French region should enjoy greater independence in governing itself. Artists and architects had appropriated the term *régionalisme* in their celebration of local aesthetic and building traditions, believing that works of art and architecture for a given site should fully reflect its unique climate, local culture, and the readily available materials nearby.[51]

Designs for huts and prefabricated houses inevitably assume that the same edifice can be made and sent anywhere – whether to the Ardennes or to Algeria – with little regard for the specifics of the local context. Because such designs featured so prominently in La Cité reconstituée, this exhibition seemed to acknowledge that rebuilding the devastated regions of France could amount to the centralized mass production and diffusion of identical buildings.

Léandre Vaillat, an art critic and defender of architectural regionalism, vehemently protested against this notion. "It is imperative that these landscapes not to be covered, by brute will, with uniform houses established according to cost tables and based on models that are indifferent to any consideration of individuals or of *terroirs*," he proclaimed in *Le Temps* after seeing La Cité reconstituée.[52] Crevel and Maigrot rallied behind Vaillat's position. "In the ensemble of the exhibited pavilions," they wrote, "nowhere do we find a regional character; [instead,] we see everywhere only the horrid chalet of the Parisian suburbs. This, in our opinion, is a big mistake that almost all of the participants have made."[53] La Cité reconstituée therefore augured what regionalists viewed as a dystopian outcome: the spread of countless off-the-shelf huts across the devastated regions of France and beyond.[54]

Here, too, critics' words on the subject of huts and housing carry loaded meanings indicative of a political stance. One can associate Crevel and Maigrot's assertion that the huts in La Cité reconstituée are characteristic of the "Parisian suburbs" with the fact that the Parisian seat of national power exercised an unusually tight grip over all French regions during the war. The danger of identical huts being designed in a central location and dispatched across the country duplicated the danger of Parisian technocrats subjugating all other parts of France to their will. Therefore, the regionalists' belief that every rebuilt house should aesthetically and materially cater to its specific site resonates with the political notion that, once the war ended, each French region should enjoy more independence from national institutions and, by extension, from the iron fist of the military as well.

In reacting to this polarizing exhibition, French commentators indirectly pondered how wartime politics, economics, and industrialism might leave a lasting mark on their country. Some argued that these secondary, self-inflicted wounds of war should be washed away without a trace. Others insisted that these marks and developments should be forever embedded into French culture, thereby altering its trajectory. All were grappling with a moment during which republican democracy had suddenly given way to militaristic autocracy just as conventional house-building methods were being challenged by modern industrialized ones. The specter that critics of La Cité reconstituée evoked time and again was that of temporary wartime disruptions becoming permanent. As Vaillat wrote, "philanthropic projects and groups, foreign or French, are cultivating amongst the ruins the multiplication of provisional huts that risk becoming definitive, and the horrors of haste and lack of foresight threaten to superpose themselves on the horrors of the war."[55]

Egged on by Vaillat, architects who took issue with La Cité reconstituée organized a counter-exhibition: L'Architecture régionale dans les provinces envahies. The influential Société des architectes diplômés du gouvernement sponsored this counter-exhibition and appointed Vaillat as its curator.[56] It opened on January 10, 1917 at the Galeries des Éditeurs Goupil in Paris.[57] The heart of the exhibition featured 80 graphite drawings by the architect André Ventre, who had painstakingly recorded historic domestic architectures in each of the French regions affected by the war. His black-and-white sketches display voluminous and steeply pitched tiled or thatched roofs draped above low-slung masonry buildings [fig. 7.6]. Chunky timber frames, large stones with rounded corners, and pocketed bricks aggregate to create houses and farms defined by irregular massing. In the exhibition space of the Galeries Goupil, paintings by other artists complemented Ventre's collection of drawings while reproducing the atmosphere and colors of each region prior to the war. Unsurprisingly, the artworks on display were organized according to the region in which their subjects had been found.[58]

Figure 7.6: Drawing by André Ventre displayed in the exhibition L'Architecture régionale dans les provinces envahies, c.1915. *Le Logis et la Maison des champs ; Exposition de l'architecture régionale dans les provinces envahies* (Paris, 1917), 33. Bibliothèque nationale de France.

One of the main objectives of L'Architecture régionale dans les provinces envahies was to take the spotlight away from the serially produced huts that had monopolized so much of La Cité reconstituée. "These examples" of huts on view at the Tuileries, declared an architect reviewing the regionalist exhibition for the journal *L'Architecture*, "clearly indicated the path that should not be followed."[59] The honorary president of the regionalist exhibition, a politician elected to represent one of the war-torn areas, asserted in his dedicatory lecture that "it is necessary to protect the resident from speculation, against those catalogs of ready-made houses, payable on installment."[60] Vaillat wholeheartedly concurred: "we cannot invoke any pretext to impose a foreign architecture on the Lorraine [region], to pour into a single mold, which lacks any character, several thousands of huts."[61] A sympathetic journalist likewise praised the organizers of L'Architecture régionale dans les provinces envahies for lobbying "against an industrial invasion deprived of any sentimentality, cynically mercantile, with its construction sites chock full of imported materials and those odious projects for symmetrical [urban] plans."[62] Against the megalomaniacal, Beaux-Arts urban plans displayed in the Jeu de Paume at La Cité reconstituée, the regionalists proffered the purported authenticity, simplicity, and irregularity of the countryside village.[63] Against the anonymous and placeless hut, they proffered the distinctively local masonry houses of ages past.

Although the organizers of the regionalist show primarily based their repudiation of huts on aesthetic grounds, their words hint at additional latent, perhaps even unconscious, anxieties. Terms like "foreign architecture," "imported," and "invasion" (from the quotes above) allude to the fact that kit-of-parts huts were synonymous with the colonial occupation of distant lands. The growing parallels between the war-torn regions of France and French colonial territories pointed toward unsettling conclusions. Accepting the use of huts for reconstruction was, in effect, commensurate with accepting that devastated French regions would be placed under the tutelage of Paris in the same way that colonies already were. The regionalists clung to visual, architectonic manifestations of French regional identity not just because warfare was eliminating the physical idiosyncrasies of the invaded regions, but also because those regions risked losing their political rights. Moreover, lodging French citizens in the same type of bland, utilitarian edifices used for colonial populations theoretically challenged what was then a foundational distinction between French citizens in the mainland and colonial subjects abroad. Proposals to don rebuilt houses in northeastern France in traditional garb can thus be interpreted as an attempt to reinstate this sharp conceptual distinction precisely as it had become blurred.

These looming political and cultural anxieties help to explain the intense disdain for huts expressed in the years that followed La Cité reconstituée. Certain architects even went as far as to argue that temporary structures – including huts – should be eliminated altogether from reconstruction plans. Doing so would reduce the officially sanctioned two-step process of reconstruction to a single step. One architect who espoused this argument was Jacques Marcel Auburtin. He had overseen the urban design section of La Cité reconstituée in the Jeu de Paume. Soon after that exhibition opened, he published an essay discounting the usefulness of both run-of-the-mill military huts as well as more advanced semi-provisional houses meant for civilized living.[64] Auburtin proposed that builders should instead develop projects for substantial permanent houses that could be erected in the devastated regions of France almost as quickly as huts, and whose use of novel cement-based building blocks – some of which were on view at La Cité reconstituée – could bypass the widespread shortages of typical construction materials.

The architect Louis Jardin seconded this opinion in an October 1, 1916 column for *Le Bâtiment* titled "Let Us Avoid Provisional Houses." "It is a singular irony," Jardin declared sardonically, "that, precisely as the orientation of our artistic renaissance is being established, our departmental engineers are returning to the primitive cabins of savages."[65] He went on to blast La Cité reconstituée for its emphasis on huts, whether high-tech or low-tech, claiming that none could sustain a satisfactory living environment:

> All those who know about buildings were able to evaluate the insalubrity of the wooden huts in this exhibition while visiting them last July. The visitor choked on the heat that persisted there and it was easy to conclude that, in winter, it would be impossible to heat these same huts because the wind, cold, and humidity would penetrate on all sides, endowing all those who sleep in them with pains and rheumatism.[66]

According to Jardin, the Tuileries exhibition had opened visitors' eyes to the civilian tragedy that was already taking place in the war-torn regions of France:

> In the northern regions, we are currently committing the grave mistake of building several thousand temporary accommodations made of wooden modules, without basements, without attics, with pine floors laid directly onto the ground, true vermin's nests that sell for 75 francs per square meter of built area.[67]

He concluded that "temporary constructions are a serious mistake, as the Exposition de la cité reconstituée demonstrated," and urged his compatriots to curb their dependence on huts for reconstruction.

Ambiguities in Regionalists' Attitude toward Wartime Huts

Despite their recurrent criticism of huts, the men who organized the regionalist counter-exhibition did not share Jardin and Auburtin's preference for only a single phase of reconstruction. The regionalists' position was rather paradoxical. They appreciated the short-term need for residential huts at this unusual juncture in their nation's history, but they rejected the idea that permanent forms of architecture should imitate huts in any way or cede their place to them. The art critic Léon Rosenthal exemplified this stance when, right after denouncing the numerous downsides of huts, he justified the need for them in a first wave of reconstruction because they "allow us to avoid rushed constructions and will give us the time to establish more thoughtful designs" in the second wave.[68] Rosenthal also emphasized, however, that huts should "be avowedly and solely provisional, destined to disappear on the day, which I do not specify, [and] which no one could specify, that definitive buildings will have been erected." Vaillat, the curator of the regionalist exhibition, similarly welcomed improved forms of huts with an extended lifespan. Agreeing with Rosenthal, he argued that such huts would allow the second wave of reconstruction to proceed at a less hurried pace. Vaillat hoped that this would in turn buy architects more time to agree on, and then perfect, a novel architectural style that properly echoed the old built environment of a given region.[69] The built craft of those final edifices would also presumably benefit from a lack of urgency.

Vaillat and his fellow regionalists' assessment that huts possess value even though they are inherently flawed recalls many French people's overall attitude toward the war. The French were generally resigned to the conflict.[70] During this period, they tended to be receptive to nationalist appeals, but they were also cognizant of the steep toll that the war was inflicting on their country. The regionalists' bipolar view of huts, both positive and negative, echoes the larger dilemma of a nation wrestling with patriotic support for its government's wartime efforts while also deploring the results of these efforts.

During the Great War, France harbored a similarly paradoxical mix of respect for and horror of the trenches of the Western Front. On the one hand, these trenches, sites of countless heroic acts, constituted a welcome first line of defense. On the other hand, soldiers' postcards and accounts in the press had, by 1916, widely publicized the terrible living conditions of those places. Ringelmann, the agricultural expert who had published extensively about construction in the colonies, pointed out that similar building practices could be used to produce either huts or the military trenches on the Western Front, since both relied on the same kind of rudimentary carpentry and earthworks without foundations.[71] This meant that occupants of both trenches and rudimentary huts were often equally forced to wallow in mud and dirt. Authors who slandered the poor living environments of huts accordingly did so in terms that recall the language used at the time to describe the "charnel house" of trenches beset with "rats, lice, vermin, and filth."[72] In their eyes, the shortcomings of living in thin-walled, leaky huts evoked the wretchedness of fighting in the trenches, both of which were widely viewed as necessary wartime evils.

An expert writing in *La Technique sanitaire et municipale* captured this fatalistic embrace, tinged with disgust, of huts when he stated that "it is eminently desirable to limit the use of provisional buildings only to strictly indispensable levels, since it will at first be necessary to resort to these to immediately shelter populations that are returning to locales destroyed by the enemy." Later, the same author noted that, because huts will need to be erected quickly and cheaply, "without foundations or basements, and inevitably cramped," they "will offer – no matter the amount of care that designers bring to the problem – unhygienic living conditions, if not entirely defective ones in many respects."[73]

The notion that huts, like the trenches, were an undesirable but inescapable part of the war relates closely to the recurring fear that huts would outlast their prescribed life. Although the military trenches were meant to be built quickly and then abandoned for the next forward position, in this war, they were proving to be much more permanent and immobile than their creators had intended. Huts could get bogged down in a given place in the same way that the war had also become bogged down in trench warfare. As Ernest Picard declared, "huts are obviously necessary," but "let us be sure to consider these huts as provisional constructions; let us not put too much credence in the word 'demountable,' since it is always difficult and expensive to transport a house that has already spent a certain amount of time in one location."[74] Picard thus preferred to think of the huts as disposable rather than as recyclable. The problem of the trenches hovers behind his argument that it is better to accept the limitations of advanced engineering rather than to blindly accept its optimistic promises.

Overall, the organizers of L'Architecture régionale dans les provinces envahies appeared to distrust the top-down, military and engineering-driven system of governance that ruled over wartime France. Yet their reluctant acceptance of huts suggests that they conceded the necessity for such a system in a time of war – as long as the rulers of this system agreed to relinquish power after the return of peace. The tension inherent in acquiescing to a disagreeable political regime reappears in architects' conflicted views about how to deploy huts as part of reconstruction. Likewise, they could not agree on the value of new and improved hut designs displayed at La Cité reconstituée. Some saw these latest designs as a threat to longstanding values, while others saw them as a useful tool that would allow for a more successful final phase of reconstruction. Such disagreement reflected the larger struggle in France about how to make sense of a momentous restructuring of national affairs precisely as the country found itself at war.

Vaillat epitomized the contradictions of regionalist attitudes toward reconstruction. Even though he lambasted huts in some newspaper columns, in others, he waxed poetic about huts and their possibilities. He even praised the interior decoration of the reconverted Adrian hut that Jacqz and Jaulmes had created for La Cité reconstituée:

> With … caned chairs, planks of white wood, trellises of boards, a little bit of color, and cotton canvas, [Jaulmes] has organized … an improvised intimacy that many would gladly adopt as their intimacy of forever; and I was thinking, while relaxing there, of that phrase by [the Enlightenment philosopher Jean-Jacques] Rousseau, when he assures us that true happiness for him would be to live in the countryside with a wife, a small house with green shutters, and a small cow. Mr. Jaulmes has unearthed the

[dream] house of Jean-Jacques, and he was careful not to forget the stable for the cow.[75]

Vaillat argued that well-furnished huts should evoke the agricultural lifestyles and settings destroyed by the war, as opposed to the large-scale industrial production that had made so much headway in France during the war and which had produced so many huts in the first place.

It is telling that, rather than rejecting huts outright, Vaillat proposed adapting them to the regionalist idyll. His ambivalence about huts – and by extension, about the entire war – echoes his uncertainty about how to view his country's military engineering. Though he dismissed the notion that engineering principles (military or otherwise) should guide architectural developments, he nonetheless appreciated a certain rusticity and local specificity that he identified in the military trench-building program. In his preface to the book compiling Ventre's drawings from L'Architecture régionale dans les provinces envahies, Vaillat stated that "the war" and its temporary constructions along the front "offered us several striking lessons," notably by confirming that each stretch of French land is defined by a unique soil and topography. "Our generals are, in essence, excellent geographers," he wrote, noting that "the earth [that they] upturned while digging the trenches … better revealed the ground of France" – and thus differences in the soil of each region – than any book ever did.[76]

Elsewhere, Vaillat declared that "we learn to build a house like we learn to cultivate a field … and even to wage war."[77] Here, too, he returned to the recurrent, and mostly implicit, idea that what was happening on the front lines was pertinent to the problem of rebuilding rural homes after the return of peace. Yet, rather than viewing this association solely in negative terms, he teased out a positive aspect of military construction that might productively inform the design of post-war villages. Clearly Vaillat saw something of value worth salvaging in the rampant militarism that had seized wartime France: something more akin to the innocuous tasks of farming and geology. These beneficial facets of military campaigns belied their dehumanizing aspects, which the army of course executed with little regard for the particularities of culture or place. Skeptics of militarized industrialism evidently searched for glimmers of hope wherever they could find them.

Conclusion

The participants who took part in La Cité reconstituée probably never imagined that their sample huts would spark such complex and passionate reactions. An exhibition that had begun as a matter-of-fact, mercantile presentation of different hut-like building systems for reconstruction became a vehicle through which France could indirectly address bigger issues. The huts of La Cité reconstituée served as protean objects upon which the French projected their hopes and fears about the direction of their country. Hut-inspired building technologies correspondingly stood for aspects of the war that could be seen as noble and positive as well as aspects of the war that were abhorrent. On the one hand, these technologies represented the promise of furthering engineering prowess and high-output industrial production in France while also harking to a bucolic ideal closely associated with simple forms of lodging. On the other hand, these technologies represented the dismal conditions of trench warfare, the imbalance of power between colonizers and colonized, and the risk that rampant technocratic, military-led industrialization might continue to permeate France even after the war, to the point of permanently refashioning its culture and society. Although some designers celebrated huts as inspiration for a new kind of inexpensive housing – one that would be lighter and quicker to erect than traditional construction – others decried that same idea. Backers of the regionalist counter-exhibition searched for yet another alternative, praising and disparaging huts in a way that mirrored conflicted views about how their nation was being reshaped by the war. At both La Cité reconstituée and L'Architecture régionale dans les provinces envahies, questions of building methods and architectural tectonics were thoroughly entangled with the political and cultural side effects of the Great War.

Notes

1   "L'Exposition de la cité reconstituée," *Le Foyer de demain* 1, no. 2 (June 1, 1916): 7.

2   Charles Du Bus, "Deux Aspects de l'art urbain; II. Vers la cité prochaine," *Gazette des beaux-arts*, no. 688 (August 1916): 388.

3   Inside the Jeu de Paume, Tony Garnier exhibited drawings of his latest large public projects for Lyon: the slaughterhouse of La Mouche, the Grange-Blanche hospital, and the Gerland stadium. "Chronologie de l'œuvre," *Tony Garnier: l'œuvre complète* (Paris: Centre Georges Pompidou, 1989), 251.

4   Ernest Picard, "La Cité reconstituée aux Tuileries," *L'Architecture*, no. 8–9 (August 1916): 143; Charles J. Storey, "La Cité Reconstituée: An Exposition on the Replanning and Reorganization of the Devastated Regions in France," *The American City* 15, no. 3 (September 1916): 254.

5   L. Revault, "La Reconstruction des immeubles détruits," *Le Foyer de demain* 1, no. 3 (June 15, 1916): 5.

6   See Philippe Nivet, *Les Réfugiés français de la Grande Guerre, 1914–1920: les "boches du nord"* (Paris: Economica, 2004).

7   Also see Leen Engelen et al., eds., *Revival after the Great War: Rebuild, Remember, Repair, Reform* (Leuven: Leuven University Press, 2020).

8   *Chalets et pavilions; constructions démontables; Système E. Gillet* (Paris: E. Gillet, 1909), 16–8; *Baraques démontables de la Société française de constructions portatives et transformables* (Paris: Berger-Levrault, 1900); Brenda Vale, *Prefabs: A History of the U.K. Temporary Housing Programme* (London: E & FN Spon, 1995), 85; Georges Espitallier, *Les Constructions démontables et leurs emplois militaires* (Paris: Berger-Levrault, 1893), 21–5; Kinda Fares, "L'Industrialisation du logement en France" (PhD diss., Conservatoire national des arts et métiers, 2012), 63–80; Hélène Vacher, "Les Terrains de la guerre et la 'construction instantanée' à la fin du XIXe siècle; Georges Frédéric Espitallier et la culture constructive du génie militaire," *Ædificare* 1, no. 1 (2017): 147–66.

9   Max Ringelmann, "Des Constructions temporaires à élever dans les régions envahies," *Bulletin de la Société d'encouragement pour l'industrie nationale* 114 (January–February 1915): 76–92. Also see Max Ringelmann, *Génie rural appliqué aux colonies; cours professé à l'École nationale supérieure d'agriculture coloniale* (Paris: A. Challamel, 1908); Max Ringelmann, *Habitations rurales et Bâtiments de la ferme des régions libérées* (Paris: Librairie agricole de la Maison Rustique, 1920).

10   See, for example, Jonah Rowen, "Strategies of Containment: Iron, Fire, and Labor Management," *Grey Room*, no. 76 (Summer 2019): 24–57.

11   See John Horne, "End of a Paradigm? The Cultural History of the Great War," *Past & Present* 242, no. 1 (February 1919): 155–92; Antoine Prost and Jay Winter, *Penser la Grande Guerre: un essai d'historiographie* (Paris: Éditions du Seuil, 2004); Patrick Fridenson, ed., *The French Home Front, 1914–1918*, trans. Bruce Little (Providence: Berg, 1992).

12   See, for example, Jay Winter, *Sites of Memory, Sites of Mourning* (Cambridge: Cambridge University Press, 1995); John Horne, ed., *A Companion to World War I* (Oxford: John Wiley and Sons, 2010); Kenneth Silver, *Esprit de Corps: The Art of the Parisian Avant-Garde and the First World War* (Princeton: Princeton University Press, 1989).

13   Horne, "End of a Paradigm?," 156. Philippe Nivet and Peter Gatrell, for example, studied the lives of refugees during and right after the war. See Nivet, *Les Réfugiés français de la Grande Guerre, 1914–1920*; Peter Gatrell, *A Whole Empire Walking: Refugees in Russia during World War I* (Indianapolis: Indiana University Press, 1999).

14   Jean-Louis Cohen, *Architecture in Uniform: Designing and Building for the Second World War* (Paris: Hazan, 2011).

15   Also see Fares, "L'Industrialisation du logement en France," and André Guillerme, Hélène Vacher, and Kinda Fares, "Le Front de l'industrialisation de la construction, 1915–1920," *Les Cahiers de la recherche architecturale et urbaine*, no. 28 (2013): 37–56. For a recent study of how the history of modern architecture intersects with the history of World War I, see Volker M. Welter, "Rebuilding, Recovery, Reconceptualization: Modern Architecture and the First World War," in *Revival after the Great War*, 107–21.

16   See, for example, Gilbert Herbert, *The Dream of the Factory-Made House: Walter Gropius and Konrad Wachsmann* (Cambridge: The MIT Press, 1984); Gilbert Herbert, *Gropius, Hirsch, and the Saga of the Copper Houses* (Haifa: Technion, Israel Institute of Technology, 1980); Brian Brace Taylor, *Le Corbusier at Pessac: The Search for Systems and Standards in the Design of Low Cost Housing* (Cambridge, Mass.: Carpenter Center for the Visual Arts, 1972); Mary McLeod, "'Architecture or Revolution': Taylorism, Technocracy, and Social Change," *Art Journal* 43 (1983): 132–47; Robert Weddle, "Housing and Technological Reform: The Case of the Cité de la Muette in Interwar France," *Journal of Architectural Education* 54, no. 3 (2001): 167–75; Gilles Ragot and Mathilde Dion, "La Modernité en chantiers: Le Corbusier et Lucien Bechmann en 1930," *Le Moniteur architecture AMC* 18–20 (February–April 1991): 48–51; Rosemarie

Höpfner and Walter Prigge, eds., *Ernst May und das Neue Frankfurt, 1925–1930* (Berlin: Ernst & Sohn, 1986).

17   The "Village France" apparently supplanted the Jeu de Paume as the metaphorical heart of the exhibition. As one journalist stated, "[t]he central highlight [*clou*] (as every exposition has a central highlight) is the Village France." "Une Visite à la 'Cité reconstituée," *Le Monde illustré* 60, no. 3053 (June 24, 1916): 418.

18   "Une Visite à la 'Cité reconstituée," 418–20.

19   Picard, "La Cité reconstituée aux Tuileries," 138.

20   *Ibid.*, 138.

21   See Nivet, *Les Réfugiés français de la Grande Guerre, 1914–1920*; Fares, "L'Industrialisation du logement en France."

22   Fares, "L'Industrialisation du logement en France," 133.

23   Pierre Vago, "Perret," *L'Architecture d'aujourd'hui* 3, no. 7 (October 1932): 16.

24   "La Vie de nos prisonniers: souvenirs de captivité en Allemagne," *L'Image de la guerre*, no. 49 (October 1915): n.p.

25   Jeanne Antelme, *Avec l'armée d'Orient: notes d'une infirmière à Moudros* (Paris: Émile-Paul Frères, Éditeurs, 1916), 101.

26   "Camp hollandais de Zeist, camp rempli de réfugies: la Hollande les traite de façon abominable," *L'Ouest éclair*, December 5, 1918, p. 2.

27   Léon Rosenthal, "La Résurrection des villes: quelques objections," *L'Humanité*, May 22, 1915, p. 3; H. Sill; "Reconstruction des villages dévastés," *L'Architecture*, no. 11 (November 1916): 175; Georges Espitallier, "Constructions civiles: la reconstruction dans les régions envahies," *Le Génie civil* 70, no. 19 (May 12, 1917): 305.

28   Louis Jardin, "Évitons les maisons provisoires," *Le Bâtiment* 53, no. 79–80 (October 1, 1916): 1.

29   Crevel and Maigrot, "Exposition de la cité reconstituée," *Le Foyer de demain* 1, no. 3 (June 15, 1916): 4.

30   *Ibid.*, 6.

31   The huts that the critic Léandre Vaillat found least offensive were the most expensive ones, or those with "a cost almost equivalent to that of an authentic house." Yet he dismissed such huts, which are "oh so expensive and which search for a compromise between the temporary shelter and the definitive setup," by arguing that the extra money would be better used on erecting permanent buildings. Léandre Vaillat, "La Cité renaissante," *Le Temps*, June 27, 1916, p. 3.

32   Rosenthal, "La Résurrection des villes," 3.

33   Georges Espitallier, "Note sur les constructions économiques et démontables," *Bulletin de la Société d'encouragement pour l'industrie nationale* 114 (May–June 1915): 544.

34   *Ibid.*, 529.

35   Georges Espitallier, "La Cité reconstituée," *Bulletin de la Société d'encouragement pour l'industrie nationale* 115, no. 2 (September–October 1916): 312.

36   Georges Espitallier, "Constructions civiles: la reconstruction dans les régions envahies (suite et fin)," *Le Génie civil* 70, no. 20 (May 19, 1917): 322.

37   Louis Gaultier, *Exposition de la cité reconstituée; esthétique et hygiène; rapport général* (Paris: Association générale des hygiénistes et techniciens municipaux, 1917), 33; Espitallier, "La Cité reconstituée," 324; "Une Visite à la 'Cité reconstituée," 423.

38   P. G., "La Fédération nationale française," *Bulletin de la Fédération nationale du bâtiment et des travaux publics* 9, no. 100 (August–October 1914): 1; "Communications de la Fédération nationale," *Bulletin de la Fédération nationale du bâtiment et des travaux publics* 9, no. 100 (August–October 1914): 2–3.

39 Victor Cambon, *Le Taylorisme* (Nancy: Imprimerie Nancéienne, 1917); Olivier Cinquealbre, "France 1913–1925, Taylor dans le bâtiment: une idée qui fait son chemin," in *Architecture et Industrie: passé et avenir d'un mariage de raison* (Paris: Centre Georges Pompidou, 1983), 198–206; Aimée Moutet, "Ingénieurs et rationalisation dans l'industrie française de la Grande Guerre au Front populaire," *Culture technique*, no. 12 (March 1984): 137–53; Aimée Moutet, "La Première Guerre mondiale et le taylorisme," in *Le Taylorisme*, ed. Maurice de Montmollin and Olivier Pastré (Paris: La Découverte, 1984): 67–81; Arthur G. Bedeian, Regina A. Greenwood, Julia Teahen, and Daniel A. Wren, "C. Bertrand Thompson and Management Consulting in Europe, 1917–1934," *Journal of Management History* 21, no. 1 (2015): 15–39.

40 Georges-Henri Soutou, *L'Or et le Sang: les buts de guerre économiques de la Première Guerre mondiale* (Paris: Fayard, 1989); Dominique Barjot, "Introduction: la mobilisation de la nation à l'époque de la guerre totale," in *Deux Guerres totales: 1914–1918, 1939–1934*, ed. Dominique Barjot (Paris: Economica, 2012), 10–20 and 57–8; Charles Maier, "Between Taylorism and Technocracy: European Ideologies and the Vision of Industrial Productivity in the 1920s," *Journal of Contemporary History* 5, no. 2 (1970): 28, 32; Jean-Louis Cohen, *L'Architecture au XXe siècle en France* (Paris: Hazan, 2014), 43; Patrick Fridenson, "Un Tournant taylorien de la société française (1904–1918)," *Annales: économies, sociétés, civilisations* 42, no. 5 (1987): 1031–60.

41 Ivan T. Berend, *An Economic History of Twentieth-Century Europe: Economic Regimes from Laissez-Faire to Globalization* (Cambridge: Cambridge University Press, 2006), 42–9.

42 The 1914 German *Werkbund* exhibition in Cologne alerted French architects about the degree to which the organizational streamlining and industrialization of their own country lagged behind that of Germany. Joan Campbell, *The German Werkbund: The Politics of Reform in the Applied Arts* (Princeton: Princeton University Press, 1978), 77.

43 See Henri Bergson, *La Signification de la guerre* (Paris: Bloud et Gay, 1915).

44 See Anne Rasmussen, Nicolas Beaupré, and Heather Jones, eds., *Dans la guerre, 1914–1918: accepter, endurer, refuser* (Paris: Les Belles Lettres, 2015).

45 Patrick Fridenson, "Introduction: A New View of France at War," in *The French Home Front, 1914–1918*, 2.

46 See Victor Cambon, *Notre avenir* (Paris: Payot, 1916), 7–8.

47 Charles-Auguste Roux, "Le Problème de la reconstruction dans les régions dévastées," *La France au travail* 1, no. 1 (December 1916): 5.

48 Crevel and Maigrot, "Exposition de la cité reconstituée," 6.

49 *Ibid.*, 4.

50 Jean Charles-Brun, *Le Régionalisme* (Paris: Bloud, 1911); Thiébaut Flory, *Le Mouvement régionaliste français: source et développements* (Paris: Presses Universitaires de France, 1966).

51 See, for example, Marcel Mayer, *Un Aspect du régionalisme: une enquête sur la sculpture bourguignonne* (Dijon: Imprimerie Darantière, 1913). The war only intensified debates between proponents and opponents of regionalist ideas. Suspicion of the powerful École des Beaux-Arts in Paris, whose students versed in neoclassical architectural idioms sometimes applied these idioms to any project regardless of its exact location, pervaded regionalist architectural discourse – even though many of its defenders had in fact studied at the Beaux-Arts. See P. Vorin, "Régionalisme," *Le Petit Messager des arts et des artistes, et des industries d'art*, no. 7 (April 21, 1915): 1; Marcel Genermont, "Pour le régionalisme," *Le Petit Messager des arts et des artistes, et des industries d'art*,

no. 14 (July 1915): 1; Léandre Vaillat, *La Maison des pays de France; les provinces dévastées* (Paris: Ernest Flammarion, 1917), 14.

52   Vaillat, "La Cité renaissante," 3

53   Crevel and Maigrot, "Exposition de la cité reconstituée," 6.

54   See Benoît Mihail, "Les Ambiguïtés du régionalisme architectural après la Grande Guerre: l'exemple de la Flandre française," in *Living with History, 1914–1964: Rebuilding Europe after the First and Second World Wars and the Role of Heritage Preservation*, ed. Nicholas Bullok and Luc Verpoest (Leuven: Leuven University Press, 2011), 104–25; Leen Meganck, "Domi or Dom-Ino? The Role of the Genius Loci in Post-war Reconstruction and Interwar Urbanism," in *Living with History, 1914–1964*, 230–43.

55   Vaillat, "La Cité renaissante," 3.

56   Jean-Claude Vigato, "L'Architecture du régionalisme: les origines du débat (1900–1950)," in *Les Trois Reconstructions 1919… 1940… 1945* (Paris: Institut Français d'Architecture, 1983), 34.

57   André Michel, "L'Architecture régionale dans les provinces envahies," *Journal des débats*, January 17, 1917, p. 2; Armand Dayot, "Pour l'art de France; la maison rustique," *Le Gaulois*, January 28, 1917, p. 2.

58   *Le Logis et la Maison des champs; Exposition de l'architecture régionale dans les provinces envahies* (Paris, 1917). An additional book published for this occasion collected Ventre's drawings with a preface written by Vaillat: Vaillat, *La Maison des pays de France*.

59   H. B., "Reconstruction des villes: l'Exposition de l'architecture régionale dans les provinces envahies," *L'Architecture*, no. 2 (February 1917): 28.

60   "Compte rendu d'une conférence de L. Revault, député de la Meuse, prononcée à l'occasion de l'Exposition de l'architecture régionale dans les provinces envahies," *Bulletin de la Société des architectes diplômés par le gouvernement* (March 1917), 57, quoted in Jacques Lucan, "Chronique d'années de guerre," *Architecture, mouvement, continuité: bulletin de la Société des architectes diplômés par le gouvernement*, no. 44 (February 1978): 71.

61   Léandre Vaillat, "La Cité renaissante; la maison en Lorraine," *Le Temps*, October 8, 1916, p. 3.

62   Dayot, "Pour l'art de France," 2.

63   Léandre Vaillat, "La Cité renaissante: le régionalisme de l'architecture," *Le Temps*, August 19, 1916, p. 3. Crevel and Maigrot similarly lamented the fact that huts displayed in La Cité reconstituée were generally "conceived for city living," not the rural lifestyle most prevalent in the French regions affected by the war. Crevel and Maigrot, "Exposition de la cité reconstituée," 4.

64   Sill, "Reconstruction des villages dévastés," 175–8.

65   Jardin, "Évitons les maisons provisoires," 1.

66   *Ibid.*

67   *Ibid.*

68   Rosenthal, "La Résurrection des villes," 3.

69   Vaillat, "La Cité renaissante," June 27, 1916, p. 3.

70   See Beaupré, Jones, and Rasmussen, *Dans la guerre, 1914–1918*.

71   Ringelmann, "Des Constructions temporaires à élever dans les régions envahies," 76–92.

72   Jules Isaac and Michel Michel, *Jules Isaac, un historien dans la Grande Guerre: lettres et carnets, 1914–1917* (Paris: Armand Colin, 2004), n.p.

73   "Reconstitution des villes et villages détruits," *La Technique sanitaire et municipale* 12, no. 6 (June 1917): 154. The author advised that "it is eminently desirable to limit the use of provisional buildings only to strictly indispensable levels," thus aligning with the view that the militarism taking over France should be limited to only what was necessary for winning the war.

74   Picard, "La Cité reconstituée aux Tuileries," 139.

75   Vaillat, "La Cité renaissante," June 27, 1916, p. 3.

76   Vaillat, *La Maison des pays de France*, 10.

77   Vaillat, "La Cité renaissante," October 8, 1916, p. 8.

Bibliography

Antelme, Jeanne. *Avec l'armée d'Orient: notes d'une infirmière à Moudros*. Paris: Émile-Paul Frères Éditeurs, 1916.

B., H. "Reconstruction des villes: l'Exposition de l'architecture régionale dans les provinces envahies." *L'Architecture*, no. 2 (February 1917): 27–31.

Baraques démontables de la Société française de constructions portatives et transformables. Paris: Berger-Levrault et Cie., 1900.

Barjot, Dominique, ed. *Deux Guerres totales: 1914–1918, 1939–1945*. Paris: Economica, 2012.

Beaupré, Nicolas, Heather Jones, and Anne Rasmussen, eds. *Dans la guerre, 1914–1918: accepter, endurer, refuser*. Paris: Les Belles Lettres, 2015.

Bedeian, Arthur G., Regina A. Greenwood, Julia Teahen, and Daniel A. Wren. "C. Bertrand Thompson and Management Consulting in Europe, 1917–1934." *Journal of Management History* 21, no. 1 (2015): 15–39.

Berend, Ivan T. *An Economic History of Twentieth-Century Europe: Economic Regimes from Laissez-Faire to Globalization*. Cambridge: Cambridge University Press, 2006.

Bergson, Herni. *La Signification de la guerre*. Paris: Bloud et Gay, 1915.

Cambon, Victor. *Le Taylorisme*. Nancy: Imprimerie Nancéienne, 1917.

———.*Notre Avenir*. Paris: Payot, 1916.

"Camp hollandais de Zeist, camp rempli de réfugiés: la Hollande les traite de façon abominable." *L'Ouest Éclair*, December 5, 1918.

Campbell, Joan. *The German Werkbund: The Politics of Reform in the Applied Arts*. Princeton: Princeton University Press, 1978.

Charles-Brun, Jean. *Le Régionalisme*. Paris: Bloud, 1911.

Chalets et Pavillons; constructions démontables; Système E. Gillet. Paris: E. Gillet, 1909.

Cinquealbre, Olivier. "France 1913–1925, Taylor dans le bâtiment: une idée qui fait son chemin." In *Architecture et Industrie: passé et avenir d'un mariage de raison*, 198–206. Paris: Centre Georges Pompidou, 1983.

Cohen, Jean-Louis. *Architecture in Uniform: Designing and Building for the Second World War*. Paris: Hazan, 2011.

———.*L'Architecture au XXe siècle en France*. Paris: Éditions Hazan, 2014.

"Communications de la Fédération nationale." *Bulletin de la Fédération nationale du bâtiment et des travaux publics* 9, no. 100 (August–October 1914): 2–3.

"Compte rendu d'une conférence de L. Revault, député de la Meuse, prononcée à l'occasion de l'Exposition de l'architecture régionale dans les provinces envahies." *Bulletin de la Société des architectes diplômés par le gouvernement* (March 1917): 57.

"Chronologie de l'œuvre." In *Tony Garnier: l'œuvre complète*. Paris: Centre Georges Pompidou, 1989.

Crevel and Maigrot. "Exposition de la Cité reconstituée." *Le Foyer de demain* 1, no. 3 (June 15, 1916): 4–5.

Dayot, Armand. "Pour l'art de France; la maison rustique." *Le Gaulois*, January 28, 1917.

Dion, Mathilde, and Gilles Ragot. "La Modernité en chantiers: Le Corbusier et Lucien Bechmann en 1930." *Le Moniteur architecture AMC* 18–20 (February–April 1991): 48–51.

Du Bus, Charles. "Deux Aspects de l'art urbain; II. Vers la cité prochaine." *Gazette des beaux-arts*, no. 688 (August 1916): 380–90.

Engelen, Leen, Rajesh Heynickx, Jan Schmidt, Pieter Uyttenhove, Luc Verpoest, and Pieter Verstraete, eds. *Revival after the Great War: Rebuild, Remember, Repair, Reform.* Leuven: Leuven University Press, 2020.

Espitallier, Georges. "Constructions civiles: la reconstruction dans les régions envahies." *Le Génie civil* 70, no. 19 (May 12, 1917): 305–7.

———. "Constructions civiles: la reconstruction dans les régions envahies (suite et fin)." *Le Génie civil* 70, no. 20 (May 19, 1917): 322–4.

———. "La Cité reconstituée." *Bulletin de la Société d'encouragement pour l'industrie nationale* 115, no. 2 (September–October 1916): 309–24.

———. *Les Constructions démontables et leurs emplois militaires.* Paris: Berger-Levrault & Cie., 1893.

———. "Note sur les constructions économiques ou démontables." *Bulletin de la Société d'encouragement pour l'industrie nationale* 114 (May–June 1915): 526–46.

"L'Exposition de la cité reconstituée." *Le Foyer de demain* 1, no. 2 (June 1, 1916): 7.

Fares, Kinda. "L'Industrialisation du logement en France, 1885–1970." PhD diss., Conservatoire national des arts et métiers, 2012.

Fares, Kinda, André Guillerme, and Hélène Vacher. "Le Front de l'industrialisation de la construction, 1915–1920." *Les Cahiers de la recherche architecturale et urbaine* 28 (2013): 37–56.

Flory, Thiébaut. *Le Mouvement régionaliste français: source et développements.* Paris: Presses Universitaires de France, 1966.

Fridenson, Patrick, ed. *The French Home Front, 1914–1918.* Translated by Bruce Little. Providence: Berg, 1992.

———. "Un Tournant taylorien de la société française (1904–1918)." *Annales: économies, sociétés, civilisations* 42, no. 5 (1987): 1031–60.

G., P. "La Fédération nationale française." *Bulletin de la Fédération nationale du bâtiment et des travaux publics* 9, no. 100 (August–October 1914): 1–2.

Gatrell, Peter. *A Whole Empire Walking: Refugees in Russia During World War I.* Indianapolis: Indiana University Press, 1999.

Gaultier, Louis. *Exposition de la Cité reconstituée; esthétique et hygiène; rapport général.* Paris: Association générale des hygiénistes et techniciens municipaux, 1917.

Genermont, Marcel. "Pour le régionalisme." *Le Petit Messager des arts et des artistes, et des industries d'art*, no. 14 (July 1915): [1].

Herbert, Gilbert. *Gropius, Hirsch, and the Saga of the Copper Houses*. Haifa: Technion, Israel Institute of Technology, 1980.

———. *The Dream of the Factory-Made House: Walter Gropius and Konrad Wachsmann*. Cambridge: The MIT Press, 1984.

Höpfner, Rosemarie, and Walter Prigge, eds. *Ernst May und das Neue Frankfurt, 1925–1930*. Berlin: Ernst & Sohn, 1986.

Horne, John, ed. *A Companion to World War I*. Oxford: John Wiley and Sons, 2010.

———. "End of a Paradigm? The Cultural History of the Great War." *Past & Present* 242, no. 1 (February 1919): 155–92.

Isaac, Jules, and Michel Michel. *Jules Isaac, un historien dans la Grande Guerre; lettres et carnets, 1914–1917*. Paris: Armand Colin, 2004.

Jardin, Louis. "Évitons les maisons provisoires." *Le Bâtiment* 53, no. 79–80 (October 1–5, 1916): 1.

Le Logis et la Maison des champs; Exposition de l'architecture régionale dans les provinces envahies. Paris: [Unknown], 1917.

Lucan, Jacques. "Chronique d'années de guerre." *Architecture, mouvement, continuité: bulletin de la Société des architectes diplômés par le gouvernement*, no. 44 (February 1978): 70–3.

Maier, Charles. "Between Taylorism and Technocracy: European Ideologies and the Vision of Industrial Productivity in the 1920s." *Journal of Contemporary History* 5, no. 2 (1970): 27–61.

Mayer, Marcel. *Un Aspect du régionalisme: une enquête sur la sculpture bourguignonne*. Dijon: Imprimerie Darantière, 1913.

McLeod, Mary. "'Architecture or Revolution:' Taylorism, Technocracy, and Social Change." *Art Journal* 43 (1983): 132–47.

Meganck, Leen. "Domi or Dom-Ino? The Role of the Genius Loci in Post-war Reconstruction and Interwar Urbanism." In *Living with History, 1914–1964: Rebuilding Europe after the First and Second World Wars and the Role of Heritage Preservation*, edited by Nicholas Bullok and Luc Verpoest, 230–43. Leuven: Leuven University Press, 2011.

Michel, André. "L'Architecture régionale dans les provinces envahies." *Journal des débats politiques et littéraires*, January 17, 1917.

Mihail, Benoît. "Les Ambiguïtés du régionalisme architectural après la Grande Guerre: l'exemple de la Flandre française." In *Living with History, 1914–1964: Rebuilding Europe after the First and Second World Wars and the Role of Heritage Preservation*, edited by Nicholas Bullok and Luc Verpoest, 104–25. Leuven: Leuven University Press, 2011.

Moutet, Aimée. "Ingénieurs et rationalisation dans l'industrie française de la Grande Guerre au Front populaire." *Culture technique*, no. 12 (March 1984): 137–53.

———. "La Première Guerre mondiale et le taylorisme." In *Le Taylorisme*, edited by Maurice de Montmollin and Olivier Pastré, 67–81. Paris: La Découverte, 1984.

Nivet, Philippe. *Les Réfugiés français de la Grande Guerre, 1914–1920: les "boches du nord."* Paris: Economica, 2004.

Picard, Ernest. "La Cité reconstituée aux Tuileries." *L'Architecture*, no. 8–9 (August 1916): 138–44.

Prost, Antoine, and Jay Winter. *Penser la Grande Guerre: un essai d'historiographie*. Paris: Éditions du Seuil, 2004.

"Reconstitution des villes et villages détruits." *La Technique sanitaire et municipale* 12, no. 6 (June 1917): 151–6.

Revault, L. "La Reconstruction des immeubles détruits." *Le Foyer de demain* 1, no. 3 (June 15, 1916): 5.

Ringelmann, Max. "Des Constructions temporaires à élever dans les régions envahies." *Bulletin de la Société d'encouragement pour l'industrie nationale* 114 (January–February 1915): 76–92.

———.*Génie rural appliqué aux colonies; cours professé à l'École nationale supérieure d'agriculture coloniale.* Paris: A. Challamel, 1908.

———.*Habitations rurales et Bâtiments de la ferme des régions libérées.* Paris: Librairie agricole de la Maison Rustique, 1920.

Rosenthal, Léon. "La Résurrection des villes: quelques objections." *L'Humanité*, May 22, 1915.

Roux, Charles-Auguste. "Le Problème de la reconstruction dans les régions dévastées." *La France au travail* 1, no. 1 (December 1916): 5–8.

Rowen, Jonah. "Strategies of Containment: Iron, Fire, and Labor Management." *Grey Room* 76 (September 2019): 24–57.

Sill, H. "Reconstruction des villages dévastés." *L'Architecture*, no. 11 (November 1916): 175–8.

Silver, Kenneth. *Esprit de Corps: The Art of the Parisian Avant-Garde and the First World War.* Princeton: Princeton University Press, 1989.

Soutou, Georges-Henri. *L'Or et le Sang: les buts de guerre économiques de la Première Guerre mondiale.* Paris: Fayard, 1989.

Storey, Charles J. "La Cité Reconstituée: An Exposition on the Replanning and Reorganization of the Devastated Regions in France." *The American City* 15, no. 3 (September 1916): 252–4.

Taylor, Brian Brace. *Le Corbusier at Pessac: The Search for Systems and Standards in the Design of Low Cost Housing.* Cambridge, Mass.: Carpenter Center for the Visual Arts, 1972.

Vacher, Hélène. "Les Terrains de la guerre et la 'construction instantanée' à la fin du XIXe siècle; Georges Frédéric Espitallier et la culture constructive du génie militaire." *Ædificare* 1, no. 1 (2017): 147–66.

Vago, Pierre. "Perret." *L'Architecture d'aujourd'hui* 3, no. 7 (October 1932): 14–7.

Vaillat, Léandre. "La Cité renaissante: la maison en Lorraine." *Le Temps*, October 8, 1916.

———."La Cité renaissante: le régionalisme de l'architecture." *Le Temps*, August 19, 1916.

———."La Cité renaissante: l'exposition des Tuileries." *Le Temps*, June 27, 1916.

———.*La Maison des pays de France; les provinces dévastées.* Paris: Éditions Flammarion, [1917].

Vale, Brenda. *Prefabs: A History of the UK Temporary Housing Programme.* London: E & FN Spon, 1995.

"La Vie de nos prisonniers; souvenirs de captivité en Allemagne." *L'Image de la guerre*, no. 49 (October 1915): n.p.

Vigato, Jean-Claude. "L'Architecture du régionalisme: les origines du débat (1900–1950)." In *Les Trois Reconstructions 1919 … 1940 … 1945*, 33–8. Paris: Institut Français d'Architecture, 1983.

"Une Visite à la 'Cité reconstituée.'" *Le Monde illustré* 60, no. 3053 (June 24, 1916): 418–24.

Vorin, P. "Régionalisme." *Le Petit Messager des arts et des artistes, et des industries d'art*, no. 7 (April 21, 1915): [1].

Weddle, Robert. "Housing and Technological Reform in Interwar France: The Case of the Cité de la Muette." *Journal of Architectural Education* 54, no. 3 (2001): 167–75.

Winter, Jay. *Sites of Memory, Sites of Mourning: The Great War in European Cultural History*. Cambridge: Cambridge University Press, 1995.

Figure 8.1: "Houses shipped from America for shelter of earthquake victims, Messina, Italy." Street view of the village Regina Elena. Library of Congress Prints and Photographs Division Washington, DIG-stereo-1s29503.

Humanitarian Relief and Confinement

The American Red Cross Refugee City in Italy during the First World War

Theodossis Issaias

Thousands of linear feet of lists and tabulation sheets carefully stored at the Hoover Archives in Palo Alto record the World War I operations of the American Red Cross (ARC) in Europe and North Africa. They have stood there, unclassified, since 1919: worksheets and schedules, itineraries of dispatched ships, invoices of collected donations, lists of missing people, receipts of items shipped and delivered, indexes of stations and dispensary locations, and shipment orders for Red Cross uniforms, insignia, and publicity material. What emerges from these records is not only the organization's leviathan bureaucracy, but also its operational modality. During the war, the ARC transformed from a relatively unknown national Red Cross society to a major humanitarian institution with programs expanding in 25 countries. As it solidified its place in the world, it became the exemplar of modern humanitarianism. To put it differently, while the outcome of "the war to end all wars" was still uncertain, an American organization defined the rules of conduct for the emerging humanitarian governance. Previous calls for Christian piety, charity, and care that had structured its humanitarian commitments were dropped and replaced by a language of efficiency and professionalism. Isomorphically with institutions of the long nineteenth century, the organization appealed to scientific management and professional expertise, and, in a cyclical process, launched relief programs, disclosed expenditures, measured tangible outcomes, and evaluated practices. Once an aid policy entered this cyclical and self-reifying process, it became an unfaltering truth – an incontrovertible humanitarian technology to be put into general use, for generations to come. The lists in the archive not only fulfilled their indexical role of managerial efficiency, but also, in this self-reifying process, had the very same capacity to impart certainty, albeit a flattening one: numbers of people who fought and of bodies who were lost, tons of flour shipped and tons delivered.

Archived among these records and certainties is the correspondence between the American consular officer in Venice (the former pastor Benajah Harvey Carroll Jr.) and the Director General of ARC's Civil Affairs in Italy (the prominent American architect Chester Aldrich), written during the unprecedented refugee crisis in Italy in the early months of 1918. After the devastating defeat of Italian forces along the Piave line, more than 500,000 refugees fled from the north to the south of the country.[1] The defeat prompted the intensification of ARC's presence in Italy and the deployment of a territorial scheme for the management of the displaced population. In the words of the consular officer: "The Red Cross fully appreciates the difficulties that are met everywhere in Italy in superimposing a refugee population on a series of communities overwhelmed with their own economic problems. As I have always believed, the only real solution is to be found in the working out of colonization plans."[2] The two officials conferred and agreed that such organization of the displaced in discreet settlements in the outskirts of cities would alleviate the aforementioned economic pressures and streamline the administering of relief. But most importantly, Carroll wrote, the plan "would prove the most effective organ of propaganda … it would appeal to the American press and to the American public."[3] Within a few weeks, a grand operation was put in place to build a pilot settlement on the outskirts of the city of Pisa, which Carroll described as the "American City" "for 15,000 people with all such conveniences as would be found in a first-class concentration camp."[4]

In this essay, I focus on the humanitarian imperatives as formulated and enacted by the American Red Cross and its permanent Commission in Italy during the First World War. I take seriously the startling admission that the American City in Pisa was conceived as "a first-class concentration camp [that] would appeal to the American public" to break apart the proposal's constituent parts, and trace its genealogy and imperatives. I argue that the humanitarian strategies proposed by Americans in Italy merged military technologies with the postulates of modern planning. They produced a settlement that carried the socially and racially inflected practices of the colonial camp, and operated in the contested space between relief, rehabilitation, and confinement. In addition, the history of this settlement serves as a paradigmatic case study for the rise of humanitarian organizations and of the institutionalization of architectural expertise within them.[5] The essay is divided into three parts. The first examines the instrumentality of publicity campaigns and mass media in the operations of the ARC: architectures of humanitarian relief mediated through magazines, exhibitions, and films served as key components in an extensive publicity apparatus that solicited empathy and donations. The second focuses on the restructuring of ARC's institutional commitments in a period leading to WWI, and traces the incorporation of architectural expertise within the ARC. Finally, the third part closely studies the proposal in Pisa, from its conception and implementation to its abrupt demise.

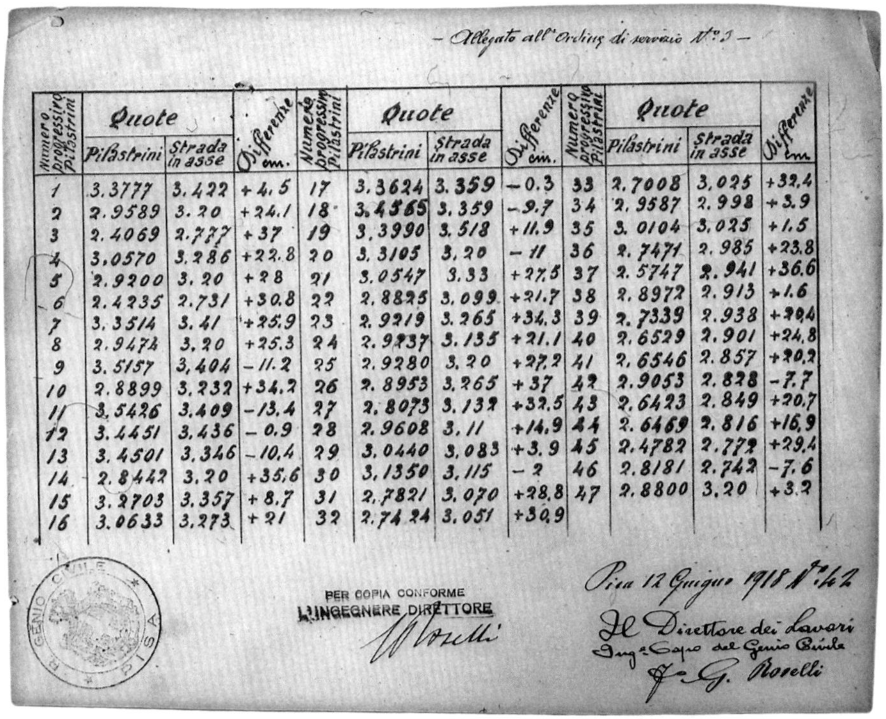

– Allegato all'Ordine di servizio N° 3 –

Numero progressivo Pilastrini	Quote		Differenze cm.	Numero progressivo Pilastrini	Quote		Differenze cm.	Numero progressivo Pilastrini	Quote		Differenze cm.
	Pilastrini	Strada in asse			Pilastrini	Strada in asse			Pilastrini	Strada in asse	
1	3.3777	3.422	+4.5	17	3.3624	3.359	−0.3	33	2.7008	3.025	+32.4
2	2.9589	3.20	+24.1	18	3.4565	3.359	−9.7	34	2.9587	2.998	+3.9
3	2.4069	2.777	+37	19	3.3990	3.518	+11.9	35	3.0104	3.025	+1.5
4	3.0570	3.286	+22.8	20	3.3105	3.20	−11	36	2.7471	2.985	+23.8
5	2.9200	3.20	+28	21	3.0547	3.33	+27.5	37	2.5747	2.941	+36.6
6	2.4235	2.731	+30.8	22	2.8825	3.099	+21.7	38	2.8972	2.913	+1.6
7	3.3514	3.41	+25.9	23	2.9219	3.265	+34.3	39	2.7339	2.938	+20.4
8	2.9474	3.20	+25.3	24	2.9237	3.135	+21.1	40	2.6529	2.901	+24.8
9	3.5157	3.404	−11.2	25	2.9280	3.20	+27.2	41	2.6546	2.857	+20.2
10	2.8899	3.232	+34.2	26	2.8953	3.265	+37	42	2.9053	2.828	−7.7
11	3.5426	3.409	−13.4	27	2.8073	3.132	+32.5	43	2.6423	2.849	+20.7
12	3.4451	3.436	−0.9	28	2.9608	3.11	+14.9	44	2.6469	2.816	+16.9
13	3.4501	3.346	−10.4	29	3.0440	3.083	+3.9	45	2.4782	2.772	+29.4
14	2.8442	3.20	+35.6	30	3.1350	3.115	−2	46	2.8181	2.742	−7.6
15	3.2703	3.357	+8.7	31	2.7821	3.070	+28.8	47	2.8800	3.20	+3.2
16	3.0633	3.273	+21	32	2.7424	3.051	+30.9				

GENIO CIVILE PISA

PER COPIA CONFORME
L'INGEGNERE DIRETTORE

Pisa 12 Giugno 1918 N° 42

Il Direttore dei Lavori

Figure 8.2: Pro-forma calculating change orders for the construction materials of the Pisa settlement. ANRCR, box 104.12, folder 2.

The essay hinges on the profound transformations on the international stage resulting from the protracted territorial instability and the involuntary population movements during the First World War and its immediate aftermath. As historian Peter Gatrell writes, the war brought the simultaneous collapse of three multiethnic empires with the emergence of modern nation-states with bounded citizenships – that is, with citizenships defined and delimited by ethnic origins.[6] In turn, the absence of space within the juridical order of the modern nation-states for anything other than the native prompted the internationalization of responses to the humanitarian crises of displacement.[7] All three factors – imperial collapses, nascent nation-states, and an international humanitarian system – found a permanent expression after the war. The creation of the League of Nations and its specialized agency, the High Commissioner for Refugees, formalized a legal framework of refugee and minority protections and set up an international system for monitoring the protracted period of displacement that followed the armistice, while the Paris Peace Conference of 1919–1920 and the Treaty of Versailles of 1923 re-apportioned the region and its peoples.[8] However, this unravelling and rebuilding had already begun during the war: between 1914 and 1919, entire communities were deported or interned because they were perceived as suspect and disloyal civilian subjects. These forceful expulsions and internments added to the already dreadful condition of civilians escaping the wrath of enemy troops from regions bordering the theaters of war.[9] At the same time, most European governments began reconstruction, nation-building projects, and programs for the consolidation of their territorial boundaries while hostilities were ravaging the region.[10] On the other side of the Atlantic, the US ascended, Adam Tooze argues, as the economic and political power of the world.[11] After three years of isolation, the Wilson administration brought the country into the war in 1917, ready to finance and dictate the terms of peace. While the US would eventually retrench and pullback from Europe, its networks of capital and humanitarian assistance would leave a profound impact in the region.

Architecture and Humanitarian Publicity

On February 25, 1918, the American consular officer in Venice sent an urgent letter to Chester Aldrich urging the entire ARC Commission in Italy to agitate for the development of a "refugee colony in Pisa." The Commission had been recently instituted by the War Council in Washington as an attempt to mitigate this humanitarian crisis in the Allied territory after the Caporetto defeat.[12] It was this new Commission that the consular officer addressed when he wrote:

> Gentlemen: This letter, which I am sending through Major Aldrich, is addressed to the entire [American Red Cross] Commission [in Italy] because it refers to a matter that, if undertaken, will demand full cooperation of every Department of the Commission [and] will furnish a concrete, tangible and visible evidence of what the Commission is capable of undertaking and will prove the most effective organ of propaganda both in Italy and America for the American Red Cross.[13]

The "matter" at hand entailed the development of discreet settlements for the displaced population to be constructed and managed by the ARC and its Commission. This was neither an original idea nor unfamiliar to the American humanitarians who had been exporting similar schemes around the world since the early 1900s. From occupied Havana (1900) to the Balkans (1912), from Sicily (1908) to the Huai River valley in

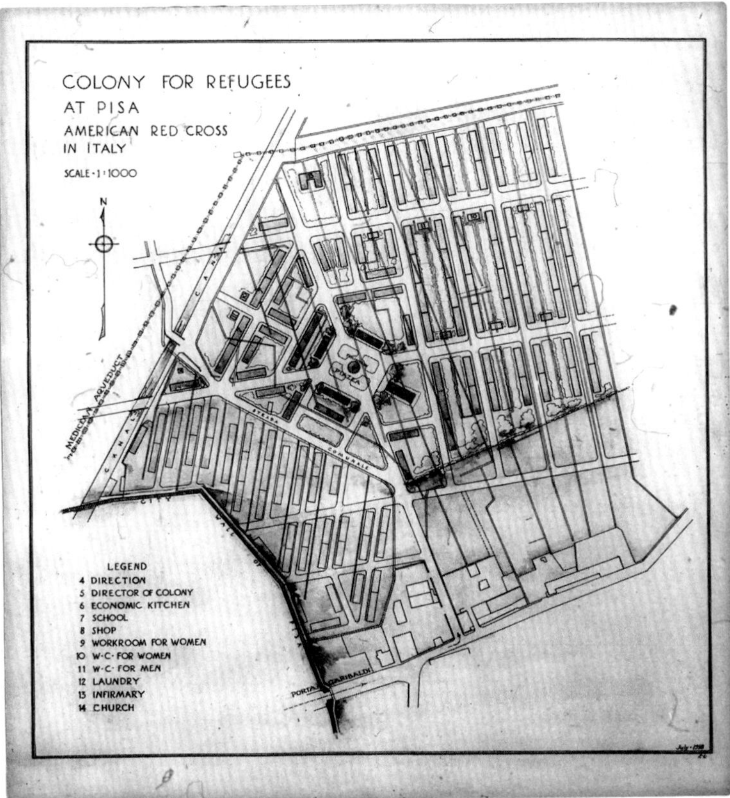

Figure 8.3: Chester Aldrich and Department of Civil Affairs in Italy. Master plan of the American City, 1918. ANRCR, box 103.15, folder 4.

China (1911), the ARC had implemented this formula for displaced populations in the aftermath of conflicts and natural disasters. However, what was at stake for the Commission was not the efficacy of the proposed "colonization plans," but rather their capacity to operate as "concrete, tangible, and visible evidence" of propaganda.

The next day, the officer followed up with a second letter containing an even more forceful plea. Addressing the entire Commission for the second time, he warned, "if we neglect this, I fear it will be a long time before we get another such opportunity."[14] If there was any question about what he meant by "opportunity," the officer volunteered a clarification:

> Such a colony would appeal to the American press and to the American public, it would lend itself to the camera and the cinema as a concrete example of what America can do when she bows her neck to it.[15]

These words were not accidental, but rather indicative of how publicity and mass media were constitutive and essential components of modern humanitarianism. With unexpected clarity, the officer affirmed the Commission's priorities and tapped into the fundamental rules that governed the ARC; what preoccupied the humanitarian experts and bureaucrats was how the organization's programs would appeal to the American public. In other words, acts of humanitarian aid were not only directed towards their beneficiaries – to those in need – but also had to be channeled back to their benefactors who had donated money, clothes, and compassion. To be sure, in order to keep the organization afloat, the ARC had to continuously relay from the front, persuade its supporters, and solicit their donations. Therefore, humanitarian solutions to specific exigencies had to perform a dual task: they needed both to fulfill their humanitarian commitments on the ground, and, as Carroll himself put it, "lend [themselves] to the camera and the cinema."[16] Therefore, the proposed territorial scheme, as much as it was intended for wartime propaganda and patriotic uplift, also belonged to a different variance of propaganda, namely the humanitarian publicity campaign of the ARC that prefigured the war and its imperatives.

Since the early 1900s, the American Red Cross had built an extensive publicity apparatus that would enlarge and intensify with America's entry in the First World War in 1917. In 1905, the organization founded an Editorial Bureau and launched its main conduit with the public, the *American Red Cross Magazine*. By 1914, the Editorial Bureau was revamped into a forceful Division for Information, run by public relations executives and advertisers.[17] And three years later, the ARC entrusted the department to Ivy L. Lee, the renowned publicity expert who had been representing the Rockefeller family, as well as major railroad companies such as Union Pacific.[18] Under the Division's control, regional publicity branches, photography departments, and a Bureau of Motion Picture would be founded and dissolved according to strategic demands, specific campaign needs, and available funds.[19] Eventually, the ARC created an extensive publicity apparatus that harnessed the power of various media technologies and launched multivalent campaigns that targeted audiences both at home and abroad.

By the early 1910s, the American public had become accustomed to a worldwide display of suffering and to a spectacle of American success and succor.[20] Through the monthly *Red Cross Magazine,* staged exhibitions, and a series of 38 commissioned movies, the organization advocated for the value of humanitarian assistance and foreign relief, and solicited private donations.[21] By pioneering the use of media and communication technologies in the service of philanthropy, the organization mastered the art of humanitarian persuasion, and transformed from a small charitable society to a mass phenomenon claiming its place in American politics. Much like a commercial enterprise, it utilized mass media to convince the public of the organization's efficacy, and competed with other philanthropic institutions for donations. As the historian

Kevin Rozario has observed, the triumph of the ARC's mass humanitarianism was assured when fundraising became a marketing exercise, and charitable giving a mass consumer activity.[22]

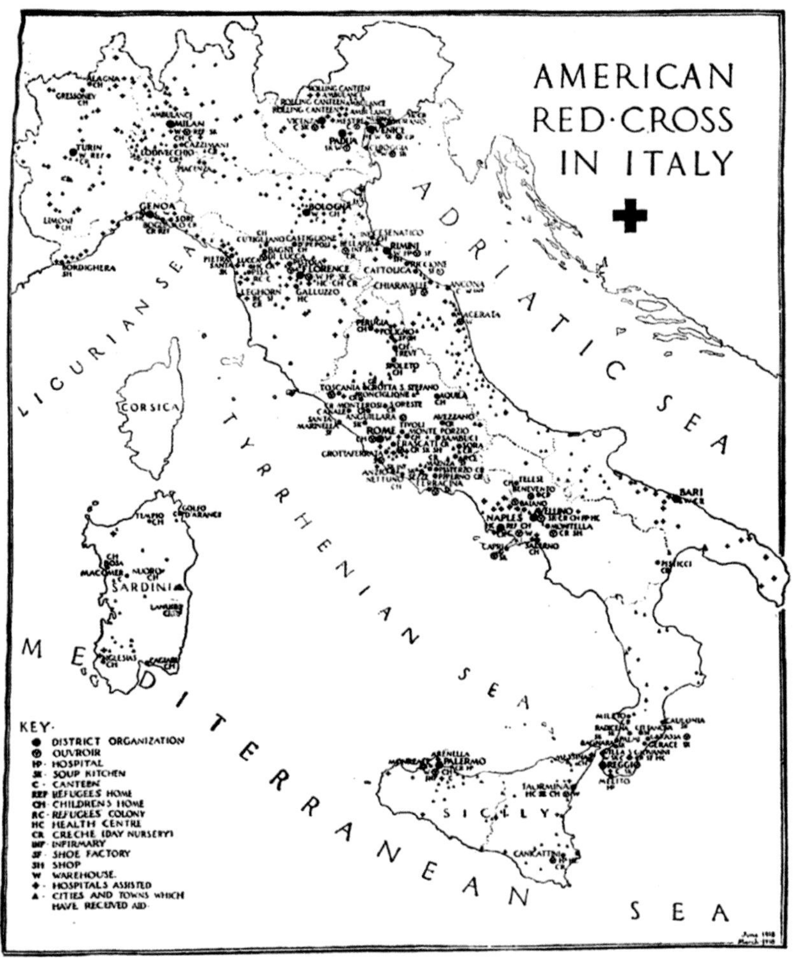

Figure 8.4: "A map showing points of American Red Cross work in Italy." William Hereford, "With the American Red Cross in Italy," *American Red Cross Magazine* 13, no. 11 (November 1918): 14–19.

The multiple media encounters put forward by the organization created a constellation of commercial advertisements, scientific developments, and images of horror. Articles on the latest public health news could be found a page away from photographs of war victims, while product advertisements stood side-by-side with heroic depictions of humanitarian workers. Accounts of "The War Orphans of France" juxtaposed advertisements of "Wrigley's Gum: The Flavor that Lasts," and images like "Gas Attack" appeared next to "The Ryzon: The Perfect Baking Powder."[23] It was not what media theorists have called sensationalism, but rather a carefully constructed cognitive dissonance between horror and consumption, empathy and guilt. This continuously shifting gaze orchestrated the proverbial spectator's dilemma, in which those exposed to the suffering of others were caught between "the egoistic ideal of self-realization and an altruistic commitment to causes which enables one to realize one-self through action."[24] To this dilemma, the humanitarian movement of the ARC, and in particular its sites of humanitarian relief, offered a resolution. Photographs of relief camps, dispensaries, and emergency shelters, and maps of humanitarian stationings supplied the coveted "concrete, tangible and visible evidence" of what America could do "for the alleviation of human suffering in times of war and peace."[25] Humanitarian architecture, as a medium and as it travelled through multiple media, became the organization's distinguishing marker, not unlike the Red Cross insignia and uniforms.

Imperial Spectacle and Humanitarian Architecture

Most indicative of such congruity was the American Red Cross exhibition presented amidst the phantasmagoric display of America's imperial vision at the Panama–Pacific International Exposition (PPIE) in San Francisco in 1915. The fair celebrated the completion of the Panama Canal, the culmination of the United States' historical trajectory of empire-building, according to which the forbidding frontier was ordered, made efficient and productive.[26] However, the narrative embodied in the fair shifted the focus from sublimity and westward expansion to a new spectacle of modernity that celebrated twentieth-century technological exploitation of resources, as well as material and moral reforms. In a case of well-crafted parallelism, just as the human-made canal of Panama merged the waters of the two oceans, so, too, the fair attempted to weave together the domestic imperatives of nation-building with the new international order.[27] For government officials and exhibition organizers, the national imaginary was contingent on America's newly assumed role as *the* ethical and modern world power. Thus, while the Great War was ravaging the Old World, America was not only to remain unscathed, but also, according to President Wilson, to assert its role as the guardian of progress and civilization. At once, the exposition enticed the public with an array of engineering wonders – "the striking evidence of the practical genius and artistic taste of America" – and visualized the efficacy of American's civilizing missions throughout the world.[28]

It was that very vision of a benevolent empire that ARC was called upon to exemplify at its staged exhibition, which strategically occupied a prominent position at the Palace of Liberal Arts, the building dedicated to governmental displays. As the

ARC officials declared at the fair, "the American Red Cross is the humanitarian arm of the United States Government, and its only recognized volunteer relief organization;" therefore, it should be "part of the government display [and] be considered a Government department."[29] If this coexistence at the exhibition grounds rendered the ARC indistinguishable from any other governmental agency, it also symbolically materialized the instrumentality of humanitarian and relief operations in American politics. While the fair glorified the figure of the engineer as the representative of America's utilitarian power, it was the humanitarian worker who wore the mantle of civilizing power and ethical judgment.[30]

Glaring flashes of light emanating from a lighthouse carrying the Red Cross insignia greeted fairgoers as they entered the Palace. Timed at six-second intervals, these flashes performed the ARC's assertion that since 1905 the organization had expended 12,000,000 dollars for the relief of human suffering worldwide; "the Beacon Light of Humanity" had spent approximately one dollar every six seconds of each working day over the previous 10 years.[31] Standing near this machine that calculated relief in dollars and watts were enlarged models of various "insect transmitters of disease … and bubonic rats burrowing though buildings."[32] Statistical charts, maps, transparencies, and didactic material for preventing contagion and infection complemented the menacing displays, mounted by the US Public Health Service. In close quarters, the Census Bureau staged a number of its computers, "electrically operated skeptical machines" capable of transcribing, classifying, and computing population data (e.g. age, race, and gender) collected in the census of 1910.[33] These "magical things shown in operation," a chronicler observed, had "the uncanny power of detecting inconsistencies and spewing statements out of its metal mouth."[34]

If the opening room of the Palace of Liberal Arts bewildered the public, the humanitarian architecture of the ARC brought this narrative linking governance, public health, and population management to a coherent close. A wall of transparencies contrasted photographs of territories ravaged by natural disasters and wars with depictions of ARC personnel administering aid in numerous affected locations. This constellation of photographs, locations, disasters, and chronologies remained unidentified and decontextualized, while the only recurring and recognizable figures were nurses dressed in white uniforms providing care to victims of disasters around the globe. The very same devices and uniforms, first aid kits and stethoscopes, traversed from the celluloid to the tactile world as they reappeared in cabinet displays to be experienced first-hand by the fairgoers under the eerie presence of the two life-size mannequins wearing Red Cross uniforms. A similar narrative was memorialized in the two-reel movie "A Day with a Red Cross Nurse," which alternated with the motion picture "Before the Doctor Comes." More importantly, the ARC exhibits at the PPIE centered around the spatial technologies and architectural protocols deployed by the humanitarian organization in two key strategic locations: the relief efforts in Messina and Reggio Calabria, Italy, after the earthquake of 1908, and the flood prevention and reclamation project in Huai Valley, China (1911–1915). These two aid initiatives, located equidistant from the city of San Francisco, traded in high symbolic value, as they represented the expanding frontier of US diplomatic and humanitarian ambitions.

Figure 8.5: "Signing the contract by which the American Red Cross agrees to build the village at Pisa housing 2000 refugee, 1918." American National Red Cross photograph collection, Library of Congress Prints and Photographs Division Washington (LC), A6196-4566. Architect Chester Aldrich is at the center with the governor of the Province of Pisa and the Pisan contractor, explaining the scheme. ARC officials can be easily identified by their military uniforms although not members of the U.S. armed forces. To emphasize its role as the official arm of the army, the U.S. government had allowed the ARC to assign its leaders military ranks.

In the center of the 4,300–square-foot space allotted to the ARC, a cyclorama illustrated two contrasting conditions: on one side of its concave walls, "a beautiful image of the ruins of Messina" was presented in the manner of a romantic landscape painting.[35] The opposite side presented an aerial view of a typical village constructed by the ARC on lands requisitioned by the Italian government in the immediate aftermath of the earthquake.[36] This immersive experience of the cyclorama was accompanied by a detailed account of the massive relief effort where five chartered cargo steamers left New York and New Orleans, loaded with more than 11 million feet of lumber, prefabricated elements, and dispatches of technical experts, architects, contractors, and medical personnel.[37] Outside the cyclorama, large-scale models of emergency shelters and of the "standard cottage" built in Messina narrated "the building bee" plan, the latest development in humanitarian architecture. This method resembled, in today's architectural parlance, the self-help building method, by which communities of displaced people came together to construct the homes with their own labor.

If the reconstruction of Messina and Reggio Calabria set out the blueprint for future interventions, the conservancy of the Huai River valley in China represented the apogee of this trajectory.[38] The project entailed an ambitious flood prevention and irrigation scheme in the rural regions of North Jiangsu and Anhui, where recurring floods, famines, and disease outbreaks had been threating the lives of Chinese civilians. Emboldened by their organizational success in Italy, the humanitarians embarked on their first disaster prevention plan in a foreign country: a development project *par excellence*, on 17,000 square miles of reclaimed land.[39] The project was part of the US "Open Door Policy" in China, which sought to guarantee American access to Chinese markets, and counteract European and Japanese dominance in a region viewed as a vast, untapped marketplace. To represent the various scales and modalities of intervention at the PPIE, the ARC responsible for the exhibition created two models. The first was a plaster cast topographic model of the Jiangsu region, which detailed the engineering project on a territorial scale, while the second zoomed into one of the pilot famine camps and represented the day-to-day operations "used by the Red Cross to house the people and their manner of living." Spectators exiting the space were then confronted with four massive bas-relief maps recording ARC operations on four continents.

Restructuring Institutional Commitments

This geographical expansion and the modes of humanitarian operations presented at the PPIE were not prefigured in the founding charter of the National American Red Cross Society of 1881; the organization did not initially aim to become the nation's principal agency for foreign assistance and diplomacy. With the founding of the National Society in the US, its first leader, Clara Barton, alongside the other signatories, declared themselves members of the International Red Cross Movement, which had been formalized in Geneva almost two decades earlier, in 1864.[40] Originally envisioned by its Swiss founders in the early 1860s, Red Cross societies in each nation were to enact the objectives of the Geneva Convention of August 22, 1864, of "civilizing war conduct." In short, each nation would have a Red Cross society that would supply medical care and relief supplies to its soldiers wounded in battle.[41] This limited scope was quickly enlarged in 1884 to also encompass the provision of relief in times of both peace and war.

However, as much as the ARC drew from its European counterparts and this latter mandate, it also developed in tandem with American missionary and charitable societies active around the world. As it joined the network of existing American missionary forces (such as the Young Women's and Young Men's Christian Association, the World's Good Habits Society, among many others), the ARC saw itself as an enterprise that would morally and materially reform the countries to which it went.[42] Respectively, if conflicts, famines, and natural disasters prompted the dispatch of aid workers, it was not emergency relief that structured ARC humanitarian commitments. Rather, ARC officials sought to export programs of civilian assistance that could increase American influence throughout the world.[43] With stationings from Cuba to Italy and from China to Russia, these *fin-de-siècle* humanitarians articulated an imperial vision – not of territorial domination, but rather of cultural expansion. As the historian Julia Irwin has shown, foreign assistance through a charitable civic society provided a viable alternative for the American polity that had long cherished, even if only in name, the Monroe doctrine, which was based on the policy of non-intervention. On the one hand, the proponents of American isolationism from both political parties deemed indirect intervention through the ARC more palatable.[44] On the other, those committed to the expansion of American interests into the world, either through the market or the military, saw international aid as a natural corollary. Eventually, as successive administrations harnessed the organization's potential, the popularity of the ARC cut across the ideological spectrum.

In 1905, Congress repealed the ARC's previous charter and enacted a new federal one that charged the organization with serving as the official US disaster relief organization responsible for "carrying on a system of national and international relief in time of peace and apply[ing] the same in mitigating the sufferings caused by pestilence, famine, fire, floods, and other great national calamities."[45] The Charter also required the organization to provide Congress with annual reports of its operations and expenditures, a mandate typically placed upon governmental entities, and provided the President of US with the power to appoint members to the organization's executive boards.[46] This federal designation of 1905 not only elevated the visibility and status of the ARC, but also effectively transformed it into a quasi-governmental instrument of the US government.[47] It is hard to overstate how radical this organizational shift was: an independent civic society which relied on private donations could now serve as an informal federal agency responsible for advancing state objectives. Since no equivalent organizational paradigm existed, the rules that structured this ambiguous synergy between humanitarian organization and government had to be negotiated, tested, and recalibrated case by case along the way, resulting in an often improvisational and unpredictable dance. However, what was certain in this choreography was that both parties could rely on and benefit from each other so long as the organization's humanitarian imperatives aligned with the government's priorities.

A new generation of military men, government officials, and technical experts – i.e. business executives, hospital administrators and architects – ousted the old guard of ARC leaders, most notably its founder Clara Barton and her circle of like-minded volunteers and nurses. If the ARC's imperatives under Barton's tutelage had been couched in the language of altruism, solidarity, and care, the new leaders claimed a new era of professionalism, efficiency, and scientific management. This transformation culminated with America's entry into World War I in April of 1917, when President Woodrow Wilson directly appointed a Red Cross War Council responsible for overseeing the organization. In the words of the new coterie of ARC officials, "the problem consists of collecting, at widely separated points, goods required, and delivering these to destination with the least possible delay. In practice, the factors controlling proper results are the same as those confronting any large business, handling a volume of, say, 100,000,000 per annum."[48]

The ARC Permanent Commission in Italy, established a few months later and headed by the industrialist Robert Perkins, exemplified this transformation. Described as "men of wide experience," three celebrated architects from the American Northeast – Guy Lowell, Chester Aldrich, and Edgar I. Williams – joined the ranks of the Commission, and respectively headed the Department of Military Affairs, the Department of Civil Affairs, and the Genoa division.[49] These three architects – and the many more who had joined the ARC cause[50] – had participated in Progressive Era reforms in the US, from advancing housing programs to setting conventions and standards for the discipline through professional societies and educational institutions.[51] While the ARC had contracted architects before, this new cast of technical experts was embedded within the institutional structure. This was not coincidental, but rather symptomatic of how humanitarian objectives and the disciplinary limits of architecture converged. To use Anooradha Iyer Siddiqi's astute observation when describing the institutionalization of architecture expertise on humanitarian relief in the 1960s and 1970s, the establishment of this professional culture fulfilled mutual desires between architecture and humanitarianism.[52] That was also the case in the earlier twentieth century for the coterie of experts who joined the ranks of the organization, shaped operational priorities, developed territorial protocols, mapped and measured destruction and population movements, directed resettlement schemes, and devised spatial technologies. On the one hand, they believed that it was imperative to intervene in a constantly evolving crisis in order to effect their objectives.[53] On the other, they shared the same anxieties of sustaining professional neutrality through which humanitarianism, as well as architecture, could appear an agent of science, technocracy, and universal good. This cast of characters had pledged their allegiance not to their Beaux-Arts training and the formal competencies it taught them, but to a political and social milieu that espoused technical expertise as a medium for progress. Chester Aldrich had done so by working with the planner and social worker Mary Kingsbury Simkhovitch as a member of the Greenwich House board, and Guy Lowell by setting professional standards for the nascent disciplines of landscape and planning as the founder of the landscape program at MIT, among others. By claiming the discipline's social function and appealing to its scientific and technocratic basis, they sought to redefine the terms of professional service. Conscription to the American Red Cross and to its commitments was one of them.

The American City in Pisa

In November of 1917, Italy suffered a devastating defeat of its forces by the German and Austro-Hungarian armies in the Battle of Caporetto, which resulted in mass casualties and the flight of more than 500,000 refugees from the northern regions of Friuli, Veneto, and Trentino to the country's south.[54] To support their American ally, members of the ARC Commission in France were dispatched to Italy to lay the groundwork. As the ARC Commissioner in Europe explained, Congress was not in session, and thus the American military was not authorized to act.[55] The ARC, a semi-governmental agency and a more agile instrument that could bypass the lengthy procedures of Washington, was called to action.[56] The ARC Permanent Commission in Italy instituted a couple of months later, in early January 1918, took control of the relief operations and increased the organization's presence in the region. Following the now-established protocol of operations, it divided its resources between military and civilian assistance. Hospital, ambulance, and canteen services addressed the needs of the Italian army, while refugee camps, hospital, dispensaries, communal kitchens, and workshops, in addition to cash allowances, comprised civilian aid, which consumed much of the Committee's attention.

Since 1914, the Italian state had created a classificatory system separating the *regnicoli*, civilians of Italian origins living in the Hapsburg lands, who were considered *refugees*, from the enemy non-combatants, who were treated as *internees*.[57] The categories were not only uncertain but also a manifestation of both the social, linguistic, and ethnic heterogeneity of the region, and cultivated an environment of fear and suspicion against the displaced.[58] These two categories came to a breaking point after the Caporetto defeat, when civilians fled from the areas of Udine, Belluno, and Venice, exacerbating disparities and internal divisions not only between refugees and internees, but also between Friulian and Venetian refugees (i.e. displaced subjects from "invaded" and "not invaded" territories), as well as between established and displaced communities. The Caporetto defeat also prompted the Italian government to establish a central Refugee High Commissariat, which instituted a policy of daily subsidies, and systematized a nationwide emergency housing program by requisitioning and renting properties on behalf of the displaced population.

Figure 8.6: "ARC city at Pisa. Trucks with material passing leaning tower, 1918." LC, A6196-5312.

Figure 8.7: "ARC city at Pisa. At work on the grounds, leaning tower in distance, 1918." LC, A6196-5318.

Devising a Plan

It was at this particular juncture that the ARC Permanent Commission in Italy proposed the deployment of a territorial management scheme long in the making. Both the consular officer in Venice and Chester Aldrich agreed that segregating the displaced population from established communities that had already been impacted by the war would be the right way forward. First, the proposed scheme conformed to the priorities of the Italian Refugee High Commissariat that had already been deterring the displaced from seeking shelter in Italy's urban centers and towns. This policy aimed at containing the defeatist sentiment prevalent among more recent refugees from the north, but also at allaying established communities' hostility towards the displaced.[59] At the same time, this separation, the ARC Department agreed, would diffuse economic pressures resulting from superimposing a refugee population on a series of cities, towns, and villages overwhelmed with their own economic problems and, at the same time, would make the administering of relief more efficient.[60] As Carroll argued, such territorial organization could bypass the "great difficulties that come from laboring with other organizations and the red tape municipal, governmental, et. al [sic], that hamper efforts at relief." In short, while the ARC had to coordinate its efforts with the High Commissariat, it sought to gain as much autonomy as possible to "effectively demonstrate what the American Red Cross is capable of doing."[61]

Figure 8.8: "ARC city at Pisa. The first building, 1918." LC, A6196-5318.

To make his proposal tangible, the consular officer drew from the history of colonial management, and without hesitation described the project as a "first-class concentration camp" for 15,000 refugees fleeing the air raids carried by the Austro-Hungarian army in the Veneto region. The technology of the "concentration camp" – that is, the indiscriminate confinement of civilians in camps – was developed in colonial contexts as a military strategy against guerrilla warfare during colonial rebellions, and was used by the Spanish in Cuba, the British in South Africa, and the Americans in the Philippines. Since the 1890s, when the strategy was first implemented, official reports and widely circulated newspapers had been recording that tens of thousands of civilians had died from malnutrition and epidemics in those camps. In addition, the strategy was widely debated in parliamentary procedures in the UK and congressional hearings in the US, as well as within the networks of humanitarian workers. What is more, Carroll did not have to resort to these public fora to learn about the inhumane treatment of civilians in the camps; he had seen them first-hand while volunteering for service in the Spanish-American War in 1898 as an *aide-de-camp* in the Texas National Guard. If this experience did not dissuade him from alluding to the colonial

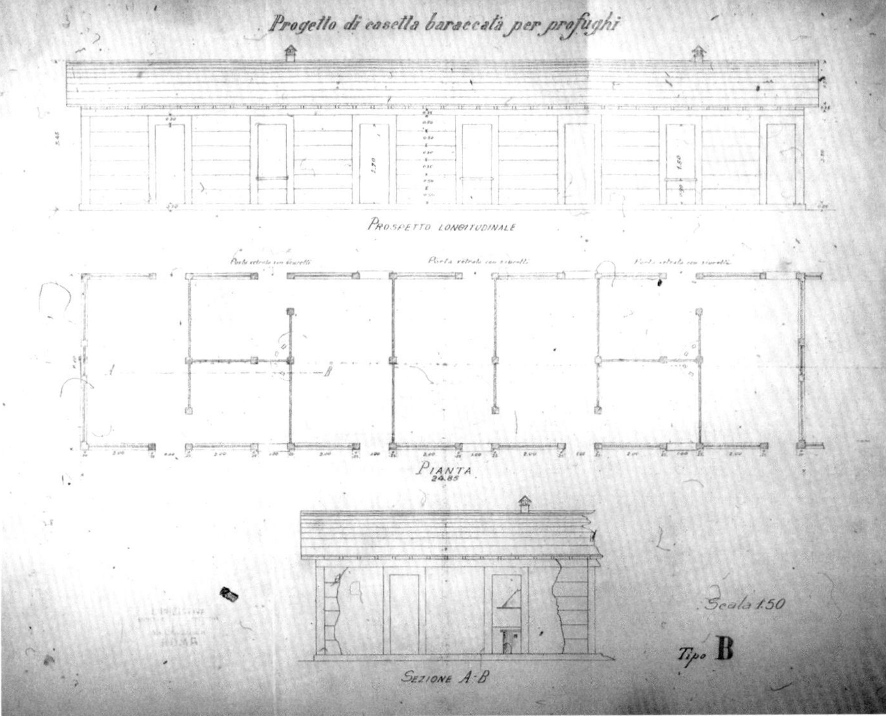

Figure 8.9: Elevation, plan and section of housing "barrack for refugees." Visible are two different typologies of the domestic units. Scale 1:50. ANRCR, box 103.15, folder 4.

technology, it was probably what made him qualify the proposed ARC scheme as a *first-class* camp. An indication that ARC officials were aware of the strategy's violent history was that this oxymoron never appeared again in official documents or press releases, and the scheme was renamed the American City. However, by invoking this spatial technology, the American officials revealed much of the underlying logic and lineage of their territorial management strategy.

It was in context of the Boer Wars (1899–1902) that the term "concentration camp" first entered the English lexicon. This military tactic can, however, be traced back to the Spanish *reconcentrados* campaign during the Cuban War of Independence (1895–1898).[62] In both cases, the concentration of civilians as a counterinsurgency measure was deployed by the colonial armies in an effort to contain guerilla warfare. To strip the guerrilla fighters of their ability to live off the land and shelter themselves among civilians, the respective colonial powers forcibly displaced and confined non-combatants in fortified camps where they would be under the control of the army. As opposed to other penal and disciplinary sites, the military tactic of the concentration camp operated according to a preemptive logic and outside any regular judicial procedure.[63] Yet camps under martial law were only one such episode in the longer trajectory of mass interment implemented by colonial powers. A well-established genealogy links the Victorian workhouses for the poor in British metropoles to the famine and plague camps of the colonies, revealing the ample overlap between the military and medical technologies of reform and exclusion.[64] As Aidan Forth explains, institutions of nineteenth-century capitalism aimed to reform and rehabilitate by excluding inmates temporary, albeit in the name of re-incorporating them as productive members of the society.[65] Structured around social, gender, and racial divisions, they sought to reform subjects by instrumentalizing labor and sanitation as pedagogical tools.

What is often omitted from this lineage is how humanitarian organizations legitimized the spatial technology of the camp and incorporated it into their operations. Clara Barton's argumentation about the ARC civilian assistance in Cuba during the war of independence in 1901 captured this moment of transference of the counterinsurgency strategy into the humanitarian repertoire. Appalled as she was by the "cruel policy of Spain in driving the reconcentrados away from their lands," she did not dispute its very rationale.[66] To the contrary, she explained that "the native guerilla [is] to be feared. There is where the danger lies [for the civilians and reconcentrados]." Her organization's mission, therefore, was to improve the conditions in the camps without making "the helpless reconcentrados professional paupers by doling out to them each day, for indefinite time, free soup and old clothes."[67] As a response, the ARC created a land cultivation scheme in the spaces of confinement and instituted sanitation protocols, which, according to Barton, were necessary since Cubans "even in their better days have never been accustomed to cleanliness."[68] Therefore, if the mass internment of enemy civilians had a military rationale of protecting the colonial regime, it also found a justification in the humanitarian claim that civilians had to be concentrated in order to be accommodated and fed amidst war hostilities and scorched-earth campaigns. Similar to the isolation of the poor in the Victorian workhouses and the quarantine of the sick in relief camps, the administrators alleged that they equally protected those inside and outside these preemptive detainment spaces. In other words, the categories deemed in need of humanitarian assistance were confined both because they were under threat and because they were perceived as a threat.[69] This Janus-faced definition of protection and exclusion structured the principles of the humanitarian camp as it returned to its place of origin during the war.

Territorial Strategy

The ARC's initial ambitious plan of accommodating 15,000 people was scaled down to a pilot settlement for 2,000 refugees, with the potential of expanding to 5,000 in a second phase. The first settlement was expected to be completed in 120 days, and would accommodate refugees from the Veneto region who had sought refuge in Tuscany. The Commission had first considered the Parco Reale San Rossore, a remote pine forest facing the Ligurian Sea to the west of Pisa as a possible location. Instead, however, they opted for a 30-acre site strategically located in exurban east Pisa. A marshland comprised of properties requisitioned by the Italian government, the grounds were delimited to the south by the historic wall and to the west and north by the Medicean Aqueduct. Aldrich's plan extended onto the site extant axes of Pisa's regulating plan with the purpose of facilitating the settlement's future integration with the city's possible expansions. Nevertheless, for this first phase, the delineation by the fortification wall and the aqueduct on three sides in conjunction with the provision of a singular entry to the site created a clearly defined enclave. As the Department of Civil Affairs put it, the site was "sufficiently segregated" to guarantee the unhindered administering of relief, but also "sufficiently near to Pisa to take advantage of the economic life [of the city]."[70]

The scheme, therefore, was isolated enough, yet adjacent to large manufacturing facilities that could employ the displaced population. The Department predicted that most refugees from Venice would be "women, since every able-bodied man in Italy whose work is not allotted to him behind the lines is fighting at the front."[71] Those not employed at the nearby cotton mills, the Department argued, would advance "traditional home industries" of Venice such as lacemaking and clothmaking. The newest Washington directive expected recipients of aid to work either in the day-to-day operations of the relief sites or in adjacent industries. This included participating in existing economic sectors of the region or in childcare, the preparation of food in communal kitchens, and the cultivation of subsistence crops in small gardens inside the camps. If economic necessity – the scarcity of resources – drove this policy, ideology provided the necessary justification; unconditional support, the officials from Washington often repeated, made the recipients of aid indolent and demoralized, leading to their "pauperization." Instead, the ARC claimed that it should solely "guide [the aid recipients] to help themselves."[72] It was this very postulate of self-help, according to officials, that distinguished traditional charity from modern humanitarianism. As the new coterie of experts declared, the ARC was no longer "a delightful but irresponsible 'fairy godmother'" – referring to the organization under Barton's leadership – but "the big brother of the Army and Navy that possessed both sentiment and sense."[73] In short, not unrestricted compassion – the proverbial "fellow feeling" – but rather pragmatism and scientific management should shape the ARC's priorities in the sites of humanitarian aid.

Again, this was not a new argument, but a well-worn one taken from the Victorian workhouse and the colonial camp; aid was conditional on labor and the ability to enter the labor market was positioned as a path to self-reliance.[74] If this language was at best paternalistic, at worst it drifted towards coercion. Since the American City would never be inhabited by refugees, official rules of conduct for the Pisa settlement were never issued by the Department of Civil Affairs. However, rules of ARC relief camps in neighboring countries illustrated how the application of this labor policy shaped the everyday life of the displaced. For example, the rules posted and distributed in Greek camps read:

> You have to obey the orders of the chiefs of your camp, you have to follow the rules they will give for the work in the camps. Every able-bodied grownup individual has to work. Those who do not work do not deserve any relief and relief will, therefore, be refused them [sic].[75]

The Settlement: On Site and in Media

The plan devised by Aldrich and his department gave form to the enactment of this labor policy and carried the socially and racially inflicted practices of the colonial camp and the workhouse into the humanitarian camp. Military technologies and nascent postulates of modern planning merged in the scheme layout and materiality, ultimately crystalizing in a form that held an ambivalent position between relief and confinement, emergency aid and paternalism. First, promoting modern sanitary and hygienic reforms in the camps was one of ARC's priorities: "To relieve this housing situation," the Red Cross equipped and operated "barracks that did not only protect the inmates from the wind and weather, but also served as a practical means of teaching cleanliness and sanitation."[76] Eighty one-story parallel blocks comprised the "living quarters" of the settlement outside of Pisa. According to the Department of Civil Affairs, its orientation along a north–south axis "secured sun and air in all the living spaces."[77] Subsistence gardens for the cultivation of vegetables and fruits were arranged linearly in between every two rows of houses.

On a rotated axis, a central square, the Piazza comunale, alongside a group of public buildings, interrupted the north–south parataxis of the housing blocks. At its center, a cubic folly adorned with inscriptions, friezes, and architraves encased a water fountain – the only source of drinking water in the settlement. This organization around a square, as well as the nomenclature (e.g. Piazza comunale, strada comunale) invoked the communal life of a village. If the appeal to Italy's vernacular typologies could foster self-reliance as exemplified in agrarian life, the plan was geared towards the labor policy and its supervision. To delimit the square, the ARC included a store selling goods produced in the settlement, a communal kitchen, and a workshop for women, overlooked by the director's office and residence. In addition, a school, a church, a nursery, and a hospital formed a second group of public amenities at the northwestern edge of the plan, behind the director's office.

All the buildings, both the housing and the public blocks, were one story high and of the same width (approximately six meters), but varied in length according to function. The structures were not intended for permanent use, though they had to endure at least 10 years of operational use. Therefore, according to the Department, they "adopted a type of construction halfway between a temporary barrack and a masonry house."[78] These barracks were constructed by prefabricated concrete elements crowned by wooden pitched roofs covered in flat ceramic tiles. Walls, ceilings, and finishes were plastered, and a coat of white paint was applied as a finish. As the Department proudly explained, this construction method was a recently "patented contrivance, a conglomerate composed with cement, volcanic lapilli mixed with moor rush."[79] Aldrich and his collaborators believed that this new patented technology would at once solve a multiplicity of interrelated issues, such as speed of construction, lack of skilled labor, and climatic conditions, among others. The lightweight conglomerate, the Department claimed, allowed for quick and easy transport and construction, making it ideal for emergency uses. At the same time, moor rushes and tephra ensured air circulation between the different layers of the conglomerate, providing basic insulation. As often as the Department advertised the innovative use of concrete prefabrication, they also alluded to its symbolism by repeating that the elements were made of "lapillo, which two [millennia] ago erupted from the Mt. Vesuvius and buried the famous cities of Pompei [sic] and Herculaneum."[80]

The endeavor and its symbolism did not go unnoticed: photographs of the site circulated in American popular media and professional journals within a few weeks of the settlement's ground-breaking ceremony. While still under construction, the American City found its place in the publicity apparatus of the ARC, and contrasted with recent war coverage depicting refugees fleeing war-ravaged territories and seeking temporary refuge in numerous historical and ancient Italian sites. These latter war photographs had linked the personal and corporeal with the geopolitical in a longer historical trajectory by juxtaposing the precarious life of the displaced with monuments and ancient Mediterranean ruins – the iconic monuments hitherto known as the sites for cultural pilgrimage through the Grand Tour. To use Michel Agier's term, these were "humanitarian pictures of the human," depictions of lives stripped bare in the degradations of suffering that reified "nothing else or other than absolute and essentialized humanity when it is suffering."[81] As humanitarian pictures of the human, they had stunned the American public and, in the hands of humanitarian publicists, had served as instruments for mobilizing compassion and donations.

However, the publicity campaign for the American City in Pisa turned this narrative on its head; it was no longer the life of the displaced stripped bare in the presence of the remains of Italy's triumphant past, but rather workers in uniform "unloading cement slabs." Detailed accounts of the American City accompanied vignettes showing material transported under the vigilant supervision of humanitarian workers in front of the Leaning Tower of Pisa. As the editor of the *ARC Magazine* explained, "the refugee problem in its immensity was nearly overwhelming," but the organization was ready to respond; "building a modern American town at Pisa" was one of its solutions. Exemplifying the ARC's publicity campaign was a picture of the American flag raised above the Medicean aqueduct, framing the orderly homes. The fluttering symbol caressed the prefabricated concrete elements, which, as the ARC officials repeated, were made of the same volcanic tephra that had buried Pompeii. Operating metonymically, the photographs carried the message home: the ARC, and by extension the US, was rebuilding Europe from its ashes.

Professional societies and their magazines, such as *The American Contractor* and *The Timberman,* saw a potential opening for the export of materials and expertise,[82] while the *Architectural Record* hailed the settlement for its modern facilities and layout. Its contributing editor and social reformer, Herbert Croly, alluded to the scheme's replicability and praised it as "an object lesson to other communities."[83] The ARC and the American government, capitalizing on this positive coverage, set in motion additional plans for refugee settlements throughout Europe, such as a "city of demountable houses" for Belgian refugees in Le Havre and a resettlement scheme for the displaced population in France, and established a Reconstruction Research and Educational Service Bureau in Europe.[84]

Despite this initial pomp, however, the Venetian refuges did not move into the American City, as it was never completed and swiftly disappeared from history. The reasons for the scheme's demise were and are paradigmatic of the recurring tensions between humanitarian organizations, recipients of aid, and local governments. From capital flows to contractual relations, the extraterritoriality of the humanitarian organization collided with the demands and conditions on the ground. First, the confidence bestowed on that material technology was one of the reasons that led to the scheme's inglorious end. The construction method using prefabricated concrete slabs proved far more complex and costly than anticipated. Raw materials, including lapillo, had to be collected from multiple locations and shipped to the manufacturer in Milan. Then the finished elements had to be transported from this off-site location to Pisa amidst war hostilities. As delays mounted, so too did frustration among humanitarians, manufacturers, and contractors.

Second, the relationship between the local contractors and American officials became combative when the former demanded better labor conditions on site. Specifically, the hired construction company, Società Cooperativa "L'Iniziativa", requested that the ARC follow Italian labor laws, which allowed workers to observe holidays and weekends. Such a concession on the part of the organization would have meant that the initial plan to complete the settlement within 120 days would have to be extended, which Aldrich and his department not only considered unacceptable but also a breach of the initial contract. To compound the problems, in the absence of an international bank for aid (such as today's World Bank), funds were to be transferred from American banks to an Italian credit union that would eventually lend its financial resources to the cooperative. In this debtor–creditor relationship, the union was required by Italian law to hold a percentage of the funds as a credit warranty, which infuriated the Americans. The Italian subjects, who had been described in the initial ARC reports as "grateful people disposed to order," who were in need of guidance to achieve self-governance, were now accused of "corruption," "insubordination," "inefficiency," and "unfaithfulness."[85] As the 120 days of construction passed and the armistice was in sight, the American Red Cross quietly withdrew from the project.[86]

With a little more than half of the buildings standing – 36 of the housing barracks and nine of the common amenities, including the public restrooms and the director's office – the American City, renamed the *Borgo veneziano* (Venetian Village), was liquidated and transferred to the Italian government. Under the government's supervision, the unfinished settlement served as a camp for prisoners-of-war, and a few years later as a sanatorium for returning Italian soldiers.[87] In 1941, the camp was eventually dismantled and converted into Casa Circondariale "Don Bosco," Pisa's largest carceral institution since its first day of operations in 1944, serving as a pre-trial detention center and a security prison with separate quarters for young adults, women, and men.[88] With a capacity of 206 inmates, it currently detains 305 people, the majority of whom are migrants from Morocco, Tunisia, and Albania. Traces of the regulating lines of the American City and its communal square can be found in the crumbling prison and its yard.

Conclusion

Policies devised during World War I – the humanitarian camp, the emergency shelter, and the cash allowance, among others – indeed reappear today, renamed and rebranded, as tried-and-tested solutions to the ever-expanding crisis of displacement. In fact, the resemblance of the endeavor of building the American City to current experiments with emergency shelters, from Shigeru Ban's paper log houses and ICON's 3D printed houses to IKEA's flat-pack refuge, deserves a mention. Aldrich's scheme and argumentation reads as one of the origin stories – if not a cautionary tale – of today's craze for experimenting, patenting, and exporting prototypes of houses to house the world's poor. More recently, there have been the "Digitally Fabricated Houses" by the World Bank and the American International Development Agency, and the 3D-printed houses made of post-industrial waste by the United Nations.[89] With renewed conviction and altruism, every generation of architects has added to a compendium of emergency solutions, intended to "provide shelter to the world's most vulnerable people." Promoted by global organizations, they transform disaster and conflict zones into sites of experimentation. The often-uttered argument is that "instead of a catastrophe, [architects] could look at this as a tremendous opportunity."[90] Whether made from lapillo, paper or agricultural waste, 3D printers or laser cutters, they might not yield the desired results in their loci of construction, but as they travel back to their places of origin through the media and reach their intended audiences steeped in their own "rule-based judgments and verifiability,"[91] they enter this self-reifying cycle.

Finally, the settlement in Pisa became the locus where the genealogy and overlap of technologies of relief and confinement, camp and city, acquired a starting materialization. To use the ARC Department's language, this genealogy became "concrete, tangible and visible." Spatial reasons for this continuity abounded – to name a few, the extramural location, a marshland, expropriated, drained, and flattened was prepared to house the "undesirables" – refugees, POWs, those awaiting trial and those convicted. In addition, the settlement's layout marked an urban memory and institutional continuity in which claims, rights, and desires were not expected to be negotiated and enacted but to be centrally supervised and managed by humanitarian workers and, later, by correctional officers. Therefore, the American City in Pisa complicates architectural historian Andrew Herscher's assertion that "while the accommodation of refugees can be at least notionally distinguished between housing, camp, and city over the course of the twentieth century, the distinctions between these architectures is collapsing in contemporary humanitarianism."[92] In this early instance of institutionalization of architectural expertise within the ARC's relief operations, these three elements – housing, camp, and city – had already collapsed into one. And thus, the normative forms of "humanitarian architecture" emerge from the sociotechnical assumptions of and about architecture as it became enmeshed in the political and managerial paradigm of humanitarian governance. Therefore, what is at stake in this story is not the site in Pisa as an isolated occurrence, but rather the topology of relations, epistemological assumptions, ideologies, and commitments of humanitarianism and its architecture.

Notes

1   Peter Gatrell, *The Making of the Modern Refugee* (Oxford: Oxford University Press, 2013), 27; for a detailed account on displacement and refugees during World War I in Italy, see Daniele Ceschin, *Gli esuli di Caporetto. I profughi in Italia durante la grande guerra* (Rome: Laterza, 2014).

2   Benajah Harvey Carroll to Chester Aldrich, "American Red Cross Relief Work," February 25, 1918, p. 3, American National Red Cross Records, Hoover Institution Library & Archives (ANRCR), box 103.15, folder 3.

3   Benajah Harvey Carroll to Chester Aldrich, "American Consular Service," February 26, 1918, p. 1, ANRCR, box 103.15, folder 3.

4   Carroll to Aldrich, "American Red Cross Relief Work," 4.

5   The essay converses with Siddiqi's scholarship that explores the institutionalization of architecture in humanitarian relief operations during the 1950–1970s. But it attempts to extend the temporal and spatial framework to the early twentieth century and the US. Anooradha Iyer Siddiqi, "Architecture Culture, Humanitarian Expertise: From the Tropics to Shelter, 1953–93," *Journal of the Society of Architectural Historians* 76, no. 3 (September 1, 2017): 367–84.

6   Gatrell, *The Making of the Modern Refugee*, 2–4; Peter Gatrell and Liubov Zhvanko, eds., *Europe on the Move: Refugees in the Era of the Great War* (Manchester: Manchester University Press, 2017); Peter Gatrell, "Introduction: World Wars and Population Displacement in Europe in the Twentieth Century," *Contemporary European History* 16, no. 4 (2007): 415–26.

7   Of the 85 million people affected by the dismemberment and reapportionment of the three empires, two-thirds were classified as citizens of one of the 28 "old enlarged, or newly created" nation-states. Thus, refugees and minorities did not represent individual cases but rather a mass phenomenon and a security concern that threatened the edifice of the post-war peace system. Joseph B. Schechtman, *European Population Transfers, 1939–1945* (New York: Russell and Russell, 1971), 4; "The whole system [was] based on a scheme of national states, with populations which fit into the scheme of nationalities," John Hope Simpson, a British Liberal politician who also served as League of Nations expert on refugees and second director of the RSC, explained. And he added, "[t]he person without nationality [did] not fit into that system." John Hope Simpson, *The Refugee Problem: Report of a Survey* (Oxford: Oxford University Press, 1939), 230; on bounded citizenship and the creation of ethnostates, see Giorgio Agamben, "Beyond Human Rights," in *Radical Thought in Italy: A Potential Politics*, ed. Paolo Virno and Michael Hardt (Minneapolis: University of Minnesota Press, 2006), 92.

8   On the system of Minority Treaties, see Mark Mazower, "Minorities and the League of Nations in Interwar Europe," *Daedalus* 126, no. 2 (1997): 47–63; for a brief account on the creation of League of Nations in the history of international organizations, see

Chapter 5 in Mark Mazower, *Governing the World: The History of an Idea, 1815 to the Present* (New York: Penguin Books, 2013); on the emergence of an international system of refugee definitions and protections, see Claudena M. Skran, *Refugees in Inter-War Europe: The Emergence of a Regime* (Oxford: Clarendon Press, 1995); on the protracted territorial instability after the war and the international agreements, see Renée Hirschon, "'Unmixing Peoples' in the Aegean Region," in *Crossing the Aegean: An Appraisal of the 1923 Compulsory Population Exchange between Greece and Turkey*, ed. Renée Hirschon (New York: Berghahn Books, 2003), 3–20.

9   Gatrell, *The Making of the Modern Refugee*, 25–35.

10   On a comprehensive account of different case studies of reconstruction and nation-building, see Luc Verpoest et al., *Revival after the Great War: Rebuild, Remember, Repair, Reform* (Leuven University Press, 2020).

11   Adam Tooze, *The Deluge: The Great War and the Remaking of Global Order, 1916–1931* (London: Penguin, 2014), 3–32.

12   "Permanent Commission to Italy Is Made Up of Men of Wide Experience," *Red Cross Bulletin. American Red Cross* 2, no. 8 (February 1918): 2.

13   Carroll to Aldrich, "American Consular Service," 1.

14   *Ibid.*

15   Carroll to Aldrich, "American Red Cross Relief Work," 4.

16   Carroll to Aldrich, "American Consular Service," 1.

17   "Division for Information Established for Public," *American Red Cross Magazine* 8, no. 3 (July 1914): 167.

18   Scott M. Cutlip, *The Unseen Power: Public Relations: A History* (London: Routledge, 2013), 67–70.

19   On the ARC's film production, see Jennifer Moore, "'Neutrality-Humanity': The Humanitarian Mission and the Films of the American Red Cross," in *Beyond the Screen: Institutions, Networks, and Publics of Early Cinema* (Bloomington, Ind.: Indiana University Press, 2016), 11–8, <https://www.jstor.org/stable/j.ctt1bmznbd>.

20   On the tension between suffering and succor in the construction of humanitarian empathy, see Didier Fassin, *Humanitarian Reason: A Moral History of the Present* (Los Angeles: University of California Press, 2011), 9.

21   Between 1915 and 1919 the American Red Cross Bureau of Pictures produced and distributed more than 38 films that ranged from propaganda and instructional to narrative films. In fact, for every dispatch of aid workers, the Bureau claimed that "the American Red Cross maintained an expert staff of camera men who are constantly taking pictures in all parts of the world." "Thirty-Eight Red Cross Films Circulating in Division," *American Red Cross Pacific Division Activities* 3, no. 6 (September 1920): 4.

22   Rozario pointedly writes that "modern 'humanitarianism' is in fact a creation of a sensationalistic mass culture. … The triumph of mass humanitarianism would not be assured until fundraising became a marketing exercise and charity-giving a mass consumer activity." Kevin Rozario, "'Delicious Horrors': Mass Culture, the Red Cross, and the Appeal of Modern American Humanitarianism," *American Quarterly* 55, no. 3 (2003): 418.

23   "Gas Attack," "The War Orphans of France," and the advertisements appear on the *American Red Cross Magazine* 13, no. 9 (September 1918): 14–9.

24   Luc Boltanski, *Distant Suffering: Morality, Media and Politics*, trans. Graham D. Burchell (Cambridge: Cambridge University Press, 1999), xiv.

25   This was the organization's credo that appeared in the covers and editorials of the monthly magazine since 1915.

26 Sarah J. Moore, *Empire on Display: San Francisco's Panama-Pacific International Exposition of 1915* (Norman, Okla.: University of Oklahoma Press, 2013), 3–9.

27 *Ibid.*, 8.

28 President Wilson's speech cited from Heidi Applegate, "Staging Modernism at the 1915 San Francisco World's Fair" (New York: Columbia University, Graduate School of Arts and Sciences, 2014), 5.

29 Lewis Stein, "The Red Cross Exhibit at the World's Fair," *American Red Cross Magazine* 10, no. 4 (April 1915): 150–4.

30 I am paraphrasing here Tichi's astute observation that the engineer was presented "as the descendent of once-powerful ministers and statesmen; his is ethical *and* utilitarian power. In an industrial era, in the gear-and-girder world, the engineer wears the mantle of civilizing and ethical power." Cecelia Tichi, *Shifting Gears: Technology, Literature, Culture in Modernist America* (Chapel Hill, N.C.: University of North Carolina Press, 1987), 99.

31 Stein, "The Red Cross Exhibit at the World's Fair," 151–2.

32 Frank Morton Todd, *The Story of the Exposition: Being the Official History of the International Celebration Held at San Francisco in 1915 to Commemorate the Discovery of the Pacific Ocean and the Construction of the Panama Canal*, vol. 4 (New York: G. P. Putnam's Sons, 1921), 106.

33 *Ibid.*, 104.

34 *Ibid.*, 104–5.

35 Stein, "The Red Cross Exhibit at the World's Fair," 153.

36 John Elliott, one of the architects working on the ground, recorded the day-to-day to operations in a memoir he coauthored with the Pulitzer-winning author Maud Howe Elliott. Maud Howe Elliott and John Elliott, *Sicily in Shadow and in Sun: The Earthquake and the American Relief Work* (Boston: Little, Brown, and Company, 1910), 148–50.

37 The director of the project chronicles the project in the memoir, Reginald Rowan Belknap, *American House Building in Messina and Reggio: An Account of the American Naval and Red Cross Combined Expedition, to Provide Shelter for the Survivors of the Great Earthquake of December 28, 1908* (New York: G. P. Putnam's Sons, 1910).

38 Arthur Powell Davis, "A Conservancy Project to Prevent Much Misery," *American Red Cross Magazine* 10, no. 1 (January 1915): 43–6.

39 Pietz links the environmental engineering of the Huai River with the construction of nationhood in the aftermath of the collapse of the Qing dynasty in 1911. Initially, the Chinese officials of the nascent Republic who had been trying to secure foreign investment for the project, welcomed the involvement of the ARC. However, the organization's paternalistic control antagonized the local administrators, making any transactional cooperation untenable. David Pietz, *Engineering the State: The Huai River and Reconstruction in Nationalist China, 1927–37* (London: Routledge, 2018); for Americans and American-trained Chinese individuals attempting to bring agrarian reforms to China, see Randall E. Stross, *The Stubborn Earth: American Agriculturalists on Chinese Soil, 1898–1937* (Los Angeles: University of California Press, 1986).

40 Marian Moser Jones, "Transatlantic Transplant," in *The American Red Cross from Clara Barton to the New Deal* (Baltimore: Johns Hopkins University Press, 2013), 21–36.

41 On the initial mandate of the International Red Cross movement and its militarization, see John F. Hutchinson, *Champions of Charity: War and the Rise of the Red Cross* (Boulder, Colo.: Westview Press, 1996).

42   Ian Tyrrell writes that "nineteenth-century moral reform was another and arguably important part of informal and formal U.S. Empire … Americans exported a wide variety of organizations designed for moral uplift. These groups were not identical in aims, structures, pet causes, or impacts, but they networked and overlapped extensively in their strategies, tactics, and ideologies." Ian Tyrrell, *Reforming the World: The Creation of America's Moral Empire* (Princeton: Princeton University Press, 2010), 2–3.

43   This argument is the subject of Irwin's inquiry. Julia F. Irwin, *Making the World Safe: The American Red Cross and a Nation's Humanitarian Awakening* (Oxford: Oxford University Press, 2017).

44   *Ibid.*, 9.

45   The American National Red Cross Charter of 1905 (33 Stat. 599–602).

46   The system granted charters to patriotic, charitable, historical, or educational non-profit organizations and ceased to exist in 1992. In its entire history there have been some 100 nonprofit corporations listed in Title 36, Subtitle I II and III, of the US Code, most of the gaining their charter after the ARC. Those organizations have been divided into three organizational categories: Subtitle I: Patriotic and National Observances and Ceremonies; Subtitle II: Patriotic and National Organizations; and Subtitle III: Treaty Obligation Organizations. This latter organizational category has only one entry, the ARC. It is there alone because it is only charter that charges an organization with fulfilling US treaty obligations under the Geneva Conventions. The American National Red Cross Charter of 1905 (33 Stat. 599–602); Name Redacted, "Congressionally Chartered Nonprofit Organizations ('Title 36 Corporations'): What They Are and How Congress Treats Them," Report, CRS Report for Congress (Congressional Research Service, 2011).

47   For the legal implications of the ambiguous designation of quasi-governmental, see Kevin Kosar, "The Congressional Charter of the American National Red Cross: Overview, History, and Analysis," Report, CRS Report for Congress (Congressional Research Service, March 15, 2006).

48   "How Department of Foreign Relief Is Organized and Operated," *Red Cross Bulletin. American Red Cross* 1, no. 34 (December 1917): 4.

49   "Permanent Commission to Italy Is Made Up of Men of Wide Experience," *Red Cross Bulletin. American Red Cross* 2, no. 8 (February 1918): 2.

50   *Ibid.*

51   Chester Holmes Aldrich (1871–1940), although more famous for his collaboration with William Adams Delano, had designed the Greenwich Settlement House for Italian immigrants in New York and had been working with the planner and social worker Mary Kingsbury Simkhovitch as a member of the Greenwich House board. On his collaboration with Delano, see Peter Pennoyer and Anne Walker, *The Architecture of Delano & Aldrich* (New York: W. W. Norton, 2003). Guy Lowell (1870–1927), the architect of Museum of Fine Arts, Boston, had founded and run the landscape program at MIT, a program that advocated for the codification of the planning and landscape standards. On the program and its objectives, see Eran Ben-Joseph et al., *Against All Odds: MIT's Pioneering Women of Landscape Architecture* (Blacksburg, Va.: IAWA, 2007). Edgar I. Williams (1885–1974), a proponent of housing reform, would eventually serve as president of the National Academy of Design and the Architectural League, and in the 1950s, alongside Richard M. Bennett and Eero Saarinen, as a member of the State Department's advisory committee of American embassies. For a short appraisal of his work, see Farnsworth Fowle, "Edgar I. Williams, Architect, Dead," *New York Times*, January 3, 1974. Among the many more architects who joined

the ranks of the organization during WWI was George Burdett Ford (1878–1930), head of the ARC Reconstruction Research and Educational Service bureau in France. Upon his return in the US in 1921, he produced planning manuals and surveys and worked as a consultant for the regional plan of New York (1929). Also involved was Philip Horton Smith, of the ARC Department of Civil Affairs in France, who had been a member of the Kilham and Hopkins firm in Boston, working on publicly financed housing schemes in the northeast and participating in the major debates on housing reform and tenement housing. On the firm's work on housing reform, see Richard M. Candee and Greer Hardwicke, "Early Twentieth-Century Reform Housing by Kilham and Hopkins, Architects of Boston," *Winterthur Portfolio* 22, no. 1 (1987): 47–80.

52   Siddiqi, "Architecture Culture, Humanitarian Expertise."

53   Arindam Dutta, "Computing Alibis: Third World Teratologies," *Perspecta* 40 (2008): 54–69; Theodossis Issaias and Platon Issaias, "Displaced in Place and in Transit," in *Transient Spaces* ed. Suzan Wang, Samantha Ong, and Loukia Tsafoulia (New York: CUNY, 2019).

54   Gatrell, *The Making of the Modern Refugee*, 27; for a detailed account on the displacement of refugees during WWI in Italy, see Daniele Ceschin, *Gli esuli di Caporetto. I profughi in Italia durante la grande guerra* (Rome: Laterza, 2014).

55   "Red Cross Raises American Flag from One End of Italy to the Other," *Red Cross Bulletin: American Red Cross* 2, no. 4 (January 21, 1918): 2.

56   Julia F. Irwin, "Nation Building and Rebuilding: The American Red Cross in Italy during the Great War," *Journal of the Gilded Age and Progressive Era* 8, no. 3 (2009): 407–39.

57   Ceschin, *Gli esuli di Caporetto*; Bruni Branca, ed., *La Violenza Contro La Popolazione Civile Nella Grande Guerra. Deportati, Profughi, Internati* (Milan: Unicopli, 2006); Matteo Ermacora, "Assistance and Surveillance: War Refugees in Italy, 1914–1918," *Contemporary European History* 16, no. 4 (2007): 445–59.

58   Ermacora, "Assistance and Surveillance," 448.

59   Ceschin, *Gli esuli di Caporetto*, 32.

60   Benajah Harvey Carroll to Chester Aldrich, "American Red Cross Relief Work," February 25, 1918, ANRCR, box 103.15, folder 3.

61   *Ibid.*; Benajah Harvey Carroll to Chester Aldrich, "American Consular Service," February 26, 1918, ANRCR, box 103.15, folder 3.

62   Iain R. Smith and Andreas Stucki, "The Colonial Development of Concentration Camps (1868–1902)," *Journal of Imperial and Commonwealth History* 39, no. 3 (September 1, 2011): 417–37.

63   Hannah Arendt was first to notice that "these camps were used for 'suspects' whose offenses could not be proved and who could not be sentenced by ordinary process of law." Building on Arendt, Agamben explains that the camps were born "not out of ordinary law (even less, as one might have supposed, from a transformation and development of criminal law) but out of a state of exception and martial law." Hannah Arendt, *The Origins of Totalitarianism* (New York: Harcourt, Brace, Jovanovich, 1973), 440; Giorgio Agamben, *Homo Sacer: Sovereign Power and Bare Life*, trans. Daniel Heller-Roazen (Stanford, Calif.: Stanford University Press, 1998), 166–7.

64   More recently Aidan Forth has addressed the links between the workhouse, the famine camp, and the counterinsurgency tactic. Aidan Forth, *Barbed-Wire Imperialism: Britain's Empire of Camps, 1876–1903* (Oakland, Calif.: University of California Press, 2017).

65   Aidan Forth, "Britain's Archipelago of Camps: Labor and Detention in a Liberal Empire, 1871–1903," *Kritika: Explorations in Russian and Eurasian History* 16, no. 3 (August 29, 2015): 655.

66   Clara Barton, "The Red Cross in Cuba," *Outlook* 38, no. 15 (April 9, 1898): 911–6.

67   William Willard Howard, "A Practical Plan of Relief in Cuba," *Outlook* 38, no. 15 (April 9, 1898): 916.

68   Barton, "The Red Cross in Cuba," 912.

69   Andrew Herscher, *Displacements: Architecture and Refugee* (Berlin: Sternberg Press, 2017), 77–126.

70   Carroll to Aldrich, "American Red Cross Relief Work," February 25, 1918, p. 3.

71   "A Red Cross Village at Pisa," *Architectural Record* 44, no. 4 (October 1918): 381.

72   Alexander Miller, "Military Importance of Red Cross Civilian Relief," *Red Cross Bulletin. American Red Cross* 2, no. 8 (February 1918): 2.

73   Editorial Board, "Sense and Sentiment Should Go Together," *American Red Cross Magazine* 11, no. 3 (March 1916): 98–100.

74   On the principle underlying the labor policies in the workhouse, see Felix Driver, *Power and Pauperism: The Workhouse System, 1834–1884* (Cambridge: Cambridge University Press, 2004).

75   Department of Medical Division in Greece to Unknown, "Propaganda Sheet (Camp Rules): Refugees!," Reel 127: Balkan States, Greece, ANRCR.

76   American National Red Cross War Council, *The Work of the American Red Cross during the War: A Statement of Finances and Accomplishments for the Period July 1, 1917, to February 28, 1919* (Washinghton, D.C.: American Red Cross, 1919), 86.

77   Department of Civil Affairs, "Notes on Village for Refugees by the American Red Cross Near Pisa," May 1919, 1, pp. 103.15–104.7, ANRCR.

78   *Ibid.*

79   Roberts Perkins to Society Cooperativa L'Initiativa and Azio Cerlini, "Construction of the Venetian Village at Pisa for the Account of the American Red Cross," December 1918, 4, pp. 103.15–104.7, ANRCR.

80   Unpublished report: Chester Aldrich and Francesco Mauro to Unknown, "Borgo Veneziano," December 1918, ANRCR, box 104.5, folder 2.

81   Michel Agier, "Humanity as an Identity and its Political Effects (A Note on Camps and Humanitarian Government)," *Humanity: An International Journal of Human Rights, Humanitarianism, and Development* 1, no. 1 (October 12, 2010): 30.

82   For example, "Americans Reconstruct Italian Village," *American Contractor* 39, no. 39 (September 28, 1918): 26; "Red Cross Work," *Timberman: An International Lumber Journal* 19, no. 1 (November 1917): 42. See also similar coverage for the Belgian settlements. "An extensive demand for lumber, which will undoubtedly be largely filled from the United States, in the rebuilding of devastated villages and cities of Belgium and Northern France, is being given foundation by the American Red Cross and by the Belgian Fond du Roi Albert." "Red Cross Model Village for Belgian Refugees," *Timberman: An International Lumber Journal* 19, no. 8 (November 1917): 89.

83   "A Red Cross Village at Pisa," *Architectural Record* 44, no. 4 (October 1918): 381.

84   The bureau in France was headed by the architect George Burdett Ford (1878–1930). Upon his return in the US he also produced planning manuals and surveys and he was a key consultant for the regional plan of New York. George Burdett Ford, *Out of the Ruins* (New York: Century Company, 1919), 929.

85 Unpublished internal memo: Chester Aldrich, "Notes on Village for Refugees Built by the American Red Cross Near Pisa, By the Department of Civil Affairs," December 1918, ANRCR, box 104.5, folder 2.

86 Capt. Mauro to Chester Aldrich, "Interpretation of the Contract with 'L'Iniaziativa,'" August 9, 1918, ANRCR, box 104.2, folder 1.

87 Chester Aldrich to Bureau of Legal Advice, "Pisa Village Matter," March 31, 1919, ANRCR, box 104.5, folder 2.

88 All information in regard to the current facility comes from the watch group Antigone, an independent observatory for the rights and guarantees in the penal system.

89 "These 3D-Printed Homes Could Provide Shelter to the World's Most Vulnerable People," PBS NewsHour, March 30, 2018, <https://www.pbs.org/newshour/science/these-3d-printed-homes-could-provide-shelter-to-the-worlds-most-vulnerable-people>; "Ecological Pavilion | Nairobi, Kenya | CEA," YALE CEA, accessed September 12, 2019, <https://www.cea.yale.edu/projects/nairobi/>.

90 *UN Environment Assembly 4: Eco-Building*, accessed September 13, 2019, <https://www.youtube.com/watch?time_continue=2&v=hUBjnsPI2d4>.

91 Arindam Dutta, "Linguistics, Not Grammatology: Architecture's A Prioris and Architecture's Priorities," in *A Second Modernism: MIT, Architecture, and the "Techno-Social" Moment*, ed. Arindam Dutta (Cambridge, Mass.: The MIT Press, 2013), 2.

92 Herscher, *Displacements*, 119.

Bibliography

Agamben, Giorgio. "Beyond Human Rights." In *Radical Thought in Italy: A Potential Politics*, edited by Paolo Virno and Michael Hardt. Minneapolis: University of Minnesota Press, 2006.

Agier, Michel. "Humanity as an Identity and Its Political Effects (A Note on Camps and Humanitarian Government)." *Humanity: An International Journal of Human Rights, Humanitarianism, and Development* 1, no. 1 (October 12, 2010): 29–45.

The American National Red Cross Charter of 1905 (33 Stat. 599–602).

Barton, Clara. "The Red Cross in Cuba." *Outlook* 38, no. 15 (April 9, 1898): 911–6.

Belknap, Reginald Rowan. *American House Building in Messina and Reggio: An Account of the American Naval and Red Cross Combined Expedition, to Provide Shelter for the Survivors of the Great Earthquake of December 28, 1908*. New York: G. P. Putnam's Sons, 1910.

Boltanski, Luc. *Distant Suffering: Morality, Media and Politics*. Translated by Graham D. Burchell. Cambridge: Cambridge University Press, 1999.

Carroll, Benajah Harvey. Letter to Chester Aldrich. "American Consular Service," February 26, 1918. Hoover Institution Library & Archives.

———.Letter to Chester Aldrich. "American Red Cross Relief Work," February 25, 1918. 103.15-–104.7. Hoover Institution Library & Archives.

Cutlip, Scott M. *The Unseen Power: Public Relations: A History*. London: Routledge, 2013.

Davis, Arthur Powell. "A Conservancy Project to Prevent Much Misery." *American Red Cross Magazine* 10, no. 1 (January 1915): 43–6.

Department of Civil Affairs. "Notes on Village for Refugees by the American Red Cross Near Pisa," May 1919. 103.15–104.7. Hoover Institution Library & Archives.

Department of Medical Division in Greece. Letter to Unknown. "Propaganda Sheet (Camp Rules): Refugees!," 1922. Reel 127: Balkan States, Greece. Hoover Institution Library & Archives.

"Division for Information Established for Public." *American Red Cross Magazine* 8, no. 3 (July 1914): 167.

Driver, Felix. *Power and Pauperism: The Workhouse System, 1834–1884.* Cambridge: Cambridge University Press, 2004.

Dutta, Arindam. "Computing Alibis: Third World Teratologies." *Perspecta* 40 (2008): 54–69.

———. "Linguistics, Not Grammatology: Architecture's A Prioris and Architecture's Priorities." In *A Second Modernism: MIT, Architecture, and the "Techno-Social" Moment*, edited by Arindam Dutta. Cambridge, MA: The MIT Press, 2013.

YALE CEA. "Ecological Pavilion | Nairobi, Kenya | CEA." Accessed September 12, 2019. <https://www.cea.yale.edu/ecological-pavilion>

Editorial Board. "Sense and Sentiment Should Go Together." *American Red Cross Magazine* 11, no. 3 (March 1916): 98–100.

Elliott, Maud Howe, and John Elliott. *Sicily in Shadow and in Sun; The Earthquake and the American Relief Work.* Boston: Little, Brown, and Company, 1910.

Fassin, Didier. *Humanitarian Reason: A Moral History of the Present.* Los Angeles: University of California Press, 2011.

Forth, Aidan. "Britain's Archipelago of Camps: Labor and Detention in a Liberal Empire, 1871–1903." *Kritika: Explorations in Russian and Eurasian History* 16, no. 3 (August 29, 2015): 651–80.

Gatrell, Peter. "Introduction: World Wars and Population Displacement in Europe in the Twentieth Century." *Contemporary European History* 16, no. 4 (2007): 415–26.

———. *The Making of the Modern Refugee.* Oxford: Oxford University Press, 2013.

Gatrell, Peter, and Liubov Zhvanko, eds. *Europe on the Move: Refugees in the Era of the Great War.* Manchester: Manchester University Press, 2017.

Herscher, Andrew. *Displacements: Architecture and Refugee.* Berlin: Sternberg Press, 2017.

Hirschon, Renée. "'Unmixing Peoples' in the Aegean Region." In *Crossing the Aegean: An Appraisal of the 1923 Compulsory Population Exchange between Greece and Turkey*, edited by Renée Hirschon, 3–20. New York, NY: Berghahn Books, 2003.

Howard, William Willard. "A Practical Plan of Relief in Cuba." *Outlook* 38, no. 15 (April 9, 1898): 916.

"How Department of Foreign Relief Is Organized and Operated." *Red Cross Bulletin. American Red Cross* 1, no. 34 (December 1917): 4.

Hutchinson, John F. *Champions of Charity: War and the Rise of the Red Cross.* Boulder, Colo.: Westview Press, 1996.

Irwin, Julia F. *Making the World Safe: The American Red Cross and a Nation's Humanitarian Awakening.* Oxford: Oxford University Press, 2017.

———. "Nation Building and Rebuilding: The American Red Cross in Italy during the Great War." *Journal of the Gilded Age and Progressive Era* 8, no. 3 (2009): 407–39.

Issaias, Theodossis, and Platon Issaias. "Displaced in Place and in Transit." In *Transient Spaces*, edited by Suzan Wang, Samantha Ong, and Loukia Tsafoulia. New York: CUNY, 2019.

Kosar, Kevin. "The Congressional Charter of the American National Red Cross: Overview, History, and Analysis." Report. CRS Report for Congress. Congressional Research Service, March 15, 2006.

Mazower, Mark. *Governing the World: The History of an Idea, 1815 to the Present*. New York, NY: Penguin Books, 2013.

———. "Minorities and the League of Nations in Interwar Europe." *Daedalus* 126, no. 2 (1997): 47–63.

Miller, Alexander. "Military Importance of Red Cross Civilian Relief." *Red Cross Bulletin. American Red Cross* 2, no. 8 (February 1918): 2.

Moore, Jennifer. "'Neutrality-Humanity': The Humanitarian Mission and the Films of the American Red Cross." In *Beyond the Screen: Institutions, Networks, and Publics of Early Cinema*, 11–18. Bloomington, Ind.: Indiana University Press, 2016.

Moore, Sarah J. *Empire on Display: San Francisco's Panama-Pacific International Exposition of 1915*. Norman, Okla.: University of Oklahoma Press, 2013.

Name Redacted. "Congressionally Chartered Nonprofit Organizations ('Title 36 Corporations'): What They Are and How Congress Treats Them." Report. CRS Report for Congress. Congressional Research Service, 2011.

Perkins, Roberts. Letter to Society Cooperativa L'Initiativa and Azio Cerlini. "Construction of the Venetian Village at Pisa for the Account of the American Red Cross," December 1918. 103.15–104.7. ANRCR.

"Permanent Commission to Italy Is Made Up of Men of Wide Experience." *Red Cross Bulletin. American Red Cross* 2, no. 8 (February 1918): 2.

Pietz, David. *Engineering the State: The Huai River and Reconstruction in Nationalist China, 1927–37*. London: Routledge, 2018.

"Red Cross Raises American Flag from One End of Italy to the Other." *Red Cross Bulletin: American Red Cross* 2, no. 4 (January 21, 1918): 2.

"A Red Cross Village at Pisa." *Architectural Record* 44, no. 4 (October 1918): 381.

Rozario, Kevin. "'Delicious Horrors': Mass Culture, the Red Cross, and the Appeal of Modern American Humanitarianism." *American Quarterly* 55, no. 3 (2003): 417–55.

Schechtman, Joseph B. *European Population Transfers, 1939–1945*. New York: Russell and Russell, 1971.

Siddiqi, Anooradha Iyer. "Architecture Culture, Humanitarian Expertise: From the Tropics to Shelter, 1953–93." *Journal of the Society of Architectural Historians* 76, no. 3 (September 1, 2017): 367–84.

Simpson, John Hope. *The Refugee Problem: Report of a Survey*. Oxford: Oxford University Press, 1939.

Skran, Claudena M. *Refugees in Inter-War Europe: The Emergence of a Regime*. Oxford: Clarendon Press, 1995.

Stein, Lewis. "The Red Cross Exhibit at the World's Fair." *American Red Cross Magazine* 10, no. 4 (April 1915): 150–4.

Stross, Randall E. *The Stubborn Earth: American Agriculturalists on Chinese Soil, 1898–1937*. Los Angeles: University of California Press, 1986.

PBS NewsHour. "These 3D-Printed Homes Could Provide Shelter to the World's Most Vulnerable People," March 30, 2018. <https://www.pbs.org/newshour/science/these-3d-printed-homes-could-provide-shelter-to-the-worlds-most-vulnerable-people>

"Thirty-Eight Red Cross Films Circulating in Division." *American Red Cross Pacific Division Activities* 3, no. 6 (September 1920): 4.

Tichi, Cecelia. *Shifting Gears: Technology, Literature, Culture in Modernist America*. Chapel Hill, N.C.: University of North Carolina Press, 1987.

Todd, Frank Morton. *The Story of the Exposition: Being the Official History of the International Celebration Held at San Francisco in 1915 to Commemorate the Discovery of the Pacific Ocean and the Construction of the Panama Canal.* Vol. 4. New York: G. P. Putnam's Sons, 1921.

Tooze, Adam. *The Deluge: The Great War and the Remaking of Global Order, 1916–1931.* London: Penguin, 2014.

UN Environment Assembly 4: Eco-Building. Accessed September 13, 2019. <https://www.youtube.com/watch?time_continue=2&v=hUBjnsPI2d4>

Verpoest, Luc, Leen Engelen, Rajesh Heynickx, Jan Schmidt, Pieter Uyttenhove, and Pieter Verstraete, eds. *Revival after the Great War: Rebuild, Remember, Repair, Reform.* Leuven: Leuven University Press, 2020.

"The War Orphans of France." *American Red Cross Magazine* 13, no. 9 (September 1918): 14–9.

PART FOUR
LANDSCAPES
REMADE

Figure 9.1: Fort Douaumont, April 9, 1916. Silver print, black and white, 13 × 18 cm.

World War I, Aerial Photography and the Emergence of Urbanism in France

Min Kyung Lee

Introduction

The First World War accelerated pioneering uses of photography for aerial reconnaissance and bombing, in which the production, use, and distribution of images were critical for French military success. Photographs from manned observation balloons, blimps, and airplanes provided the means to see and know the terrain in order to identify targets. They also functioned to confirm the results of attacks, extending visually through their reproduction and publications the violent effects of warfare. These aerial capabilities changed the theater of war. From this new aerial vantage point, cities, not individual soldiers, became an object of frontline military engagements; all buildings, not only defense structures, turned into potential targets, and civilians, not just combatants, became engaged in war and its after effects.

The Treaty of Versailles formally ended the Great War, but the interwar period was no less militarized. France maintained the largest armed forces in Europe and deployed them to consolidate and expand into new territories, for which aerial photography found a utility in new colonial urban projects. These territories became critical sites for the emergent practice of urbanism, an interdisciplinary field that had developed parallel to the war. Having been impeded from implementing its programs in the Paris metropole, the colonies became laboratories to test the diverse practices and social programs that had been outlined by the new professional association founded in 1911, the Société Française des Architectes Urbanistes (SFAU). More than simply a tool, the specific and immediate incorporation of this photographic medium and its aerial viewpoint established foundational epistemic values for the new field of urbanism.

These images were understood to be unmediated representations insofar as they were mechanically produced and thus uncorrupted by the human hand and human fallibility. Accordingly, if the field of urbanism wanted to consolidate itself as an institutionalized scientific practice – "a practice of reason," to borrow a term from Paul Rabinow – photography and its rhetoric of objectivity provided a perfect fit.[1] Aerial photography converted what had already long been visualized, via the terrestrially measured map, into something that was now thought to be seen and known as neutral and scientific. The belief that these images represented the terrain also allowed for the site of the battlefield to expand beyond the physical ground to remote offices. The terrain on which battles were fought and where cities were destroyed, discovered, and built, became distanced at the same time that they were made more accessible to a wider public through reproductions. The distancing effects of this shared visual culture of war and urbanism allude to the devastating consequences for the people who inhabited those cities and whose lives remained invisible.

This essay examines the historical context of aerial photography in France during the First World War. While there has been much written about the use of aerial photography in the Second World War and its post-war applications, particularly in the *banlieues* of Paris, there is considerably less written on this military technology in the context of urban planning history during the early decades of the twentieth century before the 1930s. The following text considers the visual culture of urbanism derived from the technologies of aerial photography developed during WWI, and demonstrates the merger of military, surveying, and planning practices that were foundational to the field of urbanism.

The Aerial View

A camera captures Fort Douaumont on April 9, 1916 [fig. 9.1]. The grainy black and white image is a vertical photograph taken from an airplane at 2,800 m as part of the French attempt to recapture a key defensive structure. Pentagonal outlines of the fortress are visibly marked and varied thin lines are etched onto the ground throughout. Pocks from artillery fire are scattered across the surface of the terrain, whose densities translate into white glares on the surface of the image.

The strategic location of Douaumont made it an important point of contact in the larger Battle of Verdun, one of the bloodiest and longest of the Great War. For the Germans, any offense from the Fort threatened their communication lines, and for the French, it was the salient of a large fortified complex comprised of 19 structures along the Meuse River. Yet, for all of its importance, the Fort was captured with little resistance by a small German party in the first days of the battle on February 25,

1916. Having observed German artillery power against Belgian forts, the French had already disarmed the area. Since 1915, they had left it largely undefended because of their calculation that fixed structures were indefensible against the German howitzers. However, the recapture of the Fort became a significant factor in French war planning for the remaining months, and on October 24, 1916, the French counter-attacked successfully and regained control of the structure, using aerial reconnaissance. It became a decisive case of aerial photography successfully deployed, and for the rest of the war, aerial flight, reconnaissance, and photography became involved in every aspect of French military operations.

The photographs of Fort Douaumont represented the rapid adoption of a new technology by the military.[2] The French were foremost among the Allies and the Germans in their aerial endeavors.[3] The Wright brothers had just taken their first flight in 1903. Soon afterwards, they set up the world's first flight school in Pau, France in 1909, where one could earn a pilot's license that the Aéro-Club de France had created. With Wilbur Wright as the pilot, Louis Paul Bonvillain took the first known aerial photograph from an airplane flying over Le Mans[4] [fig. 9.2]. The French military, recognizing the tactical value of air flight, immediately set up their own *aérostation* in Chalais-Meudon, with the result, as General Duval ultimately noted, that "aerial photography had been the eyes of the army," leading to the Allied victory.[5]

Figure 9.2: *La Vie au grand air: revue illustrée de tous les sports*, 373. November 28, 1908. Caption reads: What one sees from the Wright airplane. This photograph is an enlargement of the first cinemographic film, taken on board an airplane, by M. Bonvillain, director of the Services des voyages de la mission Pathé.

The complex mechanical, material, and logistical apparatus constructed for the production and use of aerial photographs belied the rhetoric of its utility that was – and still is – based on their universal legibility and objectivity.[6] The seeming capacity to capture the whole situation of a given terrain and for that information to appear unmediated was compelling, and the recognition of aerial photography's tactical advantages was immediate. The French first developed a hand-held camera with a 26 cm focal length and a magazine holding 12 glass plates that, from 1915, was developed into versions with 50 and 120 cm focal lengths, becoming the mainstay of French aerial photography during the war [fig. 9.3].[7] While these images offered advantageous views of the spatial organization and context of a given site, the capabilities of the cameras had much to improve over the course of the war. Their limitations required the pilot to fly close to the terrain, risking being shot down from the ground. To avoid attack, they would otherwise fly higher, but lose accuracy.

Figure 9.3: Installation of a photographic apparatus onto a reconnaissance plane, 1918. Camp d'aviation de Chaudun (Aisne), November 1917. Epreuve 12 × 17 cm. MHC, Alb 8 (Musée d'histoire contemporaine). *Vues en haut: la photographie aérienne pendant la guerre de 1914–1918* (Paris: Musée de l'Armée, 1988), 10.

The earliest reconnaissance planes were Cauldron G4 biplanes with twin engines and front propellers and the Maurice Farman XI with a propulsion motor. In both, the camera was attached to the front. One of the leading aerial photographers, Maurice

Marie Eugène Grout, first photographed German batteries at Fort Douaumont in the Verdun sector on October 7, 1914. Based on his aerial efforts, the French army initiated their operational aerial photographic activities – the Section Photo-Aerienne (SPAe) of the Service Aeronautique – on October 23, 1914.[8] These pilot-photographers were called *observateurs*, and shot on fragile glass plates placed in large and cumbersome cameras that hung on the exterior of equally fragile airplanes flying precariously above battlefields [fig. 9.4]. To privilege observation, the planes adopted a design of a two-seater with a propulsion engine that allowed the viewer on a balcony, a feature that was later catastrophic for fighter planes that could attack from behind.

Figure 9.4: Preparation for a photographic mission on board the Caudron G4. The camera was 1.20 m focal range with the boxes of glass plates. Charles Christienne and Pierre Lissarrague, *Histoire de l'aviation militaire française* (Paris: Limoges, Charles-Lavauzelle, 1986), 101.

Once the pilots landed safely, the cameras and their valuable glass plates were transported to development laboratories, designed and set up by May 1915 [fig. 9.5]. They were run by a team of officials, including an officer of photographs, a sergeant of drawing, a sergeant of photography, and a sergeant of expeditions [fig. 9.6]. A plan from the French squadron SPAe 38, stationed in Melette, north of Châlons-sur-Marne illustrated the complex procedures.[9] The cameras were first broken down, separated, and cleaned (1). If any repairs were needed, they were noted. The glass plates were separately handled (4) and washed, dried, and treated (5–7). They were then taken to the *bureau de dessin* or drawing room (8), the largest space made available, where landmarks and significant information were identified and marked. From there, prints were pulled on paper (8–13), and placed into sealed envelopes and taken to

Figure 9.5: Mobile photographic laboratory for a squadron, November 1917. Camp d'aviation de Chaudun (Aisne) Epreuve 12 × 17 cm. MHC, Alb 8. *Vues en haut: la photographie aérienne pendant la guerre de 1914–1918* (Paris: Musée de l'Armée, 1988), 70.

the officers who were trained in their interpretation. Often, the glass plates were also projected as lantern slides, and discussed in the conference room (21). There was also an underground room outfitted as a secondary lab in case of bombardment (23). As part of the SPAe, these spaces processed all of the photographs taken during the war, and at its peak, in the years 1915–1917, processed 30,000 shots taken from the front, making the Western Front "the most scrutinized area on earth."[10]

Because of the poor resolution as well as the amount of unfiltered information they presented, the images required expert interpretation. As André Carlier, a WWI photographic interpreter, wrote in his manual to aerial photography, "the technique of aerial photography is one of the principal sources of information, but used alone it would never be sufficient to allow a military commander to form an opinion, with absolute certainty, of the intentions of the enemy."[11] Initial identification of sites was first made by the *observateurs*, who could verify certain landmarks and battle formations. But the photos needed extensive annotation, and officers had to be trained in reading these sensitive images. Often, images were taken in an array, creating a serial montage. These images in particular required precise alignments, and had to be compared with maps and other documentation, in order for distances and dimensions to be well contextualized and verified. Conversion tables were created as an aid for calculating distances based on the altitude of the airplane. There was also the use of stereoscopic images for three-dimensional views of trenches. Their development as well as their use demanded training in the photographic medium, which was eventually required for all recruits to all sectors of the army.

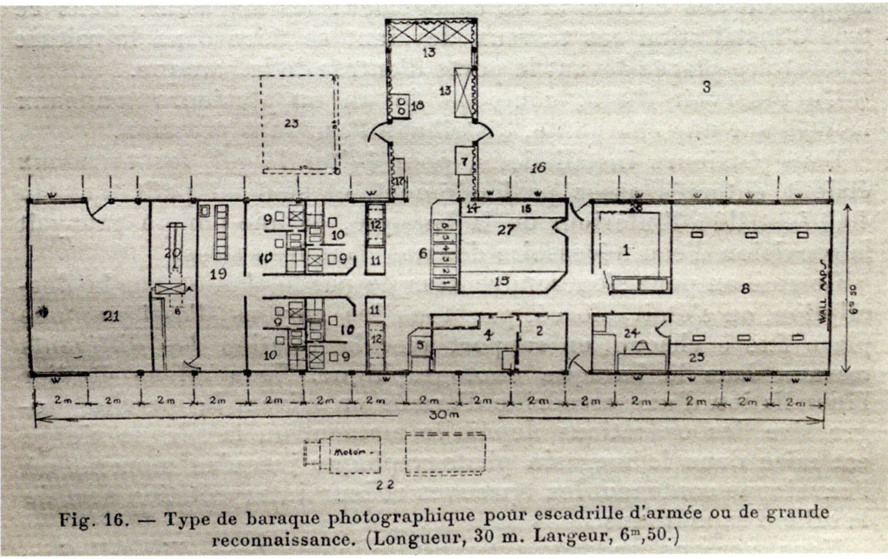

Fig. 16. — Type de baraque photographique pour escadrille d'armée ou de grande reconnaissance. (Longueur, 30 m. Largeur, 6ᵐ,50.)

Figure 9.6: Plan for a photography booth for an army squadron or of reconnaissance. André H. Carllier, *La Photographie aérienne pendant la guerre* (Paris: Librairie Delagrave, 1921), 70.

Even if the images were not entirely precise in their low resolution, photographs as products of an objective eye were believed to be accurate.[12] Once that belief was secure, the image and its information became mobile and could stand in for the terrain.[13] Paradoxically, the very realism of the photograph allowed for a "growing derealization of military engagement."[14] Commands could be and were made outside the direct battlefield; war became mediated through images, or as Paul Virilio writes, war became virtual. These aerial capabilities paradigmatically changed the theater of war. Beyond photographic reconnaissance and observation, the tactical value of flight was that airplanes reduced the geographic and temporal distance between enemies, while simultaneously reducing the possibility for human contact.[15] Thus, the target from this "high altitude" was not the individual soldier. Peter Sloterdijk has argued that the aerial view changed the main target of war, so that it "was no longer the body, but the enemy's environment."[16] As visible objects, cities became the front line of aerial warfare, and the longstanding distinctions between legitimate military and immune non-military targets collapsed. The battlefield as a contained and demarcated line of trenches with shots thrown horizontally expanded volumetrically with the potential of bombs dropping vertically.[17] In this way, flight became part of both a defensive and offensive strategy: through aerial reconnaissance, commanders could plan and plot maneuvers; through aerial bombing, those same commanders could execute those plans.

The Historical View

The technology of aerial photography was born through the confluence of the invention of the airplane and developments in photography during WWI. However, these aerial images were not merely technological products. They were part of a longer history of scopic regimes tied to painting and cartography, dating back to the early modern period and its imagined aerial views. Even in the early years of the war, aerial observation was not uncommon and achieved through the dirigibles or observers verbally reporting their findings from elevated positions on the ground or in fixed balloons, in the vein of Félix Nadar shooting pictures of Paris from his balloon.[18]

During the Renaissance, ground perspectival views dominated urban maps. They depicted a regional approach into town through the surrounding countryside, providing a picture and profile of an urban scene as a calvary view. When the bird's-eye view was introduced, it was revolutionary in offering a comprehensive aerial view of the city that had not been possible in earlier cartographic representations. These new mapped descriptions made the city illusionistically visible in a manner that was unavailable to direct experience but possible through imagined flight. Yet, while these bird's-eye views represented a departure from the calvary views by elevating the viewer's position, they continued to use the same pictorial strategies as the earlier views, emphasizing building facades and the city as an agglomeration of geometric masses. The major shift from bird's-eye to orthogonal views in the eighteenth and nineteenth centuries was paradigmatic.[19] Visual comparisons between map and city were no longer possible, as the city was now represented in a flattened and diagrammatic form, often showing the urban features that were not visible to the human eye. In fact, these features, such as property and administrative boundaries, did not exist outside its representation. Here the logic was different from photographs: the linear qualities of orthographic images were tied to an aim no longer to reproduce a visual experience of the urban built environment, but to represent the structure of a city whose graphic accuracy lay precisely in the inability to compare it to direct experience. Unlike photographs, its legitimacy as an accurate description rested on the regular geometric methods used to produce the measures of the terrain and its plan, not on its visual verisimilitude.

The oblique angle of the aerial photographs was produced from the side of first a balloon and then a propeller plane. It was in line with the older cartographic modality of the bird's-eye view that had been replaced by orthographic modes and diagrammatic forms of representing the terrain. The French army's cartographic division produced maps at a ratio of 1:5,000 and they were considered some of the most precise representations of the terrain. As in the oblique-angle shot, the vertical photograph mimicked this established cartographic mode. Thus, the novelty of aerial photography was not in the viewpoint. Instead, it was located in the belief in its accuracy, which relied on a mechanical operation as well as the realism of the image produced. It merged both the possibility of production untainted by the fallible human hand and verisimilitude between terrain and image.

These detailed maps were developed for military purposes, drawn and measured by surveyors employed by the military for conquest and control. The aerial photographs were no different in this respect. In the service of the state, the particular development of aerial photography during the Great War augured, as Peter Adey and others have termed it, "epistemologies of geographical knowledge production" that were tied to violence.[20] These new forms of knowledge replaced earlier visual representational practices devoted to locating and identifying sites and features with practices that were explicitly linked to war. The veracity located in the realism of the photographic images obscured their ideological function within a state apparatus that used these visual forms and methods for domination.

Moreover, their aesthetics of abstraction, in which the distance that was offered specifically by the aerial view allowed for images of massive destruction to be reduced to patterns, vacated any affective response. As Davide Deriu has argued, not only did these photographs inure the beholders to the scale of the violence, but they also generated an aesthetics of ruination that simultaneously preserved and desensitized traumatic effects.[21] They represented a way of seeing, whose characteristics of objectification and distancing created the conditions for new relations towards the terrain, and whose visual modality found direct use in urban planning, a field that emerged in the years prior to the First World War.

The Urban View

In describing the requirements for these photographic interpreters, Carlier noted that artists, photographers, and, notably, architects were the most qualified.[22] These skilled personnel were inclined, as Jeanne Haffner explains, to be able to connect "visible topographical information … with invisible knowledge," that is, the tacit knowledge of how to move through different kinds of spaces and perceive strategic intentions.[23] The photographs even in their blurry resolution revealed comprehensive information about geography and military formations. Yet, paradoxically, the great amount of visual information evinced through these images also obscured significant sites by flattening out objects to the same exposure as well as easily concealing camouflaged soldiers, trenches, objects, and even towns. Thus, men trained in the particularities of topographic representations were crucial for understanding the nuances of the photographic medium.

Carlier's specific mention of architects was not random. Many young men who had been trained as architects and engineers found themselves in the trenches on the Western Front.[24] And many soldiers assigned to aerial operations found work after the war for geographers, archaeologists, and planners. Moreover, with military officers having held administrative posts, many of them in the colonies and directly overseeing planning activities before and after the war, communication among architects, engineers, and the military was fluid. Among the most influential was Hubert Lyautey, Resident-General of French Morocco, who was one of the first members of the SFAU founded in 1911.[25] First led by Eugène Hénard as founder and president, the members of this association would be the primary agents involved in the reconstruction of many cities in France and in the colonies during the interwar years as well as the post-war period.

Even before the outbreak of war, architects and urban planners were enamored with aerial technologies. With the numerous aviation events and spectacles of 1909, and with a press exuberantly reporting the aerial developments to a wider public, it gave rise to new urban visions. Nathalie Roseau describes the development of Eugène Hénard's planning ideas from those that saw a city that could accommodate planes to those that were oriented around it. In a lecture, "Les Villes de l'Avenir," at the Town Planning Conference held at the Royal Institute of British Architects on October 14, 1910, Hénard imagined a city where the circulation and traffic of airplanes – "aerial motor cars" – would determine its functions and forms:[26]

> The profound revolution in thought generated by aviation is so powerful and opens such enormous perspectives that all manner of dream is possible. Air conquest will usher in an era of peace and wealth. The cities of tomorrow will be easier to transform and to embellish: their magnificent towers will welcome giant birds from all points on the horizon and perhaps, in time, the major capitals will build their beacons closer and closer to the stars.[27]

In the first decade of the twentieth century, Hénard's buoyant perspective was counterbalanced by weighty social problems, especially concerning the urban working classes.[28] Aerial flight and, as a consequence, the aerial city seemed to propose technologist solutions to the problems facing many French cities, but particularly Paris: a dearth of open spaces and parks, traffic congestion, overcrowding, and a lack of a centralized urban planning structure. His optimistic view was, however, blind to the violent consequences of aerial flight by the military.

Reformers such as Hénard, and others associated with the Musée Social (from which the SFAU emerged), actively worked to make these social problems visible. In particular, their repeated efforts were directed at passing legislation that would give more executive power as well as a systematic set of rules, especially regarding expropriation, for planning. While publicizing the chronic problems of French cities related to social inequality, density, congestion, and associated insalubrious health conditions, they offered solutions that were spatial, thereby affirming the necessity of urban planning as a profession. In 1915, Donat Alfred Agache, the secretary general of the SFAU under Hénard, along with two of his colleagues, Auburtin and Redont, published an outline of their arguments for comprehensive urban planning solutions. *Comment reconstruire nos cités détruites* made no mention of airplanes and showed no particular fascination with aerial technologies, but it introduced a new term: *l'urbanisme*.[29]

Anticipating an Allied victory, the authors projected that the end of the war would be an opportunity to reorganize the urban fabric of French cities and the administrative and financial infrastructure that undergirded all municipal decisions. The proper hygienic improvements to cities would necessarily assure moral improvement for renewed French national solidarity.[30] Their objective was to make a claim for the value of the coordinated management of the built environment that viewed the entire urban agglomeration as a unified form. Circulation, hygiene, and aesthetics – the central aspects of the reformers – were to be addressed on the scale of the entire city by an empowered elite:

> The engineer will provide logistical solutions, the architect will know how to adorn the city with noble or picturesque constructions: but it is reserved for the Urbanist to coordinate all of these values into one overall design [*une conception d'ensemble*], in a nutshell: a beautiful plan.[31]

Advocating for the expertise of the urban planner, the authors took a technologist and top-down perspective. The *plan d'ensemble* (overall plan) was cited as the central instrument to coordinate and control the building as well as the conceptualization of the city.[32] It visualized the city as a contained object, with clear boundaries, parts, and systems. Unlike the uses of the plans in the now spurned era of Haussmann and the Second Empire, here the plan was tied to new disciplines and methods, including sociology and statistics to suggest causalities between the social and spatial.[33]

The totalizing perspective of the *plan d'ensemble*, and its capacity to visualize urban parts within a whole city, was the advantage of this type of representation. Many of these early urbanists saw a new relation in which culture and social phenomena were rooted in geography.[34] For leading geographers, such as Pierre Gourou, Paul Vidal de la Blache, and his student Jean Brunhes, the incorporation of aerial photography not only illustrated but also generated their social claims. As Haffner argues, the *vue d'ensemble* (overall view) was inextricably tied to the aerial view.[35] Her central claim is that the notion of "social space," one that emerged within the urban planning discourses of the early twentieth century and that synthesized statistical and geographic methods to offer spatial solutions, had its genesis in air flight and particularly the instrument of aerial photography. Yet while Haffner argues that this aerial view emerged around the Second World War, the consolidation of diverse interdisciplinary practices under a new institutionalized category of urbanism was essentially a rational and scientific practice that was contingent on the visual culture of aerial photography that had already been prompted by the First World War.

In fact, aerial photography itself did not offer a radically new paradigm of vision. Its immediate adoption was due to the epistemological ground cultivated, with totalizing views already present in many of these fields. As Marie-Claire Robic has described, geographers found in aerial photography a resolution for "modern geography" that oscillated between a rationalist practice that found direct visual description to be too subjective and fragmentary and thus relied on contemporary and ancient maps, and a descriptive practice that valorized direct observations and sought unmediated information about the terrain.[36] The view from above taken by a mechanical apparatus – the *vue raisonnée* – proposed a terrestrial description, untainted by the human hand, that could be synoptic and panoramic. To define and normalize the visual composition of that rational view, geographers borrowed directly from World War I photography. In his survey of the field, *La géographie humaine*, Jean Brunhes includes plates taken during the war, incorporating their visuality and aesthetics into the field of geography.[37]

Correspondingly, the emergent field of urbanism was already ideologically ripe for the visuality offered by aerial photography. Its advocacy of the necessity of drawing master plans – as a scientific practice and thus potentially more capable of resolving the nation's moral issues than the political solutions offered in earlier regimes – made the incorporation of these images easier. The reformers associated with the Musée Sociale used aerial views extensively, combining socio-scientific practices with their urban analyses. Through these instruments and representational modalities, they secured urban planning as a technocratic practice that found its clearest realization abroad and in the French colonies.[38] The manipulable effects of distancing and closeness that aerial photography allowed made it an ideal tool for the social paternalism of the colonial urbanists.

After having served in Indochina and Madagascar, Lyautey was posted as the first Resident-General of Morocco as a French protectorate, and actively tried to execute the hygienic urbanism espoused by the SFAU. In 1913, Lyautey appointed Henri Prost as his *chef des services d'architecture* and outlined broad directives. Motivated by his belief that cultural hybridization was one reason for the depravity and decline of French modern society, his objectives were first to preserve the artistic and social integrity of the existing cities, and – seemingly contradictory – second, to develop a program of constructing *villes nouvelles* (new cities) that could be a model for the insalubrious and chaotic French cities.[39] (This would be enacted into official legislation a year later.) His efforts were executed by many architects, including Albert Laprade and Jean Marrast, who were both injured in the early years of the war and found work under Prost after being discharged from the military.[40] The results were new French cities built adjacent to Moroccan ones – "dual cities" – enabled through the administrative power of expropriating properties, levying taxes, and directing land-use policies, all under the rationale of modernization.[41] Yet any notion of progress was isolated to the French colonial settlements.[42] Provisions for change were not made and sometimes even hindered existing cities in their *plans d'ensembles.*[43]

For Morocco specifically, urban planning programs were to be controlled by a *plan directeur.*[44] This "master plan" comprised a series of urban maps that would organize the various layers of development, including primarily sewers, roads, transport, and habitation. They were totalizing and their authority dominant, setting all standards and norms to which the existing city had to conform. Prost provided a survey of his urban planning efforts from 1914 to 1923 in Morocco in his contribution to the seminal volume *L'Urbanisme aux colonies et dans les pays tropicaux* from 1931, directed and edited by Jean Royer, with whom he founded the journal *Urbanisme* that same year. Aerial photographs are used extensively to illustrate and justify the priorities of his work in the French protectorate. They included an aerial view of Casablanca from the harbor, and an aerial photograph nostalgically labeled *vol d'oiseau* (bird's-eye view) of Fez, with a new boulevard in the center heading in the direction of the mountains pictured the background. Another aerial view taken from a high altitude of "a new indigenous town," and an aerial photograph of the new Medina in Morocco, showed the gridded and ordered habitations [fig. 9.7].

Built between 1918 and 1919, the Medina became a model of urban study, an attempt to synthesize the objectives that Lyautey had originally set out.[45] With Laprade, Prost directed a project that decomposed and objectified architecture at scales from a town to a wall into formal and typological components to be reconfigured and composed into new towns. Photography became central to the formal objectification that defined planning practice. His team built an entire neighborhood, with markets, courtyards, baths, schools, and mosques – all services for the local population – within an envelope of white. If the color brought shifting historical valences, from one of the Muslim Orient in the French imaginary to hygienic modernity in Prost's execution, then in the photographs it represented photographic visibility.[46]

Figure 9.7: The New Medina from Henri Prost's survey of his urban planning efforts from 1914 to 1923 in Morocco. Jean Royer, *L'Urbanisme aux colonies et dans les pays tropicaux* (Paris: Les Éditions d'urbanisme, 1935).

Aerial photography and its function of detecting objects and movements were also put to use on Berber-controlled territories, supported directly by Lyautey. With his backing, from 1917 to 1918, Jules Blache gained extensive experience flying over Morocco and especially in areas that were inaccessible by foot. In an interview, he spoke of the Atlas mountains:

> In this 100 km-long stretch, the sight that the plane alone allows one to study, both in its entire expanse and in all of its detail, is extremely varied. Photographs of this landscape, taken at high altitude, have enabled the establishment of a reconnaissance map and represent geographical documents of the highest order.[47]

He published his images in several journals, including the *Revue de géographie alpine* and the *Annales de géographie*, accompanied by annotations and extensive textual descriptions. These publications defined expectations not only for those producing the aerial photographs but also for their viewers, establishing aesthetic norms for these distant spaces. His writings served as instructions for taking photographs under differing conditions. They also revealed their descriptive limitations in regard to detail, as Brunhes had also understood. Blanche admits, "Are the volcanic outpourings directly or indirectly responsible for these infillings? It was difficult to estimate without being there, on the ground."[48] The consequences of these inaccessible places now made visible but with blurred features created a false sense of connection between the viewer and the terrain that projected a site of imagination without accountability.

These aerial flights expanded the reach of the colonist, engendering a sense of greater control through surveillance and of improved vision that was often at odds with the photographic representation. While Blache would claim that these were images of "the highest order," the pictures themselves were grainy and blurry. The details of the terrain, the urban forms, and architecture remained largely illegible. And yet, they were still used to formulate comprehensive plans of new urban developments, whose projections spoke of the colonist's desire to fill in the "blank" spaces.

The Temporal View

The confluence of military and colonial ambitions expanded control not only of space but also of time through the developing parallel field of archeology, in which aerial photography also played a central role.[49] Individuals with archaeological training were purposefully enlisted into the French air corps for their service in photography and mapmaking, whose aerial coverage of North African and Middle Eastern territories occasioned the "discovery" of sites.[50] Not only did archaeologists have the skills of geographical discernment prized by the military, but the new discipline itself provided the legitimacy for territorial occupation. Aerial surveys of and archaeological missions in the Middle East during the war were possible because of the still-standing remains and the absence of anti-aircraft artillery.[51] Antoine Poidebard, a Jesuit priest and a reserve officer in the French air force, flew over Syria, following many pioneers of aerial photography who established their skills in the region, such as Leon Rey in Macedonia, Carl Schuchhardt in Dobrudja, Theodor Wiegand in the Negev Desert, and G. A. Beazeley in what became Iraq.

France had longstanding colonial interests in securing the area that was formalized in the context of the Mandate for Syria and Lebanon (1923–1946). However, their claims to the Levantine region began much earlier in the nineteenth century, along cultural lines, through Catholic associations, educational establishments and archaeological research efforts.[52] When the Ottoman Empire fell apart at the end of WWI, French planners used these institutions to justify their interest in elevating the value of these local cultures, who, they argued paternalistically, did not know how to valorize their own history and heritage. As Idir Ouahes explains, the French use of archaeology as a colonizing practice was part of a strategy to appropriate the region's past in order to affirm France's "supremacy as a result of historical links."[53] Political gains were couched in cultural terms, and archaeology was a key piece of this agenda.

The French archaeological mission took its first aerial image in 1916 of ancient Macedonian sites. WWI only further served to stimulate the development of aerial photography and its archaeological applications, creating a new subfield of aerial archaeology. Starting in 1919, aerial photography missions were regularly undertaken for cartographic purposes, ultimately contributing to official surveys by the Geographical Service of the French Army. Léon Aufrère, a French geographer extolling the virtues of aerial photography for archaeology, said, "[a] palimpsest is revealed, on which is inscribed a whole history that had seemed to have vanished without a trace from the ground."[54] Not only could aerial photography reveal large-scale patterns for current cities, but also the traces of past ones.

In 1925, Antoine Piodebard was given a commission by the French Geographical Society to undertake the first French aerial survey of Syria, tracing ancient Roman roads and irrigation systems from his biplane. From this, 219 photographs were then printed in the two-volume publication *La Trace de Rome*, understood as the traces of the ancient Roman civilization lost since the "Arab conquest." The intention was to argue for the French restoration of the pre-Arab civilization that would connect France's history to the region, thus justifying its presence. Admitting the project's specific military links, Poidebard wrote:

> [The French High Commissioner and the successive Commandant-Generals] felt that the reconstruction of the military and economic organization of the desert in the Roman era would provide useful indications towards the present-day security and development of the desert regions.[55]

Accompanied by sketches and a fold-out map, various sites were recorded through oblique and vertical angles that had by this decade become standard practice [fig. 9.8a–b]. Accordingly, the photographic atlas followed nineteenth-century conventions of scientific atlases, which presented the archaeological sites in sequence in the bounded folio, visually constructing them as objects of taxonomic scientific inquiry.[56] The epistemological claim of this method of presentation was based on the premise of revelation, not interpretation, insofar as the aerial view by a camera revealed the past's truths. Material traces were given, only to be discovered, and time was construed as objective not contingent.[57]

This alignment with scientific norms based on a belief that photography was an unmediated technique had two important consequences. The first was that the wide distribution of Poidebard's photographs of an ancient civilization in *L'Illustration*, as well as in *Syria*, a specialized journal, constructed an image of a lost urban civilization in the imagination of the French metropolitan public. The images created a stable and concrete reference out of a precarious political situation of the Mandate. Although many sites from the Umayyad period were mislabelled as being Roman, the reception of these images created the desire and provided the justification for future archaeological research and subsequent ground occupation.[58] The second consequence was that the photographic techniques and norms for their presentation through these images became incorporated into the discourse of urban planning of this same period, which was seeking to stabilize its own methodological procedures.

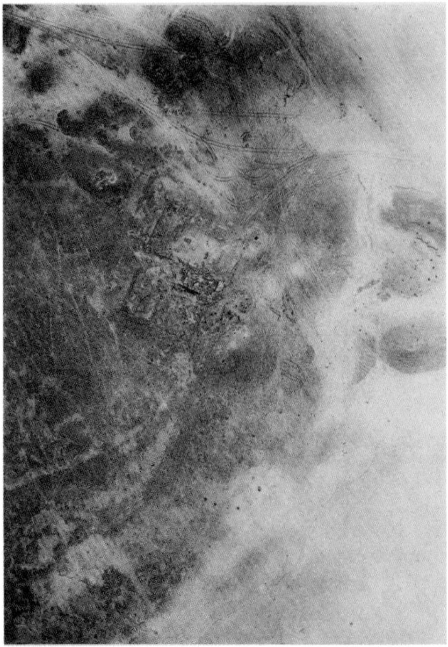

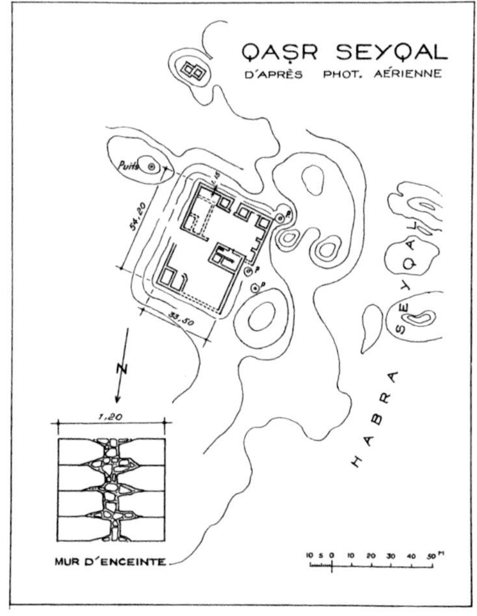

Figure 9.8a: Plate XVII: Aerial photograph of Qasr Seyql. Antoine Poidebard, *La trace de Rome dans le désert de Syrie* (Paris: Librairie Orientaliste Paul Geuthner, 1934).

Figure 9.8b: Plate XVIII: Site plan drawn based on the aerial photograph. Antoine Poidebard, *La trace de Rome dans le désert de Syrie* (Paris: Librairie Orientaliste Paul Geuthner, 1934).

The techniques used by Poidebard – the oblique and vertical views – were based on aerial reconnaissance practiced used by the 39th Aerial Observation Regiment that had been stationed in the region from October 1923. Collaborating with Colonel Orthlieb and Colonel Antoynat, and the pilots under their command, Poidebard developed maps of the northern deserts of Syria, outlining specific procedures for recording these sites.[59] These included detailed specifications, including those related to the time of day, using the sun for strategic illumination, or to the time of year, when ground cover would be minimal, etc.[60] Fifty-seven photographs were selected from the military's surveying work and published in 1926 as an album titled *Vues aériennes de Syrie et du Liban*. Similar to *La Trace de Rome*, the photographs center their objects through standardized views. Yet, unlike Poidebard's publication, which focused only on ancient sites, this album alternated between images of contemporaneous living cities and those of archeological ruins and abandoned cities with little commentary, collapsing time and creating an appearance that the region was frozen in an atemporal space, following a similar logic to the new cities that had been planned and built alongside the older ones under Prost. Composed only of images and without any captions, the album gave the viewer a sense of imagined flight over not just a spatial terrain but also another time, in which both spatial and temporal distance contracted within the album's bindings and within the French public's colonial imagination. A virtual land was pictured, paradoxically through the purported objective photograph.

These images were in wide circulation among urbanists and some were also included in *L'Urbanisme aux colonies et dans les pays tropicaux*. Its publication on the occasion of the Congrès International de Géographie in Paris as well as the Colonial Exposition in 1931 created a perverse simulacrum with images and temporary buildings that showcased the practice of urbanism and its social program to a professional and mainstream public. In this context, the French colonies were understood as laboratories for social and urban ideas and policies that had yet to be accepted and implemented in the metropole, and architects, such as Prost discussed earlier, but also Ernest Hébrard in the Pacific, Jacques Lambert in Latin America, and many others, found opportunities to realize many projects that otherwise would not have found traction in the capital.[61]

Unlike past iterations of colonial displays, the 1931 Colonial Exposition sought to avoid sentimental images of the colonies and instead to present accurate representations of them and the positive effects of urban planning policies. Accordingly, the site plan for the exposition's grounds mirrored the divisions in the planning of colonial cities, creating segregated sections for metropolitan, colonial and foreign sites. As Patricia Morton has described, the visitor "progressed from the civilizations of Europe outward to the far-flung antipodes of their empires, from the advanced societies of the present to the archaic, prehistoric ones."[62] The plan and its architecture served to represent the difference between France and the colonies, but as Morton further explains, the simultaneity of these differing temporal representations also demonstrated the inherent contradiction of the colonial display: to present the people of the colonies as savage in order to justify colonization, but not to present the civilizing mission as too successful such that colonization would no longer be justified.[63]

This temporal difference and simultaneity – or "heteroglossia," to use Mikhail Bakhtin's term, which Gwendolyn Wright has applied to the French colonial context – carried directly into the publication of the Congrès International de Géographie.[64] With Du Vivier de Streel as director of the Colonial Exposition composing its introduction, *L'Urbanisme aux colonies et dans les pays tropicaux* served as the scientific support for and endorsement of the exhibition at large. The text was organized by colonial regions, including North Africa, Tropical Africa, the Orient, Far East, America, and Ancient Cities, and compiled communications of the urbanists, administrators, and military officers directing and governing the major cities of the French empire. The volume's organization paralleled that of the plan of the Colonial Exposition. By juxtaposing images of archaeological sites with contemporary cities without any accompanying commentary, the implication was that these different temporal states were commensurate and interchangeable, thereby framing the cities as both timeless and undeveloped.

The fully incorporated aerial perspective reinforced this strategy of objectification. Fifty-eight aerial photographs were placed in every section of the volume. In the contemporary photographs of the colonial cities, European sectors were meant to be easily identified by form and composition [fig. 9.9]. For example, a photograph of Algiers was taken from the harbor that placed the French district in the foreground, distinguished by the large building blocks and the linear street network, while the "Kasbah" is pictured in the background as a rough mass of white whose specific features cannot be differentiated. The distance of the aerial view allowed for no detail [fig. 9.10a–b]. In a photographic example of Tortose, reproduced from *Vues aériennes de Syrie et du Liban* without credit, the airplane is flying at low altitude.[65] In the middle distance, the cathedral is visible, with its bulky buttresses and general form, and its façade is distinct in its massive form from the surrounding buildings, which are clusters of cubes spreading out along the coastline. In the background is the expanse of the waters, with a single sailboat coming into shore on the left edge of the image. This aerial image provides an overview of the dense urban surroundings of the religious monument, but the details remain illegible, and the visual information is impressionistic at best. Because of the oblique view and the low resolution, street patterns are not visible; people are not captured by the camera; the boundary between the water and the land is unclear. Other than a squat structure that seems to stand at the water's edge, the cathedral is the only distinguishable monument. The blurry visuals of the reproduced photograph relates to a "politics of resolution," that is, how the conditions of visibility are mediated by the modes of representation.[66] In this case, it is precisely the impossibility of the photographic medium to represent certain urban elements that constituted a means for control.

Figure 9.9: Photograph of Algiers. Jean Royer, ed. *L'Urbanisme aux colonies et dans les pays tropicaux* (Paris: Les Éditions d'urbanisme, 1935).

Figure 9.10a: Tartous. Armée du Levant, *Vues aériennes de Syrie et du Liban*, photographs by G. David, Loquinaire, and L. Piat (1926–1927). View 18.

Figure 9.10b: Tartous. Jean Royer, ed. *L'Urbanisme aux colonies et dans les pays tropicaux* (Paris: Les Éditions d'urbanisme, 1935).

Unlike the two aforementioned photographic albums, *L'Urbanisme aux colonies et dans les pays tropicaux* combined both text and image. The atemporality of the photograph in reproduction is then reframed through text. An excerpt reads:

> The traveler who has arrived from Chartres or Tours is immediately surprised to meet a former neighbor settled in Terre-Sainte. He provides an enchanting picture of this new life. He who possessed one field in the plains of Beauce or on the banks of the Loire, is now a big landowner in Palestine and has many servants; he has married a Saracen woman who converted and he has abandoned any idea to return.[67]

The perspective of the text takes a ground view, mixing spatial and familial details that the aerial photograph does not provide in its hazy resolution. It fills in the details with imaginary and romantic fiction. Elsewhere in the volume, when an aerial view is provided, the text refers to men promenading down a particular street. When a photograph of the front facade of a monument is shown, the text provides a broad historical overview of missionaries in the region and the organization of their charity work. These telescopic manipulations of time and space through "grounded" text and "aerial" images instill a disconnected experience based on the distance that is shaped by the photograph. This disjointed reading between text and image, however, created a sense neither of closeness nor of shared space. Rather, it created a virtual world, ultimately removing from the reader and the photographer any connection to time and people.

The Ground View

The distant aerial view, while offering the synoptic, could not offer precise detail. The quality of the photography was relatively poor. Its transfer to prints, and then paper reproductions, only reduced clarity. At the beginning of the war, the low resolution capacity of the technology was at odds with the rhetoric of photography's unparalleled accuracy and precision. Accordingly, the need for interpreters skilled in deciphering the blurry forms conveyed the camera's limitations. This limitation, while problematic for offensive action during war, became a critical factor in devising defensive strategies during WWI.

The advent of mechanized flight had preceded imagined aerial bombings. One early example from 1670 by Jesuit monk Francesco Lana fantasized an "aerial ship" that "would create many disturbances in the civil and political governments of mankind."[68] The fear of attack from above was so terrifying that Victor Hugo in 1862 imagined that aircraft would compel the universal abolition of international borders and eventually lead to a great world peace.[69] While many were optimistic about aerial technology's consequences, they all relied on the clear awareness that an aerial war meant a new kind of terror. As military historians agree, the principal objective of aerial warfare during the World Wars was to induce fear in people on the ground of an invisible enemy from above.[70] As Le Corbusier, ever fascinated with aerial flight, would reflect, "[t]hen came a day when offensive weapons made a mock of military enclosures, when the advent of the airplane meant that fortresses no longer had ceilings – a recent event, since it dates from the First World War."[71]

The earliest recorded aerial raid was in 1849 when the Austrians penetrated the defenses of the short-lived Venetian Republic, sending around 200 unmanned linen and paper balloons towards the city. The venture was only partially successful because while some of the projectiles carried by the balloons did reach the ground, others were blown back across Austrian lines by shifting winds. There was little impact on the defenders, but the Austrian press immediately understood its significance. As an omen of the outbreak of WWI, the Italians dropped bombs from dirigibles and airplanes on Libya during the Italo-Turkish War of 1911–1912. This time the damage was more substantial, and the coverage of the war was explicit in pointing out that the effects of aerial bombing were "decidedly moral rather than material."[72] The lesson was clear: war was three-dimensional. A new terrain had become open, that of the skies above cities – an atmospheric terrain, in which attackers had unrestricted freedom of movement and selection of targets, while the targets – cities and civilians – were immobile and effectively defenseless.[73]

The only defense that cities had against aerial reconnaissance and bombing was photographic concealment. French cities that were vulnerable to German aerial attack devised earthly solutions: camouflage nets. Web-like textiles were shaped with raffia, hay, branches, and all manner of material to mimic the flora of the local area, stretching like vines across the urban terrain.[74] From 1916 to 1917, these nets, produced by the French Camouflage Section, were hung across beams to cover streets, buildings, and all sorts of objects, extending over seven million square yards.[75] There were also observation posts that were disguised as tree stumps. From the plane, the graphic patterns of the nets became territorial patterns of fields, brush, and forest. As Hannah Rose Shell argues, this type of serial camouflage was a response specifically to the camera and historically defined by practices to circumvent the aerial technologies developed during the First World War. They constituted a politics of resolution, referring to Paul Virilio's idea of the "regulation of points of view," who argued that the battles of WWI concerned the control of ground and aerial perspectives.[76]

Considerations of a city's vulnerabilities to aerial reconnaissance and attack were a key concern of the French army throughout the war, as the bombing of towns and villages throughout the country left many of them decimated and in ruin.[77] While urbanists, architects, academics, politicians, and the military were debating the terms of urban reconstruction, a creative defensive proposal was submitted to prevent any further and future aerial attacks on the most important French city: Paris. On January 29, 1916, a German Zeppelin had launched 17 bombs onto eastern part of the capital, causing the deaths of 26 people in the districts of Belleville and Ménilmontant[78] [fig. 9.11]. While the Germans had used maps and photography to identify and launch the targets, the French press in their reportage were ironically not permitted to map or photograph the locations and the extent of the bombings. Between 1914 and 1918, about 275 Parisians died and close to 1,500 were wounded in 24 air raids and three Zeppelin attacks.[79] These German attacks on Paris paired with the night raids on London on November 19 and 20, 1917 created an urgency to develop an anti-aircraft urban defense system that included projectiles, anti-aircraft guns, and the improbable idea to camouflage the French capital.

Figure 9.11: *Le Figaro,* January 30, 1916.

Just before the end of the war in 1918, Fernand Jacopozzi, a Florentine electrical engineer who is better known for having illuminated the Eiffel Tower for the Exhibition of Decorative Arts in 1925, proposed the creation of a "faux Paris" (fake Paris) using illuminated decoys of the city's major landmarks. The French government ran with the idea and called upon industry to design and built it. The first step was to find a location that could fool pilots. The discussion of potential sites centered around nocturnal visibility from the air. After 1917, daytime aerial bombing missions were discontinued, with anti-aircraft defense systems in place on both sides. Thus, pilots would fly at night without radar and navigate by moonlight, relying on natural land-marks such as rivers and built forms such as towers and roads. In the end, three sites were selected: a site north of Paris where the curve in the Seine River resembled its course through the capital; another northeast of Paris at L'Orme de Morlu that could mimic the rail lines running to Gare du Nord and Gare de l'Est, and replicate the buildings of Saint-Denis and the factories of Aubervilliers; and a third site to the east of the city simulating the industrial zones of Chelles, Hournay, Vaires-sur-Marne, Champs, Noisiel, and Torcy.[80]

This was a city of simulacra, made for aerial vision, to be destroyed by aerial attack. Described in *L'Illustration* after the project had been cancelled, it was scenographic: "All we could do was set up a few acetylene lamps, alongside the dirt roads, so as to give the impression of avenues where the lights hadn't been turned out."[81] Props such as nets were deployed in French towns, while "simulating the rail tracks was done by just placing canvasses on the ground."[82] Entirely new structures were even built, including "buildings, platforms, trains standing at platforms and trains moving, the beginnings of tracks and signals, and a factory with buildings and functioning furnaces." These wooden buildings were then enveloped with "painted canvasses, where were stretched and translucent, so as to imitate the dirty glass roofs of the factories."[83] In the end, "faux Paris" was never tested. Construction was completed only after September 1918 and the November armistice put an end to the entire project. Yet the plans revealed how fully a culture of aerial visuality had pervaded government actions, which intertwined urbanism and military defense. It was not merely that military commanders and urban planners functioned in a world of simulations; they also built them.

Conclusion

The military development of aerial photography mapped directly onto the early practices of French urbanists. As André Balleyguier, secretary general of the Compagnie Aérienne Française, explained, the military, urban planning, and photography worked hand-in-hand:

> The urbanist arrives in effect to the colony after the solder, after the photography ... That documentation is acquired as complete as possible, so that he can establish his plans, launching into the future their logical, harmonious and practical previsions for the best organization of existing cities, the creation of new cities, and for the rational organization of the rural regions that will support the urban centers.[84]

As institutionalized through the SFAU right before the outbreak of WWI, the emergent field of urbanism synthesized methods and concepts from a variety of other disciplines, namely geography, sociology, ethnography, statistics, and architecture, in order to propose spatial solutions especially as they related to cities and their development. For a practice that was committed to demonstrating its basis as scientific, the photographic modes of representation combined, through its mechanical apparatus, the demands of objectivity and of realism that had been distinct in cartographic representation forms. What photography did was convert what had already long been visualized through maps into something that seemed to reach complete verisimilitude.

Aerial photography changed the meaning and experience of distance and closeness. Remote places were suddenly visually accessible and created an illusion of closeness, and yet that intimate visuality simultaneously allowed for violence to be enacted at a distance. This distortion was further conveyed in how these images were presented to and consumed by the public, with their temporal qualities juxtaposed to create sites that were outside of time altogether. Photographic surveys could reveal ancient monuments, but they were presented out of historic context. In their uses and reception, these aerial photographs were both accurate and blurred, both specific and vague. Having been printed from fragile glass plates, their dissemination also denied the particular materiality of their production, and instead the images came to be valued through their reproductions.

Significantly, the photographs did not necessarily provide greater vision. The details of the cities remained largely illegible due to the poor resolution of these aerial views, alluding to destructive military results as well as defensive strategies. As far as the urban planning efforts in the colonies were concerned, the consequences were devastating on many fronts. For urban programs in the colonies, they led to policies of segregation and isolation that were well pictured but not well lived for the local population. Aerial photography, while providing the overview, created a sense of distance that ultimately stripped the image of any accountability to the colonial subjects, while at the same time seeming to provide solutions that were specific to a given terrain. For the French defense against the Germans, the lack of visibility was used as an advantage in concealment. Towns and urban areas were camouflaged and built for the camera and the aerial photograph. It was precisely the sense of distance that allowed the army to create with precision an inaccurate terrestrial image. In both cases, the terrain was rendered a virtual site in which the distinctions between context and detail through photography were manipulated for the linked actions of destroying and planning cities.

Notes

1   Paul Rabinow, *French Modern: Norms and Forms of the Social Environment* (Cambridge, Mass.: The MIT Press, 1989), 20.

2   Charles Christienne and Pierre Lissarrague, *Histoire de l'aviation militaire française* (Paris: Limoges, Charles-Lavauzelle, 1986), 61.

3   On July 25, 1909, Louis Blériot flew across the English Channel from Calais to Dover. The French were the first to capitalize on the Wright brothers' invention, immediately giving them both a venue and press attention. French aviators followed very quickly afterwards.

4   James Streckfuss, *Eyes all over the sky: Aerial Reconnaissance in the First World War* (Oxford: Casemate, 2016), 10.

5   Général Duval, "Preface," in André H. Carlier, *La Photographie aérienne pendant la guerre* (Paris: Librairie Delagrave, 1921), 5. By the time the war broke, in France there were 162 aircrafts and five dirigibles. For comparison, the Germans had 232 planes, and 12 dirigibles, of which nine were Zeppelins.

6   Gérald Garry, *Environnement et aménagement*, vol. 3, *L'Usage des photographies aériennes* (Paris: Édition du Service technique de l'urbanisme, 1992).

7   Terrence Finnegan, *Shooting the Front: Allied Aerial Reconnaissance in the First World War* (Stroud, Gloucestershire: Spellmount, 2011).

8   By the beginning of 1915, the SPAe model had prompted both British and Belgian equivalents.

9   André H. Carlier, *La Photographie aérienne pendant la guerre* (Paris: Librairie Delagrave, 1921), 84.

10 Terrence Finnegan, "Shaping 20th century military intelligence through a static battlefield," in *Images of Conflict: Military Aerial Photography and Archaeology*, ed. Birger Stichelbaut, Jean Bourgeois, Nicholas Sanders, and Piet Chielens (Newcastle: Cambridge Scholars, 2009), 56.

11 Carlier, *La Photographie aérienne*, 139.

12 Precision refers to consistency and accuracy refers to correspondence. For a further discussion on the distinction between precision and accuracy, see M. Norton Wise, ed., *The Values of Precision* (Princeton: Princeton University Press, 1995).

13 The concept of "immutable mobiles" is relevant here. See Bruno Latour, "Visualisation and Cognition: Drawing Things Together," *Knowledge and Society: Studies in the Sociology of Culture Past and Present* 6 (1986): 1–40.

14 Paul Virilio, *War and Cinema: The Logistics of Perception* (London: Verso, 2000), 1.

15 See Paul Virilio, *The Vision Machine* (Bloomington, Ind.: Indiana University Press, 2007).

16 Peter Sloterdijk, *Terror from the Air* (Los Angeles: Semiotext(e), 2009), 14.

17 In an international attempt to create some protections for cities, Hague conventions on human rights were proposed in 1907 and 1922. However, they only made the vulnerability of cities and their inhabitants more clear: Article 25 from 1907 outlawed the bombardment of undefended towns but allowed attacks on military targets within such towns. This ambiguity was continued in 1922, which similarly forbade both "terror bombing" and "city bombing" but accepted "accidental civilian casualties." See Lee B. Kennett, *A History of Strategic Bombing* (New York: Scribner, 1983).

18   At beginning of the war, there were six dirigibles in service: three Clément-Bayard: *L'Adjudant-Vincenot, le Dupuy-de-Lôme*, and *le Montgolfier*; one Astra: *le Conté*; one Zodiac: *le Commandant-Coutelle*; and one Chalais-Meudon: *le Fleurus*. During the Battle of Verdun, two dirigibles were deployed, but both the *Adjudant-Vincenot* and the *Champagne* were shot down easily. On the whole, they proved to be extremely vulnerable targets, and were phased out quickly by 1917.

19   Min Kyung Lee, "An Objective Point of View: The Orthogonal Grid in Eighteenth-Century Plans of Paris," *Journal of Architecture* 17, no. 1 (February 2012): 11–32.

20   Peter Adey, Mark Whitehead, and Alison J. Williams, "Introduction: Air-target, Distance, Reach and the Politics of Verticality," *Theory, Culture and Society* 28, no. 7–8 (2011): 176–7.

21   Davide Deriu, "Picturing Ruinscapes: The Aerial Photograph as Image of Historical Trauma," in *The Image and the Witness: Trauma, Memory and Visual Culture*, ed. Frances Guerin and Roger Hallas (New York: Wallflower Press, 2007), 189–203.

22   Carlier, *La Photographie aérienne*, 131.

23   Jeanne Haffner, *The View from Above: The Science of Social Space* (Cambridge, Mass.: The MIT Press, 2013), 13

24   Among many examples, two French architects in particular, Jacques Carlu and André Deboos, recorded their trench experiences in sketchbooks, the former having a recent exhibition of his watercolors at the Cité de l'architecture in Paris, <https://www.citedelarchitecture.fr/fr/un-architecte-dans-la-grande-guerre>, and the latter having his watercolors and sketches displayed at the Musées de la Ville de Sens.

25   The association was officially registered just a few months before the outbreak of the war on March 10, 1914.

26   *L'Architecture* 13 (November 1910): 383–7.

27   Cited in Nathalie Roseau, "Reach for the Skies: Aviation and Urban Visions circa 1910," *Journal of Transport History* 30 (December 2009): 131.

28   See Paul Rabinow, *French Modern*, 254, and more generally; David Harvey, *Paris: Capital of Modernity* (London: Routledge, 2006).

29   Agache, Auburtin, and Redont, *Comment reconstruire nos cités détruites* (Paris: Librarie Armand, 1915), 5.

30   *Ibid.*, ix–xvi.

31   *Ibid.*, 5.

32   Specifically listed were (1) an overall plan at 1:5,000; (2) an overall plan of the city's underground infrastructure; (3) an overall plan of the park systems; and (4) an overall plan of the public transport. See Agache, Auburtin, and Redont, *Comment reconstruire*, 15.

33   Enrico Chapel, *L'Oeil raisonné. L'Invention de l'urbanisme par la carte* (Geneva: Metispresses, 2010).

34   For a specific discussion of Agache's causal theories, see David K. Underwood, "Alfred Agache, French Sociology and Modern Urbanism in France and Brazil," *Journal of the Society of Architectural Historians* 50, no. 2 (June 1991): 130–66.

35   Haffner dates the connection between planning and aerial views to be in the 1940s. See Haffner, *The View from Above*, 52.

36   Marie-Claire Robic, "From the Sky to the Ground: The Aerial View and the Ideal of the Vue Raisonnée in Geography during the 1920s," in *Seeing from Above: The Aerial View in Visual Culture*, ed. Mark Dorrian and Frédéric Pousin (London: Tauris, 2013), 161.

37   *Ibid.*, 170–1.

38   Agache proposed plans for Rio di Janiero, and other members won prizes in international urban planning competition, such as Jaussely in Barcelona (1903) and Hébrard in Guayaquil (1910). There were also Jacques Gréber's proposals for Philadelphia.

39   See Spencer Segalla, "Natural Disaster, Globalization, and Decolonization: The Case of the 1960 Agadir Earthquake," in *French Mediterraneans: Transnational and Imperial Histories*, ed. Patricia M. E. Lorcin and Todd Shepard (Lincoln, Nebr.: University of Nebraska Press, 2016), 106; more broadly, see Janet Abu-Lughod, *Rabat: Urban Apartheid in Morocco* (Princeton: Princeton University Press, 2016).

40   Maurice Culot, Anne Lambrichs, and Dominique Delaunay, *Albert Laprade: architecte, jardinier, urbaniste, dessinateur, serviteur du patrimoine* (Paris: Norma, 2007).

41   Brian Brace Taylor, "Planned Discontinuity: Modern Colonial Cities in Morocco," *Lotus International* 36 (1976): 52–66.

42   Between 1912 and 1924, 36.5 km of sewers were built in the new cities of Casablanca, Fez, and Rabat, and only 4.3 km in the older sections of the same cities. See Louis Sablayrolles, *L'Urbanism au Maroc: les moyens d'action, les résultats* (Paris: Albi, 1925), 109.

43   Zeynep Celik, "Le Corbusier, Orientalism, Colonialism," *Assemblage* 17 (1992): 58–77.

44   Rabinow, *French Modern,* 291.

45   Gwendolyn Wright emphasizes the significance of the French colonial cities as laboratories for two disciplines in particular: urbanism and social sciences. See Gwendolyn Wright, "Tradition in the Service of Modernity: Architecture and Urbanism in French Colonial Policy, 1900–1930," *Journal of Modern History* 59, no. 2 (June 1987): 297–8.

46   Jean-Louis Cohen and Monique Eleb, "The Whiteness of the Surf: Casablanca," *ANY*, no. 16 (1996): 16–9.

47   Jules Blache, "De Meknès aux sources de la Moulouya. Essai d'exploration aérienne du Maroc," *Annales de géographie* (1919): 292–3.

48   *Ibid.,* 295.

49   Michael Greenhalgh, "French Military Reconnaissance in the Ottoman Empire during the Eighteenth and Nineteenth Centuries as a Source for Our Knowledge of Ancient Monuments," *Journal of Military History* 66, no. 2 (2002): 359–88.

50   Georg Gerster, *The Past from Above: Aerial Photographs of Archaeological Sites* (Los Angeles: Getty Publications, 2005).

51   Jean Bourgeois and Birger Stichekbaut, "Images of Conflict: An Introduction," in *Images of Conflict: Military Aerial Photography and Archaeology*, ed. Birger Stichelbaut, Jean Bourgeois, Nicholas Sanders, and Piet Chielens (Newcastle: Cambridge Scholars, 2009), 4.

52   Philip S. Khoury, *Syria and the French Mandate: The Politics of Arab Nationalism, 1920–1945* (London: Tauris, 1987), 44–5. For a discussion of the role of the notion of culture, and the importance of the rhetoric of the *mission civilisatrice* more generally, see Jennifer M. Dueck, *The Claims of Culture at Empire's End: Syria and Lebanon under French Rule* (Oxford: Oxford University Press, 2010).

53   Idir Ouahes, *Syria and Lebanon under the French Mandate: Cultural Imperialism and the Workings of Empire* (London: Tauris, 2018), 9.

54   Jean Royer, ed., *L'Urbanisme aux colonies et dans les pays tropicaux* (Paris: Les Éditions d'urbanisme, 1935).

55   "On estima qu'à reconstituer l'organisation militaire et économique du désert à l'époque romaine, on gagnerait d'utiles indications pour assurer de nos jours la sécurité et la mise en valeur des régions désertiques." See Antoine Poidebard, *La Trace de Rome*

dans le désert de Syrie. Le Limes de Trajan à la conquête arabe. Recherches aériennes, 1925–1932 (Paris: Librairie Orientaliste Paul Geuthner, 1934), xviii.

56   Lorraine Daston and Peter Galison, *Objectivity* (New York: Zone Books, 2007), 19–27.

57   See Daniela K. Helbig's discussion comparing Marc Bloch and Antoine Poidebard's historiographic hermeneutics. Daniela K. Helbig, "La Trace de Rome? Aerial Photography and Archaeology in Mandate Syria and Lebanon," *History of Photography* 40, no. 3 (2016): 291.

58   *Ibid.*, 285.

59   Antoine Poidebard, "Missions dans le desert de Syrie en 1931," *Comptes rendues des séances de l'Académie des Inscription et Belles-Lettres* (1931): 354–8.

60   Poidebard, *La Trace de Rome*, 8.

61   For a fuller discussion of the valence of this term, "laboratory," in reference to the colonies, see Wright, "Tradition in the Service of Modernity," 298.

62   Patricia Morton, "A Study in Hybridity: Madagascar and Morocco at the 1931 Colonial Exposition," *Journal of Architectural Education* 52, no. 2 (November 1998): 77.

63   *Ibid.*, 78.

64   Wright, "Tradition in the Service of Modernity," 291–2; and Mikhail Bakhtin, "Discourse in the Novel," in *The Dialogic Imagination: Four Essays*, ed. Michael Holquist, trans. Caryl Emerson and Michael Holquist (Austin: University of Texas Press, 1981), 259–422.

65   Armée du Levant, *Vue aériennes de Syrie et du Liban*. Photographs by G. David, Loquinaire, and L. Piat (1926–1927).

66   The term is borrowed from Mark Dorrian, who discusses new political relationships that are defined by the "image resolutions and upload periodicity of data sets" instead of national borders, for instance. See Mark Dorrian, "On Google Earth," in *Seeing from Above: The Aerial View in Visual Culture*, ed. Mark Dorrian and Frédéric Pousin (London: Tauris, 2013), 301.

67   "Le voyageur qui arrive de Chartes ou de Tours, est tout surpris de rencontrer un ancien voisin s'est fixé en Terre-Sainte. Celui-ci lui fait un tableau enchanteur de sa nouvelle existence. Lui qui ne possédait qu'un champ dans la plaine de Beauce ou sur les bords de la Loire est maintenant grand propriétaire en Palestine et il a de nombreux serviteurs; il a épousé une Sarrasine qui a reçu le baptême et il a abandonné toute idée de retour." Royer, *L'Urbanisme aux colonies*.

68   Francesco Lana, quoted in Sir Walter Raleigh, *The War in the Air*, vol. 1 (Oxford: Oxford University Press, 1922), 29–30.

69   Victor Hugo quoted in I. F. Clarke, *Voices, Prophesying War, 1763–1934* (London: Oxford University Press, 1966), 3.

70   See M. Bateman and R. C. Riley, *The Geography of Defence* (London: Routledge, 2015); Michael Stohl, *The Politics of Terrorism* (New York: M. Dekker, 1988); and Kenneth Hewitt, "Place Annihilation: Area Bombing and the Fate of Urban Places," *Annals of the Association of American Geographers* 73, no. 2 (June 1983): 257–84.

71   *Looking*, 43. For a fuller discussion of Le Corbusier's interest in aviation, see M. Christine Boyer, "Aviation and the Aerial View: Le Corbusier's Spatial Transformations in the 1930s and 1940s," *Diacritics* 33, no. 3/4 (2003): 113.

72   "The Aeroplane in War," *Scientific American*, June 28, 1913.

73   See Richard Hallion, *Strike From the Sky: The History of Battlefield Air Attack, 1910–1945* (Tuscaloosa: University of Alabama Press, 2010); Tami David Biddle, *Rhetoric and Reality in Air Warfare* (Princeton: Princeton University Press, 2009).

74   Also in this tactic the French colonies played a critical role. Madagascar provided the dried raffia palm to compose these nets. See Hannah Rose Shell, *Hide and Seek: Camouflage, Photography, and the Media of Reconnaissance* (New York: Zone Books, 2012), 110.

75   See Raymond Myerscough-Walker, "Camaflour and his Craft, part 2," *Building* 157 (October 1939), 457. Also Shell, *Hide and Seek,* 81.

76   Virilio, *War and Cinema,* 92.

77   See Annie Deperchin, "Des destructions aux reconstructions," in *Encylopédie de la Grande Guerre, 1914–1918: Histoire et culture,* ed. Stéphanie Audoin-Rouzeau and Jean-Jacques Becker (Paris: Bayard, 2004), 1125–39.

78   Maurice Thiéry, *Paris bombardé par Zeppelins, Gothas et Berthas* (Paris: Éditions E. de Boccard, 1921), 28–44.

79   These numbers exclude the long-range guns stationed on the ground to bombard the city. If those are calculated, there were a total of almost 600 deaths. See Susan Grayzel, "'The Souls of Soldiers': Civilians under Fire in First World War France," *Journal of Modern History* 78, no. 3 (September 2006): 595–6.

80   Pierre-Marie Gallois, *Quand Paris était une ville-lumière* (Lausanne: Éditions L'Age d'homme, 2001).

81   *L'Illustration,* no. 4048 (October 2, 1920): 245.

82   *L'Illustration,* no. 4048 (October 2, 1920): 246.

83   *La View du Rail* (November 11, 1968): 75

84   "L'urbaniste arrive en effet à la colonie après le soldat, après le photographe … Ce n'est qu'une fois acquise cette documentation, la plus complète possible, qu'il peut établir ses projets, lançant vers l'avenir ses prévisions logiques, harmonieuses et pratiques pour la meilleur ordonnance des cités existantes, la création des villes nouvelles et pour l'organisation rationnelle des régions rurales qui feront vivre les centres urbaines." Royer, *L'Urbanisme aux colonies.*

Bibliography

Abu-Lughod, Janet. *Rabat: Urban Apartheid in Morocco.* Princeton: Princeton University Press, 2016.

Adey, Peter, Mark Whitehead, and Alison J. Williams. "Introduction: Air-target, Distance, Reach and the Politics of Verticality." *Theory, Culture and Society* 28, no. 7–8 (2011): 176–7.

"The Aeroplane in War," *Scientific American,* June 28, 1913.

Agache, Auburtin and Redont. *Comment reconstruire nos cités détruites.* Paris: Librarie Armand, 1915.

L'Architecture (November 13, 1910): 383–7.

Armée du Levant, *Vue aériennes de Syrie et du Liban.* Photographs by G. David, Loquinaire, and L. Piat, 1926–1927.

Bakhtin, Mikhail. "Discourse in the Novel." In *The Dialogic Imagination: four essays,* edited by Michael Holquist, translated by Caryl Emerson and Michael Holquist, 259–422. Austin: University of Texas Press, 1981.

Bateman, M., and R. C. Riley. *The Geography of Defence.* London: Routledge, 2015.

Biddle, Tami David. *Rhetoric and Reality in Air Warfare.* Princeton: Princeton University Press, 2009.

Blache, Jules. "De Meknès aux sources de la Moulouya. Essai d'exploration aérienne du Maroc." *Annales de géographie* (July 15, 1919): 293–314.

Bourgeois, Jean, and Birger Stichekbaut. "Images of Conflict: An Introduction." In *Images of Conflict: Military Aerial Photography and Archaeology*, edited by Birger Stichelbaut, Jean Bourgeois, Nicholas Sanders, and Piet Chielens, 1–12. Newcastle: Cambridge Scholars, 2009.

Boyer, M. Christine. "Aviation and the Aerial View: Le Corbusier's Spatial Transformations in the 1930s and 1940s." *Diacritics* 33, no. 3/4 (2003): 93–116.

Carlier, André H. *La Photographie aérienne pendant la guerre.* Paris: Librairie Delagrave, 1921.

Celik, Zeynep. "Le Corbusier, Orientalism, Colonialism" *Assemblage* 17 (1992): 58–77.

Chapel, Enrico. *L'oeil raisonné. L'invention de l'urbanisme par la carte.* Geneva: Metispresses, 2010.

Christienne, Charles, and Pierre Lissarrague. *Histoire de l'aviation militaire française.* Paris: Limoges, Charles-Lavauzelle, 1986.

Cohen, Jean-Louis, and Monique Eleb, "The Whiteness of the Surf: Casablanca" *ANY: Architecture New York,* no. 16 (1996): 16–9.

Clarke, I. F. *Voices, Prophesying War, 1763–1934.* London: Oxford University Press, 1966.

Culot, Maurice, Anne Lambrichs, and Dominique Delaunay. *Albert Laprade: architecte, jardinier, urbaniste, dessinateur, serviteur du patrimoine.* Paris: Norma, 2007.

Daston, Lorraine, and Peter Galison. *Objectivity.* New York: Zone Books, 2007.

Deperchin, Annie. "Des destructions aux reconstructions." In *Encylopédie de la Grande Guerre, 1914–1918: Histoire et culture,* edited by Stéphanie Audoin-Rouzeau and Jean-Jacques Becker, 1125–39. Paris: Bayard, 2004.

Deriu, Davide. "Picturing Ruinscapes: The Aerial Photograph as Image of Historical Trauma." In *The Image and the Witness: Trauma, Memory and Visual Culture,* edited by Frances Guerin and Roger Hallas, 189–203. New York: Wallflower Press, 2007.

Dorrian, Mark. "On Google Earth." In *Seeing from Above: The Aerial View in Visual Culture,* edited by Mark Dorrian and Frédéric Pousin, 290–308. London: Tauris, 2013.

Dorrian, Mark, and Frédéric Pousin, eds. *Seeing from Above: The Aerial View in Visual Culture.* London: Tauris, 2013.

Dueck, Jennifer M. *The Claims of Culture at Empire's End: Syria and Lebanon under French Rule.* Oxford: Oxford University Press, 2010.

Finnegan, Terrence. *Shooting the Front: Allied Aerial Reconnaissance in the First World War.* Stroud, Gloucestershire: Spellmount, 2011.

Gallois, Pierre-Marie. *Quand Paris était une ville-lumière.* Lausanne: Éditions L'Age d'homme, 2001.

Garry, Gérald. *Environnement et aménagement.* Vol. 3, *L'Usage des photographies aériennes.* Paris: Édition du Service technique de l'urbanisme, 1992.

Gerster, Georg. *The Past from Above: Aerial Photographs of Archaeological Sites.* Los Angeles: Getty Publications, 2005.

Grayzel, Susan. "'The Souls of Soldiers': Civilians under Fire in First World War France." *Journal of Modern History* 78, no. 3 (September 2006): 588–622.

Greenhalgh, Michael. "French Military Reconnaissance in the Ottoman Empire during the Eighteenth and Nineteenth Centuries as a Source for Our Knowledge of Ancient Monuments." *Journal of Military History* 66, no. 2 (2002): 359–88.

Haffner, Jeanne. *The View from Above: The Science of Social Space*. Cambridge, Mass.: The MIT Press, 2013.

Hallion, Richard. *Strike From the Sky: The History of Battlefield Air Attack, 1910–1945*. Tuscaloosa: University of Alabama Press, 2010.

Harvey, David. *Paris: Capital of Modernity*. London: Routledge, 2006.

Helbig, Daniela K. "La Trace de Rome? Aerial Photography and Archaeology in Mandate Syria and Lebanon." *History of Photography* 40, no. 3 (2016): 283–300.

Hewitt, Kenneth. "Place Annihilation: Area Bombing and the Fate of Urban Places." *Annals of the Association of American Geographers* 73, no. 2 (June 1983): 257–84.

Kennett, Lee B. *A History of Strategic Bombing*. New York: Scribner, 1983.

Khoury, Philip S. *Syria and the French Mandate: The Politics of Arab Nationalism, 1920–1945*. London: Tauris, 1987.

Latour, Bruno. "Visualisation and Cognition: Drawing Things Together." *Knowledge and Society: Studies in the Sociology of Culture Past and Present* 6 (1986): 1–40.

Lee, Min Kyung. "An Objective Point of View: The Orthogonal Grid in Eighteenth-Century Plans of Paris." *Journal of Architecture* 17, no. 1 (February 2012): 11–32.

Morton, Patricia. "A Study in Hybridity: Madagascar and Morocco at the 1931 Colonial Exposition." *Journal of Architectural Education* 52, no. 2 (November 1998): 76–86.

Ouahes, Idir. *Syria and Lebanon under the French Mandate: Cultural Imperialism and the Workings of Empire*. London: Tauris, 2018.

Poidebard, Antoine. "Missions dans le desert de Syrie en 1931." *Comptes rendues des séances de l'Académie des Inscription et Belles-Lettres* (1931): 354–8.

Poidebard, Antoine. *La Trace de Rome dans le désert de Syrie. Le Limes de Trajan àla conquéte arabe. Recherches aériennes, 1925–1932*. Paris: Librairie Orientaliste Paul Geuthner, 1934.

Rabinow, Paul. *French Modern: Norms and Forms of the Social Environment*. Cambridge, Mass.: The MIT Press, 1989.

Raleigh, Sir Walter. *The War in the Air*. Vol. 1. Oxford: Oxford University Press, 1922.

Robic, Marie-Claire. "From the Sky to the Ground: The Aerial View and the Ideal of the Vue Raisonnée in Geography during the 1920s." In *Seeing from Above: The Aerial View in Visual Culture,* edited by Mark Dorrian and Frédéric Pousin. London: Tauris, 2013.

Roseau, Nathalie. *Aerocity. Quand l'avion fait la ville*. Marseille: Parenthèses, 2012.

———. "Reach for the Skies: Aviation and Urban Visions: Paris and New York circa 1910." *Journal of Transport History* 30 (December 2009): 121–40.

———. "Du future au miroir: les paradoxes des villes aériennes." In *De l'histoire des transports à l'histoire de la mobilité?,* edited by Vincent Guigueno and Mathieu Fonneau, 207–19. Rennes: Presses universitaires de Rennes, 2009.

Royer, Jean, ed. *L'Urbanisme aux colonies et dans les pays tropicaux*. Paris: Les Éditions d'urbanisme, 1935.

Sablayrolles, Louis. *L'Urbanism au Maroc: les moyens d'action, les résultats*. Paris: Albi, 1925.

Segalla, Spencer. "Natural Disaster, Globalization, and Decolonization: The Case of the 1960 Agadir Earthquake." In *French Mediterraneans: Transnational and Imperial Histories*, edited by Patricia M. E. Lorcin and Todd Shepard, 101–28. Lincoln, Nebr.: University of Nebraska Press, 2016.

Shell, Hannah Rose. *Hide and Seek: Camouflage, Photography, and the Media of Reconnaissance*. New York: Zone Books, 2012.

Sloterdijk, Peter. *Terror from the Air*. Los Angeles: Semiotext(e), 2009.

Stichelbaut, Birger, Jean Bourgeois, Nicholas Sanders, and Piet Chielens, eds. *Images of Conflict: Military Aerial Photography and Archaeology.* Newcastle: Cambridge Scholars, 2009.

Stohl, Michael. *The Politics of Terrorism.* New York: M. Dekker, 1988.

Streckfuss, James. *Eyes all over the sky: Aerial Reconnaissance in the First World War.* Oxford: Casemate, 2016.

Taylor, Brian Brace. "Planned Discontinuity: Modern Colonial Cities in Morocco." *Lotus International* 36 (1976): 52–66.

Thiéry, Maurice. *Paris bombardé par Zeppelins, Gothas et Berthas.* Paris: Éditions E. de Boccard, 1921.

Underwood, David K. "Alfred Agache, French Sociology and Modern Urbanism in France and Brazil." *Journal of the Society of Architectural Historians* 50, no. 2 (June 1991): 130–66.

Virilio, Paul. *War and Cinema: The Logistics of Perception.* London: Verso, 2000.

———. *The Vision Machine.* Bloomington, Ind.: Indiana University Press, 2007.

Wise, M. Norton, ed. *The Values of Precision.* Princeton, N.J.: Princeton University Press, 1995.

Wright, Gwendolyn. *The Politics of Design in French Colonial Urbanism.* Chicago: University of Chicago Press, 1991.

———. "Tradition in the Service of Modernity: Architecture and Urbanism in French Colonial Policy, 1900–1930." *Journal of Modern History* 59, no. 2 (June 1987): 291–316.

Figure 10.1: Group photo on Carso with the Col. dir. A. Jervolino, 2 Zone 3 Army, May 27, 1917, "Direzione Lavori Genio Militare, Ufficio staccato Tapogliano." War Album 1915–18 (Alberto Griffini Collection, Milan).

The "Landscapes" of the Great War
The Role of Italian Engineers and Architects

Massimiliano Savorra

Introduction

At the end of the First World War, it became apparent that four years of conflict had left just the wrecks of homes in valleys, hills, and mountains, and lawns and pasturelands scattered with barbed wire and torched woods. Fields had turned into graveyards, empty lots had been invaded by armies of crosses, factories were devastated, churches torn out, and, above all, an endless firmament of trench lines and craters seamed the land. To the men who served and survived, this wounded landscape was a constant reminder of the horror of watching fellow soldiers suffer and die in the mud.[1] Among those haunted by such nightmare images were the many architects and engineers who served the war effort by manning posts on the front, working for the Corps of Military Engineers, and building defense facilities, trench lines, and roads, among other works of infrastructure.[2] Architects and engineers formed an elite corps of educated commissioned and non-commissioned officers, many of them volunteers, whose expertise in architecture and engineering went hand-in-hand with a shared faith in the "Fatherland."[3] Although little is known today about the bereavement and process of coping with trauma of this architectural and engineering elite, it is possible to trace their work at the front, beyond what Marc Bloch defined as the "psychology of witnessing" applied to the Great War.[4] At the same time, it is also necessary to analyze the "war-related work" that they completed both during and immediately after the fighting.

The aim of this essay is to analyze three different meanings of "landscape." The contribution is therefore divided into three sections. The first part, "The Wounded Landscape," will explain how young engineers and architects knew and modified the landscape of the war when they found themselves at the front to fight against the

Austro-German soldiers. The second part, "The Reconstructed Landscape," concerns how architects and engineers rebuilt houses and churches on the basis of a specific idea of "landscape." Finally, the third part, "The Commemorated Landscape," deals with the theme of the "evoked landscape" in the monuments to the fallen and in the war memorials built both on the battlefields and in the squares of every Italian city.

The Wounded Landscape

After what was often a brisk training stint in military academies before leaving for the front, architects and engineers (students in their final year of higher education, new graduates or those who had already entered the profession) were incorporated automatically among the officers of the "Genio" (Corps of Military Engineers): the Mining Engineers, the Railway Engineers, the Bridge Builders, and the Flamethrowers[5] [fig. 10.1, 10.2]. The Corps of Bridge Builders, which also included large numbers of engineers and architects, was made up in 1915 of 12 companies, which soon grew to 16. This Corps was in charge of river-crossing operations, especially for the

Figure 10.2: Corps of Flamethrowers, "Direzione Lavori Genio Militare, Ufficio staccato Tapogliano." War Album 1915–18 (Alberto Griffini Collection, Milano).

Piave, the Tagliamento and the Isonzo. At the time of the battle of Vittorio Veneto, 26 bridge-building companies were operational, grouped into six battalions. Many young graduates from Bologna University and the Polytechnic Institutes of Turin and Milan worked in the Corps of Bridge Builders,[6] but they were also particularly numerous in the Corps of Sappers and in the Corps of Mining Engineers,[7] which dealt with trenches and galleries, in addition to carrying materials for the construction and reinforcement of roads and advanced frontline positions. The number in the "Genio" overall grew from the initial 43 companies in May 1915 to 236 companies by November 1918, employed both in the defense lines behind the front and on the front lines. These groups laid down barbed wire fences and built defensive works, such as the intricate and imposing "galleria Vittorio Emanuele" under the peak of Mount Grappa.[8]

Moreover, mine warfare, and as a result countermine warfare, was still considered a valid strategy to conquer or destroy "enemy" positions:[9] in this regard, it should be remembered that the actions of the Mining Engineers led to the irreparable transformation of mountain morphology, for example at Mount Col di Lana, which lost its summit, the south face of Mount Lagazuoi, which was completely destroyed, or Mount Colbricon, which suffered the loss of one of its three jagged peaks.[10] These mountains were extensively transformed, not only on the surface, but also under the ground, even under glaciers, through many kilometers of communication trenches, dugouts, and galleries. All of these spaces housed electric power stations, laboratories, workshops, kitchens, and depots, and were often used to range bomb-throwers, grenade-throwers, flame-throwers, and machine-gun positions. These galleries created new "underground landscapes," which were added to the other "landscapes" composed of fortifications – permanent ones, on the battlefields, or temporary – and complexes of trenches and barbed wire fences.[11] While designing infrastructure essential for the deployment of troops, the Corps of Engineers also built roads crucial to the organization and supply of the front lines, such as the "strada Cadorna" between Romano d'Ezzelino and Cima Grappa planned in the fall of 1916 and finished in November 1917, the so-called "road of Heroes" on the Pasubio Massif, and the renowned "52-gallery road," a road which made a graded ascent of almost 700 m.[12] During the war, a new specialized corps was even created, that of the cableway engineers. This strategic unit which was able to lay down in under a week cable-cars that climbed well over 1,000 meters in altitude, when the army was squatting between the Paradiso Pass and the Mondrone Glacier,[13] where, thanks to their technical skills, they were actually able to create "citadels,"[14] such as "El Milanin," built on Mount Pasubio and housing up to 1,000 men in a number of sheds and shelters.

Of course, all the young engineers and architects who worked in these military corps had to have drawing skills. In the period preceding their departure for the front's hotspots, they were often instructed in "drawing for warfare purposes." A professor at the Royal Military College and at the Albertina Academy of Fine Arts in Turin, Mario Ceradini, for example, expounded his ideas regarding "military panoramic drawing," defined as a form of communication made by the scouting officer to his commander. To this end, drawing was called "communication," since the illustration side was preponderant, although written instructions were added to it: according to Ceradini, soldiers would report not so much what they could see, but rather what they deemed interesting in terms of military value. Said communication, written and drawn, had to be done on the spot, in a "fast, certain, concise way."[15] It was imperative to have knowledge of drawing from life and of applied geometry.

The architects and engineers, as well as other artists,[16] were able to sketch, draw places and architecture, and design medals and pennants, not only while resting behind the front lines, but also at the front between each attack.[17] Many of them took photographs,[18] drew caricatures of their superiors and portraits of fellow soldiers,[19] or concocted image-based tales on postcards addressed to wives, mothers, far-away friends, and relatives. From these visual documents emerged – at times distantly, at times starkly – a picture of the landscape: observed, drawn out, transmogrified, ravished.[20] Those drawings showed ruins, fields fenced off by barbed wire, smoking ground, and burning trees.[21] Architects' and artists' drawings would actually be a way of documenting, in the words of Arturo Lancellotti, "the savage mountains from which our Alpini soldiers look out in order to take the enemy by surprise, the horrendous roads over which whole convoys of trucks are made to travel, the faith of soldiers going to mass at 2,700 m altitude … the speed at which our combatants are building military bridges and barracks: in one word, the whole complex of military and logistic work and services which animates our front."[22]

These "drawn" observations were often taken from the top of belfries as well as from trenches and shelters. Towers and belfries were used as preferred vantage point for reconnoitering local areas, or as observation points for military operations. Such was the case of the belfry in Campolongo, a strategic spot for operations on the Isonzo front (where necessary, recourse was made to purpose-built wooden watch towers). The landscape was widely refashioned by the shelters for reinforcements and stocks, for example through basement-like structures with observatories built on the Tapogliano line, a beltway of trench works in addition to the "[l]ine of settlements for the defense of towns and villages.[23] At the back of the trench lines, about a hundred meters away, the Corps of Engineers built at regular intervals artillery positions and reinforced shelters for reinforcement troops, which were especially necessary for the slaughter-field of the Carso. The landscape thus underwent profound transformations, even before the great battles fought in a few well-defined theaters of operation, from the line on the Adige to that on the Isonzo [fig. 10.3].

Figure 10.3: Defensive elements and lunette, "Direzione Lavori Genio Militare, Ufficio staccato Tapogliano." War Album 1915–18 (Alberto Griffini Collection, Milano).

The militarization of the Alps, which had started at the beginning of the century with the fortifications on the Altopiano dei Sette Comuni, took a decisive turn in the summer of 1914, when, in the light of foreseen hostilities, the work of the Corps was speeded up for defense preparations. The army's top echelons considered the following forts masterpieces of defense engineering: Fort Verena, overlooking the Val d'Assa, Fort Campolongo, which dominated the Val d'Astico, and Fort Corbin, with its reinforced turning spires. These forts left an unmistakable mark on the landscape as soon as they were put up, even more so once they were attacked, occupied, or destroyed, leaving behind sites pockmarked with discouraging wounds. Yet, those forts were already obsolete even before the battles started, since infrastructure built in plain concrete was unable to withstand the Škoda howitzers that Austria's Imperial Army had recently acquired.[24]

As a result, the work undertaken by the Corps concerned the vast areas on the border which – it was understood from the start – would be involved in trench warfare,[25] even though bombardiers at times hit towns lying relatively far from the front line. The many outlying areas of so many villages, the countryside, and the towns lying on the front line were abandoned, bombed, occupied, sometimes totally destroyed and razed to the ground.[26] The medium- and large-caliber batteries that the Corps built were not enough to plug the serious holes in the armory equipment of the Italian army.[27] The countryside, where woods had been seriously depleted after months of cannon fire, the hillsides, and the mountain ranges, at times levelled by mines, were invaded by military works, such as lunettes, parts of a defense system fanning out from the countryside to reach hill country, which was supposed to act as a bridgehead.[28]

The Reconstructed Landscape

Quite often architects and engineers also oversaw works intended for the civilian population, which, admittedly, should have helped to heal the wounds left by the destruction, and – once the war was over – to build national cohesion.[29] As soon as the armistice was signed, a debate arose regarding how to rebuild, preserve, protect, and promote the landscape, especially in the many localities on the front. For a long time, castles, forts, military sheds, batteries, and the trenches themselves were used as temporary and precarious dwellings by the displaced people made homeless by the war, and as places to celebrate religious services since few churches were safe. Thus, while the damage was being evaluated, the authorities studied how to go about salvaging what was left of the country's artistic and architectural heritage.[30] They also carried out the timely restoration of countless public buildings and road infrastructure. A process was set in motion to rebuild houses, churches, castles, and squares through plans that were able to "make use of local building and decorative features, crystallized through centuries of slowly accumulated expertise by local craftsmen."[31] Much concern was expressed as to the features of "model" constructions, which – as feared by Ambrogio Annoni in 1920 – might be "brought about by laws and regulations."[32]

Some of these projects were intended for precisely those engineers and architects who had been on active duty in the Corps of Engineers and had known those places in battle:[33] such projects came about due to the Opera nazionale per la ricostruzione dei paesi danneggiati dalla guerra (National Institute for Reconstruction), which was founded in Milan by the Comitato d'azione dei Mutilati di Guerra (Action Committee for War Amputees), and thanks to the Touring Club Italiano (TCI). In January 1918, the latter organization had already remarked in the columns of its monthly magazine on the seriousness of the situation of the war-torn landscape, with the hope that rural homes and businesses in the provinces that had been invaded would be quickly rebuilt. With the funds made available by the industrialist Ercole Marelli, the TCI ran a competition for engineers and architects, with the aim of redesigning the destroyed landscape.[34] The numerous proposals submitted to the jury from all over Italy - 186 in total - were the work of designers who showed themselves to be well acquainted with the desolate landscapes. Virtually all of the proposals shared one aim, that of redesigning the landscape through the reworking of rural typologies, which had been studied, and often drawn, at the time of the truce in the northeast [fig. 10.4].[35]

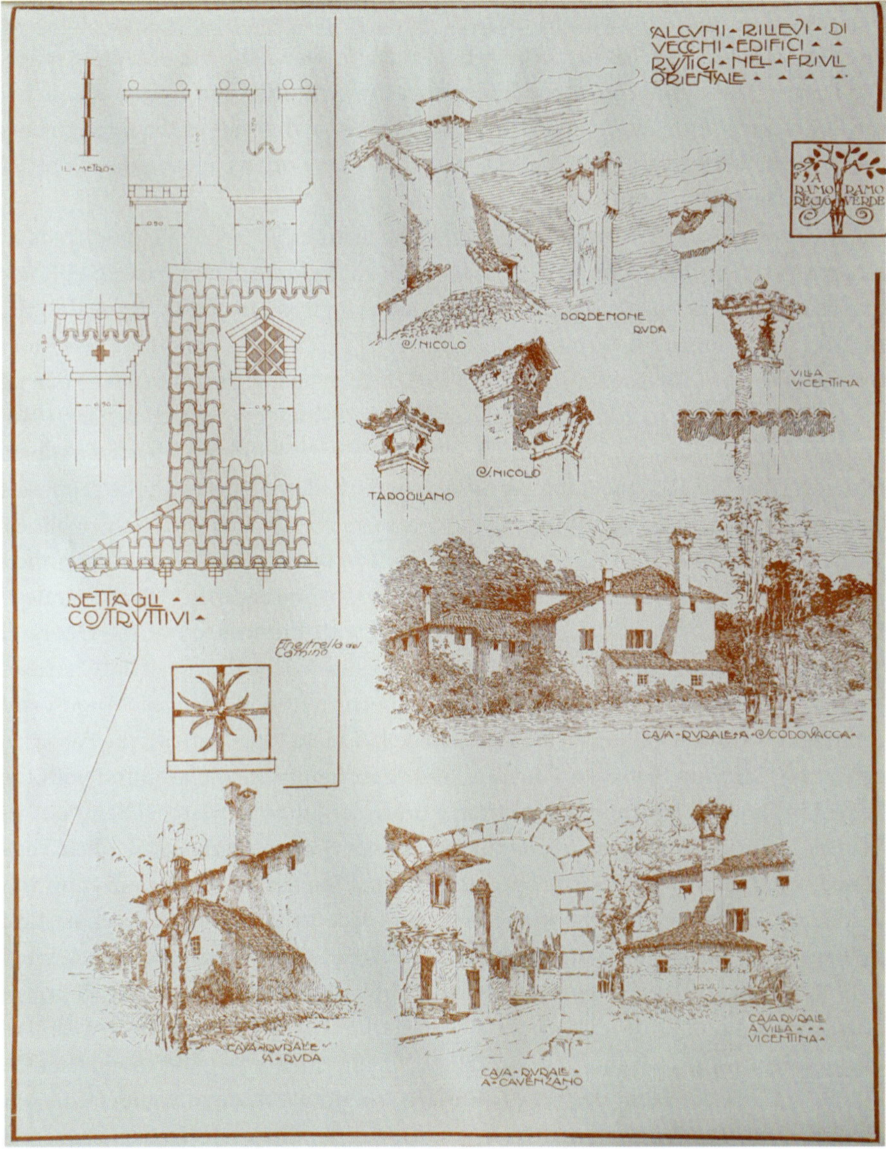

Figure 10.4: Enrico Agostino Griffini and Paolo Mezzanotte, Farmhouse project for high and medium plain area (Progetto di casa colonica per zona di alta e media pianura), Marelli Competition TCI, 1918–19 (From *Concorso "Ercole Marelli" per progetti di ricostruzione di piccoli edifici rurali nei territori devastati dalla guerra*. Edited by Touring Club Italiano. Milano: Mondaini, 1919).

Thus, the "reconstruction" also became an opportunity to reflect on the traditional aesthetic features of dwellings located in the so-called *terre irredente*, those parts of Italy that were formerly under foreign rule.[36] In fact, in countless drawings submitted to the jury it was clear that the authors were trying to define the landscape, by singling out a "harmonious and pleasant" look, good proportions, consistency of lines, the use of color effects in a variety of materials, and the use of ledges, reliefs and frames, as they appeared from the houses drawn at the front.[37] After all, such a methodological framework was also widely shared by the staff of the departments for the preservation of national heritage, and by many others among the country's architects, not just locally.[38]

These proposals were often inspired by the features of farmers' homesteads in mountain-side and hill-side areas or in the high and middle plains, based on photographs and sketches taken directly on the spot, as well as on studies devoted to the rural art of the northeast.[39] Among those who took part in the competition was Paolo Mezzanotte, who published his studies in 1920, which he had drawn from life during the war. His studies included a significant series of drawings, dated January 1918, on the rural character of the buildings in the areas that had been invaded. As part of the work of the TCI, the jury's report was published, together with the proposals chosen, in a text made available to the appropriate institutions and municipalities. The aim was to provide "a rough solution for a few typical issues, as guiding principles for practical cases that were widely different from one another."[40] Such a strategy for the "construction" of the landscape meshed with the strategy of the Opera di Soccorso per le chiese devastate dalla Guerra (Institute for the Rescue of the Churches Destroyed by the War). This organization had been envisioned between August and September 1918 by Countess Giulia Persico della Chiesa together with the Patriarch of Venice, Cardinal Pietro La Fontaine, and Monsignor Celso Costantini with the help of his brother Giovanni Costantini, a professor at the Patriarchal Seminary of Venice. Their idea became a reality on November 5 of the same year, when Pope Benedict XV approved the articles of association. The aim of the organization was to manage and coordinate the whole process of reconstruction of the ecclesiastical heritage, monitoring the work of the architects and engineers.[41] From December 1918 to January 1919, the Opera put out a call to all the bishops and parish priests of Italy to let them know they could receive money to aid in the reconstruction of their churches and their interior decorations.[42] After making a good estimate of the number of damaged and destroyed churches,[43] a notice of open competition was published in *Arte Cristiana* magazine,[44] addressed to all architects, engineers, and artists in Italy[45] [fig. 10.5].

Figure 10.5: Vito Rastelli, Alpine church project (Progetto di chiesetta alpina), 1920 (From *Arte Cristiana*, no. 3 (March 1920).

In this instance too, the request was for proposals that were "in tune with the environs" and the landscape. Once again, the solutions that were put forward were based on sketches and prototypes of countryside churches made in rural areas and in theaters of war. In the drawings (over 100 proposals were submitted to the competition) there were a plethora of bell towers, called *campanilesse*, making reference to such churches as that in Fratta (lower Isonzo valley) and the ruins of small churches that could be seen in the Monfalcone countryside or along the valleys of the Brenta or the Piave.[46]

As well as promoting the reconstruction of the landscape in accordance with the principle of *where it was, as it was*, the Opera was committed to supervising the whole task with the aim of giving a uniform character to everything that was going to be built in the Veneto, the Trentino and the Friuli-Venezia Giulia, requiring, where necessary, changes to the projects and to the decorative elements: it was not for nothing that Giovanni Costantini, the secretary and veritable *deus ex machina* of the Opera, asked the Minister of Newly Freed Lands, Cesare Nava, to authorize the Opera to give its seal of approval to all the church plans so that it could coordinate and keep each individual job of work under one roof. After the competition, the Opera acquired ever greater power in deciding who should have the right to inspect new proposals. There were a number of clashes with the Committee for War Damages Compensation as well as with individual dioceses, for example on the issue of the artistic features of the churches along the Piave or concerning surveillance methods and compensation grants. Stylistically, the Diocese of Treviso pitted its *E ruinis pulchriores* declaration against the rather rigid principles of the Opera, so as to highlight the austere and constrictive aspects of the slogan adopted for the rebirth of the churches that had been destroyed. As a result, in practice, a rather wide interpretation arose: the principle of faithful reconstruction was appropriate for churches that had received slight damage, but along the Piave front line it was a question of working on heaps of ruins, and in the case of new urban developments, reconstruction also had to be undertaken in areas other than those where the destroyed churches used to stand.[47]

The Commemorated Landscape

Alongside the many instances of reconstruction of the landscape in the areas that had been affected by the battles, in the few months after the conclusion of World War I, the areas of the front became pilgrimage destinations for veterans and the relatives of the fallen [fig. 10.6].[48] Between 1918 and 1922, a new interest arose in the landscapes that had served as theaters of war. These landscapes became on the one hand politicized, and on the other commemorative. While the Alps were exalted as a natural bulwark and an impassable border of the Nation, architects, engineers, and artists found in landscapes the raw essence for commemorative works.[49] The intimate awareness of a landscape that they had known first-hand, as aforementioned, played a significant role, both in the countless opportunities for work on war memorials and in the number of monuments put up in the main square of each individual town.[50]

It is critical to remember that in the years immediately after the war, the euphoric early days of peace went hand-in-hand with the tragedy of millions of deaths, so much so that solemn celebrations were accompanied by memorial services, as an expression of the gratitude felt for the sacrifice of the soldiers lost in battle.[51] It goes without saying that the contrast between exaltation and condemnation of the war influenced the meaning given to the monuments and memorial shrines. For example, the notorious competition for Mount San Michele al Carso,[52] to commemorate the simple foot soldier, is emblematic of the construction of an idea of landscape – as well as of the "myth of the war experience," as defined by Paul Fussell – which may be made to include the experience of engineers and architects. The battle of Mount San Michele had, in fact, been among the cruelest, when, following the Hungarians' gas attack on June 29, 1916, over 6,000 Italian soldiers alone lost their lives (between Podgora-Monte Calvario and San Michele, between May 1915 and October 1917, it is thought that 1 million men died, or 800,000 according to official estimates).[53]

Figure 10.6: Cemetery of the Undefeated (Cimitero degli Invitti della III Armata sul Colle Sant'Elia), Redipuglia 1924 (Postcard, Private Collection, Milan).

The competition for San Michele saw the participation of a large number of architects, engineers, and artists, almost all of whom were veterans of the Corps of Engineers, either officers or foot soldiers, who tried to celebrate victory and at the same time honor death in works that could reflect the meaning of the surrounding landscape [fig. 10.7]. Whether they were isolated temples on top of a hill or charnel houses fitted into the trenches, the proposed works shared a common desire to interpret the places, at times by reusing existing fortifications, at times by proposing a vision that was a far cry from the ruins of the war but close to the idea of a rhetorical commemoration of the lost landscape. In fact, when the time came for the first great event after the war, an issue that had long since been debated came to the fore regarding the symbolic meaning conveyed by a monument consisting in a communal burial ground and involving a host of landscapes and theaters of war. What were the appropriate images and languages to express the universality of loss? How to to convey the sacred essence of the landscape, when in fact in many quarters people were trying to forget the horror they had gone through? What were the appropriate forms for places where people could assemble for commemoration? Was perpetuating the memory of fortifications really necessary? These were the questions most commonly asked by professionals called upon to "plan the memory, defend the holy remnants of our dead."[54]

Figure 10.7: Enrico Agostino Griffini and Paolo Mezzanotte, Study sketch for Monument to the Fante, 1920–21 (Alessandra Griffini Collection, Milan).

The idea of a "theatrical landscape" was present in many proposals submitted for the competition, in particular one by Eugenio Baroni (an immense cross balanced on a hill).[55] At the time of the competition for the monument to the Fante (foot soldier) the conditions were ripe for a monument-shrine that took into account the sacred nature of the landscape itself, accommodated a multiplicity of symbols, and supported the different political views of the pre-fascist era, including those of the military.[56] The landscape could have been considered a monument in itself, as in the proposal by Guido Manacorda, who had also fought on the Carso and on the Piave. The decree of October 20, 1922 laid down that large numbers of war areas (San Michele and Sabotino on the Carso, the Grappa, the so-called "island of the dead" along the Piave) that were to be declared monumental areas devoted to the remembrance of veterans and amputees who would revisit them in moving pilgrimages.

The bereavement liturgies that were celebrated between the end of the war and the start of the Fascist regime were crucial for the definition of a new "war landscape." These years were decisive for a "faith rite" that was not just meant for consolation. A sense of pride, the remembrance of suffering, and the mourning process were linked, for survivors, by the awareness that they had sacrificed themselves for a noble cause in the theaters of war.[57] This idea was also in tune, as is well known, with that rhetoric of power through which Benito Mussolini tried after 1931 to acquire mass consensus also with regard to war, which was considered "just" and necessary for the liberation of Italy from foreign powers.[58] After the Fante competition, the monument-shrine set within the landscape finally became simply a "shrine," confirming its status as the supreme space – with a highly artistic, symbolic, and, above all, spiritual character – of those deadly terrains. The movement from charnel-house to shrine, which was not simply lexical, also came about because the experience of mass sacrifice solidified some fundamental Christian motifs while at the same time directing traditional religious sentiment toward new trends of secular devotion.

Obviously, the theaters of war in the Veneto, Trentino, and Friuli-Venezia Giulia, which had seen the selfless sacrifice of Italian soldiers, were the most "visited" locales, and not just for pilgrimages or communal trips, including precisely what was deemed to be the first "altar of death," San Michele al Carso. The Fante competition thus led the way to laying the foundations for a new secular cult of the war landscape rooted in a modern idea of faith linked to Fascist power.

A new sensibility arose toward landscapes that had become "untouchable" precisely as a result of their sacredness. In the wake of some events of the Risorgimento,[59] places that were themselves defined as "monuments" – as were the wishes of Monsignor Costantini for the hill of San Michele – became part of the celebrations: the landscape as much as the "road" toward it, which was set within the appropriate elegiac frame. With the military shrines of the 1930s,[60] as with proposals by the sculptor Baroni and others, the motif of the promenade, of the triumphal stairway or of the Via Crucis, took on significant value, and not just in terms of composition, as an ascending path in a secular pilgrimage undertaken by veterans and their families, but by school parties, political party groups, and other city organizations.

From 1923 onward, the representation of the fallen was no longer selective or confined to theaters of war alone. Following the example set by the German *Totenburgen*, the relationship with the natural landscape created by the shrines was the characteristic feature of the debate that had arisen in Italy after the Fante competition.[61] After 1926, the higher echelons of the legions of the Comando delle legioni della Milizia Forestale (Forestry Militia) took over the parks – where "a tree could" be dedicated "to each and every soldier," as wished by Junior Minister for Education Dario Lupi[62] – which also played a decisive role in the creation of a shared memory. In this respect, the process of landscape sacralization led to the rise in many cities of monument-shrines set within "natural décors" – tree-lined gardens, parks, and remembrance avenues (in a few cases "Fascist woods")[63] – watched over at times by veritable memorial lighthouses[64] [fig. 10.8, 10.9].

Figure 10.8: Arduino Berlam, Victory Lighthouse (Faro della Vittoria), Trieste 1923–27 (Postcard, Private Collection, Milan).

Just like everywhere in Europe, as well as in the United States, popular initiatives to create urban memorial landscapes, evoking theaters of war (made up of charnel-houses-temples with an appropriate layout of the surrounding areas), came about as a result of the return of the soldiers' mortal remains.[65] Such initiatives in Italy were strengthened by celebrations and anniversaries organized by committees of disabled amputees and former combatants, together with the local clergy promoting veritable Christian-patriotic liturgies tied to the war. The war landscapes were no longer – or at least not exclusively – those that had seen military combat, but had instead to become evoked and recreated in every place, in every square in Italy. Images of that landscape needed to be produced to offset an absence, as a reaction to the trauma of death. Such a monument, as a kind of "externalized remembrance" of the war landscape, was supposed to represent collective remembrance. Said remembrance, ever since the armistice, was constantly nourished by the experience of veterans who took it upon themselves to promote the erection of sculptures, stelae, and altars in many Italian squares at least until 1927.[66] Only subsequently was the Italian citizenry weaned off this remembrance by a flattering regime that tried to persuade survivors to be the protagonists, as well as the instigators, of the new and victorious national season [fig. 10.10].

Figure 10.9: Ferruccio Chemello, Memorial to the Fallen Soldiers (Sacrario Ossario ai caduti), Pasubio 1926–27 (Postcard, Private Collection, Milan).

Figure 10.10: Giovanni Greppi, Giannino Castiglioni, Memorial to the Fallen Soldiers (Sacrario), Redipuglia 1935–38 (Postcard, Private Collection, Milan).

In cities too, or in the nearest surroundings, or again in places that had already been consecrated to remembrance, the landscape of the front had to be evoked with the appropriate stagecraft, moving iconography, and eloquent set-ups with hieratic figures, rhetorical slogans, machine guns, cannons, and a panoply of war relics.[67] An array of statues of "heroes" characterized a new urban landscape of war: for the first time in history the lowly soldier was celebrated without any difference in military rank.[68] Moreover, the iconographic theme of the soldier dying in the arms of his fellow soldier was widely exploited by artists, who scattered emotionally resonant works all over Italy.[69] There were also countless statues of tearful mothers, devastated by grief, holding the body of their son in their lap, evoking the theme of Christian piety. Between 1861 and the First World War, the clash between Church and Army had made it impossible to unite two different ways of understanding the bereavement process, through liturgies and rituals based, on the one hand, on the cult of the martyr, and, on the other, on the myth of the hero. Italy's entrance into the war saw instead a rapprochement between the two institutions, at least in the intentions of military chaplains ministering to the memory of the fallen, which made for an understanding of the sacredness of a life lost but given to the cause of the Fatherland. The image of the soldier fallen into Christ's arms, which had already become widespread during the war years through postcards and leaflets handed out on either side of the Alps, was universally accepted in city monuments in the early 1920s.[70] In this way, veterans, relatives, and the new generations of Italians could live through the memory of the events and a vision of the war landscape as a sacred experience within their own city, town, or village.

Conclusions

During battles, architects and engineers experienced cruel landscapes. As they embarked on reconstructing them, they had in mind a bucolic and romantic idea of a landscape that no longer existed, and that helped in forgetting the horrors of the war. But when they found themselves evoking the landscape in the monuments to the fallen, the "landscapes of the war," they had experienced returned through grotesque fields of more or less scrambled human remains, which could not be buried. Such vivid images of pain and loss would stay alive for many a decades to come.

The landscape thus left by the so-called "white war," whether remembered or real, was made of stones and rocks, marble and bronze, but also of tears and grief. These were not the idealized alpine scenes, showing bold, athletic soldiers coming down on skis like daredevils. Such imagery became popular during the first World War through films put out by the propaganda machine and was based on material from the photography department of the army.[71] These rhetorical devices suggested they could do without the horror and banality of bloodshed. But eventually they were captured in the landscapes of memory of the Great War.

Notes

1   Over the years I have presented my research on the topic of monuments to the fallen soldiers and the war landscape at symposia and colloquia. Among these, I would like to mention my lecture *Landscapes of remembrance. Military shrines, monuments to fallen soldiers and war cemeteries between 1861 and Post-war Reconstruction*, given on November 20, 2014 for the MA course in "Design and Marketing of Cultural Landscapes," Università degli studi del Molise; my lecture *War landscapes: engineers, architects and artists in the trenches*, given on June 29, 2016 at the conference "L'architettura e l'urbanistica alla svolta della prima guerra mondiale. Da Bologna all'Europa" at Archiginnasio di Bologna; and my contribution *Landscapes of remembrance and remembrance of landscapes* at the international study summit "Castelli in guerra. Dai contesti medievali alle fortificazioni del Primo conflitto mondiale," held on October 5–6, 2018 at RFA Associazione Ricerche Fortificazioni Altomedievali-Museo storico italiano della guerra (The Italian War Museum), Rovereto (the proceedings, in Italian, are published with SAP Società Archeologica, edited by Annamaria Azzolini). The first paragraph of the present essay appeared in *Ark*, without notes (Savorra, "Il paesaggio ferito. Il Genio Militare durante la Grande Guerra," *Ark* 25 (2018): 68–74). My heartfelt thanks go to my friends and colleagues, for a most helpful exchange of views: Nicholas Adams, Annamaria Azzolini, Chiara Baglione, Beatrice Bettazzi, Giuliano Gresleri, Fabio Mangone, and Davide Pagliarini. I thank also Erin Sassin and Sophie Hochhäusl for the accurate reading and for the useful comments. I'd like to give special thanks to the Griffini family.
     In addition to the well-known works of Emilio Gentile, Antonio Gibelli, Mario Isnenghi and Nicola Labanca, an updated treatment of the history of World War I may be found in the latest volumes of Stéphane Audoin-Rouzeau and Jean-Jacques Becker, eds., *Enciclopédie de la Grande Guerre, 1914–1918: histoire et culture* (Paris: Bayard, 2004); Mark Thompson, *The White War. Life and Death on the Italian Front, 1915–1919* (London: Faber and Faber, 2009); Lawrence Sondhaus, *World War One: The Global Revolution* (Cambridge: Cambridge University Press, 2011). Furthermore, on the topic of remembrance and mourning, the works by Fussell 1975 and Leed 1979 still hold fast. Readers are also referred to Oliver Janz et al., eds., *1914–1918 Online. International Encyclopedia of the First World War*, <http://www.1914-1918-online. net> (accessed July 2021). See also Nicholas Bullock and Luc Verpoest, eds., *Living with History, 1914–1964: Rebuilding Europe after the First and Second World Wars and the Role of Heritage Preservation* (Leuven: Leuven University Press, 2011); and Luc Verpoest et al., eds., *Revival after the Great War: Rebuild, Remember, Repair, Reform* (Leuven: Leuven University Press, 2020).

2   It must be remembered that during the war the Ministry of Roads and Works was also mobilized to work with the Italian Royal Army pursuant to Royal Decree no. 1462 of December 1, 1912.

3   Numerous books and articles exist on the concept of "Fatherland" or "Homeland" in Italy during the years of the Great War; in any case see Sergio Bertelli, ed., *La Chioma della Vittoria: scritti sull'identità degli italiani dall'Unità alla seconda Repubblica* (Firenze: Ponte alle Grazie, 1997); Gilles Pécout, *Il lungo Rinascimento. La nascita dell'Italia contemporanea (1770–1922)* (Paris: Nathan, 1997).

4   Marc Bloch, "Reflexions d'un histoien sur les fausses nouvelles de la guerre," *Revue de Synthèse Historique* 33 (1921): 13–35.

5   This last corps, made up of many young engineers, went into action on April 20, 1916 on the Carso. Once the effectiveness of such a weapon was seen, more manpower and resources were devoted to it and its use was extended to several points on the Austrian front line. Giovanni Michelucci, for example, moved from the Mining Engineers to the Flamethrowers (the flamethrowers squadrons reported to the Divisions; on the eve of the battle of Vittorio Veneto there were nine active companies). All information on the Royal Corps of Engineers is from <http://www.storiaememoriadibologna.it/arma-del-genio-57-organizzazione> (accessed July 2021).

6   Some were still undergraduates who had suspended their studies in order to join the army, like Gio Ponti who served as a captain in the Corps of Bridge Builders and was awarded a bronze medal and the Croix de Guerre for military valor. See Gloria Arditi and Cesare Serratto, *Gio Ponti. Venti cristalli di architettura* (Venice: Il cardo, 1994), 201.

7   It is worth remembering that Pier Luigi Nervi, before he joined the Airship Battalion as second lieutenant in the Corps of Engineers, had also been a member of the 69th Company of Sappers in Bologna from March 1, 1916 and was later mobilized to a war zone. Claudio Greco, *Pier Luigi Nervi. Dai primi brevetti al Palazzo delle Esposizioni di Torino, 1917–1948* (Lucerne: Quart Edizioni, 2008), 37.

8   The "galleria" was planned by engineer Nicola Gavotta, was 5 km long, and could accommodate over 15,000 soldiers.

9   See *Riassunto delle esperienze di Mina eseguite dal 1900 al 1910 presso il 5 reggimento Genio per distruggere gallerie ferroviarie* (Rome: Tipografia E. Voghera, 1912).

10   See *La conquista di Col di Lana, 16 aprile 1916: considerazioni sulla guerra di mina, diagramma per la distruzione di gallerie, a cura della Scuola all. uff. Genio [di] Pavia* (Pavia: Cucchi, 1934).

11   See Attilio Borrozzino, *Reticolati* (Rome: Ardita, 1933).

12   The gallery road was designed by engineer Leopoldo Motti, planned by engineer Giuseppe Zappa, and dug out in the winter of 1916 by the 33rd company of Mining Engineers of the 5th regiment of the Corps. Engineers and architects also worked in the Corps of Motor Engineers and of Telegraph Operators, like Alessandro Rimini. See Ornella Selvafolta, "Alessandro Rimini: profilo di un architetto," in *Il primo grattacielo di Milano. La casa torre di piazza San Babila di Alessandro Rimini* (Cinisello Balsamo: Silvana Editoriale, 2002), 11–31; Giovanna D'Amia, "Un architetto milanese del Novecento," in *Alessandro Rimini. Opere e silenzi di un architetto milanese*, ed. Giovanna D'Amia (Santarcangelo di Romagna: Maggioli Editore, 2011), 7–41.

13   This exceptional feat allowed the Garibaldi Hut to be transformed into a modern base for the Mount Adamello army unit, which was able to house up to 1,000 men, as well as a 140-bed infirmary and an operating theater. See Marco Mondini, *Andare per i luoghi della Grande Guerra* (Bologna: Il Mulino, 2015), 26.

14   In some cases with the help of companies such as Ceretti & Tanfani, the most important industry in the field. See Alessandro Martinelli, "Gli impianti a fune e gli eventi bellici: dal Piave alla montagna," in *Luoghi e architetture della Grande Guerra in Europa. I sistemi difensivi dalle teorizzazioni di Karl von Clausewitz alla realtà della Prima Guerra*

Mondiale (Milano, 16–17 novembre 2011), ed. Maria Antonietta Breda (Oxford: BAR Publishing, 2012), 213–20.

15   Mario Ceradini, *Il disegno panoramico militare* (Turin: Libreria F. Casanova, [1912] 1916).

16   During the war years a number of art exhibitions were held of those drawings made on the front; see L. A. "Il concorso nazionale per la nostra Guerra," *Emporium* 46, no. 273 (1917): 166–8; Arturo Lancellotti, "La guerra vista dagli artisti italiani," *Emporium* 46, no. 275 (1917): 268–77. Between November and December 1916, thanks to Prince Jacques de Brogue and H.R.H. the Duchess Elena of Aosta, an exhibition was held at Palazzo della Permanente in Milan called *The Allies' Art Exhibition*, as a benefit event for the Italian Red Cross and other charities. In 1917 the Società per le Belle Arti ed Esposizione Permanente held a national competition "For our war's sake," whereas the exhibition held in Milan at Palazzo Sociale in Via Principe Umberto I 32, by the same organization, housed a "special hall" devoted to *Impressions of the war*.

17   In addition to his role as an officer in the operational area, Giuseppe Bergomi was charged with the task of drawing medals and pennants. In August 1915, Bergomi joined the 1st Regiment of the Corps of Engineers Pavia; in April 1916 he was one of the officers charged with defensive works on the Swiss border, while in October 1917 he was working in the 15th area, 7th army unit; in April 1918 he was made a liaison officer with the Central Command; the same year, in December, he was active at the Corps Headquarters in Riva di Trento. He was awarded the Croix de Guerre for military valor and returned to civilian life in March 1919, when he took up his post again as a professor at the University of Pavia. See Sestiano Giuseppe Locati, *Giuseppe Bergomi* (Pavia: estr. Annuario della R. Università di Pavia, 1934–1935), 3–4.

18   See i.f., "Dal Col di Lana alle Tofane. Fotografie artistiche dell'architetto Piero Portaluppi," *L'Illustrazione Italiana* 10 (March 5, 1916): 197–202.

19   See Elena Pontiggia, "La satira e la Grande Guerra. Aspetti dell'espressione satirica in Bonzagni, Gio Ponti, Sironi, Viani," in *La danza macabra della Grande Guerra. A cento anni dello scoppio della Prima Guerra Mondiale le opere satiriche dei grandi artisti del tempo raccolte nella collezione Isolabella*, ed. Cinzia Bibolotti et al. (Ospedaletto: Pacini, 2014), 19–23.

20   Such as the extraordinary ones by Paolo Caccia Dominioni. On the exhibition *Paolo Caccia Dominioni. Un artista sul fronte di guerra* (Gorizia, Trieste, and Brussels, 2013–2015), curated by Marianna Accerboni, see <http://www.collezioni-f.it/museo/paolo/paolo.html>; <http://www.artslife.com/2015/06/30/paolo-caccia-dominioni-un-artista-sul-fronte-di-guerra/> (accessed July 2021).

21   In attacks, forests and woods were destroyed in order to build defensive systems while at the same time lumber – as is well known – was among the basic materials as warfare technology, from sheds to telegraph posts and cross-bridges. The botanist Lino Vaccari, at the time, reckoned that at least two million cubic meters of wood were destroyed, before the conflict as well as during the battles. See Marco Armiero, *A Rugged Nation: Mountains and the Making of Modern Italy* (Winwick, Cambridgeshire: White Horse Press, 2011), 106.

22   Lancellotti, "La guerra vista dagli artisti italiani," 276.

23   Alberto Griffini's heirs still hold a priceless photograph album documenting the very great work of the Corps of Engineers in the Campolongo Tapogliano on the defense line between Torre and Isonzo. Other information, however, can be found at <http://www.comune.campolongotapogliano.ud.it/fileadmin/user_campolongotapogliano/territorio/storia/TRINCEE/2.Mostra.pdf> (accessed July 2021).

24 Fort Verena, for example, built between 1910 and 1914, was destroyed on June 12, 1915, after less than a month of operational activity.

25 On the building of trenches see Amerigo Raddi, *Il risanamento delle trincee in Guerra* (Milan: Soc. Editrice Libraria, 1918).

26 San Donà di Piave and Asiago, for example, were completely devastated in the course of the *Strafexpedition,* while San Martino was turned into a heap of ruins and a trench vanguard by the Austro-Hungarians. See Gian Paolo Treccani, *Monumenti e centri storici nella stagione della Grande Guerra* (Milan: FrancoAngeli, 2015).

27 See Filippo Cappellano, "Armi e sistemi d'arma," in *Dizionario storico della Prima guerra mondiale,* ed. Nicola Labanca (Rome and Bari: Laterza, 2014), 91–9.

28 One of the most renowned was the Cesare Battisti lunette, which, as well as looking out on the strategic bridge of Versa, acted as a defense pivot between the line of the levees of the Torre and that of the villages. It should be remembered that the so-called "vestiges of the Great War" would subsequently offer several opportunities (such as the setting up of war museums as well as numerous academic symposia) to scholars in various disciplines to reflect on the conservation and promotion, as well as the recovery, of the nation's historical heritage, as foreseen under Law no. 78 of 2001. See Marica Piva and Camillo Zadra, eds., *La memoria della Grande Guerra in Trentino. Progetti e iniziative di recupero e valorizzazione nel quadro della legislazione nazionale e provinciale (Rovereto, 22 marzo 2003)* (Trento: Soprintendenza dei beni architettonici della Provincia autonoma di Trento, 2005); Alessandra Quendolo, eds., *Paesaggi di guerra. Memoria e progetto* (Udine: Gaspari, 2014); Maria Bergamo and Andrea Iorio, eds., *Strategie della memoria. Architettura e paesaggi di guerra* (Rome: Università Iuav di Venezia-Aracne, 2014).

29 An example is the square and fountain built by Captain Alberto Griffini and Lieutenant Paolo Mezzanotte in a small reconquered village by the Isonzo, as reported in an article from an unidentified daily. The article cutting, dated September 23–30, 1917, without indication of title, is held by Alberto Griffini's heirs.

30 See Andrea Moschetti, *I danni ai monumenti e alle opere d'arte delle Venezie nella guerra mondiale MCMXV–MCMXVIII* (Venice: Premiate officine grafiche C. Ferrari, 1928), 5–44.

31 Paolo Mezzanotte, "Case e chiese nelle regioni devastate dalla Guerra," *Giornale dell'Associazione Nazionale degli Ingegneri Italiani* 1, no. 1–2 (1920): 5.

32 Ambrogio Annoni, "Problemi d'arte del dopoguerra," *Emporium* 51, no. 302 (1920): 70–82.

33 See Massimiliano Savorra, "Il paesaggio ferito. Il Genio Militare durante la Grande Guerra," *Ark* 25 (2018): 68–74.

34 See Touring Club Italiano, ed., *Concorso "Ercole Marelli" per progetti di ricostruzione di piccoli edifici rurali nei territori devastati dalla guerra* (Milan: Mondaini, 1919), 4–17. A reconstruction of the events is in Massimiliano Savorra, *Enrico Agostino Griffini. La casa, il monumento, la città* (Naples: Electa Napoli, 2000), 15–29, 146–8.

35 On these typologies, see Savorra, *Enrico Agostino Griffini,* 15–29.

36 On the matter of *terre irredente,* see Marco Mondini, *Veneto in armi. Tra mito della nazione e piccola patria, 1866–1918* (Gorizia: Leg, 2002).

37 At the end of the selection, the jury, chaired by Angelo Redaelli, chief engineer of the Ufficio Tecnico at Ospedale Maggiore in Milan, awarded the first two prizes to the proposals by Griffini-Mezzanotte. See *Concorso,* 1919; "I risultati del concorso Marelli," *Touring Club Italiano. Rivista mensile,* no. 9–10 (September–October 1919): 242; "Un interessante concorso. Per la ricostruzione dei paesi devastati dalla Guerra,"

La Domenica del Corriere, November 23, 1919.

38   On the issue of the reconstruction in Trentino-South Tyrol, there is a wide literature. On the role of some of the protagonists, such as Giorgio Wenter Marini, see Massimiliano Savorra, "Stile rustico e identità montane: Giorgio Wenter Marini e il dibattito fra tradizione e modernità," in *L'architettura dell'"altra modernità,"* ed. Marina Docci and Maria Grazia Turco (Rome: Gangemi, 2010), 280–9.

39   See Paolo Mezzanotte, "Il focolare friulano," *Edilizia Moderna* 26, no. 12 (1917): 66–8.

40   *Concorso*, 3. See also Massimiliano Savorra, "Il paesaggio della Grande Guerra e il concorso Ercole Marelli del Touring Club Italiano," *Storia dell'urbanistica*, no. 1 (2021): 124–147.

41   For a detailed analysis of the whole enterprise, see Francesca Zanella, "La ricostruzione delle chiese del Piave nel Primo dopoguerra: la permanenza del revival," *Venezia Arti. Bollettino del Dipartimento di storia e critica delle arti "Giuseppe Mazzariol" dell'Università di Ca' Foscari di Venezia* 9 (1995): 77–88; Treccani, *Monumenti e centri storici nella stagione della Grande Guerra*, 188–232.

42   The influence of the Organization was decisive when it came to modifying Law no. 426 of March 27, 1919, on war damages compensation, and Law no. 925 of June 8 of the same year, on reconstruction regulations in the Veneto, which did not deem the churches essential public buildings. See Costante Chimenton, *L'Opera di Soccorso e la ricostruzione delle chiese nei paesi del lungo Piave* (Treviso: Tipografia Editrice Trevigiana, 1930), 14–5.

43   There were 167 damaged churches in total. See *L'Opera di Soccorso per le chiese rovinate dalla guerra (Palazzo Patriarcale-Venezia). Brevi cenni sull'origine, la costituzione e lo scopo dell'Opera e sul suo lavoro a tutto giugno 1920, con carta geografica del Veneto e delle nuove Provincie dove sono indicati i paesi la cui chiesa è rovinata e i confini della diocesi della regione veneta* (Venice: Tipografia San Marco, 1920), 9–11.

44   After it became the official mouthpiece of the "Opera," the magazine's editorial board was at the Patriarchal Seminary in Venice. See Celso Costantini, "La gran pietà delle nostre chiese sul fronte," *Arte Cristiana* 6, no. 3 (March 1918): 33–44; "L'Opera di Soccorso per le chiese rovinate dalla Guerra," *Arte Cristiana* 6, no. 11 (November 1918): 174; "Cronaca. L'Opera di Soccorso per le chiese rovinate dalla Guerra," *Arte Cristiana* 7, no. 1 (January 1919): 15–6; *Arte Cristiana* 7, no. 2 (February 1919): 33–4; "Mostra Nazionale d'Arte Sacra," *Arte Cristiana* 7, no. 10 (October 1919): 181–2; "Relazione sul concorso per le chiese da riedificare al fronte," *Arte Cristiana* 8, no. 3 (March 1920): 65–7; "Progetti di chiese approvati," *Arte Cristiana* 8, no. 3 (March 1920): 67–73; "Inaugurandosi la Mostra Nazionale d'Arte Sacra a Venezia (9 settembre 1920)," *Arte Cristiana* 8, no. 9–10 (September–October 1920): 162–6; "L'Opera di Soccorso per le chiese rovinate alla fronte," *Arte Cristiana* 9, no. 1 (January 1921): 26–31.

45   The competition was closed on September 30, 1919. The winning entries were made public in February 1920. The Report, dated Venice, February 18, 1920, was published in the March issue of *Arte Cristiana* 8, no. 3 (March 1920): 65–71.

46   Among the many proposals there were some remarkable ones: among others, those by architects Prospero Battistin, Griffini and Mezzanotte, Annibale Zucchini, Giovan Battista Ceas, Vito Rastelli, Brenno del Giudice, Domenico Rupolo and Aldo Andreani. See "Relazione sul concorso per le chiese da riedificare al fronte," 66.

47   See Costante Chimenton, *E ruinis pulchriores. Perdite e risarcimenti artistici nelle chiese del lungo Piave. Relazione sui danni di guerra e sulle nuove opere artistiche fornite alle chiese della diocesi di Treviso e documenti interessanti le nuove ricostruzioni* (Treviso: Tipografia Editrice Trevigiana, 1934).

48 The present paragraph re-elaborates, as well as enlarges upon, some material in Massimiliano Savorra, "Da ossari a sacrari. Il monumento al fante e le retoriche della Grande Guerra," in *Pietre ignee cadute dal cielo. I monumenti della Grande Guerra*, ed. Martina Carraro and Massimiliano Savorra (Venice: IUAV-Ateneo Veneto, 2014), 25–53; see 33–68.

49 On the monuments to the fallen put up in Italian towns, the literature on the subject has seen several new studies lately (also as a result of the work done by the Special Committee for the preservation of the historical heritage of the First World War, instituted by Law 78/2001). For specific geographical areas, please see Gianni Isola, ed., *La memoria pia. I monumenti ai caduti della prima guerra mondiale nell'area trentino-tirolese* (Trento: Dipartimento di scienze filologiche e storiche, 1997); Patrizia Marchesoni and Massimo Martignoni, eds., *Monumenti della Grande Guerra. Progetti e realizzazioni in Trentino, 1916–1935* (Trento: Museo storico di Trento, 1998); Vittorio Vidotto et al., eds., *La memoria perduta. I monumenti ai caduti della Grande Guerra a Roma e nel Lazio* (Rome: Argos, 1998); Giuseppe Trevisan, *Memorie della grande guerra. I monumenti ai caduti di Verona e provincia* (Sommacampagna: Cierre, 2005); Daniela De Angelis, ed., *I monumenti ai caduti della Grande Guerra nei castelli romani. La luce e l'ombra* (Rome: Gangemi, 2006); Maria Mangiavacchi and Laura Vigni, eds., *Lontano dal fronte. Monumenti e ricordi della Grande Guerra nel Senese* (Siena: Nuova Immagine, 2007); Anna Maria Spiazzi et al., eds., *La memoria della Prima Guerra Mondiale. Il patrimonio storico tra tutela e valorizzazione* (Vicenza: Terra Ferma, 2008); Mario Balossini and Emiliana Mongiat, *Fummo soldati d'Italia. Monumenti ai caduti delle province di Novara e Verbania* (Novara: Interlinea, 2009); Maria Rosaria Nappi, ed., *La Campania e la grande guerra. I monumenti ai caduti della provincia di Salerno* (Rome: Gangemi, 2009); Domenique Charles Fuchs and Renata Gottschalk, eds., *In victoria vita. I monumenti ai caduti della prima guerra mondiale nell'Aretino* (Florence: Edifir, 2010); Nicola Labanca, ed., *Pietre di guerra. Ricerche su monumenti e lapidi in memoria del primo conflitto mondiale* (Milan: Edizioni Unicopli, 2010); Maria Rosaria Nappi, ed., *La Campania e la grande guerra. I monumenti ai caduti di Napoli e provincia* (Rome: Gangemi, 2011); Lia Brunori, ed., *Monumenti ai caduti. Firenze e provincia* (Florence: Polistampa, 2012); Alberta Cazzani, ed., *I monumenti e i giardini celebrativi della grande guerra in Lombardia. Il censimento per le province di Brescia, Milano e Monza Brianza* (Udine: Gaspari, 2012); Marco Mantini, *La zona monumentale del monte San Michele. Carso 2014+: da teatro di guerra a paesaggio della memoria* (Udine: Gaspari, 2016).

50 See Savorra, "Stile rustico e identità montane."

51 See Alessandro Miniero, *Da Versailles al Milite Ignoto. Rituali e retoriche della Vittoria in Europa (1919–1921)* (Rome: Gangemi, 2008).

52 See Massimiliano Savorra, "La rappresentazione del dolore e l'immagine dell'eroe: il monumento al Fante," in *L'architettura della memoria in Italia. Cimiteri, monumenti e città, 1750–1939*, ed. Maria Giuffrè et al. (Milan: Skira, 2007), 365–73.

53 Some data available in Lucio Fabi, *Soldati d'Italia. Esperienze, storie, memorie, visioni della Grande Guerra* (Milan: Mursia, 2014).

54 Roberto Papini, "Il concorso per il monumento al fante," *Emporium* 52, no. 307–308 (1920): 89–96.

55 The idea was later returned to by Giovanni Greppi and Giannino Castiglioni, in the shrines they were commissioned to make by General Ugo Cei who replaced Giovanni Faracovi as committee member for honoring the fallen. It should be remembered that Greppi had been a member of the competition committee for the monument to the

Fante and had been among the greatest supporters of the proposals that paid attention to landscape, such as those by Eugenio Baroni and by Griffini and Mezzanotte. On the shrines made by Greppi and Castiglioni, see Anna Maria Fiore, "La monumentalizzazione dei luoghi teatro della Grande Guerra: i sacrari di Giovanni Greppi e di Giannino Castiglioni (1933–1941)" (PhD diss., Università Iuav of Venice, 2001).

56   Marco Mondini, "La festa mancata. I militari e la memoria della Grande Guerra, 1918–1923," *Contemporanea. Rivista di storia dell'800 e del '900* 4, no. 7 (2004): 555–78. See also Marco Mondini, *Veneto in armi. Tra mito della nazione e piccola patria, 1866–1918* (Gorizia: Leg, 2002); "Le sentinelle della memoria. I monumenti ai caduti e la costruzione della rimembranza nell'Italia Nord Orientale (1919–1939)," *Annali della Fondazione Luigi Einaudi* 40 (2006): 273–93.

57   See George L. Mosse, *Fallen Soldiers: Reshaping the Memory of the World Wars* (Oxford: Oxford University Press, 1990). Jay M. Winter, *Sites of Memory, Sites of Mourning: The Great War in European Cultural History* (Cambridge: Cambridge University Press, 1995).

58   It should be remembered, after all, that at the time of the competition for San Michele, the experience of the war was not used instrumentally in Italian politics, whereas later, during the 1920s, the sites of mourning and memory were occupied by the regime with the aim of total indoctrination by the Fascist credo.

59   See Savorra, "La rappresentazione del dolore e l'immagine dell'eroe. "

60   Beside the 12 shrines made by Greppi and Castiglioni (Grappa, Redipuglia, Caporetto, Timau, San Candido, Passo Resia, Colle Isarco, Pian di Salesei, Bezzecca, Feltre, Pola, Zara), we may remember those in Bassano, Stelvio, Fagarè, Tonale (Pietro del Fabbro); Castel Dante, Rovereto (Ferdinando Biscaccianti); Pocol, Cortina (Giovanni Raimondi); Asiago (Brenno del Giudice, Orfeo Rossato); Oslavia (Ghino Venturi); and Montello (Felice Nori). A map of the shrines made between 1928 and 1939 was published in *Le vie d'Italia* 45, no. 11 (1939).

61   It must be stressed, moreover, that the proposals submitted for the competition for the monument to the Fante, exhibited in public shows in Rome and Milan, influenced those who took part in the competition for the French Ossuaire de Douaumont (1922–1923). See Stéphanie Quantin et al., *L'Ossuarire de Douaumont. Cathédrale de la Grande Guerre* (Ars-sur-Moselle: Serge Domini Éditeur, 2015).

62   See Dario Lupi, *Parchi e viali della Rimembranza* (Florence: Bemporad, 1923).

63   It should be remembered, moreover, that, starting from late December 1931, following the death of Arnaldo Mussolini, chairman of the National Forestry Committee, who was considered an activist for the rebirth of woods, every municipality in the Kingdom had to plant trees to the "Venerable Memory" [of fallen soldiers]. On Remembrance parks, see Michela Rosso, "Gli alberi del ricordo: il Parco della Rimembranza di Torino," in *L'architettura della memoria in Italia. Cimiteri, monumenti e città, 1750–1930*, ed. Maria Giuffrè et al. (Milan: Skira, 2007), 375–83.

64   The most iconic being those in Trieste (Arduino Berlam, 1923–1927), Minervino Murge (Aldo Forcignanò, 1923–1932), Turin (Edoardo Rubino, 1923–1928), and Besozzo (Diego Brioschi, 1927). See Marco Pozzetto, *Giovanni Andrea, Ruggero, Arduino Berlam: un secolo di architettura* (Trieste: Editoriale Lloyd MGS Press, 1999), 140–51; Franca Dalmasso, ed., *Eclettismo e Liberty a Torino: Giulio Casanova e Edoardo Rubino* (Turin: Il Quadrante Edizioni, 1989), 193.

65   See Kirk Savage, *Monument War: Washington, D.C., the National Mall, and the Transformation of the Memorial Landscape* (Berkeley: University of California Press, 2005).

66   On a "theory of the monument," see Andrea Pinotti, "Antitotalitarismo e antimonumentalità. Un' elettiva affinità," in *Memorie di pietra. I monumenti delle dittature*, ed. Gian Piero Piretto (Milan: Raffaello Cortina, 2014), 17–33. On the construction of the memory of war instead, see Maurizio Ridolfi, ed., *Rituali civili. storie nazionali e memorie pubbliche nell'Europa contemporanea* (Rome: Gangemi, 2006).

67   Iconic examples of these were the archi-sculptural ensembles by Leonardo Bistolfi at Casale Monferrato (1922–1923) and those by Saverio Dioguardi in the cemetery in Bari (1923).

68   Suffice to observe the combatant lying dead on the rocks, a work by Egisto Caldana, looking since 1922 over the piazza of Breganze, the lookouts holding sway since the late 1920s over the city centers of Santhià, San Francesco al Campo or Maddaloni (by sculptors Attilio Gartmann, Michelangelo Monti and Santino Tuntillo, respectively), or the frozen battle scenes made perennial in marble and bronze, showing soldiers armed only with a flag and lying side-by-side with allegories of victory, in the works by Francesco Jerace in Torre Annunziata (1929–1930) and Aversa (1936).

69   Such as Enrico Quattrini, who made a sculpture of two forlorn soldiers in his monument in Gualdo Tadino (1925), or Ruperto Banterle, with his touching image of the fallen soldier held up by a fellow soldier in front of the House of the Amputee in Verona (1931–1933).

70   This trend was started by Edmondo Furlan with his Christ in the Trench or Pietà (1916–21) made for the cemetery of heroes next to the basilica in Aquileia.

71   See the text published in 1916 by Treves, *La guerra in alta montagna,* and the issues of *Domenica del Corriere*, with the covers drawn by Achille Beltrame. The Treves publications may be seen at <http://www.cimeetrincee.it/albumdepoca.htm> (accessed July 2019). See also Roberta Basano and Sarah Pesenti Campagnoni, eds., *Al fronte. Cineoperatori e fotografi raccontano la Grande Guerra* (Cinisello Balsamo: Silvana Editoriale, 2015).

Bibliography

Annoni, Ambrogio. "Problemi d'arte del dopoguerra." *Emporium* 51, no. 302 (1920): 70–82.

Arditi, Gloria, and Serratto, Cesare. *Gio Ponti. Venti cristalli di architettura*. Venice: Il cardo, 1994.

Armiero, Marco. *A Rugged Nation: Mountains and the Making of Modern Italy*. Winwick, Cambridgeshire: White Horse Press, 2011. (Italian translation, *Le montagne della patria. Natura e nazione nella storia d'Italia. Secoli XIX e XX*. Turin: Giulio Einaudi editore, 2013.)

Audoin-Rouzeau, Stéphane, and Jean-Jacques Becker, eds. *Enciclopédie de la Grande Guerre, 1914–1918: histoire et culture*. Paris: Bayard, 2004. (Italian translation, *La prima guerra mondiale*, edited by Antonio Gibelli, 2 vol. Turin: Giulio Einaudi editore, 2007.)

Balossini, Mario, and Mongiat, Emiliana. *Fummo soldati d'Italia. Monumenti ai caduti delle province di Novara e Verbania*. Novara: Interlinea, 2009.

Basano, Roberta, and Sarah Pesenti Campagnoni, eds. *Al fronte. Cineoperatori e fotografi raccontano la Grande Guerra*. Cinisello Balsamo: Silvana Editoriale, 2015.

Bergamo, Maria, and Andrea Iorio, eds. *Strategie della memoria. Architettura e paesaggi di guerra*. Rome: Aracne, 2014.

Bloch, Marc. "Reflexions d'un histoien sur les fausses nouvelles de la guerre." *Revue de Synthèse Historique* 33 (1921): 13–35. (Also in Joseph Bédier and Marc Bloch, *Storia psicologica della prima guerra mondiale*, edited by Francesco Mores, 83–114. Rome: Castelvecchi, 2015.)

Borrozzino, Attilio. *Reticolati*. Rome: Ardita, 1933.

Brunori, Lia, ed. *Monumenti ai caduti. Firenze e provincia*. Florence: Polistampa, 2012.

Bullock, Nicholas, and Luc Verpoest, eds. *Living with History, 1914–1964: Rebuilding Europe after the First and Second World Wars and the Role of Heritage Preservation*. Leuven: Leuven University Press, 2011.

Cappellano, Filippo. "Armi e sistemi d'arma." In *Dizionario storico della Prima guerra mondiale*, edited by Nicola Labanca, 91–9. Rome and Bari: Laterza, 2014.

Cazzani, Alberta, ed. *I monumenti e i giardini celebrativi della grande guerra in Lombardia. Il censimento per le province di Brescia, Milano e Monza Brianza*. Udine: Gaspari, 2012.

Ceradini, Mario. *Il disegno panoramico militare*. Turin: Libreria F. Casanova & C., [1912] 1916.

Chimenton, Costante. *L'Opera di Soccorso e la ricostruzione delle chiese nei paesi del lungo Piave*. Treviso: Tipografia Editrice Trevigiana, 1930.

Chimenton, Costante. *E ruinis pulchriores. Perdite e risarcimenti artistici nelle chiese del lungo Piave. Relazione sui danni di guerra e sulle nuove opere artistiche fornite alle chiese della diocesi di Treviso e documenti interessanti le nuove ricostruzioni*. Treviso: Tipografia Editrice Trevigiana, 1934.

Costantini, Celso. "La gran pietà delle nostre chiese sul fronte." *Arte Cristiana* 6, no. 3 (March 1918): 33–44.

"Cronaca. L'Opera di Soccorso per le chiese rovinate dalla Guerra." *Arte Cristiana* 7, no. 1 (January 1919): 15–16; 7, no. 2 (February 1919): 33–4.

D'Amia, Giovanna. "Un architetto milanese del Novecento." In *Alessandro Rimini. Opere e silenzi di un architetto milanese*, edited by Giovanna D'Amia, 7–41. Santarcangelo di Romagna: Maggioli Editore, 2011.

Dalmasso, Franca, ed. *Eclettismo e Liberty a Torino: Giulio Casanova e Edoardo Rubino*. Turin: Il Quadrante Edizioni, 1989. Exhibition catalog.

De Angelis, Daniela, ed. *I monumenti ai caduti della Grande Guerra nei castelli romani. La luce e l'ombra*. Rome: Gangemi, 2006.

Fabi, Lucio. *Soldati d'Italia. Esperienze, storie, memorie, visioni della Grande Guerra*. Milan: Mursia, 2014.

Fiore, Anna Maria. "La monumentalizzazione dei luoghi teatro della Grande Guerra: i sacrari di Giovanni Greppi e di Giannino Castiglioni (1933–1941)." PhD diss., Università Iuav of Venice, 2001.

Fuchs, Domenique Charles, and Renata Gottschalk, eds. *In victoria vita. I monumenti ai caduti della prima guerra mondiale nell'Aretino*. Florence: Edifir, 2010.

Fussell, Paul. *The Great War and Modern Memory*. Oxford: Oxford University Press, 1975. (Italian translation, *La Grande Guerra e la memoria moderna*. Bologna: Il Mulino, 1984.)

Greco, Claudio. *Pier Luigi Nervi. Dai primi brevetti al Palazzo delle Esposizioni di Torino, 1917–1948*. Lucerne: Quart Edizioni, 2008.

i.f. "Dal Col di Lana alle Tofane. Fotografie artistiche dell'architetto Piero Portaluppi." *L'Illustrazione Italiana* 10 (March 5, 1916): 197–202.

"Il concorso del T.C.I. per progetti di ricostruzione." *Corriere della Sera*, May 3, 1919.

"Inaugurandosi la Mostra Nazionale d'Arte Sacra a Venezia (9 settembre 1920)." *Arte Cristiana* 8, no. 9–10 (September–October 1920): 162–6.

"I risultati del concorso Marelli," *Touring Club Italiano. Rivista mensile*, no. 9–10 (September–October 1919): 242.

Isola, Gianni, ed. *La memoria pia. I monumenti ai caduti della prima guerra mondiale nell'area trentino-tirolese*. Trento: Dipartimento di scienze filologiche e storiche, 1997.

L. A. "Il concorso nazionale per la nostra Guerra." *Emporium* 46, no. 273 (1917): 166–8.

Labanca, Nicola, ed. *Pietre di guerra. Ricerche su monumenti e lapidi in memoria del primo conflitto mondiale*. Milan: Edizioni Unicopli, 2010.

La conquista di Col di Lana, 16 aprile 1916: considerazioni sulla guerra di mina, diagramma per la distruzione di gallerie, a cura della Scuola all. uff. Genio [di] Pavia. Pavia: Cucchi, 1934.

Lancellotti Arturo. "La guerra vista dagli artisti italiani." *Emporium* 46, no. 275 (1917): 268–77.

Leed, Eric J. *No Man's Land: Combat and Identity in World War I*. Cambridge: Cambridge University Press, 1979. (Italian translation, *Terra di Nessuno. Esperienza bellica e identità personale nella prima guerra mondiale*. Bologna: Il Mulino, 1985.)

Locati, Sestiano Giuseppe. *Giuseppe Bergomi*. Pavia: estr. *Annuario della R. Università di Pavia*, 1934–5.

"L'Opera di Soccorso per le chiese rovinate dalla Guerra." *Arte Cristiana* 6, no. 11 (November 1918): 174.

L'Opera di Soccorso per le chiese rovinate dalla guerra (Palazzo Patriarcale-Venezia). Brevi cenni sull'origine, la costituzione e lo scopo dell'Opera e sul suo lavoro a tutto giugno 1920, con carta geografica del Veneto e delle nuove Provincie dove sono indicati i paesi la cui chiesa è rovinata e i confini della diocesi della regione veneta. Venice: Tipografia San Marco, 1920.

"L'Opera di Soccorso per le chiese rovinate alla fronte." *Arte Cristiana* 9, no. 1 (January 1921): 26–31.

Lupi, Dario. *Parchi e viali della Rimembranza*. Florence: Bemporad, 1923.

Mangiavacchi, Maria, and Laura Vigni, eds. *Lontano dal fronte. Monumenti e ricordi della Grande Guerra nel Senese*. Siena: Nuova Immagine, 2007.

Mantini, Marco. *La zona monumentale del monte San Michele. Carso 2014+: da teatro di guerra a paesaggio della memoria*. Udine: Gaspari, 2016.

Marchesoni, Patrizia, and Massimo Martignoni, eds. *Monumenti della Grande Guerra. Progetti e realizzazioni in Trentino, 1916–1935*. Trento: Museo storico di Trento, 1998. Exhibition catalog.

Martinelli, Alessandro. "Gli impianti a fune e gli eventi bellici: dal Piave alla montagna." In *Luoghi e architettura della Grande Guerra in Europa. I sistemi difensivi dalle teorizzazioni di Karl von Clausewitz alla realtà della Prima Guerra Mondiale (Milano, 16–17 novembre 2011)*, edited by Maria Antonietta Breda, 213–20. Oxford: BAR Publishing, 2012.

Mezzanotte, Paolo. "Il focolare friulano." *Edilizia Moderna* 26, no. 12 (December 1917): 66–8.

———."Case e chiese nelle regioni devastate dalla Guerra." *Giornale dell'Associazione Nazionale degli Ingegneri Italiani* 1, no. 1–2 (1920): 5.

Miniero, Alessandro. *Da Versailles al Milite Ignoto. Rituali e retoriche della Vittoria in Europa (1919–1921)*. Rome: Gangemi, 2008.

Mondini, Marco. *Veneto in armi. Tra mito della nazione e piccola patria, 1866–1918*. Gorizia: Leg, 2002.

———."La festa mancata. I militari e la memoria della Grande Guerra, 1918–1923." *Contemporanea. Rivista di storia dell'800 e del '900* 4, no. 7 (2004): 555–78.

———."Le sentinelle della memoria. I monumenti ai caduti e la costruzione della rimembranza nell'Italia Nord Orientale (1919–1939)." *Annali della Fondazione Luigi Einaudi* 40 (2006): 273–93.

Moschetti, Andrea. *I danni ai monumenti e alle opere d'arte delle Venezie nella guerra mondiale MCMXV–MCMXVIII*. Venice: Premiate officine grafiche C. Ferrari, 1928.

Mosse, George L. *Fallen Soldiers: Reshaping the Memory of the World Wars*. Oxford: Oxford University Press, 1990. (Italian translation, *Le guerre mondiali. Dalla tragedia al mito dei caduti*, Rome and Bari: Laterza, 1990.)

"Mostra Nazionale d'Arte Sacra." *Arte Cristiana* 7, no. 10 (October 1919): 181–2.

Nappi, Maria Rosaria, ed. *La Campania e la grande guerra. I monumenti ai caduti della provincia di Salerno*. Rome: Gangemi, 2009.

———,ed. *La Campania e la grande guerra. I monumenti ai caduti di Napoli e provincia*. Rome: Gangemi, 2011.

———.*Andare per i luoghi della Grande Guerra*. Bologna: Il Mulino, 2015.

Papini, Roberto. "Il concorso per il monumento al fante." *Emporium* 52, no. 307–308 (1920): 89–96. (Also in *Cronache di architettura, 1914–1957. Antologia degli scritti di Roberto Papini*, edited by Roberto De Simone, 11–4. Florence: Edifir, 1998.)

Pinotti, Andrea. "Antitotalitarismo e antimonumentalità. Un'elettiva affinità." In *Memorie di pietra. I monumenti delle dittature*, edited by Gian Piero Piretto, 17–33. Milan: Raffaello Cortina, 2014.

Piva, Marica, and Camillo Zadra, eds. *La memoria della Grande Guerra in Trentino. Progetti e iniziative di recupero e valorizzazione nel quadro della legislazione nazionale e provinciale*. Trento: Soprintendenza dei beni architettonici della Provincia autonoma di Trento, 2005.

Pontiggia, Elena. "La satira e la Grande Guerra. Aspetti dell'espressione satirica in Bonzagni, Gio Ponti, Sironi, Viani." In *La danza macabra della Grande Guerra. A cento anni dello scoppio della Prima Guerra Mondiale le opere satiriche dei grandi artisti del tempo raccolte nella collezione Isolabella*, edited by Cinzia Bibolotti et al., 19–23. Ospedaletto: Pacini, 2014. Exhibition catalog.

Pozzetto, Marco. *Giovanni Andrea, Ruggero, Arduino Berlam: un secolo di architettura*. Trieste: Editoriale Lloyd MGS Press, 1999.

"Progetti di chiese approvati." *Arte Cristiana* 8, no. 3 (March 1920): 67–73.

Quantin, Stéphanie, et al. *L'Ossuarire de Douaumont. Cathédrale de la Grande Guerre*. Ars-sur-Moselle: Serge Domini Éditeur, 2015.

Quendolo, Alessandra. *Paesaggi di guerra. Memoria e progetto*. Udine: Gaspari, 2014.

Raddi, Amerigo. *Il risanamento delle trincee in Guerra*. Milan: Soc. Editrice Libraria, 1918.

"Relazione sul concorso per le chiese da riedificare al fronte." *Arte Cristiana* 8, no. 3 (March 1920): 65–7.

Riassunto delle esperienze di Mina eseguite dal 1900 al 1910 presso il 5 reggimento Genio per distruggere gallerie ferroviarie. Rome: Tip. E. Voghera, 1912.

Ridolfi, Maurizio, ed. *Rituali civili. storie nazionali e memorie pubbliche nell'Europa contemporanea*. Rome: Gangemi, 2006.

Rosso, Michela. "Gli alberi del ricordo: il Parco della Rimembranza di Torino." In *L'architettura della memoria in Italia. Cimiteri, monumenti e città, 1750–1930*, edited by Maria Giuffrè et al., 375–83. Milan: Skira, 2007.

Savage, Kirk. *Monument Wars: Washington, D.C., the National Mall, and the Transformation of the Memorial Landscape*. Berkeley: University of California Press, 2005.

Savorra, Massimiliano. *Enrico Agostino Griffini. La casa, il monumento, la città*. Naples: Electa Napoli, 2000.

———."La rappresentazione del dolore e l'immagine dell'eroe: il monumento al Fante." In *L'architettura della memoria in Italia. Cimiteri, monumenti e città, 1750–1939*, edited by Maria Giuffrè et al., 365–73. Milan: Skira, 2007. (Also in *Le pietre della memoria. Monumenti sul confine orientale*, edited by Paolo Nicoloso, 70–91. Udine: Gaspari, 2015.)

———."Stile rustico e identità montane: Giorgio Wenter Marini e il dibattito fra tradizione e modernità." In *L'architettura dell'"altra modernità,"* edited by Marina Docci e Maria Grazia Turco, 280–9. Rome: Gangemi, 2010.

———."Da ossari a sacrari. Il monumento al fante e le retoriche della Grande Guerra." In *Pietre ignee cadute dal cielo. I monumenti della Grande Guerra*, edited by Martina Carraro and Massimiliano Savorra, 33–68. Venice: IUAV, 2014. Exhibition catalog. (Also in *Rivista dell'Ateneo Veneto*, terza serie, 202, no. 14/1 (2015).)

———."Il paesaggio ferito. Il Genio Militare durante la Grande Guerra." *Ark* 25 (2018): 68–74.

———."Il paesaggio della Grande Guerra e il concorso Ercole Marelli del Touring Club Italiano." In *Storia dell'urbanistica*, no. 1 (2021): 124–147.

Selvafolta, Ornella. "Alessandro Rimini: profilo di un architetto." In *Il primo grattacielo di Milano. La casa torre di piazza San Babila di Alessandro Rimini*, 11–31. Cinisello Balsamo: Silvana Editoriale, 2002.

Sondhaus, Lawrence. *World War One: The Global Revolution*. Cambridge: Cambridge University Press, 2011. (Italian translation, *Prima guerra mondiale: la rivoluzione globale*. Turin: Giulio Einaudi editore, 2014.)

Spiazzi, Anna Maria, et al., eds. *La memoria della Prima Guerra Mondiale. Il patrimonio storico tra tutela e valorizzazione*. Vicenza: Terra Ferma, 2008.

Thompson, Mark. *The White War: Life and Death on the Italian Front, 1915–1919*. London: Faber and Faber, 2009. (Italian translation, *La guerra bianca. Vita e morte sul fronte italiano, 1915–1919*. Milan: Il Saggiatore, 2009.)

Touring Club Italiano, ed. *Concorso "Ercole Marelli" per progetti di ricostruzione di piccoli edifici rurali nei territori devastati dalla guerra*, 4–17. Milan: Mondaini, 1919.

Treccani, Gian Paolo. *Monumenti e centri storici nella stagione della Grande Guerra*. Milan: FrancoAngeli, 2015.

Trevisan, Giuseppe. *Memorie della grande guerra. I monumenti ai caduti di Verona e provincia*. Sommacampagna: Cierre, 2005.

"Un interessante concorso. Per la ricostruzione dei paesi devastati dalla Guerra." *La Domenica del Corriere*, November 23, 1919.

Verpoest, Luc, Leen Engelen, Rajesh Heynickx, Jan Schmidt, Pieter Uyttenhove, and Pieter Verstraete, eds. *Revival after the Great War: Rebuild, Remember, Repair, Reform*. Leuven: Leuven University Press, 2020.

Vidotto, Vittorio, et al., eds. *La memoria perduta. I monumenti ai caduti della Grande Guerra a Roma e nel Lazio*. Rome: Argos, 1998.

Winter, Jay M. *Sites of Memory, Sites of Mourning: The Great War in European Cultural History*. Cambridge: Cambridge University Press, 1995. (Italian translation, *Il lutto e la memoria. La Grande Guerra nella storia culturale europea*. Bologna: Il Mulino, 1998.)

Zanella, Francesca. "La ricostruzione delle chiese del Piave nel Primo dopoguerra: la permanenza del revival." *Venezia Arti. Bollettino del Dipartimento di storia e critica delle arti "Giuseppe Mazzariol" dell'Università di Ca' Foscari di Venezia* 9 (1995): 77–88.

Figure 11.1: Refugee camp Gmünd, church and school building, 1915. Stadtarchiv Gmünd.

Camps or Cities

The Urbanism of World War I Refugee Camps in the Austro-Hungarian Empire

Antje Senarclens de Grancy

Beginning in the fall of 1914, a series of large barrack camps were quickly erected over the course of just a few months in the heartland of Cisleithania,[1] the northern and western part of Austria-Hungary.[2] In each of these, up to 30,000 refugees and forced evacuees from the battle zones were gathered together and interned by order of the government, brought first from Bukovina and Galicia, and later also from parts of Trentino and the Austrian Littoral. Contemporary architects and architectural publicists described the construction of these "Imperial-Royal Refugee Camps" (*k.k. Flüchtlingslager*)[3] as "town planning in wartime."[4] Even in the daily papers and among visitors a general consensus soon prevailed that these camps for refugees – all civilian citizens of the monarchy – should be regarded as modern cities or residential colonies.[5] The primary decipherable urban codes identifying them as such included the grid plan of their streets, the variety of building types, and the camps' modern infrastructure. A description written by the Danish author Karin Michaëlis provides a good example of this interpretation. Michaëlis maintained contacts with the intellectuals and artists of the Vienna avant-garde around 1900, and took an active role in charity work during the war.[6] In 1917, following a visit to one such camp in Lower Austria [fig. 11.1], she wrote: "Each refugee camp is a city, created by a word of command, stamped out of the earth, a city with a water supply, sewage system, and electricity, with churches, schools, factories, hospitals, craftsmen and scholars, government and law."[7] And further: "The streets, straight as an arrow, form rectangular blocks like those in America."[8]

At that time, the concept of these refugee camps as artificial cities was closely linked to a vision of an ideal community, which could be projected onto the camps.[9] In some cases, the descriptions of them even resemble utopian novels of the nineteenth century. An account published in 1916 by the Polytechnic Club of Graz describes a camp in Styria in glowing terms: "An improbability made reality from Bellamy's 'The

Year 2000' stands before us and earns our sincere admiration, even in a social respect."[10] The author was referring to the novel *Looking Backward* (1888)[11] by the American writer Edward Bellamy, which enjoyed international success and was well known in Austrian circles. It also later inspired Ebenezer Howard's concept of the garden city. But what all these city descriptions of the refugee camps failed to mention were the mechanisms of control and registration, the surveillance systems and military guard details, the cleaning and disinfection stations, the quarantine barracks, the detention facilities, and the camp cemeteries as visible signs of epidemics and mass mortality.

The refugee camps were organized as self-contained but interconnected systems, and were administered by the governor's offices of the respective crown lands (Moravia, Bohemia, Lower Austria, Styria, Carinthia, and Upper Austria). They were surrounded by fences, and often also by barbed wire, the inhabitants' comings and goings were strictly controlled by soldiers and gendarmes at the camp gates, and a number of compulsory hygienic measures (quarantine, disinfection) were imposed. Despite the strict, centralized organization, catastrophic conditions prevailed in the camps, and the refugees suffered from illness, hunger, cold, squalor, overcrowded barracks, and extreme psychological stress. The rudimentary sleeping arrangements – simple cots with straw mattresses – were assigned to each refugee by the administration, and the barrack commandants[12] inspected the living areas, which were open to view, and disciplined the inhabitants at their daily tasks. Even if the Austro-Hungarian monarchy was not a colonial power in the conventional sense,[13] numerous photographs, propaganda publications, and exhibitions of the refugee camps present a colonialist view of the camps' inhabitants, and thus reveal the social hierarchies and asymmetries of political power at play here.

The perception of these camps as more or less ideal cities could in fact only function if the actual living conditions of the inhabitants and the power structures governing their daily life were completely ignored, a result of a massive propaganda campaign promoted by the government, ministries, and administration in the sense of the "home front." Nevertheless, as I will show, urbanistic concepts and visions of the city did indeed explicitly form the foundation for the planning of these camps during the First World War. Along with inspiration from military architecture and urban homeless shelters, these visionary architectural principles were shaped into a *dispositif* of state refugee assistance.[14] In practice, the categorical boundaries between city and camp proved fluid, and hybrid spatial constructs developed.

Camps in the Colonial Context

The refugee camps of the Habsburg monarchy marked the beginning of an era that continues to this day, which Zygmunt Bauman has called the "Century of Camps."[15] In contemporary parlance around 1900, the term "camp" was primarily associated with military camps of troop barracks. "Camp" meant a space temporarily used for lodgings, with clearly delineated and closed boundaries to the outside world, used for military troops or other clearly defined groups of people.

The colonial concept of the "concentration camp" was known in Austria before the First World War (still free of the later connotation of the extermination camp). The news media primarily addressed the British concentration camps in South Africa and quoted the English activist Emily Hobhouse's accounts of the colonial government's brutal treatment of Boer women and children, who were exposed to hunger, cold, and inhumane hygienic conditions in these tent camps.[16] Even though by comparison the general situation in the Austrian refugee camps was better, with these facilities the Habsburg monarchy nonetheless in fact resorted to the precise practice of isolating and interning civilians and military troops in camps typically used by colonial powers as a measure of state crisis and war management. Since the late nineteenth century, such camps had already become a global mass phenomenon, beginning in Cuba, the Philippines, South Africa, and German South West Africa.[17] Around 1900, the colonial empires were closely interconnected via transnational media, and their respective methods of imposing colonial authority closely resembled each other, especially with regard to the implementation of concentration practices and camps as rapidly erected, provisional mass housing.

During the First World War, the spatial configuration of the camp ultimately reached its peak as a biopolitical tool applicable to millions of people worldwide, whether as a prisoner-of-war camp, an internment camp for foreign civilians, a refugee camp,[18] or a hospital camp. In recent years, various twentieth-century camp types have formed the focus of scholarly investigation in the fields of contemporary history and philosophy, postcolonial studies, and refugee studies, as well as architectural history.[19] Current research particularly focuses on the "early" camps "before Auschwitz," such as the refugee camps of the Austro-Hungarian Empire, addressing a wide variety of interdisciplinary questions.[20]

"Town Planning in Wartime"

A Camp System for War Refugees

The *k.k. Flüchtlingslager* ("Imperial-Royal Refugee Camps")[21] of 1914–1918 were the Austrian government's reaction to a wartime situation that posed massive social and hygienic problems.[22] Beginning in the summer of 1914, hundreds of thousands of people from the war zones in the northeast and south of the country arrived in the heartland, including both voluntary refugees and those displaced in the process of the forced evacuation ordered by the government and implemented by the military.[23] The mass accumulation of people in the urban centers, especially in the metropolis of Vienna, but also in other cities such as Prague, Brno, and Graz, led to chaotic supply conditions and a dramatic increase in the already blatant housing crisis. The state was thus forced to find an expedient solution. In a meeting on September 13, 1914, the Austrian Ministry of the Interior laid out procedures for the entire country.[24] On the one hand, the government sought to protect the local population from feared dangers, such as the outbreak of epidemics or social conflicts, but also to bring those who appeared politically suspect under control. On the other hand, the creation of temporary mass housing for the newly homeless was also intended as a humanitarian measure for public welfare. These measures primarily affected those refugees who were destitute.[25]

For this purpose, the government did not consider it sufficient to build temporary barrack settlements away from large cities and provide the refugees with food and medical care. Rather, it was deemed unavoidable to organize these facilities as camps, that is, as self-contained entities closed off from the outside world with an elaborate system of surveillance, control, and discipline, and to implement a series of compulsory hygienic measures, including quarantine and disinfection. The fact that from the outset the directives drafted by the Ministry of War regarding the internment and detention of nationals and foreigners "dangerous to the state" served as the basis for the government's refugee policy provides some explanation for this approach.[26]

The enclosed spaces for the temporary concentration of a certain segment of the population were thus architectural manifestations of a process of othering, which – fueled by anti-Slavic and anti-Semitic resentments and collective suspicions of espionage – consisted of an emphatic ostracization of those classified as "different." In addition, in order to avoid conflict, the refugees were strictly segregated according to nationality and religious affiliation: separate camps were set up for Jewish refugees (the first group for whom camps were established in Moravia), as well as for Polish, Ruthenian, Slovenian, and Italian refugees, and so on.

The refugee camps also corresponded to modern exclusion camps, which Giorgio Agamben defines as spaces of "a permanent state of exception."[27] Although they were civilian citizens of the monarchy, the people housed in the camps found themselves excluded from legal protection.[28] These facilities were officially called "collective settlements" (*Sammelniederlassungen*),[29] or, in reference to the building types, "barrack camps" or "barrack towns," thus obscuring their actual purpose. Unofficially, for example in the daily newspapers, they were often referred to as "concentration camps," which initially simply meant collective accommodation in a single place as opposed to a more individualized residential situation scattered throughout cities, which was difficult to control. The term "concentration camp," however, also clearly denoted an internment situation, and implied, as mentioned above, a reference to the South African colonial camps used by the British Empire in the Boer War.

Since the "foreigners" were by no means meant to be settled permanently at the camp sites, and since the logic of war required financial commitments to be focused primarily in the military sphere, the construction of the camps had to be carried out as economically as possible. Wooden barracks seemed the ideal building type for this purpose: they could be produced serially and cheaply, were easy to dismantle, and their neutral design allowed for various uses.[30] The often catastrophic living conditions of the refugees in the overcrowded giant barracks, designed to accommodate up to 500 people, the extremely high mortality rate, and the internment and disciplinary measures were, however, hidden from the public as much as possible.

Order, Control, and City

From the beginning, the population of the camps was estimated at several thousand, in some cases 20,000–30,000 people per camp, thus exceeding that of many smaller cities in Austria-Hungary. The ministerial adoption of the camp system in September 1914 derived from the view that surveillance strategies would allow for control over social processes and the containment of health hazards. The architecture of the camps provided a suitable instrument for this purpose, in which the efficiency-oriented administration and technical planning interlocked like clockwork.

As Michel Foucault writes in *Discipline and Punish*, "the [military] camp is the diagram of a power that acts by means of general visibility," and represents a basic principle that was to have a long-lasting effect "in urban development, in the construction of working-class housing estates, hospitals, asylums, prisons, schools."[31] When it came to establishing order, control, and discipline in the refugee camps and guaranteeing the observance of hygienic standards, however, the planners obviously needed to draw on methods of modern urban planning, not only military models. Containing chaos through regulatory intervention, directing movement in public space, and establishing networks of infrastructure – all these internationally well-established techniques of urban development could be regarded as inspiration for the planning of the camps.

The technical and urbanistic transformations and dramatically increasing need for housing had developed into a formidable dynamic in the industrialized city of the nineteenth century. In the case of the refugee camps, these processes now had to be greatly accelerated under extreme wartime conditions. Thousands of refugees needed housing, not in months or years, but under extreme time pressure, within a few weeks. In the Wagna camp, for example, residents already referred to an "Old Town" and a "New Town" after the construction of a new section of the camp, barely a year after the camp initially opened in 1915. The older section may have reminded them of the miserable, overcrowded tenement blocks of large cities, while by comparison the smaller barracks and green spaces of the new section more closely resembled recent suburban developments.[32] Due to the state of emergency caused by the war, existing urban norms, regulations, and standards, for example those limiting the number of inhabitants in residences, were often far exceeded or ignored.

By comparison with many small or even large cities in Austria-Hungary, in the refugee camps modern standards in the sense of urban supply, sanitation, and traffic systems were relatively high.[33] These consisted of sewage systems and treatment plants, electrification and street lights, as well as in many cases light railways running through the camps, wooden sidewalks, and partially paved streets for automobiles and bicycles. The explicitly modern elements of the camps also included the various specialized buildings: hospitals, disinfection facilities, showers and bathtubs, and quarantine barracks. A wide variety of building types that could be regarded as urban elements were also built: children's homes and orphanages, synagogues and churches, buildings for entertainment and education, such as theaters, cinemas and other multifunctional community buildings, along with cafeterias, department stores, and tobacconists' kiosks. By contrast to a bourgeois urban society, which built such modern infrastructure for its own use, in the camps all these standards were of course not primarily intended to provide the refugees with a comfortable metropolitan lifestyle, but instead to optimize control and sanitation in the sense of a biopolitical *dispositif* and to guarantee social quiescence.

Urban Planning and Urban Sanitation around 1900

The architectural design of the refugee camps was inscribed within the contemporary discourses and practices of urban planning and its hygienic, technological, and aesthetic requirements. Since the second half of the nineteenth century, urban planning and sanitation had long been recognized and popularized as public and above all municipal responsibilities. Urban development intensified shortly before the outbreak of the First World War, and around 1910 we see "the true heyday of modern urban planning"[34] as a comprehensive and multidisciplinary objective. Around 1900, urban planning was already integrated into the curriculum at German-speaking polytechnic institutes, as well as in Vienna from 1906. By the time the war began, an extensive array of scholarly literature on the subject was widely available, including numerous reference works and manuals by authors including Joseph Stübben, Theodor Fischer, and Theodor Fritsch. Raymond Unwin's *Town Planning in Practice* was also published in German translation in 1910.[35] Beginning in 1904, Camillo Sitte and Theodor Goecke published the journal *Der Städtebau*, which concentrated on the spatial and aesthetic aspects of urban planning, and addressed topics such as building codes, design competitions, urban layout, and traffic management.

In the Austrian milieu of the camp planners, the discourse on urban development was primarily influenced by two personalities, who in many respects represented contrasting ideas. In his 1889 book *City Planning According to Artistic Principles*,[36] Camillo Sitte had developed an aesthetic approach inspired by studies of historical cities in Germany and Italy, and in reaction to the architecture of the Ringstrasse in Vienna. Otto Wagner, on the other hand, formulated a clear affirmation of the potentially "unlimited" metropolis with its modern achievements.[37] Despite their different approaches to solving the problem, both realized that the true basis of contemporary urban planning had to be meeting the requirements of the immediate present.[38] The idea of the garden city, first published by Ebenezer Howard in 1898 in his influential book *To-Morrow. A Peaceful Path to Real Reform*,[39] also played a role in the planning of the refugee camps. This model of an economic and hygienic alternative to the unhealthy and chaotic metropolis was also the subject of intense discussion in Austria.

Closely related to urban planning, and in some aspects overlapping with it, the field of urban hygiene in the sense of a system of public healthcare also evolved in the nineteenth century, mainly in response to the devastating cholera and typhoid epidemics sweeping through crowded industrial cities. This field encompassed the design of water supply, sewage, and garbage disposal systems. Along with structural interventions, it also involved regulations and legislation, including those addressing sociopolitically motivated problems. The beginning of the First World War marked the end of the "implementation phase"[40] of urban redevelopment and urban hygiene.

Camp Planners

The entire planning and administration of the refugee camps was organized and executed by the respective governor's offices of the crown lands. The establishment of this internment and supply system was by no means understood as a subordinate, purely technical task. Thus, in addition to the civil engineers of the state building departments,[41] the planners also employed independent specialists from the fields of public hygiene, hospital planning, and architecture. One of the experts involved was Adalbert Stradal (1861–1943), a highly trained ministry official and a well-informed expert in international discussions on urban development and city sanitation systems. He helped design two camps in Styria (Wagna) and in Lower Austria (Oberhollabrunn).

Stradal had studied in Prague, and joined the Ministry for Public Works in 1909. His interests ranged from public hygiene and healthcare technology,[42] urban planning, and technology, to questions of housing reform and building exhibitions. He was involved in transnational networks of experts that emerged in the late nineteenth century,[43] took part in numerous international conventions on architecture and urban hygiene, and visited exhibitions on construction, urban planning, urban redevelopment, and public hygiene in various European countries and in the USA. In Austria he reported on these subjects in professional journals and lectures,[44] for example in his 1907 essay on *Die Wohnungsfrage in England* (The Housing Question in England),[45] in which he discussed the concept of the garden city. All these experiences formed a pool of knowledge and experience on which he could draw when developing the principles for the refugee camps.

Along with the government engineers, academically trained architects were also employed in planning the refugee camps. These included Max Joli (1879–1946), a former student of Otto Wagner's at the Akademie für Bildende Künste (Academy of Fine Arts) and a member of prominent architects' associations.[46] He was specifically responsible for designing temporary churches and synagogues in the Lower Austrian camps, along with community buildings like a *Volkshalle* or People's Hall. For his church projects he worked hand-in-hand with the artist Berthold Löffler, a member of the Vienna Secession who also taught at the Kunstgewerbeschule (School of Applied Arts).[47] Up until 1912, Joli had worked for the Silesian architect Eugen Fulda, who had primarily designed apartment buildings and villas for the local bourgeoisie. He was one of the few independent architects in Austria who received large government commissions during the war, for which he sometimes employed over 20 workers.[48] Camp construction therefore provided some architects with a lucrative war business in an otherwise stagnant economic climate.

Elements of the Metropolis Designed for the Masses

Grid, Rows, Zones

Both camp planning and modern urban development shared the goal of using structural elements to gain control over large masses of people, disorder, and chaos. In both cases, the orthogonal grid plan appeared to be a practical means of using straight streets with good visibility to create order and guarantee the smoothest possible flow of traffic. The case of the Gmünd refugee camp, where construction began in

January 1915, provides a good example of the planning process.[49] The entire plan of the camp was developed from a regular rectangular grid which divided the area into easily recognizable cells [fig. 11.2] . These rectangular blocks each accommodated two sets of four barracks housing 250 people each, with a kitchen barracks placed between them. One block held the church and school, marking it as a sort of city center, while another housed the hospital facilities.

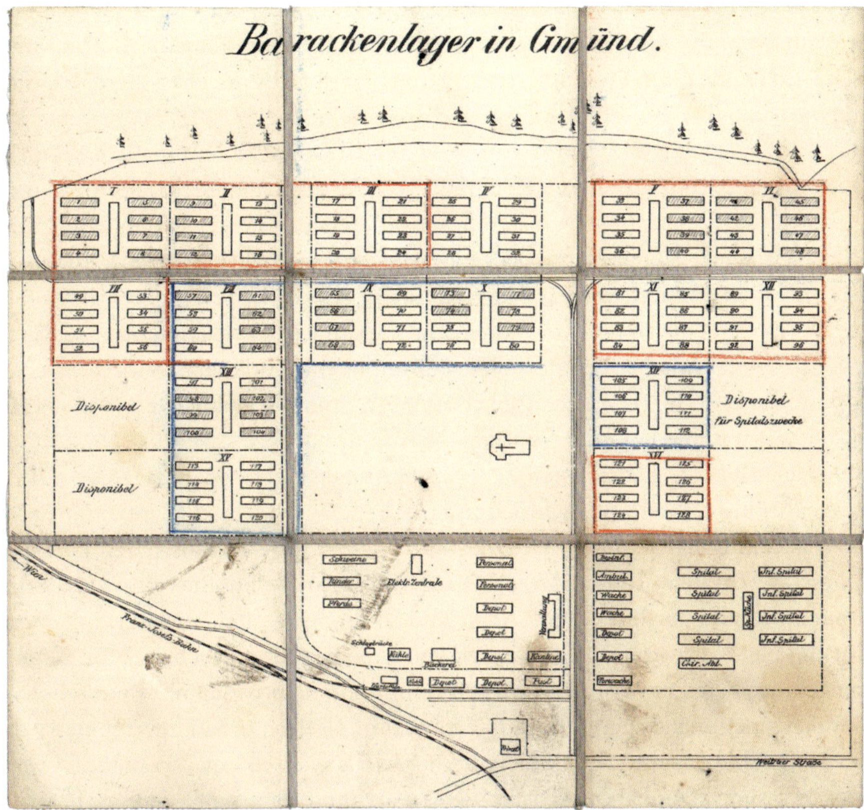

Figure 11.2: Map of refugee camp Gmünd, 1914/15. Stadtarchiv Gmünd.

This arrangement of parallel, uniform blocks, a system already used in ancient Roman military camps, as well as those of the nineteenth century, was applied in the refugee camps primarily in the areas for the residential barracks. It is precisely this grid that characterizes our current, now almost canonical, image of "the camp," because of the widely disseminated photographs of the concentration camps of various twentieth-century regimes. Just as the biopolitical *dispositif* of the modern camp emerged in the nineteenth century, however, the orthogonal grid simultaneously also became a commonplace of modern, rational urban planning and development, as reflected in the repeated characterization of the refugee camps as "American cities."[50] Urban grid planning, however, was by no means a new phenomenon unique to this period. Since Antiquity, the grid pattern has repeatedly characterized city design.[51] This urban form had proven versatile and durable, and allowed for order and regulation, facilitated navigation and spatial orientation, and lent itself to rapid design and adaptability.

By contrast to the perimeter block development seen in traditional cities, especially the historicist nineteenth-century Viennese neighborhoods of the *Gründerzeit*, the planners of the Austrian refugee camps employed the method of row building, also based on the grid. If we understand camp planning as modern urban planning, then the camps can indeed be interpreted as a preliminary step in the introduction of this urban structure in central Europe. Comparison of the camp plans with the layouts of modern housing estates of the 1920s reveals a high degree of similarity, at least in two dimensions. One significant difference, however, stands out. In the camps, the linear layout of the barracks was designed with the requirements of control, administration, and easy accessibility in mind. The primary motivation of the later housing developments, namely the maximum use of sunlight as achieved in the strict east–west orientation of, for example, the Allotment Dammerstock in Karlsruhe (1929) or the Westhausen complex in Frankfurt am Main (1929–1931), was not taken into account in planning the camps.[52]

At a glance, the plans of the refugee camps immediately reveal a clear separation between residential and other functions. The regular rows of residential barracks, which accommodated all the activities of daily life, were each assigned kitchens, schools, and theaters. The various other zones set apart within the camp for administration, hospital facilities, workshops, and so on, were often enclosed by fences, allowing better control of the refugees' movements.[53] The psychiatric or general clinics constructed in Austria after 1900 using a modular pavilion system followed a similar functional structure.[54] In the context of modern urban development, the principle of the separation of urban functions had already emerged as an idea several times in various national contexts in the years around 1900, half a century before it became the international standard of modern urban planning after the end of the Second World War as a result of the CIAM congress *The Functional City* (1933) and Le Corbusier's *Charter of Athens* (1943). In 1898, the urban separation of functions was paradigmatically formulated in Ebenezer Howard's garden city model, and in 1913 Karl Scheffler addressed this principle in *Die Architektur der Großstadt*[55] (The Architecture of the Metropolis), as did Tony Garnier in *Une cité industrielle*[56] (An Industrial City, 1904/1917).

The Austrian refugee camps of the First World War, however, differ from these in another essential point: while ideal cities or models thereof are usually conceptualized radiating outward from a defined center, placed at the intersection of important axes of communication and thus intentionally open, the camps were planned starting from the entrance gate as an interface between the camp and the outside world. The prominent location of the entrance determined the entire logic of this special form of "city," and can also be seen as a unifying characteristic of the later exclusion camps of the twentieth century. From this starting point, the functional arrangement of the building groups then reflects the priorities of the camp management, as well as the procedures carried out in the camp. We must therefore contrast Ebenezer Howard's star-shaped city diagram with a diagram of the camp as a sack-like structure.

Plazas as "Air Centers"

Beyond grids and zoning as direct elements of order and control, the "public space" of the refugee camps was also shaped by the open plazas, as seen in the example of the (ideal) camp plan of Mitterndorf an der Fischa [fig. 11.3].[57] The consecutive construction phases of the refugees' barracks – *Lager I* and *Lager II* (Camps I and II) – are clearly recognizable. Public buildings such as schools and administrative offices are situated between the residential areas, embedded within a type of park. Both sections of the camp are more or less square, and characterized by the geometric grid. *Lager I* incorporates an open, park-like plaza surrounding a *Volkshalle* or People's Hall, with a cinema as the cultural center of the residential area. The same formula appears again in the second section of the camp, this time with a church placed even more clearly in the center. This arrangement centered on a "public" building at least

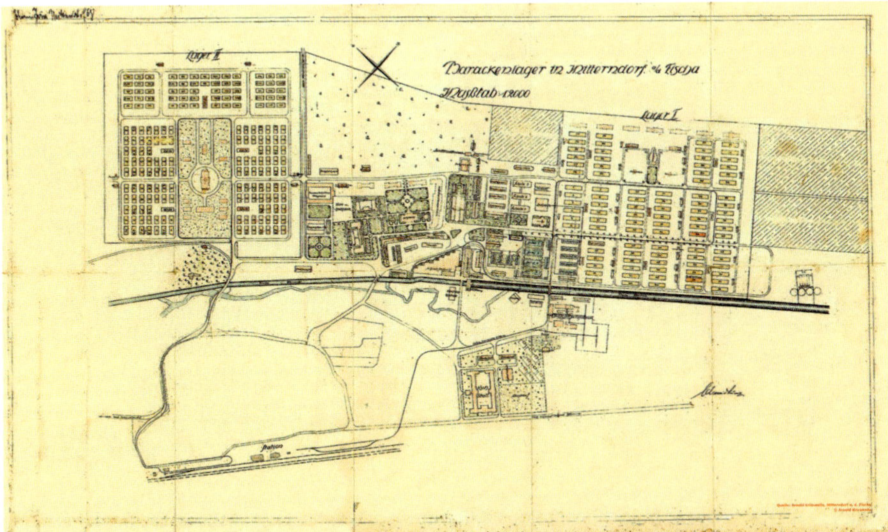

Figure 11.3: Map of refugee camp Mitterndorf a.d. Fischa, around 1915. Private collection Arnold Krizsanits.

suggests a certain attempt to emulate the European tradition of the ideal city. In a 1916 article in the journal *Der Architekt*, the architectural publicist Hartwig Fischel emphasized the fact that "the camp plans already [had] a unified overall disposition with central church squares and a garden-like design,"[58] with buildings such as schools or administrative offices arranged regularly around these squares.

Comparing the plans of Mitterndorf, Gmünd, or Deutschbrod (Havlíčkův Brod) with an ideal plan from Otto Wagner's 1911 study *Die Großstadt* (The Metropolis), mentioned above, reveals several parallels [fig.11.4]. For the largely autonomous districts of the modern metropolis, Wagner developed a large open space[59] – what he called a *Luftzentrum* or "Air Center" – with public buildings, cultural centers, and parks as the backbone of each district. The rational orthogonal plan of Wagner's "unlimited metropolis" corresponds to the idea of the potentially equally "unlimited camp."[60] Given the camp directors' urbanistic ambitions and the professional profiles of the individuals involved, an association between the camps and Otto Wagner's concept, which was well known in such circles, is not implausible.[61] In this case, the idea may have come from Wagner's former student Max Joli. Direct comparison, however, only truly applies to the two-dimensional aspect of the plans, as a look at Wagner's bird's-eye view of a neighborhood with its grand, multi-story buildings clearly reveals. Even though the streets of the refugee camps were mainly character-ized by the monotonous wooden walls of the residential barracks, the camp plans clearly demonstrate at least the ambition to visually improve these dreary places through urban design.

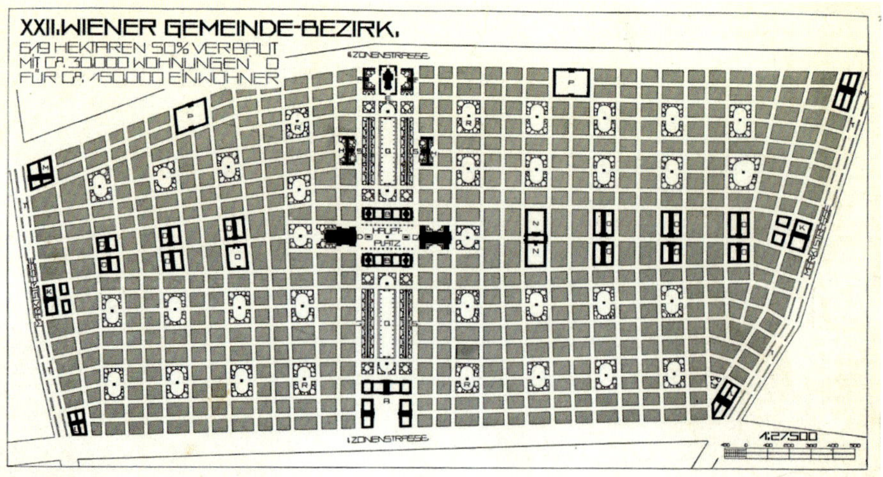

Figure 11.4: Otto Wagner, map of a fictitious XXII District of Vienna. Otto Wagner, *Die Großstadt. Eine Studie über diese* (Vienna: Schroll, 1911).

Simulated Small Towns

Pacification and Opportunities for Identification

In the first phase of the construction of refugee camps beginning in the fall of 1914 the main goal was to provide mass housing and the necessary infrastructure and hygienic facilities. Despite all the architectural measures, however, the internment and the stress caused by overcrowding and lack of adequate care for the refugees led to numerous riots, rebellions, and social conflicts, as well as escape attempts and depression. After only a few months, therefore, the camp planners introduced new goals in a second phase in order to minimize these problems and guarantee social peace. As the war progressed, the need to establish some form of normalcy and familiarity seemed unavoidable in order to make a longer stay within the more or less closed camp borders bearable. Measures needed to be taken to create something resembling a community, and provide opportunities for residents to develop a sense of shared identity. Especially from 1915 onwards, the ministry and planners now repeatedly spoke of "barrack towns" in reference to the accommodation for refugees, a term that shifted the perception of the camps from a focus on their temporary nature toward an idea of permanence.[62] In addition, a code switch (from camp to (small) town) also better lent itself to propaganda purposes, allowing officials to downplay the misery of the camps in public.

In the intended simulation of an urban situation, the paradigm of the idyllic, tranquil small town was more suitable than the code of the modern metropolis,[63] which implied anonymity and uniformity, especially since the refugees primarily came from rural and small-town backgrounds. The camp and its characteristics were overwritten and recoded using idyllic images associated with tradition, without, however, actually reducing the degree of internment. Initially, starting in the second year of the war, the residential areas received an architectural upgrade as a result of protests from the residents themselves, but also from visitors and aid committees. The organizational form of the large-capacity barrack for hundreds of inhabitants gave way to smaller residential units. The camp planners did not take metropolitan, collective forms of housing such as one-kitchen houses into consideration; instead, the new, smaller barrack types more closely resembled the houses of suburban communities and country houses, almost like villas. This architectural strategy to alleviate the tense situation in the camps can be compared to the intended deproletarianization in the so-called *Stadtrandsiedlungen* ("suburban settlements") of the interwar period, where individualization and attachment to property and land were intended to reduce excess social energy.[64]

The term "colony,"[65] which planners and visitors often used in reference to the camps, closely correlates with the concept of the camp as a (small) town. In this term two contemporary meanings overlapped: on the one hand, that of migration and appropriation of land (thus implying a type of internal colonization in reference to the refugee camps), and on the other, that of a planned suburban housing estate or garden city.[66] In both respects, this implied that the refugees were actually settlers and the camps peaceful settlements on fallow new land, downplaying or veiling the fact that the situation had resulted from a centrally organized program of deportation and forced resettlement carried out by the military and segregated from the local population.

A propaganda publication of the Wagna refugee camp in Styria[67] [fig. 11.5] shows the camp planners' intention to take the sting out of the instrument of internment. Illustrations show scenes of camp life: an open, inviting entrance gate, women strolling around with shopping baskets, residents at the kiosk, young girls doing handicrafts, barrack buildings with smoking chimneys and laundry hung out to dry. Here we see a constructed ideal image of a tranquil small town with residents who seem content. The drawing style corresponded to the practices of the *Heimatschutz* ("homeland protection") movement, which, beginning in the years after 1900, propagated a traditional modernism with German nationalist traits in Austria as well.[68] Before the war, advertising for garden city settlements and workers' colonies on the outskirts of the large cities used similar atmospheric images (mostly, however, without residents), such as the illustrations in the works of Raymond Unwin, Theodor Fischer, and Heinrich Tessenow. Geographically closer to the Wagna camp were the garden suburbs designed by Adolf von Inffeld and Franz Polzer for the outskirts of Graz.[69]

In accordance with these guiding principles, the (re)design of the refugee camps was now based on habits of seeing and on traditional proportions, forms, and ornamentation. Heimat Style or Cottage Style, sometimes with echoes of Art Nouveau and a moderate Secessionism, gave the camp areas a romanticized small-town flair in keeping with the housing estates of the pre-war period. Some of the residential buildings, pre-schools, daycare facilities for children, and administrative buildings were now also erected in stone. While the very first camp plans provided for only a minimal elaboration of "public" space, the later versions included avenues of trees, lawns, teaching gardens, and parks reminiscent of contemporary projects by city beautification associations. Within the residential areas, churches of the various denominations and synagogues were primarily intended to provide a sense of identity and cultural belonging. Church furnishings were colorfully painted "in the style of village churches,"[70] and the camp church of Wagna was equipped with a large organ. The synagogue in the camp at Bruck an der Leitha, which served simultaneously as an assembly hall and a common room, in its turn followed in the tradition of Eastern European wooden synagogues. To accommodate the customs of the Jewish inhabitants, who came from Eastern Europe, the bema was placed in the center of the room.[71]

Figure 11.5: Scenes from the camp life, refugee camp Wagna. Franz Haimel, *Flüchtlingslager Wagna bei Leibnitz* (Graz, 1915).

Housing Projects for the Post-War Period

The reinterpretation of the camps as small towns and residential colonies, however, went even further. Since the construction of the temporary camps required significant financial investment, beginning in the second year of the war attempts were made to reconceptualize the camps as more profitable facilities, and to make them more sustainable and more suitable for later purposes and other target groups. This changed their character. The original function of the camps as a means of segregating a group of people perceived as "strangers" was supplemented by their function as potential housing for the resident population as well as for the soldiers returning home from war and for disabled persons (*Kriegerheimstätten*, "Veterans' Homes"). This gave rise to hybrid forms of "normalized" wartime housing, and the categorical difference between camp and city was finally intentionally dissolved by the camp planners. Even during the war, the names used in numerous sources to refer to the refugee camps – for example Barackenstadt Neu-Gmünd, Bruck-Neustadt or Neu-Oberhollabrunn – reflect the idea that they effectively formed new districts of the nearby communities.

Figure 11.6: Administration building of the refugee camp Oberhollabrunn, around 1918. Private collection Friedrich Ecker.

The refugee camp of Oberhollabrunn, erected in the early months of 1916 and administered by the governor's office of Lower Austria, exemplifies this tendency particularly clearly [fig. 11.6].[72] A glance at the plan immediately reveals that the usual grid-like layout of the refugee camps has been replaced here by curved streets that are obviously adapted to the hilly terrain and recall the picturesque urban patterns inspired by Camillo Sitte. This unusual variation on the camp plan owes its existence to the negotiation and intervention of Rudolf Kolisko, mayor of Oberhollabrunn and a German nationalist, with the Ministry of the Interior and the regional authorities. His goal was to allow for a later use of the camp "as a veterans' home and summer resort."[73] Adalbert Stradal, one of the planers of this camp, had already taken an interest in the garden city model as put forth by Ebenezer Howard, and in 1908 had reported on Letchworth, the first garden city actually built in England.[74] The hybrid "camp/garden city" Oberhollabrunn reflected the contemporary trends in urban planning discourse: both in Austria and internationally, the garden city, primarily conceptualized as a suburban garden settlement or colony, was propagated as the residential model of the future during the First World War, and promoted as the ideal pattern for reconstruction in the post-war period.[75] In fact, beginning in the 1920s, the surviving portions of the former Oberhollabrunn camp were adapted as a "garden city" and villa suburb of the nearby town.

Figure 11.7: Refugee camp Gmünd, church and school building, 1915. Stadtarchiv Gmünd.

Conclusion

The refugee camps of the Austro-Hungarian Empire [fig. 11.7], created under extreme wartime conditions, can be read as part of the trajectory of European or Central European modernist architecture and urban planning history. In these instruments of internment and biopolitical *dispositifs* of the monarchy, rooted in global colonial histories, architecture played a defining role in shaping space and providing a sense of identity. By applying structural methods of order and control and simulating an urban situation, the planners combined two actually contradictory models of urban development: the metropolis designed to accommodate the masses, and the small-scale garden city. The camp plans revealed tendencies towards suburbanization and, in part, anticipated elements of urban planning that would become prevalent in the interwar period. In practice the boundary between "camp" and "city" proved quite fluid. The later planning of the refugee camps developed into a kind of strategic housing program for the post-war period. From this perspective, it represented a preliminary stage of mass social housing as it emerged after World War I as a communal and cooperative undertaking.

The essential distinction between camp and city, or camp and suburban settlement, was only partially reflected in the architecture and spatial arrangement. Instead, the primary difference lay in the system of rule, as manifested in the camp fence, the guarded entrance, and the procedures of control and discipline. Once these elements were removed after the end of the war, the former camp complexes fulfilled the function of new suburban residential areas, and in many cases the buildings, street grids, and sewage systems of the former camps remain in use today.

Notes

1   The official name of Cisleithania was "The Kingdoms and Lands represented in the Imperial Council" (*Die im Reichsrat vertretenen Königreiche und Länder*).

2   This essay builds on the author's research project at the Graz University of Technology addressing "Modern Architectures of Camps."

3   Two types of camps for civilians from the front areas prevailed in the Austro-Hungarian Empire during the First World War: refugee camps for destitute internally displaced persons or forced evacuees, and internment camps for those under political suspicion.

4   Julius v. Bük, "Kriegsausstellung Wien 1916 (Fortsetzung)," *Der Bautechniker* 36 (1916): 241–3, esp. 243. See also Richard Staudinger, "Kriegsbau-Kunst und Kitsch," *Der Bautechniker* 36 (1916): 267–8, esp. 267.

5   See, for example, "Eine neue Stadt in Niederösterreich. Die hölzerne Stadt bei Gmünd," *Arbeiter-Zeitung*, January 24, 1915, p. 24; "Die Stadt aus Holz," *Wiener Illustrierte Zeitung*, November 14, 1916, pp. 2–3, esp. 3.

6   Birgit S. Nielsen, "Die dänische Schriftstellerin Karin Michaelis und der erste Weltkrieg," *Text & Kontext* 22, no. 1/2 (2000): 20–40.

7   Karin Michaëlis, *Opfer. Kriegs- und Friedenswerke an der Donau* (Wien and Leipzig: Manz, 1917), 1.

8   *Ibid.*, 5.

9   See, for example, "Das Flüchtlingslager in Mitterndorf," *Arbeiter-Zeitung, Morgenblatt*, September 5, 1916, p. 6; K. M., "Weihnachtsverkauf von Flüchtlingsarbeiten," *Reichspost*, December 7, 1916, p. 10; Ernst Decseys, "Steiermarks italienische Stadt. Ein Besuch in Wagna," *Neue Freie Presse, Morgenblatt*, March 30, 1916, pp. 1–3.

10   "Vereinsberichte. Polytechnischer Club in Graz," *Der Bautechniker* 36 (1916): 53–4, esp. 53.

11   Edward Bellamy, *Looking Backward. 2000–1887* (Boston: Ticknor, 1888).

12   German: *Barackenkommandant*; Italian: *Capo di barraca*, Polish: *Wojt*.

13 See, for example, Johannes Feichtinger, Ursula Prutsch, and Moritz Csáky, eds., *Habsburg postcolonial. Machtstrukturen und kollektives Gedächtnis* (Innsbruck: Studienverlag, 2003).

14 Regarding the aspects of the refugee camps as a disciplinary instrument, see Antje Senarclens de Grancy, "Different Housing Spaces – Space, Function, and Use of Barrack-Huts in World War I Refugee Camps," *Reflections on Camps – Space, Agency, Materiality, zeitgeschichte* 45, no. 4 (2018): 457–82.

15 Zygmunt Bauman, "A Century of Camps?," in *The Bauman Reader*, ed. Peter Beilharz (Oxford: John Wiley, 2001), 266–80. See Joël Kotek and Pierre Rigoulot, *Le Siècle des Camps. Détention, concentration, extermination. Cent ans de mal radical* (Paris: J.-C. Lattès, 2000).

16 See, for example, Evelyn Asinelli, "Emily Hobhouse und ihr Werk im Transvaal," *Neues Frauenleben* 18 (March 1906): 7–9.

17 See, for example, Aidan Forth, *Barbed-Wire Imperialism: Britain's Empire of Camps, 1876–1903* (Berkeley: University of California Press, 2017); Jonas Kreienbaum, *A Sad Fiasco: Colonial Concentration Camps in Southern Africa, 1900–1908* (Oxford and New York: Berghahn Books, 2019); Matthew Stibbe, "The Internment of Political Suspects in Austria-Hungary during the First World War: A Violent Legacy?," in *Gender and Modernity in Central Europe: The Austro-Hungarian Monarchy and its Legacy*, ed. Agata Schwartz (Ottawa: University of Ottawa Press, 2010), 203–18.

18 The only other refugee camps constructed in Europe during the First World War with a comparable level of architectural elaboration were those built in the Netherlands for Belgian refugees. See Michaël Amara, "Belgian refugees during the First World War (France, Britain, Netherlands)," in *Europe on the Move: Refugees in the Era of the Great War*, ed. Peter Gatrell and Liubov Zhvanko (Manchester: Manchester University Press, 2017), 197–214.

19 See, for example, Irit Katz et al., eds., *Camps Revisited: Multifaceted Spatialities of a Modern Political Technology* (London: Rowman and Littlefield, 2018).

20 Bettina Greiner and Alan Kramer, eds., *Welt der Lager. Zur "Erfolgsgeschichte" einer Institution* (Hamburg: Hamburger Edition, 2013); Christoph Jahr and Jens Thiel, eds., *Lager vor Auschwitz. Gewalt und Integration im 20. Jahrhundert* (Berlin: Metropol-Verlag, 2013).

21 Refugee camps were erected in the following states in the Austrian part of the empire: Lower Austria, Upper Austria, Styria, Carinthia, Bohemia, and Moravia.

22 Walter Mentzel, "Die Flüchtlingspolitik der Habsburgermonarchie während des Ersten Weltkrieges," in *Aufnahmeland Österreich. Über den Umgang mit Massenflucht seit dem 18. Jahrhundert*, ed. Börries Kuzmany and Rita Garstenauer (Vienna: Mandelbaum, 2017), 126–55; Walter Mentzel, "Kriegserfahrungen von Flüchtlingen aus dem Nordosten der Monarchie während des Ersten Weltkrieges," in *Jenseits des Schützengrabens. Der Erste Weltkrieg im Osten: Erfahrung – Wahrnehmung – Kontext*, ed. Bernhard Bachinger and Wolfram Dornik (Innsbruck: Studien Verlag, 2013), 359–90; Martina Hermann, "'Cities of Barracks': Refugees in the Austrian Part of the Habsburg Empire during the First World War," in *Europe on the Move: Refugees in the Era of the Great War*, ed. Peter Gatrell and Liubov Zhvanko (Manchester: Manchester University Press, 2017), 129–55; Julia Thorpe, "Displacing Empire: Refugee Welfare, National Activism and State Legitimacy in Austria-Hungary in the First World War," in *Refugees and the End of Empire: Imperial Collapse and Forced Migration in the Twentieth Century*, ed. Panikos Panayi and Pippa Virdee (Basingstoke: Palgrave Macmillan, 2011), 102–26.

23 This first affected Galicia, Bukovina and the Balkans, then South Tyrol, Trentino, Gorizia and Gradisca, Friuli, Istria and the Austrian Littoral.

24 Walter Mentzel, "Kriegsflüchtlinge in Cisleithanien im Ersten Weltkrieg" (PhD diss., University of Vienna, 1997), 219.

25 "Socially superior" refugees with sufficient financial means were accommodated in apartments, hotels, guesthouses, etc. in various communities.

26 Mentzel, "Die Flüchtlingspolitik."

27 Giorgio Agamben, *Means without End: Notes on Politics* (Minneapolis: University of Minnesota Press, 2000), 37–45, esp. 39.

28 Only after the reconvening of the Austrian Imperial Council was a law passed on December 31, 1917 "concerning the protection of war refugees."

29 K.k. Ministerium des Innern, ed., *Staatliche Flüchtlingsfürsorge im Kriege 1914/15* (Vienna, 1915), 11.

30 See, for example, Walther Lange, *Der Baracken-Bau mit besonderer Berücksichtigung der Wohn- und Epidemie-Baracken* (Leipzig: Baumgärtner's Buchhandlung, 1895).

31 Michel Foucault, *Discipline and Punish: The Birth of the Prison*, trans. Alan Sheridan (New York: Random House, 1977), 171–2. Regarding the relationship of military camps to collective housing, see Teresa Zarebska, "Théories militaires et habitations collectives," *Archithese* no. 8 (1973): 9–14.

32 "Ein Besuch im Flüchtlingslager Wagna (Grazer Volksblatt)," *Lagerzeitung für Wagna*, February 24, 1916, p. 2.

33 Dieter Schott, *Die Vernetzung der Stadt. Kommunale Energiepolitik, öffentlicher Verkehr und die "Produktion" der modernen Stadt. Darmstadt – Mannheim – Mainz 1880–1918* (Darmstadt: Wissenschaftliche Buchgesellschaft, 1999).

34 Wolfgang Sonne, "Blütezeit des Städtebaus in Europa und den USA," in *Stadtvisionen 1910/2010. Berlin Paris London Chicago. 100 Jahre Allgemeine Städtebau-Ausstellung in Berlin*, ed. Harald Bodenschatz et al. (Kiel and Berlin: DOM publishers, 2010), 30–7, esp. 30.

35 Raymond Unwin, *Town Planning in Practice: An Introduction to the Art of Designing Cities and Suburbs* (London: T. F. Unwin, 1909).

36 George R. Collins and Christiane Crasemann Collins, *Camillo Sitte: The Birth of Modern City Planning. With a translation of the 1889 Austrian edition of his City Planning According to Artistic Principles* (New York: Rizzoli, 1986).

37 Otto Wagner, *Die Großstadt. Eine Studie über diese* (Vienna: Schroll, 1911).

38 Wolfgang Sonne, "Großstadtbaukunst. Otto Wagners Städtebau im internationalen Kontext," in *Otto Wagner*, ed. Andreas Nierhaus and Eva-Maria Orosz (Salzburg and Vienna: Residenz, 2018), 52–9.

39 Ebenezer Howard, *To-Morrow. A Peaceful Path to Real Reform* (London: Swan Sonnenschein, 1898).

40 Peter Münch, *Stadthygiene im 19. und 20. Jahrhundert. Die Wasserversorgung, Abwasser- und Abfallbeseitigung unter besonderer Berücksichtigung Münchens* (Göttingen: Vandenhoeck & Ruprecht, 1993), 340.

41 Mario Schwarz, "Architekt Heymann, Ingenieur Gröger und das k.k. Flüchtlingslager Oberhollabrunn," *Steine sprechen* 46/2, no. 132 (2006): 8–16.

42 See, for example, Adalbert Stradal, "Krankenhäuser," in *Atlas und Lehrbuch der Hygiene. Mit besonderer Berücksichtigung der Städte-Hygiene*, ed. Wilhelm Prausnitz (Munich: J. F. Lehmann's Verlag, 1909).

43 Philipp Wagner, *Stadtplanung für die Welt? Internationales Expertenwissen, 1900–1960* (Göttingen: Vandenhoeck & Ruprecht, 2016); Helen Meller, ed., *Ghent Planning Con-*

gress, 1913. Premier Congrès International et Exposition Comparée des Villes* (London: Routledge, 2014).

44   See, for example, A. G. Stradal, "Die Bauordnungen von New-York und Chicago," *Zeitschrift des Österreichischen Ingenieurs- und Architekten-Vereins* 46 (1894): 155–61 and 167–71.

45   A. G. Stradal, "Die Wohnungsfrage in England," *Allgemeine Bauzeitung* 73 (1908): 75–88.

46   Max Eisler, Österreichische Werkkultur (Vienna: Schroll, 1916), 245 and 249; Marco Pozzetto, *Die Schule Otto Wagners 1894–1912* (Vienna and Munich: Schroll, 1980), 230 and fig. 155–7; "Joli, Max Hans," accessed December 17, 2019, <http://www.architektenlexikon.at/de/262.htm>. In the 1920s Joli worked for the "Red Vienna" housing complex, Quellenstraße, Vienna (1928/29). See Helmut Weihsmann, *Das Rote Wien. Sozialdemokratische Architektur und Kommunalpolitik, 1919–1934* (Vienna: Promedia, 2002), 248.

47   Gerd Pichler, "Bertold Löffler. Leben und Werk" (PhD diss., University of Vienna, 2017), 72–3.

48   "Schweizer Architekten bevorzugt," *Deutsche Presse*, December 12, 1916, p. 2.

49   See the versions of the plan in the Stadtarchiv Gmünd, as well as in the Österreichische Staatsarchiv, Archiv der Republik, Kriegsflüchtlingsfürsorge.

50   Ernst Decseys, "Steiermarks italienische Stadt. Ein Besuch in Wagna," *Neue Freie Presse, Morgenblatt,* March 30, 1916, pp. 1–3; "Die Ausstellung in der Bognergasse (Flüchtlingsfürsorge)," *Neue Freie Presse,* January 21, 1916, pp. 1–3, esp. 1.

51   Piet Lombaerde and Charles van den Heuvel, eds., *Early Modern Urbanism and the Grid: Town Planning in the Low Countries in International Context: Exchanges in Theory and Practise, 1550–1880* (Turnhout: Brepols, 2011); Reuben Rose-Redwood and Liora Bigon, eds., *Gridded Worlds: An Urban Anthology* (Cham: Springer, 2018).

52   Ute Poerschke, "The Sun for All: Social Equity and the Debate on Best Solar Orientation of High Modernist Housing," *EAAE ARCC Conference Proceedings 2016* (Lisbon, 2016), 367–73. At least in German-speaking countries, Theodor Fischer's Alte Heide housing complex in Munich (1919–28) is often cited as the first example of a modern row settlement aligned according to the position of the sun.

53   This zoning appears particularly clearly in the site plans of the Wagna camp, produced in 1915 for exhibition, where the zones are even marked in different colors. Franz Haimel, *Flüchtlingslager Wagna bei Leibnitz. Mit einer Abhandlung über die Alt-Römerstadt Flavia Solva* (Graz, 1915).

54   This is particularly true of the Niederösterreichische Landes Heil- und Pflegeanstalt für Geistes- und Nervenkranke am Steinhof (Lower Austrian State Sanatorium and Home for the Insane and Mentally Ill "Am Steinhof") near Vienna, and the state hospital in Graz. See Heinrich Schlöss, *Die Irrenpflege in Österreich in Wort und Bild* (Halle a.S.: Marhold, 1912).

55   Karl Scheffler, *Die Architektur der Großstadt* (Berlin: Cassirer, 1913).

56   Tony Garnier, *Une Cité industrielle. Étude pour la construction des villes* (Paris: Massin, 1917).

57   The plan was not implemented in its entirety, and should be understood as an ideal design. Regarding the Mitterndorf camp see Friederike Scherr, "Jakob Levy Moreno im Flüchtlingslager Mitterndorf a.d. Fischa – eine Spurensuche," *Zeitschrift für Psychodrama und Soziometrie* 12, no. S1 (2013): 3–126.

58   Hartwig Fischel, "Bauanlagen der staatlichen Flüchtlingsfürsorge," *Der Architekt* 21 (1916/1918), 15–24, esp. 21–2.

59   Wagner demonstrates this principle using the example of a fictitious XXII District of Vienna.

60   The camp barracks, by contrast, form rows as described above, instead of the peripheral block construction typical of Wagner's urban planning.

61   Eisler, *Österreichische Werkkultur*; "Die Arbeit des Oesterreichischen Werkbundes," *Reichspost*, October 22, 1916, p. 11.

62   K.k. Ministerium des Innern, ed., *Staatliche Flüchtlingsfürsorge im Kriege 1914/15* (Vienna, 1915), 10.

63   Britta Hentschel and Harald Stühlinger, eds., *Recoding the City: Thinking, Planning, and Building the City of the Nineteenth Century* (Berlin: Jovis, 2019).

64   Werner Suppanz, "Entproletarisierung in der Stadtrandsiedlung – eine gegen/moderne Strategie," in *Architektur. Vergessen. Jüdische Architekten in Graz*, ed. Antje Senarclens de Grancy and Heidrun Zettelbauer (Vienna, Cologne, and Weimar: Böhlau, 2011), 202–4.

65   From the very beginning outsiders had often referred to the refugee camps as "colonies" (*Kolonien*). See, for example, "Oesterreichische Flüchtlingsstädte," *Salzburger Chronik, Sonntagsbeilage*, June 4, 1916, pp. 14–5.

66   In German-speaking countries the word "colony" (*Kolonie*) refers to a district connected to a core city or town, which served primarily for residential purposes. The term was used both for middle-class establishments ("villa colony," *Villenkolonie*) and for workers' colonies and housing for the homeless. Only in the interwar period did the term "settlement" (*Siedlung*) displace "colony." See Anna S. Brasch, *Moderne – Regeneration – Erlösung. Der Begriff der 'Kolonie' und die weltanschauliche Literatur der Jahrhundertwende* (Göttingen: V&R Unipress, 2017).

67   Haimel, *Flüchtlingslager Wagna bei Leibnitz*.

68   Antje Senarclens de Grancy, "Konservative Reform. Die Anfänge des Vereins für Heimatschutz in Steiermark," in *Identität – Politik – Architektur. Der "Verein für Heimatschutz in Steiermark*," ed. Antje Senarclens de Grancy (Berlin: Jovis, 2013), 31–54.

69   Franz Polzer, *Die Cottageanlage St. Josef im Kroisbachtale bei Graz* (Vienna, 1906); "Gartenstadtprojekt ausgearbeitet von den Schülern des V. Bauwerkmeisterkurses an der k.k. Staatsgewerbeschule in Graz," *Wiener Bauindustrie-Zeitung* 31, no. 40 (1914): 239 and 241–2, plates 77–8.

70   Hartwig Fischel, "Bauanlagen der staatlichen Flüchtlingsfürsorge," *Der Architekt* 21 (1916/1918): 15–24, esp. 21.

71   Heinrich Schreiber, "Das jüdische Barackenlager von Bruck a. L.," *Dr. Bloch's Österreichische Wochenschrift*, July 30, 1915, pp. 582–3. See also Pierre Genée, "Die neuzeitlichen Synagogen in Niederösterreich," *David. Jüdische Kulturzeitschrift* 1 (April 1989): 7–11, 8.

72   Werner Lamm, *Vom Flüchtlingslager zur Gartenstadt, mit Beiträgen von Walter Johann Fittner. Begleitband zum Film "Die Gartenstadt" von Ferry Seher* (Hollabrunn: Hollabrunner Museumsverein, 1999).

73   "Flüchtlingslager," *Wochen-Zeitung für das Viertel unter dem Manhartsberg*, January 21, 1916.

74   Stradal, "Die Wohnungsfrage in England."

75   See, for example, Theodor Bach, "Der Friede und das Siedlungswesen," *Der Bautechniker* 35 (1915): 202–4; Theodor Bach, *Krieg und Gartenstadt* (Prague: Mercy, 1916); Österreichischer Ingenieur- und Architekten-Verein, ed., *Wien nach dem Kriege. Denkschrift verfaßt vom ständigen Ausschusse für die bauliche Entwicklung Wiens des Österr. Ingenieur- und Architekten-Vereines* (Vienna, 1916), 47–50.

Bibliography

Agamben, Giorgio. *Means without End: Notes on Politics.* Minneapolis: University of Minnesota Press, 2000.

Amara, Michaël. "Belgian refugees during the First World War (France, Britain, Netherlands)." In *Europe on the Move: Refugees in the Era of the Great War*, edited by Peter Gatrell and Liubov Zhvanko, 197–214. Manchester: Manchester University Press, 2017.

Bauman, Zygmunt. "A Century of Camps?" In *The Bauman Reader*, edited by Peter Beilharz, 266–80. Oxford: John Wiley, 2001.

Brasch, Anna S. *Moderne – Regeneration – Erlösung. Der Begriff der 'Kolonie' und die weltanschauliche Literatur der Jahrhundertwende.* Göttingen: V&R Unipress, 2017.

Collins, George R., and Christiane Crasemann Collins. *Camillo Sitte: The Birth of Modern City Planning. With a translation of the 1889 Austrian edition of his City Planning According to Artistic Principles.* New York: Rizzoli, 1986.

Eisler, Max. Österreichische Werkkultur. Vienna: Schroll, 1916.

Feichtinger, Johannes, Ursula Prutsch, and Moritz Csáky, eds. *Habsburg postcolonial. Machtstrukturen und kollektives Gedächtnis.* Innsbruck: Studienverlag, 2003.

Forth, Aidan. *Barbed-Wire Imperialism: Britain's Empire of Camps, 1876–1903.* Berkeley: University of California Press, 2017.

Foucault, Michel. *Discipline and Punish: The Birth of the Prison.* Translated by Alan Sheridan. New York: Random House, 1977.

Kreienbaum, Jonas. *A Sad Fiasco: Colonial Concentration Camps in Southern Africa, 1900–1908.* Oxford and New York: Berghahn Books, 2019.

Garnier, Tony. *Une Cité industrielle.* Étude pour la construction des villes. Paris: Massin, 1917.

Genée, Pierre. "Die neuzeitlichen Synagogen in Niederösterreich." *David. Jüdische Kulturzeitschrift* 1 (April 1989): 7–11.

Greiner, Bettina, and Alan Kramer, eds. *Welt der Lager. Zur "Erfolgsgeschichte" einer Institution.* Hamburg: Hamburger Edition, 2013.

Haimel, Franz. *Flüchtlingslager Wagna bei Leibnitz. Mit einer Abhandlung über die Alt-Römerstadt Flavia Solva.* Graz, 1915.

Hentschel, Britta, and Harald Stühlinger, eds. *Recoding the City: Thinking, Planning, and Building the City of the Nineteenth Century.* Berlin: Jovis, 2019.

Hermann, Martina. "'Cities of Barracks': Refugees in the Austrian Part of the Habsburg Empire during the First World War." In *Europe on the Move: Refugees in the Era of the Great War*, edited by Peter Gatrell and Liubov Zhvanko, 129–55. Manchester: Manchester University Press, 2017.

Howard, Ebenezer. *To-Morrow. A Peaceful Path to Real Reform.* London: Swan Sonnenschein, 1898.

Jahr, Christoph, and Jens Thiel, eds. *Lager vor Auschwitz. Gewalt und Integration im 20. Jahrhundert.* Berlin: Metropol-Verlag, 2013.

K.k. Ministerium des Innern, ed. *Staatliche Flüchtlingsfürsorge im Kriege 1914/15.* Vienna, 1915.

Katz, Irit, et al., eds. *Camps Revisited: Multifaceted Spatialities of a Modern Political Technology.* London: Rowman and Littlefield, 2018.

Kotek, Joël, and Pierre Rigoulot. *Le Siècle des Camps. Détention, concentration, extermination. Cent ans de mal radical.* Paris: J.-C. Lattès, 2000.

Lange, Walther. *Der Baracken-Bau mit besonderer Berücksichtigung der Wohn- und Epidemie-Baracken.* Leipzig: Baumgärtner's Buchhandlung, 1895.

Lombaerde, Piet, and Charles van den Heuvel, eds. *Early Modern Urbanism and the Grid: Town Planning in the Low Countries in International Context: Exchanges in Theory and Practise, 1550–1880.* Turnhout: Brepols, 2011.

Meller, Helen, ed. *Ghent Planning Congress, 1913. Premier Congrès International et Exposition Comparée des Villes.* London: Routledge, 2014.

Mentzel, Walter. "Die Flüchtlingspolitik der Habsburgermonarchie während des Ersten Weltkrieges." In *Aufnahmeland Österreich. Über den Umgang mit Massenflucht seit dem 18. Jahrhundert,* edited by Börries Kuzmany and Rita Garstenauer, 126–55. Vienna: Mandelbaum, 2017.

Mentzel, Walter. "Kriegserfahrungen von Flüchtlingen aus dem Nordosten der Monarchie während des Ersten Weltkrieges." In *Jenseits des Schützengrabens. Der Erste Weltkrieg im Osten: Erfahrung – Wahrnehmung – Kontext,* edited by Bernhard Bachinger and Wolfram Dornik, 359–90. Innsbruck: Studien Verlag, 2013.

Mentzel, Walter. "Kriegsflüchtlinge in Cisleithanien im Ersten Weltkrieg." PhD diss., University of Vienna, 1997.

Michaëlis, Karin. *Opfer. Kriegs- und Friedenswerke an der Donau.* Vienna and Leipzig: Manz, 1917.

Münch, Peter. *Stadthygiene im 19. und 20. Jahrhundert. Die Wasserversorgung, Abwasser- und Abfallbeseitigung unter besonderer Berücksichtigung Münchens,* Göttingen: Vandenhoeck & Ruprecht, 1993.

Nielsen, Birgit S. "Die dänische Schriftstellerin Karin Michaelis und der erste Weltkrieg." *Text & Kontext* 22, no. 1/2 (2000): 20–40.

Pichler, Gerd. "Bertold Löffler. Leben und Werk." PhD diss., University of Vienna, 2017.

Poerschke, Ute. "The Sun for All: Social Equity and the Debate on Best Solar Orientation of High Modernist Housing." *EAAE ARCC Conference Proceedings 2016,* 367–73. Lisbon, 2016.

Rose-Redwood, Reuben, and Liora Bigon, eds. *Gridded Worlds: An Urban Anthology.* Cham: Springer, 2018.

Scheffler, Karl. *Die Architektur der Großstadt.* Berlin: Cassirer, 1913.

Scherr, Friederike. "Jakob Levy Moreno im Flüchtlingslager Mitterndorf a.d. Fischa – eine Spurensuche." *Zeitschrift für Psychodrama und Soziometrie* 12, no. S1 (2013): 3–126.

Schlöss, Heinrich. *Die Irrenpflege in Österreich in Wort und Bild.* Halle a.S.: Marhold, 1912.

Schott, Dieter. *Die Vernetzung der Stadt. Kommunale Energiepolitik, öffentlicher Verkehr und die "Produktion" der modernen Stadt. Darmstadt – Mannheim – Mainz 1880–1918.* Darmstadt: Wissenschaftliche Buchgesellschaft, 1999.

Schwarz, Mario. "Architekt Heymann, Ingenieur Gröger und das k.k. Flüchtlingslager Oberhollabrunn, *Steine sprechen* 46/2, no. 132 (2006): 8–16.

Senarclens de Grancy, Antje. "Different Housing Spaces – Space, Function, and Use of Barrack-Huts in World War I Refugee Camps." *Reflections on Camps – Space, Agency, Materiality, zeitgeschichte* 45, no. 4 (2018), 457–82.

———. "Konservative Reform. Die Anfänge des Vereins für Heimatschutz in Steiermark." In *Identität – Politik – Architektur. Der "Verein für Heimatschutz in Steiermark,"* edited by Antje Senarclens de Grancy, 31–54. Berlin: Jovis, 2013.

Sonne, Wolfgang. "Blütezeit des Städtebaus in Europa und den USA." In *Stadtvisionen 1910/2010. Berlin Paris London Chicago. 100 Jahre Allgemeine Städtebau-Ausstellung in Berlin*, edited by Harald Bodenschatz et al., 30–7. Kiel and Berlin: DOM publishers, 2010.

Sonne, Wolfgang. "Großstadtbaukunst. Otto Wagners Städtebau im internationalen Kontext." In *Otto Wagner*, edited by Andreas Nierhaus and Eva-Maria Orosz, 52–9. Salzburg and Vienna: Residenz, 2018.

Stibbe, Matthew. "The Internment of Political Suspects in Austria-Hungary during the First World War: A Violent Legacy?" In *Gender and Modernity in Central Europe: The Austro-Hungarian Monarchy and its Legacy*, edited by Agata Schwartz, 203–18. Ottawa: University of Ottawa Press, 2010.

Suppanz, Werner. "Entproletarisierung in der Stadtrandsiedlung – eine gegen/moderne Strategie." In *Architektur. Vergessen. Jüdische Architekten in Graz*, edited by Antje Senarclens de Grancy and Heidrun Zettelbauer, 202–4. Vienna, Cologne and Weimar: Böhlau, 2011.

Thorpe, Julia. "Displacing Empire: Refugee Welfare, National Activism and State Legitimacy in Austria-Hungary in the First World War." In *Refugees and the End of Empire: Imperial Collapse and Forced Migration in the Twentieth Century*, edited by Panikos Panayi and Pippa Virdee, 102–26. Basingstoke: Palgrave Macmillan, 2011.

Unwin, Raymond. *Town Planning in Practice: An Introduction to the Art of Designing Cities and Suburbs*. London: T. F. Unwin, 1909.

Wagner, Otto. *Die Großstadt. Eine Studie über diese*. Vienna: Schroll, 1911.

Wagner, Philipp. *Stadtplanung für die Welt? Internationales Expertenwissen, 1900–1960*. Göttingen: Vandenhoeck & Ruprecht, 2016.

Weihsmann, Helmut. *Das Rote Wien. Sozialdemokratische Architektur und Kommunalpolitik, 1919–1934*. Vienna: Promedia, 2002.

Zarebska, Teresa. "Théories militaires et habitations collectives." *Archithese* no. 8 (1973): 9–14.

About the Editors

Sophie Hochhäusl is an Assistant Professor in Architectural History and Theory at the University of Pennsylvania where she is also a board member in the Gender, Sexuality, and Women's Studies program. Her scholarly work centers on modern architecture and urban culture with a focus on spatial histories of dissidence, intersectional feminism, queer theory, and environmental history. Currently, she is working on two book projects: an interdisciplinary history and translation project titled *Memories of the Resistance: Margarete Schütte-Lihotzky* and the *Architecture of Collective Dissidence, 1918–1989,* as well as the monograph *Housing Cooperative: Politics, Architecture, and Urban Imagination in Vienna, 1904–1934.* She received a PhD and MA in History of Architecture and Urbanism from Cornell University and an MArch from the Academy of Fine Arts, Vienna. She is currently an Alexander von Humboldt Senior Fellow and a Fellow at the Mandel Center for Advanced Holocaust Studies at the United States Holocaust Memorial Museum.

Erin Eckhold Sassin is an Associate Professor of the History of Art and Architecture at Middlebury College, Vermont, where she teaches modern architectural history and theory. She received her PhD in the History of Art and Architecture from Brown University in 2012. Her research is closely linked to her teaching interests: she has published articles on gender and feminism, the intersection of architecture, power, and ethnicity on the borders of the German Empire, as well as on Acoustic Ecology and the built environment. Her 2020 book, *Single People and Mass Housing in Germany and Beyond (1850-1930)—(No) Home Away from Home,* was awarded a 2019 fellowship from the Graham Foundation for Advanced Studies in the Fine Arts. It is the first complete study of single-person mass housing in Germany and the pivotal role this class- and gender-specific building type played for pre-war German architectural culture and society, the transnational Progressive reform movement, and Architectural Modernism in the 1920s.

List of Contributors

Deborah Ascher Barnstone is Professor of Architecture and Head of School at the University of Technology Sydney. She holds a PhD in architectural history and theory from the Technical University, Delft; an MArch degree from Columbia University; and a Bachelor of Arts degree cum laude with high honors from Barnard College. She is a licensed architect as well as an historian. Barnstone's primary research interests are in interrogating the origins of modernism and exploring the relationships between art, architecture, and culture more broadly. Her monographs include *The Break with the Past: German Avant-garde Architecture, 1910–1925* (Routledge, 2018) and *Beyond the Bauhaus: Cultural Modernity in Weimar Breslau, 1918–1933* (University of Michigan Press, 2016). Recent publications include articles in *Journal of Architecture, Journal of Design History,* and *New German Critique. The Color of Modernism: Paints, Pigments and the Transformation of Modern Architecture in 1920s Germany* is in press at Bloomsbury Academic for a 2022 release.

David Caralt is an Assistant Professor of Architecture at Universidad San Sebastián, Chile. His research focuses mainly on the nightscapes and urban nocturnes during the interwar period, and on the intersection between technologies of spectacle and architecture. He received a MArch and a BArch from the Polytechnic University of Catalonia, Barcelona. His PhD thesis in progress analyses the water and electric light systems displayed at the Barcelona World's Fair in 1929. His recent publications include the books *An Accidental Masterpiece: Mies van der Rohe's Barcelona Pavilion* and *The Barcelona Pavilion: One Hundred Texts since 1929* (both in Birkhäuser, 2020), with Dietrich Neumann. David teaches architectural design and is Director of the School of Architecture at Universidad San Sebastián in Concepción, Chile.

Theodossis Issaias is an architect and educator, and recently joined the Heinz Architectural Center at the Carnegie Museum of Art as Associate Curator. He earned his Diploma of Architecture at the National Technical University of Athens and a Master of Science in Architecture and Urbanism from the Massachusetts Institute of Technology. His PhD dissertation, "Architectures of the Humanitarian Front" at Yale University, explored the nexus of humanitarian organizations and architecture and their relation to conflict, displacement, and the provision of shelter. Since 2009, he has been practicing as a founding member of Fatura Collaborative, an architecture and research collective. Their work has been presented in museums, conferences, and exhibitions including the 2014, 2016, and 2020 Venice Architectural Biennales, Manifesta, and the Benaki Museum of Athens, among others.

Da Hyung Jeong is a PhD candidate at the Institute of Fine Arts, New York University. His dissertation, entitled "Soviet Architectural Postmodernism, 1977–1991" and supervised by Professor Jean-Louis Cohen, is the first book-length study devoted to the subject. He has published book chapters and articles on such topics as Italo-Soviet architectural exchanges during the 1980s, Soviet architectural presence in Southeast Asia and the British reception of the work of the Italian architectural collective Superstudio. He was a 2019–2020 Mellon-Marron Research Consortium Fellow at the Museum of Modern Art, New York, where he undertook curatorial research in connection with an upcoming exhibition on architectural modernism in South Asia, paying particular attention to the works of Minnette de Silva and Yasmeen Lari. Currently, he is a 2021–2022 Predoctoral Fellow at the Getty Research Institute, Los Angeles, where his research project, entitled "The Postmodern Fragment in the Architecture of the Soviet 'Periphery,'" examines the emergence of semiotic approaches to architectural design in the so-called peripheral republics of the Soviet Union. He has served as an adjunct professor at the City College of New York and New York University.

Aubrey Knox is a PhD candidate in Art History at The Graduate Center of The City University of New York. Her dissertation uses the transformation of the Grand Palais into a military hospital during World War I as an entry point into a wider exploration of the intersection of art and medicine through the media of architecture, painting, sculpture, and photography. She has published about art and pandemic in *Art in America* and vernacular architecture in *Platform*. She holds an MA in Art History from Columbia University, where she studied the history of collecting and museums. She is also the Senior Operations Manager for Design at The Metropolitan Museum of Art.

Min Kyung Lee is an Assistant Professor in the Growth and Structure of Cities Department at Bryn Mawr College. Her research concerns urban representations and especially the relations between mapping and architectural practices from the late eighteenth century to the present. Her forthcoming monograph, *The Tyranny of the Straight Line: Mapping Modern Paris,* studies the surveying of the French capital during the nineteenth century, situating the emergence of specific modalities of urban representation in their scientific, cultural, and historical contexts. Based on this project, she was the inaugural Banister Fletcher Global Fellow at the University of London Institute in Paris, the Bartlett School of Architecture, and Queen Mary University of London, where she conceived of a public program on the quantification of urban space. The events sought to engage scholars in discussing the process and consequences of how space is represented through numbers and data. She is currently a New Directions Mellon Foundation Fellow, now working on a project on Korean migration and the American built environment, and a visiting scholar at the Heyman Center for Humanities at Columbia University. She received a PhD and MA from Northwestern University and a BA cum laude from the University of Pennsylvania.

Etien Santiago is an Assistant Professor of Architecture at Indiana University. He specializes in architectural history and theory from the late nineteenth century to the present, architects' explorations of materials and construction methods, as well as theoretical debates about technological change. He received a PhD in Architecture from Harvard University, an MArch with distinction from the Harvard Graduate School of Design, as well as a BArch and BA cum laude from Rice University. His PhD dissertation uncovers how World War I ignited and shaped modern architects' obsessive search for mass-produced housing based on advanced construction techniques. Etien teaches architectural studio, architectural history, and structures courses in the J. Irwin Miller Architecture program based in Columbus, Indiana.

Massimiliano Savorra is a Professor in History of Architecture at the University of Pavia. He received a PhD in History of Architecture from Iuav University of Venice (1999), and a Master's degree in Architecture from the University of Naples Federico II (1994). He has participated in numerous conferences and lectured in Italian and foreign universities. He has obtained fellowships and grants in Italy and abroad, and he has conducted studies in France, Canada, and the United States. He has also curated conferences and exhibitions, among them *"Pietre ignee cadute dal cielo". I monumenti della Grande Guerra* (Venice, 2014). He has published monographic volumes in editorial series and articles in important specialized journals. Among his books are *Enrico Agostino Griffini. La casa, il monumento, la città* (Electa, 2000); *Charles Garnier in Italia. Un viaggio attraverso le arti 1848–1854* (Il Poligrafo, 2003); *Capolavori brevi. Luciano Baldessari, la Breda e la Fiera di Milano* (Electa, 2008); *La forma e la struttura. Félix Candela, gli scritti* (2013); *Carlo Sada 1849–1924. Committenti, architetture e città nella Sicilia orientale* (Torri del vento, 2014); *Questioni di facciata. Il "completamento" delle chiese in Italia e la dimensione politica dell'architettura, 1861–1905* (FranoAngeli, 2018); and *Per la donna, per il bambino, per la razza. L'architettura dell'ONMI tra eutenica ed eugenica nell'Italia fascista* (LetteraVentidue, 2021).

Antje Senarclens de Grancy is an Assistant Professor at Graz University of Technology, Institute of Architectural Theory, Art History and Cultural Studies where she teaches architectural history. Her areas of expertise are the field of tension between architecture and politics/society, modern reform movements (Werkbund, Heimatschutz), processes of canonization of architectural history, and the architectural history and theory of the nineteenth and twentieth centuries in Austria and Central Europe. She studied Art History and History at University of Graz, and Anthropology at Paris 8 University Vincennes-Saint-Denis, and received a PhD in Art History from University of Graz. Currently she is preparing a book on the relationship between the camp and modern architecture, using the example of the refugee camps of the Habsburg Monarchy during the First World War.

Emma Thomas received her BA from Yale University and completed her PhD in American Studies at Boston University in 2021. Her expertise is in American material and visual culture, primarily of the long nineteenth century, and her interdisciplinary work aims to expand the geographic boundaries that have typically defined the study of nineteenth-century American art. Currently, her research focuses on Polynesia and the Pacific Rim, following the completion of her dissertation, "Art Against Docility: Visual Culture and Imperialism in late 19th-century Hawai'i."

Katti Williams is a Research Fellow in Australian architectural history in the Faculty of Architecture, Building & Planning, at the University of Melbourne, Australia. Her research interests lie at the intersections of art, architectural, military, and cultural histories. Her PhD thesis, completed in 2017 at the University of Melbourne, comprised the first sustained academic study of Australian-born architect and prolific architectural commentator William Lucas, with a specific exploration of his unbuilt designs for First World War memorials. Her published work has focused on the design and interpretation of First World War commemorative architecture; manifestations and transformations of classical precedent; and unbuilt competitive designs. Her interest in soldier architects and architectural biography underpins her recent work with Julie Willis on the international travels undertaken by Australian architects and the networks that these journeys enabled.

Julie Willis is a Redmond Barry Distinguished Professor of Architecture and Dean of the Faculty of Architecture, Building & Planning at the University of Melbourne, Australia. Her research concentrates on the history of Australian architecture, with a focus on institutional buildings and the profession. Recent projects have focused on development of modern hospital architecture in Australia; the importance of small public buildings in community and civic identity; architecture during wartime and its subsequent impact on practice and production; the development of innovative school architecture in Australia; and equity and diversity in the Australian architectural profession. Her work on the history of women architects in Australia garnered significant attention, being awarded a commendation in the category of Best Art Book Published in 2001 by the Art Association of Australia and New Zealand and the National Bates Smart Award for Architecture in the Media in 2002. The book was also named a Year of the Built Environment Exemplar in 2004. Major published works include the *Encyclopedia of Australian Architecture* (Cambridge University Press, 2012), *Designing Schools: Space, Place and Pedagogy* (Routledge, 2017), and *Architecture and the Modern Hospital: Nosokomeion to Hygeia* (Routledge, 2019).

Index of Names, Locations, and Keywords

Index of Locations

Index of Keywords

Apichatpong Weerasethakul and team on the set of *Mekong Hotel*
Nong Khai Province, Thailand, 2012

Colophon/Impressum

Jahresring 63
Annual of Fine Arts/Jahrbuch für Kunst
SouthEastAsia
Spaces of the Curatorial/Räume des Kuratorischen

Edited on behalf of the Association of Arts and Culture of the German Economy at the Federation of German Industries/Herausgegeben im Auftrag des Kulturkreises der deutschen Wirtschaft im BDI e.V.

This book is published in collaboration with/Dieses Buch ist veröffentlicht in Zusammenarbeit mit NTU Centre for Contemporary Art Singapore.

Editors/Herausgeberinnen: Ute Meta Bauer, Brigitte Oetker
Editorial consultant/Editorischer Berater: Lee Weng Choy
Managing editors/Redaktion: Cheong Kah Kit, Isabel Podeschwa
Copyediting/Lektorat: Aaron Bogart, Nina Köller
Translation/Übersetzung: Anne Breimaier (Gaweewong),
Barbara Hess (Bauer, Flores, Seng), Karl Hoffmann (Butt, Godfrey, Taylor),
Danilo Scholz (Ker, Legaspi-Ramirez, Soon, Teh), Jochen Stremmel (Chua)
Design/Grafische Gestaltung: Markus Weisbeck, Victor Kassis,
Surface, Berlin/Frankfurt am Main
Lithography/Bildbearbeitung: der ripperger, Medienproduktion GmbH
Printing/Druck: BUD Potsdam

ISBN 978-3-95679-260-1

Sternberg Press
Caroline Schneider
Karl-Marx-Allee 78
D–10243 Berlin
www.sternberg-press.com